The Collected Poems of George Mackay Brown

George Mackay Brown was born in 1921 in Stromness in the Orkney Islands, where he spent much of his life. He was awarded the James Tait Black Memorial Book Prize in 1988, and won the Saltire Scottish Book of the Year Award in 1994. In the same year his novel *Beside the Ocean of Time* was shortlisted for the Booker Prize. He died in 1996, having published over fifty works, including poetry, plays, novels, short stories, essays, children's books and his autobiography.

The editors of this collected volume are uniquely qualified. **Archie Bevan** is George Mackay Brown's literary executor and **Brian Murray** is co-author of *Interrogation of Silence*, a critical study of the works of George Mackay Brown (published by John Murray).

'*The Collected Poems* is a rich gift . . . This much-needed volume is a testament to the inspiration of a distinctive poet who lived on the margins yet saw into the centre'
Herald

'Extraordinarily eff . . . George Mackay Brown really does possess the magician's touch'
Observer

'A dazzling writer'
Guardian

'A brilliant writer . . . He combines great imagination, which takes him into the realms of the mystical, with a firm rooting in reality and a deep understanding of humanity'
The Spectator

'The reader embarks on a voyage – which is how Mackay Brown himself saw his work – through the elemental world of his cliff-girt, craggy isles'
The Times

The Collected Poems of
GEORGE MACKAY BROWN

The Collected Poems of

GEORGE MACKAY BROWN

Edited by Archie Bevan
and Brian Murray

JOHN MURRAY

The publisher gratefully acknowledges subsidy from the Orkney Islands Council and the Scottish Arts Council towards the publication of this volume.

First published in Great Britain in 2005 by John Murray (Publishers)
A division of Hodder Headline

Paperback edition 2006

3

A CIP catalogue record for this title is available from the British Library

ISBN-13 978-0-7195-6884-8

Typeset in 9.75/12.75 Adobe Sabon by Servis Filmsetting Ltd, Manchester

Printed and bound by Clays Ltd, St Ives plc

Hodder Headline policy is to use papers that are natural, renewable and recyclable products and made from wood grown in sustainable forests. The logging and manufacturing processes are expected to conform to the environmental regulations of the country of origin.

John Murray (Publishers)
338 Euston Road
London NW1 3BH

Contents

Preface

'His Collected Poems are overdue. A wider readership would represent real progress.' If Dennis O'Driscoll's comment on the need for a much more substantial and varied gathering of George Mackay Brown's poetry was justifiable in 1989, sixteen years and ten titles on, the necessity is a pressing one. The four volumes of *Selected Poems* issued in Brown's lifetime (1971, 1977, 1991 and 1996) were an inadequate representation of his work's quantity, range and quality. This book offers all the collections he published in book form, together with selections from the posthumously printed *For the Islands I Sing, Stained Glass Windows* and *Northern Lights* and the whole of *Travellers*. The total of 421 poems should be set beside the 86 of the 1996 *Selected*, which occupied less than 160 pages of text.

The qualitative case for a genuine *Collected Poems* is equally simple to address. We have noted how Brown's reputation has grown steadily among fellow poets, critics and the general public, who have endorsed the powerful claim of Seamus Heaney, recording his appreciation of how Brown 'has added uniquely and steadfastly to the riches of poetry in English' by his impressive content and technique. Vernon Scannell's reflection on how a writer's *Collected Poems* 'put him on trial for his life' seems a fair assessment, one from which Brown's work emerges as a major contribution to poetry, on a par with the best of modern times while taking its place in the line of permanently recognised and appealing poets.

Note: it proved impossible to trace the publisher of *The Sea and the Tower* (1994), a very small part of a work in progress. Accordingly, it is not represented here. Nor is *Orkney: Pictures and Poems* (published shortly after Brown's death in 1996) owing to copyright problems.

Archie Bevan and Brian Murray
Orkney, 2005

Acknowledgements

Many of the poems in this book were first published in or by one of the following: Aquarius; Babel; Birds; The Breckness Press; The Celtic Cross Press; Chapman; Clanjamfrie; Edinburgh University Press; First and Always; Glasgow Herald; The Herald; Honour'd Shade; Lines Review; The Listener; Morning Star Publications; New North; New Poetry; New Statesman; The Orcadian; The Orkney Herald; Perpetua Press; Phoenix; Poetry Canada Review; Poetry Ireland Review; Poetry Supplement; Poetry Wales; Poets and Peasants; The Scotsman; A Second Scottish Anthology; Shorelines; Spectrum; The Tablet; Temenos; A Touch of Flame; The West Highland Free Press; Trees; Zeugma.

Introduction

Prologue

For the islands I sing
   and for a few friends;
not to foster means
   or be midwife to ends.

* * *

For Scotland I sing,
   the Knox-ruined nation,
that poet and saint
   must rebuild with their passion.

For workers in field
   and mill and mine
who break earth's bread
   and crush her wine.

Go, good my songs,
   be as gay as you can.
Weep, if you have to,
   the old tears of man.

Praise tinker and saint,
   and the rose that takes
its fill of sunlight
   though a world breaks.

Many readers will recognise the opening line of this early poem by George
Mackay Brown. It was written in 1952 as the prologue to his first collec-
tion of verse, *The Storm And Other Poems*, and was chosen more than forty
years later by the poet's editors as an appropriate title for his posthumously
published autobiography.

   The Storm was printed by a local newspaper, the long defunct *Orkney
Herald*, for which Brown had worked as Stromness correspondent and also
as a weekly columnist. Clearly there was no great expectation of a bumper
sale for the book. Only 300 copies were printed, and when they sold out

within a fortnight the type had already been dismantled, leaving no possibility of a reprint.

The book contained a foreword by George Mackay Brown's friend and mentor Edwin Muir. Brown had recently studied under him at Newbattle Abbey College, of which Muir was then Warden. In his introduction Muir speaks glowingly of his fellow poet and fellow Orkneyman:

> His main theme is Orkney, past and present, but it is as a poet, not only as an Orkney poet, that I admire him. I read these poems first when Mr Brown was at Newbattle Abbey, and what struck me then was their fresh and spontaneous beauty. Now, after reading them again, I am impressed by something which I can only call grace. Grace is what breathes warmth into beauty and tenderness into comedy. Grace is what I find in all these poems, both the serious and the lighter ones. Orkney should be proud of this book celebrating its life, and proud above all that it has produced a young poet of such high gifts.

Finally, one of the revelations of this little book is the extent to which the poet has already mapped out his territory. We can hear it in these verses from the prologue and in the poems which follow, where he introduces the themes he will explore with increasing depth and technical mastery during the next four decades. His principal subject matter is of course the place and the people of Orkney, with their long and frequently turbulent history reaching back beyond the Viking era to the Stone Age, and their great treasure house of lore and legend. Here too is the celebration of farmer and fisherman, tinker and saint. The title poem of this collection is notable for its religious and autobiographical overtones, and its reminder of Brown's debt to fellow poets whom he held in high esteem (p. 3).

It was five years after *The Storm* that Brown's poetry found a national publisher. The initiative came from Edwin Muir who sent a number of the poems to the Hogarth Press. These were published under the significant title of *Loaves and Fishes*. The volume contains a reworking of the best poems from *The Storm*, and although some of the other poems still show the influence of fellow poets such as Yeats and Dylan Thomas and Muir himself, it is an influence which has been largely assimilated. Increasingly we have a poet speaking in his own distinctive voice.

We can hear this in 'Hamnavoe' (p. 24), the great elegiac poem in memory of his father, the town postman, who died in 1940. It is also a celebration of his native town Stromness, the 'Hamnavoe' of his poetry and stories. (Hamnavoe – Haven Bay – is the old Viking name for the lovely harbour of Stromness.) Brown wrote six versions of this poem over a period of more than forty years. The one used in this collection is the fourth – and probably still the best.

Loaves and Fishes contains several sonnets of quite remarkable quality.
'The Old Women' paints an unflattering picture of those kill-joys of the community who 'fix on you from every close and pier/ An acid look to make your veins run sour' (p. 16). In sharp contrast to this bleak picture is the fine elegiac sonnet commemorating the death of the poet's friend Peter Esson ('Tailor, Town Librarian, Free Kirk Elder') (p. 18).

Undoubtedly one of the finest poems in *Loaves and Fishes* is the poet's 'Elegy' (p. 32) for a young friend who died in childbirth – herself a poet of high promise and a beautiful singer. The conjunction of the agricultural and Christian cycles and rituals was to become a strong and increasingly familiar element in the poet's work. The parable of the sower and the seed provided a universal image

> 'which seemed to illuminate the whole of life for me . . . It included within itself everything from the most primitive breaking of the soil to Christ himself with his parables of agriculture and the majestic symbolism of his passion, and death, and resurrection . . . You will find it at the heart of many of my stories and poems.'*

It is undoubtedly given powerful expression in this early poem. The word 'Magnustide' in the opening line is used to signify Spring, and much more. Forty years later, the poet himself would be buried on St Magnus Day, the anniversary of the saint's martyrdom.

George Mackay Brown's third volume of poems, *The Year of the Whale*, was published in 1965. By this time Brown had returned to Orkney from his university sojourn in Edinburgh. He had taken an honours degree in English, and had ▇▇▇▇▇ two years of post-graduate study on Gerald Manley Hopkins. A▇▇▇ver these years he had suffered a recurrence of the TB which had afflicted him intermittently since the age of 20, and which required fairly lengthy hospital treatment.

The Year of the Whale is an impressive achievement. Much of it is concerned with death and mortality – death by shipwreck (p. 38), the death of Ally Flett the fisherman, and of Ward the farm labourer, the death of a community in the title poem (p. 47), and even the death of a hawk (p. 51) in one of the first and finest of his many animal poems. And where life still lingers, as in his studies of 'Halcro' (p. 27) and the 'Old Fisherman With Guitar' (p. 46) the ambience is distinctly geriatric.

This is equally true of the next poem, as we turn from sea to soil – 'from grey furrow to black furrow', as the poet would put it – and listen to Ward the farm labourer on his deathbed:

> 'God, am I not dead yet?' said Ward, his ear
>   Meeting another dawn . . . (p. 46)

---

* Brown, George Mackay, *Writer's Shop*, Chapman, Edinburgh, 1976, p. 23.

Despite the apparent morbidity of the subject matter in these poems, the overall effect is life-affirming and elegiac – and there is no sentimentality.

By the time this book was published, Brown's talents had been recognised by another distinguished Orkney writer, Eric Linklater. And Linklater was not stinting in his praise:

> George Mackay Brown has become a recognised feature of Orkney's landscape . . . and that eminence has been fairly won by poetry of a quite individual distinction, in which he has translated his sharp-sighted vision into language of a marvellous and ringing felicity. His genius has been recognised and rewarded . . . but more important to the islands of his birth is the fact that George Mackay Brown is a good poet, a true poet, and essentially a poet of Orkney. Orkney is his persistent theme and constant inspiration.*

Linklater also comments on a characteristic poetic mode which we encounter frequently in Brown's poetry, and to which he gives the name 'processional', where:

> the poet watches, in imagination, the passers-by at a wedding, a funeral, a country fair – solemn or riotous, but apprehended with a visionary understanding.†

Linklater's point is well made, and serves to remind us of just how much of Brown's poetry has this strong narrative impulse. The processional is already evident in 'Hamnavoe', which moves in time through a typical day in the life of the town. Eric Linklater chose another Hamnavoe poem to illustrate his point. 'Har⬛⬛⬛arket' (p. 49) is the story of seven countrymen who visit the to⬛⬛⬛rket day to experience all the fun of the fair, and return under ⬛⬛⬛s, leaving one of their number in a ditch – 'his mouth full of ⬛⬛g fires'. Brown himself described this piece as 'a highly condensed short story'. It is indeed a small miracle of compression.

George Mackay Brown's fellow Orkneymen were not alone in hailing the arrival of this talented poet with the unique northern voice and the island agenda, who was already a significant figure in the Scottish Literary Renaissance. Younger contemporaries such as Ted Hughes, Seamus Heaney and Ian Crichton Smith were quick to recognise the achievement of a kindred spirit whose poetic concerns were very much their own.

And it was Douglas Dunn – distinguished poet and scholar of a younger generation – who identified *The Year of the Whale* as a vital poetic watershed for George Mackay Brown. Having proclaimed his credo in the

---

* Linklater, Eric, *Orkney and Shetland*, London, Robert Hale, 1971, p. 256.
† ibid. p. 256.

1952 Prologue, Brown now finds a distinctive Orcadian voice with which to give it utterance. According to Dunn,

> 'the collection marks an exhilarating advance. Many of its poems could be described as 'documentary lyrics'. From the very first poem, too – 'The Funeral of Ally Flett' – we are introduced to the finest poetry written this century in the British islands which celebrates a community, which lyricises and portrays a people and a place.'*

Praise indeed! – and all the more pity that the poet chose to banish this little masterpiece (p. 37) from his *Selected Poems*. There is a justifiable suspicion that here as elsewhere Brown was exercising a degree of self-censorship in removing 'unseemly' material from his texts – and even complete texts from his canon.

Brown was regarded by most of his fellow poets with affection as well as admiration. His friend Stewart Conn – former Head of Radio Drama and the first Makar (Laureate) of Edinburgh – remembers how Brown at first acquaintance 'seemed something of a still centre, not one for high falutin' chat; if I asked what something in one of his poems meant, like as not he'd start intoning 'Pied Beauty' or hum a few bars from Beethoven's Ninth.'†
Apart from writing numerous plays for Festival performance, Brown's principal task as Vice President of the St Magnus Festival was to invite a fellow poet to a Festival residency involving a few poetry readings and much conviviality. Needless to say, the poets – including Ted Hughes, Seamus Heaney, Iain Crichton Smith, Norman MacCaig, Stewart Conn, Liz Lochhead, Douglas Dunn, and Edwin Morgan – gladly accepted the opportunity to visit an old friend, and savour the atmosphere of a great island event. Indeed, almost all of them paid a return visit to the Festival. Yet Brown himself never performed in public, here in Orkney or anywhere else.

Over the next thirty years Brown was to publish five new volumes of verse, three volumes of selected poems, and a number of poem sequences such as *Stone* and *Orkney: Pictures and Poems* in collaboration with photographer Gunnie Moberg, and *The Scottish Bestiary* in which he collaborated with a number of distinguished Scottish artists. Later sequences including the *Brodgar Poems, Tryst on Egilsay*, and *Foresterhill* (the poet's tribute to the Aberdeen hospital where he was a patient in 1990) were to be followed posthumously by *Stained Glass Windows, Northern Lights*, and *Travellers* in 2001. One of his finest achievements in this huge body of work is the great Rackwick poem cycle *Fishermen With Ploughs*, which takes its title from an early poem in *The Storm*. Some of these texts appeared originally in limited editions published by Celtic Cross Press (beautifully

---

* Dunn, Douglas, ed. Spear, Hilda D., *George Mackay Brown – A Survey of his Work and a Full Bibliography*, Lampeter, Edwin Mellen Press, 2000, p. 26.
† Conn, Stewart, *Distances*, Dalkeith, Scottish Cultural Press, 2001, p. 78.

illustrated by Rosemary Roberts), by Babel, the Perpetua Press, and the Breckness Press.

It is now more than thirty years since an encounter with one of George Mackay Brown's books, *An Orkney Tapestry*, led Peter Maxwell Davies to visit Hoy one bleak Sunday in the summer of 1970. And it was there in Rackwick that the avant-garde composer first met the island poet. It was a meeting which fired the composer's imagination and began a lifelong friendship and a fruitful collaboration which still continues on what might be called a unilateral basis. Several of Maxwell Davies's most recent choral works have been inspired by Brown's texts. These include substantial song cycles from *Fishermen With Ploughs* and *Following a Lark*.

The first of George Mackay Brown's poems to be set to music by Peter Maxwell Davies was 'Stations of the Cross', later retitled 'From Stone to Thorn' (p. 178), a spiky atonal piece which requires more than one hearing to reveal its undoubted quality. The most celebrated collaboration of that early period was the Davies adaptation of Brown's novel *Magnus* into the chamber opera *The Martyrdom of St Magnus* which launched the St Magnus Festival in 1977.

'Lullaby for Lucy' (p. 383), however, is an example of their collaboration at its simplest and most hauntingly beautiful. Lucy Rendall was born in 1981, the first Rackwick child in many years. George celebrated her arrival with a lovely acrostic, to which Max responded with music of great tenderness, using only 'the white notes' to produce a sublimely simple cradle song.

What can be said in a few sentences about all of Brown's later body of verse, bearing in mind that from 1967 onwards he was also producing a large number of short stories, novels and essays of quite exceptional quality? The Orcadian themes still predominate, though the treatment is perhaps more archetypal than before. The religious note becomes increasingly dominant, and processional poems such as 'Countryman' (p. 222) tend to focus on our swift progress from birth to death.

That poem also reminds us of the poet's long love affair with the mystical number seven. In earlier days he used it to beautiful effect in lovely miniatures such as 'Country Girl' (p. 50). It appeared also in 'Taxman' (p. 104), which is perhaps the shortest of all his so-called 'short stories in verse'. But the most celebrated example of this genre is undoubtedly 'Beachcomber' (p. 123), which happily reappears here in its original form.

As the years pass, Brown's attachment to the number seven as a poetic device is matched by a growing preoccupation with the seven ages of man and the fourteen Stations of the Cross. And despite the lighthearted moments and the many flashes of humour, the prevailing tone is one of gravitas.

What is never in doubt is the poet's supreme control of his medium. He was a consummate wordsmith, and remained so throughout his life. As his style matured, it became increasingly honed, with images that were integral

to his narrative and lyrical purpose, as we can see most strikingly in short
poems such as 'Kirkyard' (p. 68) and 'Shroud' (p. 104), the latter of which
Brown unaccountably omitted from his *Selected Poems*. The poet's fascin-
ation with what he called 'the heptahedron – the seven-faceted poem or
story' – can be seen at its most compelling in his posthumous collection
Northern Lights, especially in his celebration of Robert Burns (p. 392), St
Magnus (p. 402), 'All Souls' (p. 418), and – autobiographically – 'An Old
Man in July' (p. 410).

Brown's reputation as a 'saga man' is justified up to a point. He certainly
learned much from the sagas – and indeed from the old Scottish ballads –
about economy of expression and the importance of uncluttered narrative;
about how to combine a laconic Viking style with some dead-pan Viking
humour.

However, this collection also demonstrates that Brown was content at
times to allow himself some breathing space, especially in the prose poems
which provide a bridge between his 'pure' metrical poetry and his short
stories. Elsewhere he confesses to 'a weakness for overlaying plain prose
with a wash of lyricism', and suggests that 'perhaps in the cold grey air of
the north the hybrid [prose poem] is most at home'.

George Mackay Brown's first collection of short stories, *A Calendar of
Love*, was published in 1967, and it marked a turning point in his career.
Until then he had been known to a comparatively small circle of readers
as a poet; but now he was opening up a rich narrative seam which would
produce eight books of short stories, six novels, several children's books
of rare quality, and several plays and collections of essays. It also attracted
a large and appreciative reading public, far beyond the borders of
Scotland, and it attracted film and TV directors of the calibre of Bill
Forsyth and the late, great James MacTaggart. While there was a strong
commercial motive ('You couldn't keep a cat on what you'd make from
poetry!' he would say), in fact Brown had been practising these other
genres from his early twenties.

In a short introduction it is not possible to dwell on more than one or two
of the qualities in his prose which make George Mackay Brown such a
superb story teller. Mention has already been made of the saga influence on
his poetry. This is also evident in the bare style of his prose, with its reliance
on short sentences, and its concentration on simple narrative without any
running commentary. This might seem like the recipe for a detached, imper-
sonal treatment of his subject; but the reality is quite different. In fact,
Brown's prose carries a powerful emotional charge, and is often deeply
moving. It articulates the joy and grief, the suffering and endurance of his
characters, many of whom are people of few words when it comes to voicing
their feelings. At times his writing blossoms into passages of rare and com-
pelling beauty, particularly in the coda to some of his most powerful stories.
These often depict loss and suffering and despair, but are nevertheless

imbued with a sense of ultimate serenity, an assurance that 'all shall be well and all manner of thing shall be well.' Like his poetry, Brown's prose at its best is suffused with that quality which Edwin Muir identified all these years ago – the quality of grace.

A frequently voiced criticism of Brown's work is that he is stuck in a time warp, neglecting or deliberately ignoring the realities of life here and now. This charge cannot be wholly dismissed, as indeed the author himself conceded. But it will be strongly contested by anyone who has read the author's prose poem 'The Return of the Women' (p. 131), or his novels *Greenvoe, Magnus, Time in a Red Coat, Vinland,* and best of all perhaps, his brilliant swansong *Beside the Ocean of Time* – short-listed for the Booker Prize in 1994.

George Mackay Brown had a deep and abiding sense of community. It permeated almost everything he wrote, and is reflected in the weekly column he contributed to the local newspaper for nearly half a century. It shows also in his repeated contention that the poet is essentially a craftsman like the joiner and the plumber. Yet he was also a visionary who recognised that the poet has a larger, deeper, and more solitary function, to which he gave memorable expression in these lines which graced the London Underground some years ago:

The Poet

Therefore he no more troubled the pool of silence.
But put on mask and cloak,
Strung a guitar
And moved among the folk.
Dancing they cried,
'Ah, how our sober islands
Are gay again, since this blind lyrical tramp
Invaded the Fair!'

Under the last dead lamp
When all the dancers and masks had gone inside
His cold stare
Returned to its true task, interrogation of silence.

Finally, in the last years of his life, came the stark but superbly resonant
poem which was to provide the poet's own epitaph:

A Work for Poets

To have carved on the days of our vanity
A sun
A ship
A star
A cornstalk

Also a few marks
From an ancient forgotten time
A child may read

That not far from the stone
A well
Might open for wayfarers

Here is a work for poets –
Carve the runes
Then be content with silence

Biographical Note

George Mackay Brown was born on 17 October 1921 in Stromness, second largest town in Orkney, with 1900 inhabitants. Son of John Brown, tailor and postman, and Mary-Jane Mackay, hotel worker, he was the youngest survivor of six children, one dying in infancy. His home life was secure and happy, although his father's illness and periodic bouts of depression led to anxiety. The local school was entirely different, a boring experience relieved only by the enjoyment of writing essays and listening to stories – the latter continuing to develop an interest first generated by his sister's recitation of ballads.

When he left school at the age of 18, Brown worked in the Post Office for a short time, until a Forces medical revealed he was suffering from tuberculosis. After a lengthy stay in hospital, Brown had no occupation until he was invited to be Stromness correspondent for *The Orkney Herald* in 1944. The reading and writing with which he had been occupying his time since his release from hospital served him well, as Brown quickly became known for the vigour and interest of his journalism.

In 1951 he left the Islands for Newbattle Abbey College, then under the wardenship of the Orkney poet and critic Edwin Muir. Muir encouraged Brown in his literary ambitions and endeavour. A recurrence of tuberculosis in the winter of 1952 forced Brown to break off his second year at Newbattle. Despite being seriously ill in Kirkwall Sanatorium, he continued to read and write, until his favourable response to new drugs justified his discharge.

Brown enjoyed the friendship of other Orkney writers, notably the scholar Ernest Marwick and poet Robert Rendall. Like Muir, and the novelist Eric Linklater, they were proof that Orkney was not altogether a literary backwater which inhibited writers. Yet Brown again began to feel the urge to try life outside Orkney, away from the undemanding way of life he had adopted – journalism, socialising and carrying on creative work. A third term at Newbattle Abbey in the summer of 1956 having intensified the desire to try his wings elsewhere, Brown left Orkney for a four-year course in English at Edinburgh University, eventually graduating with second-class honours, in 1960. He continued to write during his course, but a brief, unsuccessful spell at teacher-training college removed one of his possible employment options – school teaching. An opportunity to delay decisions for two years was provided by postgraduate research at Edinburgh University, on the poet Gerard Manley Hopkins. When this came to an end, Brown returned to Orkney having made, in effect, the ultimate career choice – he would be a full-time writer. By now, another major step had been taken – Brown became a Catholic in 1960, after some years of enquiry and observation.

As his list of publications and his reputation grew, despite intervals of illness, Brown settled into a routine and rhythm of work which suited him, satisfying his appetite for writing. He was now able to live with increasing financial security. His literary standing increased, and he was awarded numerous bursaries, prizes and honorary degrees, including the OBE in 1974 and the James Tait Black Memorial Prize in 1988. In 1994 his novel *Beside the Ocean of Time* was shortlisted for the Booker Prize. His work was translated into many languages, and he received critical acclaim from readers and writers alike. But none of these achievements altered his characteristically modest demeanour and lifestyle. Nor did they prevent him from issuing a stream of publications, which increased significantly in his last years. In addition, he left a considerable amount of posthumous work of a high standard – seven volumes of which have already been published. He died after a short illness on 13 April 1996, with his funeral taking place three days later from St Magnus Cathedral – on St Magnus Day. The huge attendance of both Orcadians and people from outwith the islands paid tribute not only to a Stromness man's literary distinction, but just as much to the personality who had been a familiar feature of the town for almost seventy-five years.

ORKNEY

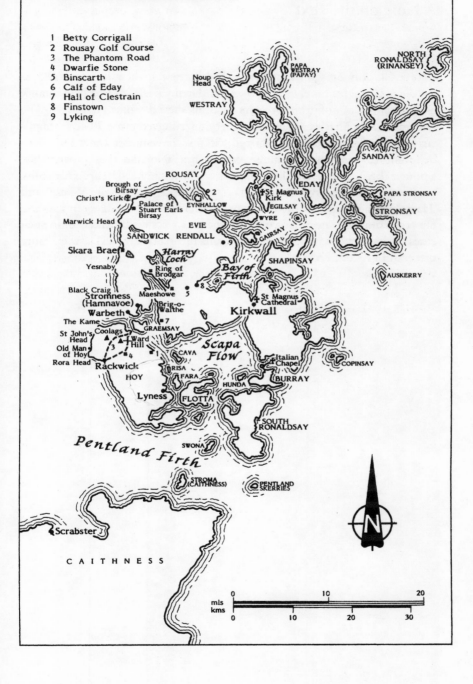

1 Betty Corrigall
2 Rousay Golf Course
3 The Phantom Road
4 Dwarfie Stone
5 Binscarth
6 Calf of Eday
7 Hall of Clestrain
8 Finstown
9 Lyking

NORTH
RONALDSAY
(RINANSEY)

Noup
Head

WESTRAY

PAPA
WESTRAY
(PAPAY)

SANDAY

ROUSAY

Brough of
Birsay

Christ's Kirk

Palace of
Stuart Earls
Birsay

Marwick Head

EYNHALLOW

St Magnus
Kirk

EGILSAY

EDAY

PAPA STRONSAY

STRONSAY

EVIE

SANDWICK RENDALL

WYRE

GAIRSAY

Skara Brae

Harray
Loch

Yesnaby

Ring of
Brodgar

SHAPINSAY

Bay of
Firth

AUSKERRY

Black Craig

Maeshowe

Stromness
(Hamnavoe)

Warbeth

Brig-o-
Waithe

St Magnus
Cathedral

Kirkwall

The Kame

St John's
Head

Coolags

GRAEMSAY

Ward
Hill

Scapa
Flow

Old Man
of Hoy

Rora Head

Rackwick

CAVA

RISA

Italian
Chapel

COPINSAY

HOY

FARA

BURRAY

Lyness

HUNDA

FLOTTA

SOUTH
RONALDSAY

SWONA

Pentland Firth

STROMA
(CAITHNESS)

PENTLAND
SKERRIES

Scrabster

CAITHNESS

N

mls
kms

0   10   20
0   10   20   30

A Note on the Text

George Mackay Brown was notoriously self-critical when it came to choosing the material for his *Selected Poems*, and many pieces of excellent quality have remained out of print for years awaiting their day of resurrection. 'The Funeral of Ally Flett' is a typical and very puzzling example. Readers familiar with the *Selected Poems* of 1996 will also have noticed that the poet's ballpoint has been busy among several of these texts, altering a word here, a phrase there, even in well known poems which had been in print for many years such as 'The Five Voyages of Arnor', 'The Year of the Whale' and 'Hamnavoe'. Frequently Brown improved the meaning, imagery or rhythm, but from time to time one or other of these aspects was weakened. In such cases we have chosen to present the poems in what we regard as their more successful original version.

The Collected Poems of

GEORGE MACKAY BROWN

The Storm (1954)

Prologue

For the islands I sing
   and for a few friends;
not to foster means
   or be midwife to ends.

Not for old Marx
   and his moon-cold logic –
anthill dialectics,
   neither gay nor tragic.

Not that extravagance
   Lawrence understood –
golden phoenix
   flowering from blood.

For Scotland I sing,
   the Knox-ruined nation,
that poet and saint
   must rebuild with their passion.

For workers in field
   and mill and mine
who break earth's bread
   and crush her wine.

Go, good my songs,
   be as gay as you can.
Weep, if you have to,
   the old tears of man.

Praise tinker and saint,
   and the rose that takes
its fill of sunlight
   though a world breaks.

The Road Home

As I came home from Kirkwall
   The ships were on the tide:
I saw the kirk of Magnus
   Down by the water side:
The blessèd brave Saint Magnus
   Who bowed his head and died.
His shining life was shorn away,
His kirk endureth to this day.
   As I came home from Kirkwall
   The ships were on the tide.

As I came home from Birsay
   A sower, all in tatters,
Strode, scattering the seed, immense
   Against the sunset bars,
And through his fingers, with the night,
   Streamed all the silver stars.
I watched him (leaning on a gate)
Scatter the glowing seeds of fate:
   As I came home from Birsay
   Against the sunset bars.

As I came home from Sandwick
   A star was in the sky.
The northern lights above the hill
   Were streaming broad and high.
The tinkers lit their glimmering fires,
   Their tents were pitched close by.
But the city of the vanished race
Lay dark and silent in that place.
   As I came home from Sandwick
   A star was in the sky.

Song: Rognvald to Ermengarde

The winds embrace you, my lover
And the quiet stars bless,
Noons touch you with ardour
And dawns with tenderness.

All these are my brothers,
They abide: I fare on.
I shall not see your like again
Beneath the enduring sun.

O mould with me a timeless love:
That we, the time-accursed,
May mock the sad and fleeting hours
And bid death do his worst.

But the hours embrace you, my lover
And the grave seasons bless,
The years touch you with wisdom
And death with gentleness.

The Storm

What blinding storm there was! How it
Flashed with a leap and lance of nails,
        Lurching, O suddenly
        Over the lambing hills,

Hounding me there! With sobbing lungs
I reeled past kirk and ale-house
        And the thousand candles
        Of gorse round my mother's yard,

And down the sand shot out my skiff
Into the long green jaws, while deep
        In summer's sultry throat
        Dry thunder stammered.

Swiftly the sail drew me over
The snarling Sound, scudding before
        The heraldic clouds now
        Rampant all around.

The sea – organ and harps – wailed miserere;
Swung me in fluent valleys, poised
        On icy yielding peaks
        Hissing spume, until

Rousay before me, the stout mast
Snapped, billowing down helpless sail.
  What evil joy the storm
  Seized us! plunged and spun!

And flung us, skiff and man (wave-crossed, God-lost)
On a rasp of rock! . . . The shore breakers,
  Stained chancel lights,
  Cluster of mellow bells,

Crossed hands, scent of holy water. . . .
The storm danced over all that night,
  Loud with demons, but I
  Safe in Brother Colm's cell.

Next morning in tranced sunshine
The corn lay squashed on every hill;
  Tang and tern were strewn
  Among highest pastures.

I tell you this, my son: after
That Godsent storm, I find peace here
  These many years with
  The Gray Monks of Eynhallow.

The Exile

So, blinded with Love
He tried to blunder
Out of that field
Of floods and thunder.

The frontiers were closed.
At every gate
The sworded pitiless
Angels wait.

There's no retreat.
The path mounts higher
And every summit
Fringed with fire.

The night is blind,
Dark winds, dark rains:
But now his blood
Pours through his veins,

His hammer heart
Thuds in his breast
'What Love devises,
That is best,'

And he would not turn,
Though the further side
Dowered his days
With fame and pride.

What though his feet
Are hurt and bare?
Love walks with him
In the menacing air.

The frontiers sealed;
His foot on the stone;
And low in the East
The gash of dawn.

Rackwick

(for Ian MacInnes)

Let no tongue idly whisper here.
Between those strong red cliffs,
Under that great mild sky
Lies Orkney's last enchantment,
The hidden valley of light.
Sweetness from the clouds pouring,
Songs from the surging sea.
Fenceless fields, fishermen with ploughs
And old heroes, endlessly sleeping
In Rackwick's compassionate hills.

Chorus: 'Soon Spring Will Come'

(for Robert Rendall)

1.

Soon Spring will come, and then the thrifty crofter
    Must yoke an ox, and drive his eager plough
Through the wet mould. The sower will follow after,
    And cast the good seed, rhythmical and slow,
    Along the furrows fringed with April snow.

2.

The fisherman will sail his black-tarred boat
    Into the west, and lower creels in the flood
For the scuttling lobster; or stretch his baited lines
    Along the ocean floor to hook the cod,
    Or wide-winged skate, if any are abroad.

3.

In her tight-thatched croft the busy wife will sweep,
    Will rock her crib, and knead the sticky dough
And turn her wheel. The ale-kirn's all her care,
    For when the liquor's clear, its amber glow
    Is stored in bottles in a shining row.

4.

Then summer suns, and fields green with young corn . . .
    We rape bright fleeces from the tremulous fold,
And dig dark fire from the droning hill,
    And whet our scythes, for now above the mould
    The ripening corn from green shimmers to gold.

5.

What happy men we are, if we only knew it!
    Like fallen seeds hoarding our darkened strength
For the long pilgrimage on perilous roads
    That crowd so thick to death, we soar at length,
    God-ripe above time's ruined labyrinth.

                                         [From a verse play]

At the first shout of dawn he woke
And strung his boots, and scratched for fleas,
Dipped his face in the throbbing burn,
And wolfed his bits of bread and cheese.

There ran the road, his lord and master,
That he must follow to the end,
Whether it soared across a hillside
Or staggered past 'The Sailor's Friend.'

Sometimes through a summer cornfield
It made a rutty golden track,
Or broadened to a city street
Bearing a million on its back.

Nothing else mattered; he must follow
Although it brushed the lip of hell,
Or strode in stone across a torrent,
Or lingered round a village well.

And yet he is a king of space
Who measures space with his own feet,
And beast and sun and harvest field
Come dancing to his red heart beat.

Death by Fire
A Newbattle Legend

(for Bob Fletcher)

WOMAN
A long time ago I saw that bud of flame.
It shook out petals, became a delicate flower.
Then they were everywhere, the crimson blossoms
Spreading on wall and floor a riotous garden.
Swords of light pierce me. Now I cannot hear
His voice in the fire's clamour.

MONK

                    Our ways end here –
Two blind lost travellers in a burning tower,
Two pilgrims from the opposite shores of time.
Strange loveliness is cast upon this girl,
Now gently breathing, as though it were a dream
Swinging across her brain from time far back
– A fabulous bough, laden with worldfall apples.
What of the night outside? Her father broods
On the dying torch in his hand. The country folk
(Tangled in wind and stars and curiosity)
Redden their faces gaping on this doom.
But we must die, fast in our web of lust.

WOMAN

The wanton flames fumbling about my heart
Will strip me skeleton-bright, beyond all passion.
A world apart, he suffers and smiles alone.
And now I see a snake slide through the garden.

MONK

And now I see a snake slide through our garden
Of twisted light. He pokes with his club face
At her shimmering foot, and rears; and then coils off
Vivid with doubt. A red rain bursts about her.
Her hair is a glory about her quiet throat.

WOMAN

Be born, redeem us now, O innocent darkness
Wombed in these flames. Their martyring tongues and blades
Hallow our rags of flesh that might have smouldered
Seventy years long. And now I take my cross
And pray to my good angel that lured me here
To such a radiant bourne.

MONK

                    Dreamily a rafter falls
Across her shoulder and wafts her to her knees.
She buries her face in flame as in a flower.

WOMAN

        A pilgrim I go
        Through three salt deserts.
        A pilgrim I linger

In a cold city.
A pilgrim I walk
By barren waves.
A pilgrim I sit
By wells of sorrow.
A pilgrim I burn
At the stake of love.
A pilgrim I seek
By tall dark trees
The Shining One.

MONK

The thunder of fire is still. My silver spirit
Swims from my body over the darkling hills.

Orcadians: Seven Impromptus

(for Edwin Muir)

1. LIFEBOATMAN

When the trawler sloped, askew on the rocks,
Drunk with the sea's cold fermentation
That February morning, and the washed decks
Mingled pitiful cries with the raving air,
And winking rockets in the zenith
Made eerie carnival, and frightened folk
Fluttered on the cliff verge, it was then you
Heroic at the wheel of the dumpy lifeboat,
Laughing at danger, set her dancing
Alongside the breaking hull, the frozen prayers
Answered, and struck surely for life
That snowy morning, while death channered
From lift and yelping wave and rasping rock;
Uncorked the rum bottle and swore merrily
At the wavering cheer from the cliff top;
Then slewed her home across the tiderace.

　　This is a legend where men drink their ale
　　By the peat glow, or under the pub's fluorescence.

And it was you, at Thorfinn o' Mucklehaa's,
When Thorfinn was south at the Highland Show,
Pushing his fingers in the flanks of bullocks
And stroking his chin over seeds and fertilisers,
It was you (none other) called on his bonny wife,
Ten years bairnless, on a simple social errand,
And laughed both moon and stars out of the night;
When Spring had scoured the tarnished sun,
And buttered the marsh with marigolds,
And made piglets nibble at the immense derelict sow,
Mucklehaa also was enriched with an heir
To the coy delight of Thorfinn and the countryside's mirth.

     This is a legend where men drink their ale
     By the peat glow, or under the pub's fluorescence.

2. FISHERMAN

The west flushed, drove down its shutter
And night sealed all.

Peaceful the air, the sea.
A quiet scattering of stars.

The great ocean
Makes the gentlest of motions about the turning world,
A thin wash through the pebbles.

No moon this night.
The creels lie still on their weeded ledges.

Not a sound, except far inland
The yelp of a tinker's dog.

Three days ago a storm blazed here, and drowned
Jock Halcrow among his lobsters.

There's one croft dark to-night in the lighted valley.

Peerie hen dandering across the road (clucking)
Dawdling, dipping, dandering (clucking)
Pecking at the tarmac (clucking)
Cocking a fierce bright eye
At a dandelion in the ditch (cluck, cluck, cluck, clucking)
Fate lours.
    It is the end.
        Goodnight, sweet gossip.

The Ford comes snoring by
In a flurry of fumes and feathers.

    'Janet lass, oot wi the pot.
    There'll be hen for wur tea the night.'

4 . CROFTER

The excisemen ferreted out
A pair of illicit stills
– Which straightway they confiscated –
Buried under the peatstack
Of the croft of Biggings.

And a week later
Mansie received his summons.

Sorry are the country folk.
They praise the fiery whisky
That Mansie distilled,
And wonder what the fine will be.

    'Sheurly tae God
    He'll no get the jail!'

They are all very distressed.

Only Walter o' Grayland
Who ten years ago
Cheated Mansie over the purchase of a field
Slaps his thighs and laughs.

5. DOCTOR

Describe Guthrie the doctor?
Little need be said:
His face a dark smirk,
His body a narrow black suit of clothes.

Oh, but very clever,
Especially with his tongue,
And therefore unpopular
With the heavy slow-spoken farmers of the parish.

So young, and so malicious,
He should be whetting his brain on the stone of some city,
Not on these gentle hills
Scattering barren wit.

Listen to him on a Saturday night
Over his glass of whisky:

'A curious hotch-potch, these people,
Proud of their purity of race.
Purity? . . .

First the aborigines
That howked Skara Brae from the sand.
Then the Picts,
Those small dark cunning men
Who scrawled their history in stone.
The Celtic fathers followed,
And many a Pictish lassie, no doubt,
Felt their power in the bed
As well as at the altar.

And then the tigers from east over sea,
The blond butchering Vikings,
Whose last worry on sea or land
Was purity of race, as they staggered couchwards
After a fill of ale.
Finally, to make the mixture thick and slab,
The off-scourings of Scotland,
The lowest sleaziest pimps from Lothian and the Mearns,
Fawning in the train of Black Pat,
And robbing and raping ad lib.

But that's not all.
For many a hundred ships have ripped their flanks
On Rora Head, or the Noup,
And Basque sailor lads and bearded skippers from Brittany
Left off their briny ways to cleave a furrow
Through Orkney crofts and lasses.

Not to speak of two world wars
And hordes of English and Yanks and Italians and Poles
Who took up their stations here:
By day the guns, by night the ancestral box-bed.
Only this morning
At Maggie o' Corsland's I delivered a bairn
With a subtle silk-selling Krishna smile.

A fine mixter-maxter!'

He laughs, his face a black snirl;
Then puts aside his whisky to answer the phone. . . .

A cry from some lonely croft behind the hill:
'Owld Jeems o' Seatter's been ta'en wi anither stroke.'

It's well after midnight.

Still sneering, he laces his boots.
Give Guthrie his due, he's conscientious.

6. SAINT

When Peter, orraman at Quoys,
Was 'saved' by Pentecostals
They dipped him in the sea.

'Peter's gey simple.'
Round blue eyes
Aimless amble of plouting feet
Birdcries on his tongue
Laughing among bairns
          simple Peter.
He knew nothing of justification,
Election or original sin,
But that morning on the beach

He heard the rocks cry out
GLORY TO GOD!
Each wave had a trumpet on its lips.
The caves were strewn with weeds and shells of praise.

Peter's mouth brimmed with psalms like a bell,
His knees bored holes in the wet sand,
His hands shivered with blessing.
For O, that ploughman's boots upon the road
Rang fire from the cobbles of New Jerusalem!

Peter the Saint
With thirty shillings a week (all found)
And his peerie black bible.

Simple Peter
Talking to a thrush on the telegraph wire.

7. THEM AT ISBISTER

Right on the very cliff verge
Is the croft of Isbister
And there old Janet lives
Who has borne four sons.

Two of them are under the hill.
One keeps a garage in Vancouver.
The youngest rarely comes home, being a sailor.

Old Janet has bright eyes
And thick brisk hands.
The parish dogs all know her.
She can tell the time by the sun
To within five minutes.

Now that Robbie is useless with rheumatics
Old Janet works Isbister.
Robbie sits by the fire smoking and spitting.
He welcomes any visitor,
Even the minister.

When Janet rails at Robbie
He rarely bothers to answer.
Sitting by the honeysuckle in July
Or under the tilley in December,
He is well contented.
He knows when it will rain
By the pains in his legs.

When a letter comes from the youngest boy
They peek at each other over their spectacles,
Spelling out the clumsy words far into the evening.

The dog barks in amazement.

When a butterfly knock comes at the door
Robbie says, 'Damn me, it's the minister.
But let him in.'

He gropes for his pipe.
Janet scurries to hang the kettle on the hook
And cries a welcome to the rattling sneck.

Loaves and Fishes (1959)

Part I The Drowning Wave

The Old Women

Go sad or sweet or riotous with beer
Past the old women gossiping by the hour,
They'll fix on you from every close and pier
An acid look to make your veins run sour.

'No help,' they say, 'his grandfather that's dead
Was troubled with the same dry-throated curse,
And many a night he made the ditch his bed.
This blood comes welling from the same cracked source.'

On every kind of merriment they frown.
But I have known a gray-eyed sober boy
Sail to the lobsters in a storm, and drown.
Over his body dripping on the stones
Those same old hags would weave into their moans
An undersong of terrible holy joy.

That Night in Troy

The wind was fire; the streets hot funnels; women
Went trailing lamentation round the walls
Searching for father or husband or son who lay
Churned in the rubble.
               Far off, where the sky
Curved like a claw upon the tawny plain
A casual smudge showed where the spoilers marched
To rouse their ships from ten years' arid slumber
(Each prow was buried deep in fleeting seapinks).

Over the carnival hill the stars trooped out.
The moon got up and walked across the sky
And laid bright fingers on the harp of Troy,
Smashed by an alien hoof.
             In one poor hovel
(So poor the enemy had passed it by
With a sneer and a spit) a girl spoke certain words
To the blind god of sheaf and shoal and cluster –
The haggard bundle whining in her arms
A redder conqueror than Agamemnon.
   Among his prisms a philosopher
(He was dying not of swords but of the brightening
Blizzard of age) said to the smiling lad
Who chafed his hands and fired his thoughtful clay:
'What was that uproar in the streets at noon?
It sounded like swift cataracts of thaw
In mountain valleys, winter's last lustration
Before the ploughman chants across the glebe
His liturgy of spring, turning a page
With every patient furrow' . . .
          On a dark plinth
(Its marble general toppled) Corydon crouched
Glowing with agony for three tall brothers
Broken beneath the wheels.
           A girl from the temple
Where lust all day had knit
Soldiers and vestals into sweating knots
Under the images whose eyes were vacant,
Stumbled upon him there.
           A crystal finger
Tuned an invisible string.
           With their first kiss
A ten years' vogue was out, and Paris died.
Since one unbroken string can lure dead stones
Into a solemn architectural dance
And lead in order through the finished gate
The horse, the wheel, the god, the golden corn,
They sealed a resurrection for the city.

Ulysses' prow over the formal waves
Led him the long way home. He turned his head
And saw far back, far back, the burning town.
He thought for an idle moment that it looked

Like a red rooted rose, symbol of love.
The spray went glancing past. He could not tell
If the drop that stung his cheek was bitter sea
Or the sudden image of a woman weaving.

The Death of Peter Esson
Tailor, Town Librarian, Free Kirk Elder

Peter at some immortal cloth, it seemed,
Fashioned and stitched, for so long had he sat
Heraldic on his bench. We never dreamed
It was his shroud that he was busy at.

Well Peter knew, his thousand books would pass
Gray into dust, that still a tinker's tale
As hard as granite and as sweet as grass,
Told over reeking pipes, outlasts them all.

The Free Kirk cleaves gray houses – Peter's ark
Freighted for heaven, galeblown with psalm and prayer.
The predestined needle quivered on the mark.
The wheel spun true. The seventieth rock was near.

Peter, I mourned. Early on Monday last
There came a wave and stood above your mast.

The Masque of Bread

What answer would he give, now he had reached
The Inquisitor's door, down seventy hungry streets,
Each poorer than the last, the last a slum
Rambling like nightmare round his winter feet?

The Inquisitor's door? The walls were all blank there,
But a white bakehouse with a little arch
And a creaking sign. . . . Against the fragrant doorpost
He clung, like drifted snow, while the shuttered oven
Opened on hills of harvest sun and corn.

The loaf the bakers laid on the long shelf
Was bearded, thewed, goldcrusted like a god.
Each drew a mask over his gentle eyes
– Masks of the wolf, the boar, the hawk, the reaper –
And in mock passion clawed the bread.
                                    But he
Who stood between the cold Plough and the embers
In the door of death, knew that this masquerade
Was a pure seeking past a swarm of symbols,
The millwheel, sun, and scythe, and ox, and harrow,
Station by station to that simple act
Of terror or love, that broke the hill apart.
But what stood there – an Angel with a sword
Or Grinning Rags – astride the kindled seed?

He knelt in the doorway. Still no question came
And still he knew no answer.

                          The bread lay broken,
Fragmented light and song.

                          When the first steeple
Shook out petals of morning, long bright robes
Circled in order round the man that died.

December Day, Hoy Sound

The unfurled gull on the tide, and over the skerry
Unfurling waves, and slow unfurling wreckage
– The Sound today a burning sapphire bough
Fretted with mimic spring.

                          The creatures of earth
Have seasons and stations, under the quartered sun
Ploughshare and cornstalk, millwheel and grinning rags.
The December seed kneels at his frosty vigil,
Sword by his side for the long crusade to the light
In trumpeting March, with the legion of lamb and leaf.

The sea grinds his salt behind a riot of masks.

Today on Hoy Sound random blossoms unfurl
Of feather and rust, a harlequin spring.

                    Tomorrow
The wave will weep like a widow on the rock,
Or howl like Lear, or laugh like a green child.

Thorfinn

Sing Thorfinn's drowning.
                    Tired of his thieving guests,
The kestrel shape that wore his hand and eye,
The stealthy-by-moon deep-litter ghost,
And the seducer of vagrant Pertelotes,
Clad in his innocent hungers Thorfinn walked
Past farmyards havering with hens and greed.

Through streets of finger-pointing folk who'd set
Iron bars between him and the sun
(They shackled not the spectre but the boy)
Went Thorfinn to the clean curve of the oar.

Heart sick of the land
Where troubles grew with every grass blade
And every rose gushed from a septic root
And every casual car was the Black Maria,

He rowed his little boat behind the holm
To take the purple samurai of the flood.
Cornless they range, the lobsters.
By weeded rock and plangent pool
God puts in their beautiful claws
Sweet algae and tiny glimmering fish
The dropping surfeits of the rich Atlantic
Ravelling its rivers through the corn-patched Orkneys
And shrinking, twice a day.
(To their peril they eat man fodder:
Explore a casual fishgut hole, they're snared
In a tarry mesh, drawn up, and drowned with air.)
Whether it chanced, the Owner of these lobsters,
Grown sour at Thorfinn as any bristling poultry man
Turned a salt key in his last door of light;

Or whether Love, abroad in a seeking wave
Lifted him from the creaking rowlocks of time
And flung a glad ghost on a wingless shore:

No one can tell.
                              A crofter at early light
Found an empty boat stuttering on the rocks
And dawn-cold cocks cheering along the links.

Themes

Tinker themes cry through
The closes of my breath –
    Straw and tapestry shaken
    With keenings of love and birth;
Odyssean corn returning
Across furrows of death;
    Women scanning the sea;
    Ploughmen wounding the earth.

Gregory Hero

Five suns lit his dust.
They're out, and for his death
We yield him images: he was
A Viking ship, a white stallion.

Twelve winds knit his strength
From fish, corn, old gravestones.
Twenty years stored his veins
With spindrift, rain, the milk
Of vanished women's mildness and the kegs
Of courage smuggled down generations.

Gregory dispersed again, down the
Throat of crabs, spun through
Long green currents of water,
Sunk to the root of seaweed and
In core of shells settled.

Tall virgins, stretching hand and breast
To catch the sun and sweet showers,
Mending nets or in the cornfield
Taking a burnish and caress of wind,
It's Gregory pursues you round the world.

Port of Venus

The holy earl, his kestrel pilgrimage
Hardly begun, furled sails in a strange port
Out of the kick of the gale and the salt siege,
And all the sailors called for a night's sport

With foreign girls and ale, eyeing their lord,
Ignorant of what sanctities he planned –
Unlock the city granaries with his sword,
Or lay a cold mouth on the prince's hand

To get fresh corn aboard his famished ships.
The square was mild with doves. The elders came
And led this hawkwing, in a barnyard choir,
To greet their prince, a girl with snooded hair
And shy cold breasts. They trembled as their lips
Welded holy and carnal in one flame.

Part II Crofts Along the Shore

The Stranger

One night he stayed with us
(Said the tall proud woman)
One night in our poor house
And then mounted his mare
And clattered thankless forth.
I've thought him ever since
A great one of the earth
– A poet or a prince –
Touched with unlucky fire.

That night when I was laid
(Sang the milking girl)
Sound in my box bed
He broke upon my rest
And in the deep midnight
Turned that first cruel pain
Into a wild delight
That buds and flowers again
When his child seeks my breast.

What was he but a tink
(Cried the obstinate man)
All rags, blether, and stink?
Yet when he slouched through that door
Begging a slice of bread
And a drop of ale in a glass
The old wife bowed her head,
And a throb went through our lass
As though an angel stood there.

Childsong

The moon's a clown
Tumbling through clouds,
His circus face
Mapped with all moods.

Stars reap the blue
Swept corn of night.
Westward they surge,
Their sickles bright.

Dayspring's a hunter
On the Orphir hills.
The grimling wolf
With his bow he kills.

But all these jewels
From the mines of space,
Not half so far-come
As that cold face.

Hamnavoe

My father passed with his penny letters
Through closes opening and shutting like legends
    When barbarous with gulls
    Hamnavoe's morning broke

On the salt and tar steps. Herring boats,
Puffing red sails, the tillers
    Of cold horizons, leaned
    Down the gull-gaunt tide

And threw dark nets on sudden silver harvests.
A stallion at the sweet fountain
    Dredged water, and touched
    Fire from steel-kissed cobbles.

Hard on noon four bearded merchants
Past the pipe-spitting pier-head strolled,
    Holy with greed, chanting
    Their slow grave jargon.

A tinker keened like a tartan gull
At cuithe-hung doors. A crofter lass
    Trudged through the lavish dung
    In a dream of cornstalks and milk.

Blessings and soup plates circled. Euclidian light
Ruled the town in segments blue and gray.
    The school bell yawned and lisped
    Down ignorant closes.

In 'The Arctic Whaler' three blue elbows fell,
Regular as waves, from beards spumy with porter,
    Till the amber day ebbed out
    To its black dregs.

The boats drove furrows homeward, like ploughmen
In blizzards of gulls. Gaelic fisher girls
    Flashed knife and dirge
    Over drifts of herring,

And boys with penny wands lured gleams
From the tangled veins of the flood. Houses went blind
    Up one steep close, for a
    Grief by the shrouded nets.

The kirk, in a gale of psalms, went heaving through
A tumult of roofs, freighted for heaven. And lovers
    Unblessed by steeples, lay under
    The buttered bannock of the moon.

He quenched his lantern, leaving the last door.
Because of his gay poverty that kept
    My seapink innocence
    From the worm and black wind;

And because, under equality's sun,
All things wear now to a common soiling,
    In the fire of images
    Gladly I put my hand
    To save that day for him.

Stars

Tae be wan o them Kings
That owre the desert rode
Trackan a muckle reid star,
The herald o God!

Tae swivel a crystal eye
Abune a mountain place
And light on an uncan star,
A tinker in space! –

Thought Tammas, rowan his boat
Fae creel tae creel aroond,
When Venus shook her hair
Owre the Soond.

The Death Bird

(i)

Pen, take no wings on you
But trail black scars across the page
Calamitously to record
For all grocers to be
That Knarston, justice of the peace, is dead,
Washed home by the last cold wave.

Or rather, on Wednesday,
The clock in his skull rang 'Time'
And startled him under the hill.
The lark was silent.
                    A bird
Winged with fivers,
Sovereigns birling in the throat,
Shrieked across his dying.

In the play of The Death Bird
All the actors came out well
Except for the hero
Who had spasms of stage fright.

        In the end, all the same
        They smothered him in flowers
        And bore him off, shoulder high.

(ii)

A week later Peero died
Feet pointing at the stars,
Thoroughly soused
In holy beer and dew.
They gave him back to God
        Without a flower or a tear.

But over the corn
A lark sang, wildly cheering
        Peero's sweet translation
        From ratflesh to light

(Thought Halcro, Peero's neighbour, his tongue
Sacramental with malt, his eyes
Grieving like angels. He stuck
A haloed candle in the wine bottle
Peero drained last week.)

Unfortunately, according to counter and pew,
    According to books of the month,
    According to singing reels and smoking guns,
    According to umbrellas and spats
Halcro is a damned liar
And his three tears
Are not angels
Nor saints of sorrow
But a drunken leak.

      (Not for all under the hill
      Over the hill a lark stammers
      Abracadabra of joy.)

Halcro

   Don't go to that old man
With daffodil-shining dove-winged words
   To hang beside his clock.
His wall is wild with ships and birds.

   Even the rum you bring
And the tobacco coiled and mellow
   He loves to chew, he'll stuff
In the oblivion of his pillow.

   Give him the salty texts
Chanted in smithy, pub, and loan –
   How the corn's ripening; how
The pier was gray with Grimsbymen

   Last stormy weekend; how
Sigurd got a pint of stout
   So riotously sour
They had to call the police out;

And how Grieg's spindly lass
With hollow neck and freckled brow
   Is suddenly grown a woman
And has two breasts like roses now. . . .

   Then see his bone-bright hands
Frail on the chair, grow firm again
   In the stillness of old brawls,
Torn nets, sweet dust, and tangled grain.

The Lodging

The stones of the desert town
Flush; and, a star-filled wave,
Night steeples down.

From a pub door here and there
A random ribald song
Leaks on the air.

The Roman in a strange land
Broods, wearily leaning
His lance in the sand.

The innkeeper over the fire
Counting his haul, hears not
The cry from the byre;

But rummaging in the till
Grumbles at the drunken shepherds
Dancing on the hill;

And wonders, pale and grudging,
If the queer pair below
Will pay their lodging.

Part III *The Redeeming Wave*

The Heavenly Stones

Three men came to our door with gifts
When I was a lightsome lad.
Yellow and red and black they stood
Against the milking shed.

'Will you take the sign of wealth?' said one
And gave me a disc of gold,
The same with which God's corn and wine
Are dearly bought and sold.

I ran with it to the midden heap
And sank it in that filth.
'If that's how you treat good gold,' laughed he,
'You lock the door on wealth.'

The red one said, 'My jar's sweet fume
Is sensuality.'
What sound was that? My father's boar
Rutting behind the sty.

I tilted the vessel with my foot
Till the dark oil shimmered out.
'If that's how you treat the dancing five,
Go wear a beggar's clout;

'Who might have had heraldic cloaks
Over your shoulder slung,
And bedded with more beautiful girls
Than ever Solomon sung.'

The third old man came shuffling up
And opened his earthen bottle:
'O what are breast and thigh but dust,
And what is yellow metal?

'Taste the bitters in my cruse,
Nor twist your face, my son.
This has grown on the tree of life
Since Adam's day began.

'And you must hang on your own tree
Watered with women's tears,
The grape of God that ripens slow
Through forty hundred years.

'The men of dust will pluck you down
And eat your flesh for food,
And angel fingered, fill their flasks
At the five gates of your blood.

'Drink this wine now, that you may know
What Adam had to suffer,
And what atonement, on that day,
A son of God must offer' . . .

I longed to spit it from my mouth
But yet I drank it down
With anguish, and the three old men
Rode onward to the town.

That hour I felt mortality
Fasten about my bones.
The gold out of the midden sang
And heaven leaked from the stones.

The shaken branch, The Voice, the draped
Whispering coil of flame,
And Eve a tall unfingered harp
Strung with desire and shame.

All the world's honey and its dust
Through my five senses falling . . .
Till from the hearth stone where she knelt
I heard my mother calling,

And heard my father's restless saw
Rasping through the wood –
Old craftsman, making crib and cross
Where simple trees had stood.

A Roman column under the moon
Passed like a gleaming wave
That time would scatter, each bright drop
To its salt separate grave.

I flung away the heavenly stones
Yellow and black and red
That I had played with all day long,
And, laughing, crept to bed.

Dream of Winter

These were the sounds that dinned upon his ear –
The spider's fatal purring, and the gray
Trumpeting of old mammoths locked in ice.
No human sound there was: only the evil
Shriek of the violin sang of human woe
And conquest and defeat, and the round drums
                    Sobbed as they beat.

He saw the victim nailed against the night
With ritual stars. The skull, a ruin of dreams,
Leaned in the wind, merry with curl and thorn.
The long robes circled. A penitential wail
For the blue lobster and the yellow cornstalk
And the hooded victim, broken to let men live,
                    Flashed from their throats,

Then all the faces turned from the Winter Man.
From the loch's April lip a swan slid out
In a cold rhyme. The year stretched like a child
And rubbed its eyes on light. Spring on the hill
With lamb and tractor, lovers and burning heather.
Byres stood open. The wind's blue fingers laid
                    A migrant on the rock.

Saint Magnus in Egilsay

Since Time folded his breath about the world,
Fixed in us wondering apes a praising tongue,
Strung his bright harps along the cold sea caves,
And broke our winter into grape and grain,
Plough, harrow, and scythe pressed on the virgin isles
Their circling kiss of peace. But one cold hill
            Locked thighs of stone against

The ardent ploughs, Penelope bound to a ghost.
They lured you there, a gentle enemy.
Bow your blank head. Offer your innocent vein.
A red wave broke. The bell sang in the tower.
Hands from the plough carried the broken saint
Under the arch. Below, the praying sea
      Knelt on the stones.

But O what love came then! Root, stalk, and flower
Twined in a riot through the acre of death
And larks cut lyrical nests deep in its turf.
Parched loin, and stringless tongue, and pearl-blind eye,
Sailed up that sound, fingered that dust, and saw
The red ploughs cleave their snow and curve for ever
      Across the April hill.

Elegy

The Magnustide long swords of rain
    Quicken the dust. The ploughman turns
      Furrow by holy furrow
        The liturgy of April.
      What rock of sorrow
    Checks the seed's throb and flow
Now the lark's skein is thrown
      About the burning sacrificial hill?

Cold exiles from that ravished tree
    (Fables and animals guard it now)
      Whose reconciling leaves
    Fold stone, cornstalk and lark,
      Our first blood grieves
    That never again her lips
Flowering with song we'll see,
      Who, winged and bright, speeds down into the dark.

Now let those risers from the dead,
    Cornstalks, golden conspirators,
      Cry on the careless wind
        Ripeness and resurrection;

How the calm wound
    Of the girl entering earth's side
Gives back immortal bread
        For this year's dust and rain that shall be man.

The Shining Ones

Shuttered in crystal webs, they gravely eyed
The man coming in, cold and remote and silent.
His foot on the last step, he turned again
And threw one wild look backward. But the night
Was a funnel of darkness, roaring with stars. Beyond
Ranged the great beasts of time.

        The watchers stood,
And still his feet came on. He could not tell
If they were light or fire, or if the road
That drove him through his death now swung him sheer
Into eternity (a flower pressed dry
By poets, preachers, all the literate humbugs)
Or was the salty cobbles of a grief
Where he must pace till morning shook the cloud
From his blunt brow, and storied Legion ale
Gushed from the lever he pressed to his tired heart.

'This *is* the gate of death,' he prayed.
            Far on
A new wave turned.
        They stood.
            There as he faltered
Under the webs of fire, twin blessings fell
From that hard cry; its echoes Bread and Breath
(Four dove-wings by his father's door) had sheltered
All his green hungers, flying in pity and peace
Through sequent arches of his growth, until
The last stone sang.

        The birds of Dread and Dearth
That all the dolorous way clung to his wrist
Shrieked down their homing gale.

He stood, a legend,
On the bright side of the bone.
A new wind rose
And stripped the rags of anguish from his shoulder
Supple as tulips, gayer than the hour
He fought Young Kelly in the Lammas booth
(The surgeon's scar still vivid on his side)
Stayed his three rounds, and won his thirty bob,
And sent that profit raging down his throat.

The sky grew tall as lupins. Far below
Wave and boat swayed like familiar dancers.
That sea must hold him now. It swung him over
To the purgatorial hill.

The silent watchers
Out of the dawn lifted their swords. They blazed.

Song: 'Further than Hoy'

Further than Hoy
the mermaids whisper
through ivory shells
a-babble with vowels

Further than history
the legends thicken,
the buried broken
vases and columns

Further than fame
are fleas and visions,
the hermit's cave
under the mountain

Further than song
the hushed awakening
of sylvan children
the harp unstroked

Further than death
Your feet will come
to the forest, black forest
where Love walks, alone.

Chapel between Cornfield and Shore

Above the ebb, that gray uprooted wall
Was arch and chancel, choir and sanctuary,
A solid round of stone and ritual.
Knox brought all down in his wild hogmanay.

The wave turns round. New ceremonies will thrust
From the thrawn acre where those good stones bleed
Like corn compelling sun and rain and dust
After the crucifixion of the seed.

Restore to that maimed rockpool, when the flood
Sounds all her lucent strings, its ocean dance;
And let the bronze bell nod and cry above
Ploughshare and creel; and sieged with hungry sins
A fisher priest offer our spindrift bread
For the hooked hands and harrowed heart of Love.

Daffodils

Heads skewered with grief
Three Marys at the cross
(Christ was wire and wax
festooned on a dead tree)

Guardians of the rock,
their emerald tapers touch
the pale wick of the sun
and perish before the rose
bleeds on the solstice stone
and the cornstalk unloads
peace from hills of thorn

Spindrifting blossoms
from the gray comber of March
thundering on the world,
splash our rooms coldly with
first grace of light, until
the corn-tides throb, and fields
drown in honey and fleeces

Shawled in radiance
tissue of sun and snow
three bowl-bound daffodils
in the euclidian season
when darkness equals light
and the world's circle shudders
down to one bleeding point
Mary Mary and Mary
triangle of grief.

The Year of the Whale (1965)

The Funeral of Ally Flett

Because of his long pilgrimage
    From pub to alehouse
        And all the liquor laws he'd flout,
Being under age
        And wringing peatbog spirit from a clout
Into a secret kettle,
    And making every Sabbath a carouse,
Mansie brought a twelve-year bottle.

Because his shy foot turned aside
    From Merran's door,
        And Olga's coat with the red button
And Inga's side
        Naked as snow or swan or wild bog cotton
Made him laugh loud
    And after, spit with scunner on the floor,
Marget sewed a long chaste shroud.

Because the scythe was in the oats
    When he lay flat,
        And Jean Macdonald's best March ale
Cooled the long throats
        (At noon the reapers drank from the common pail)
And Sanders said
    'Corn enough here for every tramp and rat',
Sigrid baked her lightest bread.

Although the fleet from Hamnavoe
    Drew heavy nets
        Off Noup Head, in a squall of rain,
Turning in slow
        Gull-haunted circles near the three-mile line,
And mouthing cod
    Went iced and salted into slippery crates,
One skipper heard and bowed his head.

Because at Dounby and the fair
    Twelve tearaways
        Brought every copper in the islands
Round their uproar
        And this one made a sweet and sudden silence
Like that white bird
    That broke the tempest with a twig of praise,
The preacher spoke the holy word.

Because the hour of grass is brief
    And the red rose
        Is a bare thorn in the east wind
And a strong life
        Runs out and spends itself like barren sand
And the dove dies
    And every loveliest lilt must have a close,
Old Betsy came with bitter cries.

Because his dance was gathered now
    And parish feet
        Went blundering their separate roads
After the plough
        And after net and peat and harvest loads,
Yet from the cradle
    Their fated steps with a fixed passion beat,
Tammas brought his Swedish fiddle.

Shipwreck

Paul grounded at Braga, a gull on his shoulder.
The milkmaids wrung him dry.
He lay that night at the fire of Lifia
And then moved inland
And keeps pigs on a black hill.
    Jan put a cut of tobacco in his teeth
When the *Maggi* struck.
They found him at the end of the kirk
Near dawn, out of the gale,
Squirting poison among the tombstones.
    For Gregory was much grief in the crofts.
The sea did not offer him with green hands
To the seven dark shawls.

His bones fouled no net or slipway.
With small diagonals crabs covered him.
    Two storms and a dove later
A man with a limpet pail
Turned a gold swathe among seaweed.
That was the hair
Of Robin, weaver of nets, in a warp of ebb.
    Peero said when the first lump of salt
Fell through wrenched timbers,
'Now it seems I can never
Hang a brass chain at my belly
Or sit in the council
Or go among doors with the holy cards' . . .
The gray lumps fell and fell and stopped his mouth.
    Peter was three years getting home from the wreck.
He found his feet at Houton.
The ale-house there kept him a week.
He stayed at Gair for harvest,
Drowned and drunk again with broken corn,
Then shipped at Hamnavoe
For the blue fish, the whales, the Davis Straits
And casks of hellfire Arctic rum.
He stood dry in his door at last.
Merrag wore a black shawl.
He read his own tombstone that evening.
    For Donald the way was not long.
His father had a dozen horse at Skaill
But Donald loved the dark net.
Indeed for Donald the day and the way were not long.
Old men had said,
'Such skill at Greek and physics and poetry
Will bring this Donald fame at last.'
But for him the day was not long.
His day was this long –
Sixteen years, four months, and two days.

Culloden:
The Last Battle

The black cloud crumbled.
                My plaid that Morag wove
In Drumnakeil, three months before the eagle

Fell in the west, curled like the gray sea hag
Around my blood.
                    We crouched on the long moor
And broke our last round bannock.
                    Fergus Mor
Was praying to every crossed and beaded saint
That swung Iona, like the keel of Scotland,
Into the wrecking European wave.
Gow shook his flask. Alastair sang out
They would be drunker yet on German blood
Before the hawk was up. For 'Look', cried he,
'At all the hogsheads waiting to be tapped
Among the rocks' . . .
                    Old iron-mouth spilled his brimstone,
Nodded and roared. Then all were at their texts,
And Fergus fell, and Donald gave a cry
Like a wounded stag, and raised his steel and ran
Into the pack.
                    But we were hunters too,
All smoking tongues. I picked my chosen quarry
Between the squares. Morag at her wheel
Turning the fog of wool to a thin swift line
Of August light, drew me to love no surer
Than that red man to war. And his cold stance
Seemed to expect my coming. We had hastened
Faithful as brothers from the sixth cry of God
To play this game of ghost on the long moor.
His eyes were hard as dice, his cheek was cropped
For the far tryst, his Saxon bayonet
Bright as a wolf's tooth. Our wild paths raced together,
Locked in the heather, faltered by the white stone,
Then mine went on alone.
                    'Come back, come back',
Alastair cried.
                    I turned.
                    Three piercing shapes
Drifted about me in the drifting smoke.
We crossed like dreams.
                    This was the last battle.
We had not turned before.

The eagle was up
And away to the Isles.
That night we lay

Far in the west. Alastair died in the straw.
We travelled homeward, on the old lost roads,
Twilight by twilight, shepherd by weeping shepherd.

My three wounds were heavy and round as medals
Till Morag broke them with her long fingers.

Weaving, she sings of the beauty of defeat.

Horseman and Seals, Birsay

On the green holm they built their church.
There were three arches.
They walked to the village across the ebb.
From this house they got milk.
A farmer cut and carted their peats.
Against their rock
Fishermen left a basket of mouthing silver.
They brought the gifts of heaven
To the new children and the suffering shapes.
They returned to the island
And mixed their bell with the seven sounds of the sea.
Eight times a day
They murmured their psalms in that steep pasture.

A horseman stood at the shore, his feet in seaweed.
He could not cross over.
The sea lay round the isle, a bright girdle.
His voice scattered in the vastness
Though from shore to shore pierced cries of gull and petrel.
What did the horseman want?
Perhaps an old man in the parish was sick,
Or he wanted a blessing on his ship,
Or he wished to argue a point in theology.
From shore to shore they blessed him.
They trooped under the arch for nones.
After the psalms the horseman was still there,
Patient in the seaweed.

The sea shone higher round the skerry.
And the abbot said, 'Cormac, you are the carpenter
A blessed occupation.
And tomorrow you will beg some boards and nails
And you will build a little boat,
So that we do not need to keep horsemen waiting on the other
    shore
Who are in need of God' . . .

And while the boat was building under the crag
Paul gathered whelks.
From the cold triangular pools he gathered handfuls
And put them in his basket.
He sang *Dominus Pascit Me*, gathering whelks in the ebb.
Twenty seals lay on the skerry.
They turned their faces towards the psalm.
The brother sang for them also,
For the seals with their beautiful gentle old men's faces.
Then the ebb subtracted one sound
From the seven-fold harmony of ocean.
The tide lay slack, between ebb and flowing, a slipped girdle.
Paul gathered whelks and sang
Till the flood set in from the west, with a sound like harps,
And one by one the seals entered the new water.

The Abbot

Here at Innertun we have seven brothers.
Havard was a shepherd
In Hoy, that huddle of blue shoulders.
In the tavern there
He broke the back of a loud fisherman.
He has given his fifty sheep to the widow,
To the three orphans his green hill.
At Innertun now, he weaves our coats.

At Rinansay, Einar was a butterfly
Over a tangled harp.
The girls miss him in that low island.
Now when candles are lit
For matins, in the warp of winter,
He drifts, our gray moth
Among the woven monotonies of God.

Sigurd sailed to Iceland, a boy,
And lost an arm there.
He was with Leif on the Greenland voyage.
He bought a Galway horse, sire of thirty
And sailed home from Norway
With tusks of walrus, proper embellishment
For hilt and helmet and ale-cup.
'Too old now', said Sigurd
'For any port but the blue of heaven,
I teach the brothers shipwit'.

We have a field at Innertun
That was full of stones last April.
Plenty of lobsters, goat milk
At our fasting tables.
Then Erling rode from Birsay, love-torn.
He laid a plough on our acre.
He gives us bannocks and new ale.

You would not wish to have seen
The *Gothenberg* at the crag
Like a hare in the cold jaw of a wolf.
You would not wish to have seen
Gulls over blind shapes on the sand.
From the timbers we made a new door
And the Swedish boy
Has Latin enough to answer the priest now.

Rolf whistled down the wild hawk.
He brought twelve rampant foals
From the hill Greenay,
Gale shapes, to the horse fair at Hamnavoe.
He put a ring in the bull's nose,

And said in a circle of drunk whalers
'There is a time to finish with beasts
And to strive with angels'.
His knee was at our line of knees next morning.

This day is a day of sheaves at Innertun
And five crisp circles.
A yellow wind walks on the hill.
The small boats in the Sound
Pluck this brightness and that from the nets.
Our cow watched a black field in March,
And deepening greens, all summer.
Today she cries over a sudden radiance,
The clean death of corn.
Christ, crofter, lay kindly on this white beard
Thy sickle, flail, millstone, fires . . .
They shout across the broken gold.
The boy has found a lark's nest in the oats.

Our Lady of the Waves

The twenty brothers of Eynhallow
Have made a figure of Our Lady.
From red stone they carved her
And set her on a headland.
There spindrift salts her feet.
At dawn the brothers sang this
       Blessed Lady, since midnight
       We have done three things.
       We have bent hooks.
       We have patched a sail.
       We have sharpened knives.
       Yet the little silver brothers are afraid.
       Bid them come to our net.
       Show them our fire, our fine round plates.
       Per Dominum Christum nostrum
       Look mildly on our hungers.

The codling hang in a row by the wall.
At noon the brothers sang this
       Holy Mother, Una the cow
       Gives thin blue milk.

Where is the golden thread of butter?
The stone in the middle of our glebe
Has deep black roots.
We have broken three ploughs on it.
Per Christum Dominum nostrum
Save Una from the axe,
Our dappled cow with large eyes.

The girls go by with pails to the byre.
At sunset the brothers sang this
   Sweet Virgin, the woman of Garth
   Is forever winking at Brother Paul.
   She puts an egg in his palm.
   She lays peats in his cowl.
   Her neck is long as spilt milk.
   Brother Paul is a good lad.
   Well he carries word and wine for the priest.
   But three red midnights
   His tongue has run loose among dreams.

Paul has broken knees at the stone.
At midnight the brothers sang this
   Queen of Heaven, this good day
   There is a new cradle at Quoys.
   It rocks on the blue floor.
   And there is a new coffin at Hamnavoe.
   Arnor the poet lies there
   Tired of words and wounds.
   In between, what is man?
   A head bent over fish and bread and ale.
   Outside, the long furrow.
   Through a door, a board with a shape on it.

Guard the plough and the nets.

Star of the sea, shine for us.

The Poet

Therefore he no more troubled the pool of silence.
But put on mask and cloak,
Strung a guitar

And moved among the folk.
Dancing they cried,
'Ah, how our sober islands
Are gay again, since this blind lyrical tramp
Invaded the Fair!'

Under the last dead lamp
When all the dancers and masks had gone inside
His cold stare
Returned to its true task, interrogation of silence.

Farm Labourer

'God, am I not dead yet?' said Ward, his ear
   Meeting another dawn.
      A blackbird, lost in leaves, began to throb
And on the pier
       The gulls stretched barbarous throats
         Over the creels, the haddock lines, the boats.
      His mortal pain
         All day hung tangled in that lyrical web.

'Seventy years I've had of this', said Ward,
   'Going in winter dark
     To feed the horse, a lantern in my fist,
Snow in my beard,
       Then thresh in the long barn
       Bread and ale out of the skinflint corn,
     And such-like work!'
       And a lark flashed its needle down the west.

Old Fisherman with Guitar

A formal exercise for withered fingers.
   The head is bent,
     The eyes half closed, the tune
Lingers
      And beats, a gentle wing the west had thrown
     Against his breakwater wall with salt savage lament.

So fierce and sweet the song on the plucked string, [47
    Know now for truth
        Those hands have cut from the net
The strong
        Crab-eaten corpse of Jock washed from a boat
    One old winter, and gathered the mouth of Thora to his
          mouth.

The Year of the Whale

The old go, one by one, like guttered flames.
    This past winter
        Tammag the bee-man has taken his cold blank mask
          To the honeycomb under the hill,
            Corston who ploughed out the moor
        Unyoked and gone; and I ask,
    Is Heddle lame, that in youth could dance and saunter
           A way to the chastest bed?
The kirkyard is full of their names
          Chiselled in stone. Only myself and Yule
           In the ale-house now, speak of the great whale year.

This one and that provoked the taurine waves
    With an arrogant pass,
        Or probing deep through the snow-burdened hill
          Resurrected his flock,
           Or passed from fiddles to ditch
        By way of the quart and the gill,
    All night lay tranced with corn, but stirred to face
          The brutal stations of bread;
While those who tended their lives
          Like sacred lamps, chary of oil and wick,
           Died in the fury of one careless match.

Off Scabra Head the lookout sighted a school
    At the first light.
        A meagre year it was, limpets and crows
          And brief mottled grain.
           Everything that could float
        Circled the school. Ploughs
Wounded those wallowing lumps of thunder and night.

The women crouched and prayed.
Then whale by whale by whale
Blundering on the rock with its red stain
Crammed our winter cupboards with oil and meat.

Trout Fisher

Semphill, his hat stuck full of hooks
Sits drinking ale
Among the English fishing visitors,
Probes in detail
Their faults in casting, reeling, selection of flies.
'Never', he urges, 'do what it says in the books'.
Then they, obscurely wise,
Abandon by the loch their dripping oars
And hang their throttled tarnish on the scale.

'Forgive me, every speckled trout',
Says Semphill then,
'And every swan and eider on these waters.
Certain strange men
Taking advantage of my poverty
Have wheedled all my subtle loch-craft out
So that their butchery
Seem fine technique in the ear of wives and daughters.
And I betray the loch for a white coin'.

The Twelve Piers of Hamnavoe

Those huge apostle feet
Stand in the ebb.
Twice daily
The god of whale and iceberg
Returns with gulls
To lay green blessings on them

Or spreads his wounds around
Threatening the nets

Or like an old blind ghost
Folds them in love and lost voices.

Hamnavoe Market

They drove to the Market with ringing pockets.

Folster found a girl
Who put wounds on his face and throat,
Small and diagonal, like red doves.

Johnston stood beside the barrel.
All day he stood there.
He woke in a ditch, his mouth full of ashes.

Grieve bought a balloon and a goldfish.
He swung through the air.
He fired shotguns, rolled pennies, ate sweet fog from a stick.

Heddle was at the Market also.
I know nothing of his activities.
He is and always was a quiet man.

Garson fought three rounds with a negro boxer,
And received thirty shillings,
Much applause, and an eye loaded with thunder.

Where did they find Flett?
They found him in a brazen circle,
All flame and blood, a new Salvationist.

A gypsy saw in the hand of Halcro
Great strolling herds, harvests, a proud woman.
He wintered in the poorhouse.

They drove home from the Market under the stars
Except for Johnston
Who lay in a ditch, his mouth full of dying fires.

Country Girl

I make seven circles, my love
For your good breaking.
I make the gray circle of bread
And the circle of ale
And I drive the butter round in a golden ring
And I dance when you fiddle
And I turn my face with the turning sun till your feet come in
     from the field.
My lamp throws a circle of light,
Then you lie for an hour in the hot unbroken circle of my
     arms.

Boy from the Shore

When horsemen at the inn-yards say
'Return to her'
I stay beside the barrel, drinking.
When the old women urge,
'Bring her a gift of fish'
I take nothing but hunger into your house.
When the elders insist
'Break bread together'
You are the witch in the flame, I the fiddler,
At the gate of loaves and fishes.
Each Sabbath silence
Our tree is crammed with birds,
And when the villages dance
Then we lie quiet all night with mixed hair.

Weather Bestiary

RAIN
The unicorn melts through his prism. Sodden hooves
Have deluged the corn with light.

WIND
A fisherman wets his finger. The eyelash
Of the gray stallion flicks his blood with cold.

SUN
A hard summer. The month I sat at the rock
One fish rose, belly up, a dead gleam.

THUNDER
Corn, lobster, fleece hotly harvested – now
That whale stranded on the blue rock!

FROST
Stiff windless flower, hearse-blossom,
Show us the brightness of blood, stars, apples.

FOG
The sun-dipped isle was suddenly a sheep
Lost and stupid, a dense wet tremulous fleece.

SNOW
Autumn, a moulted parrot, eyes with terror
This weird white cat. It drifts the rose-bush under.

The Hawk

On Sunday the hawk fell on Bigging
    And a chicken screamed
    Lost in its own little snowstorm.
And on Monday he fell on the moor
    And the Field Club
    Raised a hundred silent prisms.
And on Tuesday he fell on the hill
    And the happy lamb
    Never knew why the loud collie straddled him.
And on Wednesday he fell on a bush
    And the blackbird
    Laid by his little flute for the last time.
And on Thursday he fell on Cleat
    And peerie Tom's rabbit
    Swung in a single arc from shore to hill.
And on Friday he fell on a ditch
    But the rampant rat,
    That eye and that tooth, quenched his flame.

And on Saturday he fell on Bigging
   And Jock lowered his gun
   And nailed a small wing over the corn.

The Image in the Hills

Language, open the sacred quarry.
   Pagan in clouds, a stone image,
She guards the field, the river, the birds.

The dark hills roll across her silence.
   Beyond their scars and tumults, she sees
A blond morning of honey and fleeces.

Build an arch of hard square words.
   April flows from her wounded hands.
The gentle beasts and legends gather.

Carved on broken stone, at the well
   A stag runs, hard in light, before
The fading tangle of hound and horn.

Stone and litany fold her now.
   Stand in the poem, nude cold girl,
Till the Word wakes and all stones die.

The Condemned Well

Turgid, sweet. The well on the brae
Wet fifteen mouths all summer.
To the sisters of Scorran
The well was lover, the water kisses and secrets.
Shall we mention Linky the tailor
Who stitched that silk through his rum?
We shall not forget that drunken cross-legs.
The horse of Quoygarth
Raised there an ecstatic streaming skull,
With square barbarous teeth, black curling lips!
This was the theatre

When Coghill, hotly pursued
By lawyer, creditor, lover
Drenched his deliberate throat with death.
Shall any complain
Because a golden bee hung here
For his tiny ration?
Fool, thou poet, thou rememberest
Ada and Mary and Ann
Who sank bright buckets here.
Poet, those were beautiful girls
Nor could thy net of words hold one.
All these, certainly more,
Drank from that rocky breast,
For always were tinkers passing
And flies that drown
And raging Sabbath thirsts from the ship beyond.
Fool, thou poet,
Tomorrow is the day of the long lead pipe.

The Sailor, the Old Woman, and the Girl

'Have you any help', cried the young sailor
Pulling against the tide,
'Have you any spell or herb to mend
This new pain in my side?'

The old woman gathering whelks
Raised her fierce gray head.
'The best cure in the world for that
Is, take her to your bed.

If watchdogs howl, there's two good places
To end a lover's moans –
The alehouse with its lamp and barrel,
The kirkyard with its stones.

Or use the black worm of the mind.
Think, when she leans up close
And all the lurings of Delilah
Break open like a rose

Against your eyes and throat and mouth,
That I am lying there,
Time's first lover stark as a thorn
In a white winter air'.

The girl sang from another shore
And the tranced oars beat on,
And the old woman's fingers went
Like roots through the gray stone.

Harald,

*the Agnostic Ale-Drinking Shepherd, Enemy
of Ploughmen and Elders and all the
Dancing Sons of Barleycorn, Walks
over the Sabbath Hill to the Shearing*

Two bells go pealing through my age,
Two mad majestic criers.
One celebrates the pastured saints,
One descants on hell fires.
They storm at me with trembling mouths
And both of them are liars.

The barman had a little bell
That swayed my soul to peace
At ten last night.
        When the mad horns
Raged in the barley lees,
From lip to bottom of my glass
Clung a shining fleece.

The 'Mirabel'

Three old men stood in storm
At the crag, saying
'Folster is sailing well'
And, 'With the sea thus
And wind in the west
A man is better home'.

They lit pipes. 'The *Mirabel*
Is a boat of small luck.
She drowned Sam, and Isaac
Who drove the first nail
Was not at the hammering of the last',
And, 'Easier stand at the barrel
Than drink that ebb'.
They stood round the barrel.
'A good fisherman
Need not be a friend of the sea',
And, 'Them at the beach, the women
Will presently forget.
The Indians are in the parish
Spreading their silk'.

Ikey on the People of Hellya

Rognvald who stalks round Corse with his stick
I do not love.
His dog has a loud sharp mouth.
The wood of his door is very hard.
Once, tangled in his barbed wire
(I was paying respects to his hens, stroking a wing)
He laid his stick on me.
That was out of a hard forest also.

Mansie at Quoy is a biddable man.
Ask for water, he gives you rum.
I strip his scarecrow April by April.
Ask for a scattering of straw in his byre
He lays you down
Under a quilt as long and light as heaven.
Then only his raging woman spoils our peace.

Gray the fisherman is no trouble now
Who quoted me the vagrancy laws
In a voice slippery as seaweed under the kirkyard.
I rigged his boat with the seven curses.
Occasionally still, for encouragement,
I put the knife in his net.

Though she has black peats and a yellow hill
And fifty silken cattle
I do not go near Merran and her cats.
Rather break a crust on a tombstone.
Her great-great-grandmother
Wore the red coat at Gallowsha.

The thousand rabbits of Hollandsay
Keep Simpson's corn short,
Whereby comes much cruelty, gas and gunshot.
Tonight I have lit a small fire.
I have stained my knife red.
I have peeled a round turnip.
And I pray the Lord
To preserve those nine hundred and ninety nine innocents.

Finally in Folscroft lives Jeems,
Tailor and undertaker, a crosser of limbs,
One tape for the living and the dead.
He brings a needle to my rags in winter,
And he guards, against my stillness
The seven white boards
I got from the Danish wreck one winter.

Fisherman and Boy

ROADS TO THE KIRKYARD

Thorfinn, there are several roads to the kirkyard
Besides the way of the pillow.
There is the way of the west –
A few carry the salt key with them always.
There is the way of patriotism
But in the year of the foreign gun
Bilk and Drew and Howie
Ate limpets a whole winter in the cave.
There is the way of rum
That enchants the feet of twenty sailors
And bewitches one gravewards.
Before a girl kills you
Think of the rattling thorn on the brae –
Once it was crammed with roses.

Firth died among rafters – that noose
Had led his stallion through the nine parishes.
And Learmonth went over the crag for a ewe
And did not return.
The sheep afterwards had twelve winter lambs.

Each herring hangs at last by its own tail.

A HOUSE BY THE SEA

Thorfinn, build your house of quarried stone.

Josiah raised these holy walls, they say
For his lamp and bible
With red random rocks from the beach.
Then Kirsty came, who baked her sweet bread
For Breck and for birds in the snow.
Kolson the fisherman was here. The walls
Were white in the morning
And black when he sailed from the west.
Then a whole winter the walls were white.
Here Merran raised her seven bastards.
The close was never so gay.
She died young, of love and poverty.
Here Tom the tailor laid a long bench.
He stitched a coat for the laird
That later the scarecrow of Skarataing wore,
Dancing rags, half wind and half light.
Breck hung his fiddle on that wall.
After 'A Lamentation for Kirsty'
It died, sweet bird, among draughts and water.
Tinkers endured for one winter only
The spider's repairs
And the growing arrogance of rat and thistle.

Carve but one name over a lintel.

GOOD GHOSTS

Thorfinn, I would not keep bread and ale
From any hunger at the door –
A patched coat may cover an angel.

When a ship breaks on the rock
Fold the drowned hands
Before the sand is strewn with rum and silk.
Do not neglect to wish him well
Who hoists a sail
Though formerly your words were crossed.
Lay an offering near the holy stones.
Many men have straddled the boughs of Freya,
Keep yourself from those apples.
Study the silence of the hawk.
You will find, seven good words
Over crossed hands
Will cancel much filth and evil from the ale-house.

A fisherman has need of good ghosts.

THE DRINKERS

Thorfinn, to 'The White Horse' on Saturday mornings
The whalers come
Who end the day in a surge and fall of fists.
A few shepherds arrive at noon, peaceable men.
Fishermen come with scales in their beards
From the drifts of herring.
They generally sit in their own blue corner.
Then the ploughmen, after the lamp is lit,
With gaping bonnets and white collarless shirts.
Lords of the corn, they dominate the house
With fiddles and bawdry!
The whalers bear their resentment off, blue thunder,
To the rum barrels in *The Moby Dick*
(Rum is the drink for seamen).
Fishermen return to the piers of gull and herring.
The shepherds carry a gentleness back to the hills.
Only a tinker is left
Among the fiddles and the endless talk of horses.

Bread and ale, the sons of Barleycorn,
Study them well,
The dove's friend, the dancer with the knife.

Thorfinn, this new boat 'Whitemaa'
Can die as many deaths as a man.
Say two boards were badly fitted.
There are rocks like wolves all up the west,
Braga and Hellyan, Yesnaby, Marwick, The Brough.
A man and his boat like a sung word, a spell,
Compel the waters.
They dance well above the salt and the savagery,
The sudden swell that bursts from the sea's heart,
The wind that sweeps like an angel's wing.
These stresses break a bad song.
The 'Serpent' was cloven by a trawler.
The 'Swift' disappeared in shining seas, westward.
But that was a better doom than 'Thetis'.
She lay in seapinks, turtled, a proud fisher
Decaying among hens.
Twelve years the nettles besieged her bursting sides.

Be the lonely cold questing eye of the gull.

THE FIRES OF LOVE

Thorfinn, that the howdie* might cry
'A bairn clean and loud as a gull.'
That the old men and the young men might say
'This boy, I think,
Will throw a good net and hold his whisky'.
That girls might whisper
'Such a one could come to my bed and welcome'.
That the merchants might say in their club
'This man owes nothing for twine
Or for hooks or meal or rum or a coat –
His name is a blank in our books'.
That an old woman might say
'He brought me to a house with fire and bed and cupboard,
A poor bright place'.
That the last road be gray with grief

* Howdie – midwife

Pray that your lust
Breaks to a red flame, then a white flame, before morning.

PLACES TO VISIT

Thorfinn, no man bides forever in one place
Like a cat or a pigeon.

In Birsay they move in their furrows, bread is broken
Half way to sacrament.
Here Magnus was born, here they laid his bones,
Here his first miracles came, seapinks
About a broken tombstone.
Hoy guards with its blue huddle of shoulders
An offering hand
That brims with corn and larks in June.
An Irish princess walked in the hall of Gairsay.
Egilsay keeps its broken kirk;
There one April were ploughs, nets, shawled women
And the rose of martyrdom.
Visit the circle of stones in Stenness;
Know then what a dark phallic sun
The martyrless Pict
Compelled upon his beasts and tillage.
A man talked with a mermaid in Deerness.
In Kirkwall a red pillar
Locks in the cloven skull of the saint;
Much curiosity, little sanctity;
A Godroot among dead stones.

Thorfinn, you will learn more in Orkney
Than Mansie did
Who made seven salt circles of the globe.

The Seven Houses

In Memory of John F. Kennedy

Man, you are at the first door.
The woman receives you.
The woman takes you in.

With joy she takes you in to her long hall.
The nine candles are burning.
Here with reptile and fish and beast
You dance in silence.
Here is the table with the first food.
This is the House of the Womb.

Man, you are at the second door.
A woman receives you.
With brief hands she holds you.
She delivers you into time,
Into light and into darkness,
Into sound and silence and a new dance.
From an outer spring
The natural water comes to your mouth.
Also on your head
A man lays seven bright drops.
This is the House of Birth.

Man, you are at the third door.
A tree in a gray courtyard.
Here the animals dare not enter.
The tree is loaded with apples.
Three women stand at the tree,
The bare bitter bloody tree.
With oil and cloths they stand at the tortured tree.
This is the House of Man.

Man, you are at the fourth door.
Ploughman, merchant, engineer
Cross in a busy street.
On the seven oceans beyond
The ships sail on,
The peoples exchanging oil and wheat and music.
The cornstalk is tall in the field.
Through those yellow tides, that peace,
One woman comes,
On her shoulder a tall jar of untasted wine.
This is the House of Corn and Grape.

Man, you are at the fifth door.
The woman has brought you to her gate.
You have drunk her wine.
She has washed your hands at the threshold.

Now she prepares a bed.
Under the seven stars you watch and wait.
Inside, flames twist and untwist their hair.
This is the House of Love.

Man, you are at the sixth door.
The enemies with sculptured faces,
Stiffly they dance
About the disordered dangerous board.
The broken pitcher spills its oil.
Dark at the wall
The harp is a tangle of strings.
The hungry sit at a narrow table
And the Golden Man
Summons another beast from the flames.
The negro hangs on his tree.
At the sixth wall
In growing darkness, you lit one lamp.
This is the House of Policy.

Man, you are at the last door.
Three small mad venomous birds
Define in your skull
A new territory of silence.
The darkness staggered.
Seventy thousand ordered days
Lay ravelled in the arms of a woman.
In a concord of grief
The enemies laid aside their masks,
And later resumed them
For epitaph, platitude, anger.
What they say is of small importance.
Through the arrogance of atom and planet
May the lamp still burn
And bread be broken at the tables of poor men
(The heads bowed
And the sweet shape of the dove at the door.)
This is the House of History.

Poems New and Selected (1971)

New Poems

The Five Voyages of Arnor

I, Arnor the red poet, made
Four voyages out of Orkney.

The first was to Ireland.
That was a viking cruise.
Thorleif came home with one leg.
We left Guthorm in Ulster,
His blood growing cold by the saint's well.
Rounding Cape Wrath, I made my first poem.

Norway hung fogs about me.
I won the girl Ragnhild
From Paul her brother, after
I beat him at draughts, three games to two.
Out of Bergen, the waves made her sick.
She was uglier than I expected, still
I made five poems about her
That men sing round the benches at Yule.
She filled my quiet house with words.

A white wave threw me on Iceland.
Sweyn's skull is there (my brother) in a round howe.
Rolf rode him down
In Tingvoe, after the council, and rode on
Through villages, red-hooved, to the sea
Far from Inga his sister
And the lawless cry in the cradle, Inga's and Sweyn's,
And the farm at Rangower.
They put an axe in my hand, the edge turned north.
Women in black stood all about me.
There were lilies and snow on the hill above Broadfirth

And Rangower silent.
In Unst two nights, coming home,
We drank the ale and discussed new metres.
For the women, I reddened the axe at a dog's throat.

I went the blue road to Jerusalem
With fifteen ships in a brawling company
Of poets, warriors, and holy men.
A hundred swords were broken that voyage.
Prayer on a hundred white wings
Rose every morning. The Mediterranean
Was richer by a hundred love songs.
We saw the hills where God walked
And the last hill where his feet were broken.
At Rome, the earl left us. His hooves beat north.

Three Fridays sick of the black cough
Tomorrow I make my last voyage.
I should have endured this thing,
A bright sword in the storm of swords,
At Dublin, Micklegarth, Narbonne.
But here, at Hamnavoe, a pillow is under my head.
May all things be done in order.
The priest has given me oil and bread, a sweet cargo.
Ragnhild my daughter will cross my hands.
The boy Ljot must ring the bell.
I have said to Erling Saltfingers, *Drop my harp
Through a green wave, off Yesnaby,
Next time you row to the lobsters.*

Viking Testament

OX
To Thorstein the Ox, I give and bequeath these furrows,
The hawk above, the seal below,
The worn runes over the lintel
> *Ingibiorg tallest of women
> carried wine to the traveller*
Let the fire watch from the hill, Thorstein.
Scour the axe at the grindstone.
Beat the plough into edges.
I expect Bui from Ireland

Now that his cheek has the bronze curl.
His father opened the quarry.
His father took the hawk on his wrist.
His father sang to the curious seals.
His father had fair dust to lie with,
Ingibiorg, tallest of women.
His father rode down to the ships.
Then one morning
His father lay crooked in seaweed,
A cold man among red swathings.
    Hoof and scarecrow are Thorstein's,
Scythe, flail, quernstones, forge.
So dowered, the ox in the furrows
May quench those Irish axes.
To Helga his wife, ale-kirn and griddle.

DOVE
To the Eynhallow kirk, my fishing-boat *Skua*,
The sail and the oar also.
Erling, our holy prodigal, is there,
Gaunt with heavenly bread.
His net is a bunch of various holes,
A thing of laughter to fish.
Lost in prayer, the hands of the brothers
Are clumsy with ploughshares.
Rooted in praise, their tongues
Compel corn and oil
From the seven ox-dragged seasons.
Their queen is a stone woman,
Their lord a scarecrow with five red tatters.
Mild as a tree of doves,
Bui's wrath is no more to them
Than a painted hawk on a sail.
The net to those long robes
Who call the codling 'little silver brothers'
Even as they suck the bones clean
All the brightening days of Lent.

ROSE
I do not forget thee, my Sigrid.
He carried thee off to Barra
(Thee and thy thirteen Aprils)
Einar thy man. Too soon
That prow unlocked the horizon.

Thy father is quiet now
Who once bore fire to the castles,
And as for thy brothers, one
Has a skull square as an ox,
And Erling glides in a trance
Through bell and psalm and secret,
A cold mouth in the godstreams.
    What can I leave thee? Thou hast
Horizons of whale and mermaid
Far in the west, a hall,
Three ships in Cornwall and Ulster, trading,
A young son with black curls
And five horses in the meadow.
Arnor has sailed to the quarries in Eday
With chisel and harp.
That stone is red as fire, roses, blood.
I pay well for my verses.
'Cut a deep rune for Sigrid, Arnor'.
Irishmen will read it perhaps
Over a fated lintel,
One fragrant stone among blackened stones.

The Coat

She bowed in her door, all ripeness.
The reaper went round and round.
Wave after wave of bread
Fell with a secret sound.
She sent the shuttle flying,
She laid the new cloth by,
And through that yellow spindrift
She sent a drowning cry.

With lie and crust and rag
Between two trees we move,
The drifting apple blossom
And the three nails of love.
Naked we come and we go.
Even the Incarnate One
Shed his seamless splendour
Under a sackcloth sun.

The old ploughman of Gyre
Laughed above his ale.
Lie after lie he stitched
Into a masterly tale.
He put down an empty mug.
The thread shore in his throat.
Between crib and coffin
You must dance in a beautiful coat.

Carol

In the first darkness, a star bled.

The war of cloud and summit, other wounds.
Hills cupped their hands
And the rain shone over knuckles of rock and dropped to the
    sources.

Precious that well-hoard.
The priests gathered in secret jars
Lustrations for the passionate and the dead.

You were blessed, young tree
With one apple.
Far on you must bear the five godwounds, prefigured and red.

The deer runs on, runs on, swiftly runs on
Before bird and arrow,
Then bends, obedient to the arrow, its branching head.

A hunter's hand has broken the wild grape
To stain and seed.
And the hunter's hill opened with a green sound,
A stalk of corn,
And the blacksmith took from his forge a powerful blade.

Now this, a cry in our atom-and-planet night –
A child wailing,
A child's cry at the door of the House-of-Bread.

Kirkyard

A silent conquering army,
The island dead,
Column on column, each with a stone banner
Raised over his head.

A green wave full of fish
Drifted far
In wavering westering ebb-drawn shoals beyond
Sinker or star.

A labyrinth of celled
And waxen pain.
Yet I come to the honeycomb often, to sip the finished
Fragrance of men.

Sea Orpheus

A plough and barley fiddle
For one tide-raped girl
Sang in the looms of the sea.
Driftweed red as lashes
Scored the strings, seals
Clustered around (old salts
They swig shanties like ale,
They shine like bottles.)
            The fiddle
Stretched one thin strand across
The warp of the ebb.
            Eurydice
Caught in the weaving streams
Was half enchanted now
To a cold mermaid.
            The Salt One
Turned the wave round. He gathered
The Song of the Five Seas
Into his loom – Suleskerry
Flashed a new eye, Ahab
Hailed Jonah across
Tumultuous whaletracks, gulls
Climbed up the Glasgow sky
Rivet in beak.

The Salt One
Had more to do than pity
A sinking mouth, or heed
One mortal cornstalk whispering
A legend of resurrection
Among the spindrift.
        The Salt One
Unrolled webs and bales
Above the drowning.
        Sea girls
Take this buttercup girl
To her salt bridal.

The Masque of Princes

SEA JARL

> Arkol the skald mingled these
> words with harp strokes
> at the Earl's Hall at
> Orphir in Orkney in the
> Yuletide of 1015.

Our salt march ended before the city.
The king said, 'Their roofs are tall.'
We closed the five roads into the city.
They threw down stones from the wall.
Bones were broken, a skull, twelve ribs.
We commandeered fields round the city
And cattle, barns, horses, women, wells.
They threw down fire from the wall.
A skull was charred.
Roofbeams hissed in the Seine.
We circled the wall with dice and wineskin.
The city rotted slowly
Like a spotted corpse in a charnel.
They threw down insult and curse
But that hurt no-one,
The men from the fjords are not sensitive.
Armand the spy reported
Now they were eating rats in the city
And fungus that creeps between stone.

The merchants (said Armand) were poor as the students
And the priests distracted
With shrivings, anointings, requiems.
When the wind lay towards the city
We turned the sputtering ox on the spit.
On the fortieth day the stones were disordered
And Ragnar stood in the gate.
Tapestry. Vats. Opal. Nakedness. Ashes.
The harp was silent. I drew my fingers through silver.
We stayed in the city seven days,
Then dragged carts to the ships at the mouth of the river.
We waited two nights for a wind.
I put the siege in a set of formal verses.
The skippers did not praise that poem.
(This is for blacksmiths and poachers.)
We arrived in Jutland in time for the spring sowing
With a cargo of silver, corn, foreign rats.

LORD OF THE MIRRORS

> A dance Bernard of Ventadour
> made, with masks and
> lutes and ladies, for
> the investiture of
> Philip Count of Narbonne
> in April 1130.

The new prince questioned a very ancient shield

Lord, the first quartering sheweth
A skull, a sheaf of corn, a mask
(Your bread is uttered on long sweet throats)

Prince, the second quartering sheweth
A skull, a sword, a mask
(Your soldiers gleam at the five gates)

Sire, the third quartering sheweth
A skull, a harp, a mask
(Poets stain your parchment with nightingale notes)

Man, the fourth quartering is blank
        'Between skull and mask
        This face, a bright withering flower'
                A breath, surge of cloud,
                        through the bronze mirror.

The new prince goes among roses, cupids, peacocks

        Beast, what is love?
        Phallus, rut, spasm

        Peasant, what is love?
        Plough, furrow, seed

        Priest, what is love?
        Prophecy, event, ritual

        Lord, what is love?
        Lys, and daunce, and viol

        Man, what is love?
        On the garden pool breezes, a
            caul of sackcloth.

                *

The new prince kneels at a rood, scarlet and black

        Man, where have you been this loud April day?
        I followed the hounds to a kill.

        Man, what have you done with the royal stag?
        Five wounds I bore to a ruined hall.

        Man, who received that sacrifice?
        A lady, stricken and still.

        Man, was there bread on her table?
        The rat had devoured the earth-gold. Silent
            the stones in the mill.

        Man, what lamp in the rafters?
        A star that pierced like a nail.

Man, was there fire in that hearth?
Breathings of ox and ass. The lady cried in
the straw. Night laid a shroud on the hill.

That vigil done,
The rood was rose 'of ravissement and ruth'.

*

Now, Mask-and-Skull, rear high among the trumpets!

PRINCE IN THE HEATHER

> The bard Alasdair MacNiall
> made this in Barra
> the day after the true
> prince left Scotland
> for France, 1746.

Who would have thought the land we grew in, our mother,
Would turn on us like a harlot?
The rock where the stag stood at dawn,
His antlers a proud script against the sky,
Gave us no shelter.
That April morning the long black rain
Bogged our feet down
But it did not douche the terrible fire of the English,
Their spewings of flame.
(I think it will rain a long time at Culloden
And steel rot under the stone.)
Who would have thought our own people,
Men of our tongue and lineage,
Would make one wall that day with barbarians?
We prayed our endless mountain tracks
Would baffle the hunters
But the armies marched like doom on the one road
To the one graveyard.
Who would have thought for a moment
But that our leaders had wisdom,
Men skilled in the ancient rites and duties of warfare?
Tinkers from a ditch
Would have directed the lines better that morning.
Casually the cannonball burst those ribs,
Removed that leg.

They harried us like rats from a granary,
A fury worse than dogs.
A great shining thing is gone forever from the glens.
Sheep drift through the halls of the chief and his lady.
The white rose is withered.
Now grandsons of hunter, fisherman, bard
Must turn high courtesy to unction,
A manner and a speech to please the Saxons,
A thing never known before.
Who would have thought our prince, that hero,
While we plucked broken steel from the forge of our valour,
Would take to the screes, a frightened stag?

WHITE EMPEROR

> A troop of irregular soldiers
> led by a woman sing these
> choruses on the road near
> Ekaterinburg, March 1918.

What are you, skeleton with the bayonet?
The Ploughman

What are you, skeleton with rifle and bullets?
The Sower

What are you, skeleton dragging a field gun?
The Harrower

What are you, scarecrow with the knife?
The Reaper

What are you, scarecrow with stones?
The Miller

What are you, shadow among the ashes?
The Baker

*

Unmasked, the Little Father and his children
     Drift on. The sky is red.
Five winters now he has doled us blood and snow
     For our daily bread.

Now in the fifth winter the rat is king
    Of furrow and mill.
That golden mask has worn you, Little Father,
    Down to the skull.

Mane and sabre whirl against the sunset.
    Those princes turn
And fade in the snow. From Omsk to Warsaw, this starfall,
    The Russias burn.

*

Who called us brothers of ox and mule?
Peasants we were,
Children of The White King.

Who calls us skeletons, rags, shadows?
Soldiers we are,
Comrades of The Red One.

We are the people. Forge and field are ours.
I am Natasha.
I measure the sun with lucent eyes.

KING OF KINGS

          The inn-keeper at Bethlehem
          writes secret letters to the
          Third Secretary (Security) at
          the door marked with dolphins
          in the fifth street north from
          Temple and Dove-market.

Came the first day of the week five guardsmen, Greeks. No sleep in the village for their choruses. Their lamp still burned at sunrise. One broken jar. Rachel's scent was in the sergeant's sheets. Came a troop of merchants, solemn men, with currants in their satchels, they were up and gone early, on four camels, southward. *Who will pay for the jar?* I said to the guardsmen. *Caesar,* said a corporal. *Rachel,* said the sergeant, *she broke it. And anyway,* said a guardsman, *the drink was bad.* God keep me from guests like them. It was this summer's wine, the leaven still moving in it, a little cloud. The Chian and Syrian are for silk purses.

*

These passed through my door yesterday – Jude and Abrim and
Saul, farmers. Jude had sold an ox at the mart. *A fire in
the back room, a lamp, dice, a skin of wine,* said Jude. An
Egyptian with scars on his face, he left the north-bound
camel train, he ate barley cakes and fish and was most
courteous and laid Ethiop coins on the table. Then
Abrim's wife, crying under the stars, *Where is Abrim? He
hasn't come home, the bull is in the marsh, his children are
hungry, he is with Rachel, I know it, she will have his last
penny.* The Egyptian leaned his knifemarked face from his
window. The wife of Abrim took one look at him, then
turned and wrapped her in night and silence. The
Egyptian looked from the stars to a chart he had on the
sill. He made comparisons, measurements.

*

The Egyptian is still here. He asks me after breakfast, could he
get a guide as far as the border? *I have certain persons to
meet in the desert,* said he. In the afternoon he left with
Simon, donkey by donkey, a muted going. This was the
sole guest today, except for a rout of farm servants and
shepherds who lay about the barrel like piglets at the teats
of a sow, and sung and uttered filth and (two of them)
David a ploughman and Amos a shepherd roared about
the alleys after Rachel. They came back with bleeding
faces, separate and silent, after midnight. Such scum.

*

My brain is reeling from a press of faces! I had no warning of
this. First came two bureaucrats, a Parthian and a
Cypriot, bearing Caesar's seal, and a boy with them. *Your
best room,* said the Cypriot. (For these chit-bearers you
get paid a half-year later.) Then came a little company of
clerks with scrolls and ledgers and wax and moneybags
and a wolf on a chain. They set up benches in the court-
yard. Then – O my God – by every road north and south
they came, a horde of hook-noses, hillmen, yokels, they
swarmed about the doors, come to pay some tribal tax,
filthy thirsty goats. *We'll sleep on the roof,* said some. And
others, *Provide beer and bread, never mind blankets.* And
Rachel shining among them like a fish in a pool. A mea-
sured clash of bronze; a column of soldiers possessed the
village. And the lieutenant, *I commandeer six rooms.
There are no six rooms,* I said. *I commandeer the whole*

inn, he said. The Cypriot stood in the door. *I commandeer the whole inn except for the rooms of Caesar's civil servants,* said the lieutenant. *And the room of the chief clerk,* said the Cypriot, *and the room of my hound, and the room of Eros.* (Eros is their catamite.) Never was such a day in this place. The till rattled, I don't deny it, a hundred throats gargled the new wine. Ditches between here and Hebron will be well dunged.

*

The skin is full of blots and scratchings and bad spellings. Put it down to this – my trade is lighting fires, listening, going with chamber pots, whispering, heating cold porridge; not scrivener's work. Know however, the yokels are back in the hills, poor as goats after the taxes and the revelry. Out of Rachel's room all morning small sweet snores. The clerks are balancing figures in their ledgers, melting wax in small flames. The bureaucrats are playing at chess in their room and sipping the old Chian. Eros, like Rachel, sleeps. The soldiers polish their greaves and drink and throw dice; two of them, bare and bronze-knuckled and bloodied, boxed in the sand at noon. There came a man and a woman from the north to pay the tax, very late, and wanted a room. This was after dark. I had one place, ox and ass kept it warm with winter breathings. I gave the man a lantern.

*

The tax-men have gone, a clash of bronze on one side, a wedge of steel on the other, the Parthian on horseback before, the Cypriot on horseback behind, the wolf chained to the money cart, Eros carried by two black men in a silk chair, swaying aloft like a tulip. The first star brought the shepherds. *The soldiers have drunk all the wine,* I said. Amos stood well back in the shadows. *You,* I said, *Amos, stay outside, never come back. I bar you from this place. You and your punch-ups and your pewkings.* I said sweetly to the others, *The Romans have dried the barrel.* The shepherds drifted on past me. One carried a new white winter lamb.

*

Most secret and urgent. Aaron will bring this on horseback, direct from inn to palace, helter-skelter, a shower of hooves and stars. The negro with the cut cheeks has come back, and

with him an Indian and one from very far east with eyes like
grass-blades. In the first light they seemed like revellers
masked and weary from a carnival. They had men servants
with them, heavy baggage on the mules, bales and jars. I lit
fires, put out sweet water, spread woven blankets over linen.
They went about the village all day with questing eyes.
I poked among the baggage – ingots, cruets, chalices, tiaras,
candlesticks, swords, thuribles, swathe upon swathe of
heavy green silk, emeralds cold as ice. They came back late.
They wrote their names in the guest book, steep square
letters like Hindu temples, like ships of Cathay. I cannot
read it, I have torn out the page for your perusal. *Please,*
I said, *to enter places of origin.* Coal Face murmured, *The
broken kingdoms of this world,* and wrote in the book.
Nothing in the room for a while but shadows and flutters.
Also enter, I said, *the nature of your business. You under-
stand, the imperial government requires this.* Bronze Face
said, *Bearers of precious gifts.* Nothing again – one star that
hung a web of glimmers and shadows about the chamber.
Blessings given to men in the beginning, he went on at last,
*that have been wrongly spent, on pomp, wars, usury,
whoredoms, vainglory: ill-used heavenly gifts. We no longer
know what to do with these mysteries. Our thrones are
broken. We have brought the old treasures here by difficult
ways. We are looking for the hands that first gave them, in
the ancient original kingdom. We will offer them back
again. Let them shine now in the ceremonies of the poor.* I lit
a cluster of seven candles at the wall. *But first we must find
the kingdom,* said Daffodil Face, smiling. *Perhaps this
kingdom does not exist. Perhaps we found it and did not
recognize it. Perhaps it is hidden so deep in birth and love
and death that we will never find it. If so, we will leave our
skulls in the desert. We do not know where we should go
from here. Perhaps the kingdom is a very simple thing.*
I kept my hands clasped and my head to one side. *Landlord,*
said Coal Face, *your guests tonight are poor lost cold
hungry kings. What have you got for us in your cellar?*
I informed them that their rooms were ready. I said that I
had bread with honey and currants and dates in it, baked
that same morning. I mentioned Rachel. I said also my inn
was famous for wines, in keg or skin or flagon. I hoped the
gentlemen would enjoy their stay. It was cold, I said, for the
time of year. They did not move. The night was a sack of
coal with one diamond in it. I turned to the door.

Press-Gang
> A man-of-war enchanted
> Three boys away.
> Pinleg, Windbag, Lord Rum returned.

Hierarchy
> A claret laird,
> Seven fishermen with ploughs,
> Women, beasts, corn, fish, stones.

Harpoonist
> He once riveted boat to whale.
> Frail-fingered now
> He weaves crab prisons.

Wreck
> The *Merle d'Or* struck at Scabra.
> One man flung shoreward,
> Cried strangely, fell.

Books
> No more ballads in Eynhallow.
> The schoolmaster
> Opens a box of grammars.

Skerries
> A fanged treeless island.
> On shipwrecked wood
> Men die, love, cry sunwards.

The Chapel of The Visitation
> Before the unuttered Christstone
> A new arch,
> Two bending women, a stone kiss.

Ruined Chapel
> Among scattered Christ stones
> Devoutly leave
> Torn nets, toothache, winter wombs.

Saint

> A starved island, Cormack
> With crossed hands,
> Stones become haddock and loaf.

Easter

> Friday, dayspring, a pealing cockerel.
> Haul west, fishermen,
> With flushed violent mouths.

Lost

> An island without roads.
> Ikey the tinker
> Stood throat-deep in the bog.

Dove and Crow

> A preacher broke our dove-stone.
> Sermons, crowflocks,
> Blackened furrow and shore.

Circle

> Cod, give needles and oil.
> Winter hands
> Must sew shrouds by lamplight.

Fish and Corn

> Our isle is oyster-gray,
> That patched coat
> Is the Island of Horses.

Runes from the Island of Horses

Winter

> Three winter brightnesses –
> Bridesheet, boy in snow,
> Kirkyard spade.

Barn Dance

> Fiddler to farm-girls, a reel,
> A rose,
> A tumult of opening circles.

Respectability

Sigurd lay with three women,
Reckoning his mother
And thwart twin sister.

Farm Girl

Spinster, elder, moth
Quiz till dawn
The lamp in Merran's window.

Entrances

Between thief and hoard
Three narrow doors –
Furrow, maidenhead, grave.

Kirkyard

Pennies for eyes, we seek
Unbearable treasure
Through a wilderness of skulls.

Mirror

Ikey unpacked a flat stone.
It brimmed
With clouds, buttercups, false smiles.

When You Are Old

Some night when you are gray
And lonely, by muttering flame
(Closed your sweet womb,
Your breasts fallen away,

The rose of one tremulous day
Haunting that loaded room)
Take up my book with your name,
Turn yellow leaves and say,

'That spring, whatever the parish talk,
We made one blessed rhyme
On a shaken branch of love.
Then the eye of the hawk
Down the huge convex of time
Measured our dove.'

Tinkers

Three princes rigged like scarecrows
Straggled along the shore
And every clucking wife
Ran in and barred her door.

Their coats hung in such shreds
The dogs barked as they came.
O but their steps were a dance,
Their eyes all black flame!

The wife's undone her pack
And spread it at our door.
Grails, emeralds, peacock feathers
Scattered over the floor.

The man flashed his bow,
His fiddle had only one string,
But where is the sun-drowned lark
Like that can sing?

The dark boy wore his rags
Like an April-wakened tree,
Or as a drift of seaweed
Glitters on the arms of the sea.

Princes, they ruled in our street
A long shining age,
While Merran peeped through her curtains
Like a hawk from a cage.

Paupers, they filthied our pier
A piece of one afternoon,
Then scowled, stank, shouldered their packs
And cursed and were gone.

Three Songs from a Play

I

THE BALLAD OF JOHN BARLEYCORN,
THE PLOUGHMAN, AND THE FURROW

As I was ploughing in my field
The hungriest furrow ever torn
Followed my plough and she did cry
'Have you seen my mate John Barleycorn?'

Says I, 'Has he got a yellow beard?
Is he always whispering night and morn?
Does he up and dance when the wind is high?'
Says she, *'That's my John Barleycorn.*

*One day they took a cruel knife
(O, I am weary and forlorn!)
They struck him at his golden prayer.
They killed my priest, John Barleycorn.*

*They laid him on a wooden cart,
Of all his summer glory shorn,
And threshers broke with stick and stave
The shining bones of Barleycorn.*

*The miller's stone went round and round,
They rolled him underneath with scorn,
The miller filled a hundred sacks
With the crushed pride of Barleycorn.*

*A baker came by and bought his dust.
That was a madman, I'll be sworn.
He burned my hero in a rage
Of twisting flames, John Barleycorn.*

A brewer came by and stole his heart.
Alas, that ever I was born!
He thrust it in a brimming vat
And drowned my dear John Barleycorn.

And now I travel narrow roads,
My hungry feet are dark and worn,
But no-one in this winter world
Has seen my dancer Barleycorn.'

I took a bannock from my bag.
Lord, how her empty mouth did yawn!
Says I, 'Your starving days are done,
For here's your lost John Barleycorn.'

I took a bottle from my pouch,
I poured out whisky in a horn.
Says I, 'Put by your grief, for here
Is the merry blood of Barleycorn.'

She ate, she drank, she laughed, she danced.
And home with me she did return.
By candle light in my old straw bed
She wept no more for Barleycorn.

II

TINKER'S SONG

'Darst thu gang b' the black furrow
This night, thee and thy song? . . .'
'Wet me mooth wi' the Lenten ale,
I'll go along.'

They spied him near the black furrow
B' the glim o' the wolf star.
Slow the dance was in his feet,
Dark the fiddle he bore.

There stood three men at the black furrow
And one was clad in gray.
No mortal hand had woven that claith
B' the sweet light o' day.

There stood three men at the black furrow
And one was clad in green.
They're taen the fiddler b' the hand
Where he was no more seen.

There stood three men at the black furrow
And one was clad in yellow.
They're led the fiddler through a door
Where never a bird could follow.

They've put the gowd cup in his hand,
Elfin bread on his tongue.
There he bade a hunder years,
Him and his lawless song.

'Darst thu gang through the black furrow
On a mirk night, alone? . . .'
'I'd rather sleep wi' Christen folk
Under a kirkyard stone.'

III
FIDDLER'S SONG

The storm is over, lady.
The sea makes no more sound.
What do you wait for, lady?
His yellow hair is drowned.

The waves go quiet, lady,
Like sheep into the fold.
What do you wait for, lady?
His kissing mouth is cold.

The Wedding Guest

Hamnavoe of water and granite and sky, at gray daystart I say
      farewell to you, I make an end now, in a morning that is
      not the morning rising monotonously upon our vanity, gray
      out of black, a many thousand beginnings till age makes of
      morning a mockery, but in a secret set-apart morning, a
      triune welling of dayspring and April and youth, when fire

and earth have their way one with another, a lovely spurt-
ing of seed and egg and spawn, on such a morning I rose
and washed in the rockpool and said farewell in particular
to the *Sigrid*'s fishermen and left the village before the girls
came out to the well for their water, to the stack for their
peats, laughing and letting on not to look at the strong arms
weaving and baiting the black fish-twine, and went on past
the cross at the end of the village to the summons and the
ceremony.

*

As I went north in mid-morning, going near the edge of crags
that are set stark between sea and clouds, slowly walking
and lingering, from shell-strewn ledges stirred the skuas,
strong beautiful birds, and circled, and fell about my head
with threat and thunderclap of wings, so that I seemed like
a man with his head in a confusion of sharp circles, and
on I went with cold bidden blood, and presently wing and
claw and beak faltered and fell away and returned to the
mothering niches, and on my feet went with no change of
pace through the salt-bitten grass, but my body was a
smithy – an assault, a wincing, a tumult of heart-strokes –
and I leaned northwards dutifully into the wind, and the
wind falling folded me in two huge dove-wings.

*

In the afternoon I came to a place called Yesnaby where the line
of western crags was broken into much confusion of rock
and sea, and there in a sudden green valley locked from
the noise of ocean I blundered across a camp of tinkers,
and above a flame one man was shaping a tin cup with a
hammer, and a boy drained blood through the throat of a
rabbit into the earth, and a young man held a hawk on his
wrist and sang sometimes and at other times whispered to
the fierce tranced head, and a girl suckled a baby, and an
old man and an old woman looked at me as indifferently
as if I were a goat, and a child came up glistering out of
the sea, and there I would have stopped to warm me a
while (these tribes exist pure, birth to death, in a fire of
simply pagan lust), but that a far behest lured me towards
a consummation so beautiful that we but echo the ecstacy
with harps and statues; as the naked tinker boy held now
to the shell of his ear a colder sea mouth.

*

Created heart of man, when were you ever clear of sorrow? – at the long beach of Skaill as north I went a huddle of gray shawls watched the sea, for, said a girl, there is one boat, the *Skarf*, that went out this morning and is not come back, and they made confusion of words and wailing, but an old woman stood a little apart from them, a fisherman's mother, and said never a word, but put a withered look on the withered sea – and I tried to comfort them, saying that I too was a fisherman and with the wind northerly and a good shoal of herring off Hoy many a boat would be reaping an Atlantic harvest to give all the parish its wintering of food and oil, and this word was a comfort to them – one gave me a scallop shell to hang at my belt – and they fluttered and mewed about me for a while like white-maas, and only the old one kept silence – but again as I left them their thin eyes prised at the oyster of the horizon.

*

Now I was come to Quoyloo, a cluster of ale houses in a valley at sunset, and each howff was the sprawled body of Barleycorn, the barrel his belly, the lamp his yellow eye, and his servingmen feasting with quarrel and song at his gross undiminished godhead, and slow went my feet past the open door of Sigurd's ale-house where an old man sat on a lobster-box with pewter and froth in his whiskers and past Thorfinn's ale-house where a ploughman sat at a board with sixty-four black-and-white squares and was silently reflected in a fisherman with sixty-four white-and-black squares (and by that mirror I knew the loneliness of man) and past Sweyn's ale-house where Applecheeks in the door cried out 'Welcome, traveller' and the smell of his malt came near to ravel the ordered beads of my intention (*A wedding? Begin here the bridal, Cana was a feast of jars – Rejoice O young man in thy youth – Drink thy wine with a merry heart*) and past the barrels at the end of the house, and out into the pasture and through a cornfield towards – O most faint desire now – a ghostly bride cup.

*

Through Marwick I dragged the struggling sack of my lusts. On I went, a beast-bearing ghost. One star stood over the hill.

There in a byre door a young woman lingered. She dipped cup in bucket. She held out white dripping warmth, cow honey, buttercup ale. My fingers gathered the cup, mouth lapped milk. She pressed against the doorpost, she gave me room to pass into the cow-dung darkness, the breathing beasts, a spread of blond straw.

Glint of sea-surf in the thickening light. Woven into the hill a first strand of sackcloth.

By the old woman's fire of peats I sat; who uttered a parish litany of deaths, births, espousals, and the changing price of goose eggs.

A man passed through with a lantern and a mash of old bannocks in a plate, going past into the pigsty.

The old woman knelt, she coughed, she mumbled prayers, she crossed herself, she eased her body, hand by elbow by shoulder by head, slowly, on to the rack of the stone floor, and covered her bones with a hide.

The man came back with a dapple of lantern-and-darkness about his knees. He glowered at me and went out to sleep among the horses.

The old one coughed for a long time, then began to snore softly, her mouth fluttering open and close.

Then came the girl from her making of cheese and butter in the cold room next the sea and stood in the dying light of the peatfire and, garment by garment, unfolded her rose and honey nakedness, faintly and secretly smiling, and lay down with the old woman, spring beside winter, and softly filled the house with buttercup breath.

I stood outside in the yard. Star by star had stepped down to fill its lamp at the sunset. Their cold fires westered slowly. A dog barked in the next farm.

*

Light and sea-noise and soil of Birsay, travelled towards you this guest a many a morning, a many a sin, a many a prayer, yet can he still by no means pass over, he must bide with his feet in a drift of seapinks, for the sea has lain with his two arms about the island all night, and glutted every cave and fissure, and now turns slowly from the island, glutted, and begins to ebb from the island with a sound like a struck harp, and *Lauds* glimmers, a frail hidden monotony, and fades, and sea lapses from crag and shelf, and from seapink to sand to washed rock advances the foot of the pilgrim, and the Bride is hidden in her chamber, she has not yet come forth all glorious in robes of spun gold with many a hand-maiden in her train, and slips from rock the sea (and two brothers drift west in a boat with creels), and *Terce* brightens, and from stone and stone and stone shrinks the sea (and three brothers come out with yoke and ox and plough to a steep half-done furrow) and the Bridegroom is in the sanctuary, hidden, there he abides, his single watch-lamp like ruby or stigma or rose, and sea falters from weed and limpet and sand (and one solitary brother stoops now with a basket among rockpools) and ocean surges at last clear of the island, and the foot of the bidden one goes cold among seaweed, a slow perilous dance between the cloven waters, and from the steeple the first bronze mouth (struck) brims, mildly they all brim then, the mass-bells (swung) and they quiver, up and down, nuptial summonings, round on round of welcome, *Here is your single cell, here all time is but the lucency of a single morning, prepare here your distillings of the Rose for the kirkyard where lie in light and peace the hundred brothers of Birsay,* and a dozen doves, clustered, query round the slipway, and enfold him, and out at sea a raven sail, wind laden, westward urgently leans.

Fishermen with Ploughs (1971)

A Poem Cycle

A ship called *Dove* sails west out of Norway in the ninth century
carrying a tribe of fisher people. Their god, the beautiful Balder,
is dead. They are in flight from starvation, pestilence, turbulent
neighbours (what the poet calls, in the shorthand of myth, the
Dragon). But also they are compelled west by the promise of a
new way of life: agriculture. The cargo in their hold is a jar of
seed corn. Fate, blind and all-wise, has woven their myth about
them. Now the same Fate sits at the helm.

That is the theme of the opening section of the poem.

The people settle in a valley called Rackwick in the Orkney
island of Hoy. Their slow evolution through the centuries
occupies the next four sections; how the climate of their
existence changed with such things as the Reformation,
annexation to Scotland, foreign wars, compulsory education.
But essentially their lives were unchanged; the same people
appear and reappear through many generations – the laird,
the crofter-fisherman, the shepherd, the tinker, the beach-
comber, and the women who watch the sea with stony
patience; all are caught up in 'the wheel of bread' that is at
once brutal and holy.

There is a slow sure improvement in the material conditions.
Why does the wheel slow down and stop (V)? By the middle
of this century the valley was almost completely depopulated.
Perhaps (the poet argues) the quality of life grows poorer as
Progress multiplies its gifts on a simple community. The dwellers
in islands are drawn to the new altars. The valley is drained of
its people. The Rackwick croft ruins are strewn with syrup tins,
medicine bottles, bicycle frames, tattered novels, rubber boots,
portraits of Queen Victoria.

In part VI the Dragon, black pentecostal fire, falls on a great
city. Once again a few people escape by boat. They return to the
valley. Their most precious possession is the sacred corn sack.
They make themselves farmers and fishermen. The women return,
unchanged yet terribly changed. But the wheel has been wrenched
from the axle-tree. The great song must begin all over again, very

far back, beyond the oxen and millstones and bronze throats of
agriculture.

George Mackay Brown
September 1969

I Dragon and Dove

Building the Ship

'A dove must fold your seed from dragon flame.'

That blind rune stabbed the sea tribe.
Fishermen sought a bird in the mountains.

Their axes kept them that year from the dragon.
Logs throttled a mountain torrent.
A goatherd gaped on the lumbering tons.

Saws shrieked, sputtered, were sharpened, sang.
Dunes were pale with strewment of boards.
Seaward a keel was set.
Sprang from that spine a vibrant cluster of ribs.

Forge and anvil begot a host of rivets.
Shavings, blond hair of excited children,
Curled from the combing adzes.
A woodman died of a rotten nail.
(Njal found, near falcons, an urn for his fires.)

Men daylaboured, were dappled with lanterns.
They beat design on the thwart timbers.
Loomed a dry dove from June leafage.
That bird would unlock the horizon westwards.
Now visit, dragon, a blank shore.
Tar pots chuckled like negroes over the fires.

Moons, seven fish, swam through that labour.
A summer whirled its golden hoof.
'Trees for this doveflight,' cried Norn among the looms,
'Would blacken the coast with yawls.'
(Njal brought Gudrun down, a cold jar.)
'We sup sawdust broth,' sang the workmen.
Thorkeld drove the hammers. Their hands bled.

The Fight with the Dragon

Thorkeld stood that night between Dragon and Dove.
Horn, hoofbeat, triumph of the blind mouth.
He left the hot bed of Norn his woman.
The moon was a huge cinder.
'Our guest is generous with his flames,' said Thorkeld.

Thorkeld stood in a smoulder of nets.
His cold mouth touched the sword.
'Into his fires, long sharp fish,' he said,
'See if this Dragon will relish you.'
The Dove was astir in the trestles.
At the shore the Dragon tasted the bronze fish.

Thorkeld turned. He splintered the stable door.
The mares were a row of charred skulls.
'Thunder,' he coaxed a garnet eye.
The stallion reared at the stars like a red wave.

Thorkeld unbolted the door of the women.
He plucked Gudrun from a hundred shrieks.
Hoof-fast Njal bore his manseed wombfurled waveward.

Thorkeld a blacksmith, the Dragon a blown forge.

Thorkeld stood at the altar of the god Balder.
He strewed that stone with dragon scales.
The village burned around like oil barrels.
'Now on a new shore,' said Thorkeld,
'This folk can give the star shoal a sweeter name.'
The dog Bran licked his charcoal hand.
The sun rose. Thorkeld gave himself to the sea.

Thorkeld brought to the blind westering Dove
A body charted with twelve wounds.

The Death of Thorkeld

The twelve wounds were like a defiance of mouths
In a mountain ambush.
They turned, a star wheel, from the gray of dawn.

They winced like fish in a hauled net.
The twelve wounds were like a map of islands.
Women were westerlings then,
Their fingers quested among that cluster.

They are glad, all women, at a man's stillness –
In the cradle lying, quiet as apples,
In the trance after love,
Even carried in from boarfang or whalequake:
In wombfold again laid, her utter man.

Steel came unclouded from stiffening mouth.
The oarsmen could not tell tears from spindrift.
Round the last stiff smile
The shrouding women came with a drift of smiles.

An oarsman slid a silver coin for ferry
Under the cold flame of the tongue.
Skald wove deathsong in the loom of his mouth.
'Go from us, Thorkeld, among purer streams.
See, they are waiting for you,
The ancient kings asleep under the aurora.'

Norn turned down her tranquil mouth.
Throats of the heroes throbbed.

The sea opened and shut on the lord of whales.
The coat with twelve red islands
Hung, silver-clasped, from Njal's throat.

At once the blind tongue blossomed with bodings, biddings.

**The Blind Helmsman of the Ship called Dove to the Tribe
that was Lately Dragon-Embattled**

Man goes, man voyages, into the blackest sun.
Nor doth hero long keep
Lithe limb or lissomness or laughter.
Honey is bitter at last in the mouth.
Fareth a shadow to the ghostly feast-halls.

And tribes decay. Northwards they seek cold fires.
Our god at last was a glacier.
Shoals departed, nets came empty to shore.
The yawl warped at the rock.
Young skippers ceased to measure the west.
Balder was ice. The mouth of the poet guttered.

But Thorkeld appraised the hooves of oxen.
Thorkeld handled the seed of the quartered sun.
Thorkeld abode a winter in Bergen
With shipwrights, westerlings, weighers of bronze.

A blind fist beat on your shutters.

It is time to turn from the solstice of black flame
And to harness the passion of oxen.
Time for the urn to be emptied.
Time for the hill to be smitten with willed fire.
Time for a hundred jars to be gathered.
Indeed it is time to forsake this ebb.
Time for the bird to seek the golden solstice.

Man goes, man voyages. Thorkeld took us
From nailing of meagre timbers.
The sailman stitched one huge gale-lover.

Man goes, man voyages. His hand swings the star wheel.
This freedom is defeat for the Dragon.

The Blind Helmsman to Njal Thorkeldson the New Chief

I think of heroes who lived in the lissom light,
How Armod sundered the jaws of a whale,
How Kol unlocked the knees of the coldest ladies,
How Sven hooded an eagle,
How Thorkeld mingled his bronze with dragon flame.

Too soon their sun was a black circle.

This and that and the other were hewn to pieces.
One died among walrus ivories.
One silvered, hapless, into silence.

Yet none hardship like this endured.
None wounded his tribe with exile.
None ventured with poorer freight, one smouldering jar.
Seek out Gudrun, the mountain bride.
That small urn still has snow in it.
Will you brim her, like a shore girl, with oil and salt?
Gudrun must be a mother of harvesters.

Shark and sardine have swum through your tough nets.
Cod wander tinkerwise, corn is true.
Dumbness of herring, windcry and burnish of wheat.
Cornstalk unlocks the door of a great king.

Lust builds a howe over the burning ghost.
Lust, bread kissed, becomes love.

The untasted cup brimming with red circles
Will be gladness to travellers out of a storm,
To the poet after his song,
To the councillor who has spoken in the debate.
Down the dark sun
Lipflush the dove will fall with five wounds.

The Blind Helmsman to the Shipwright

In Hoy and Unst, the western landfall, shipwright,
Dry be thy beams.
Keep thy cunning from strakes awhile.
Make a door for a man and woman to stand at sunset,
A bed for mixing of hair.
Tree and tribe must mingle quiet branches.

Keep thy wit from the doomed gunwale.
Gray leafage covered those hulls.
Our fathers were shaken deathward like cold gleams.

What's Thorkeld? Torrents of silent fish.

Njal must rule from a high dovetailed bench.
Keep thy hammer from barren keels.

But the earthship, the plough, breaking frail furrows across
The slow surge of the hills,
Learn well that cleave and curve and plunge.
We are pilgrims with seed, vat-bearers.
The earthship, the coffin, under the hill drowned,
Honour that hoard of seventy years.
Njal must trade for bronze in the black grave.

Broad be your timbered barn, the great earth-ark,
To hold the cargoes of summer.
The voyagers are not lost in the loam wave.
Down the dark sun
Hurtles the dove, his beak a blazon of corn.

But still the winter images will not leave us.
We track the sun beast to his bloody lair.
At dawn our hands are red and empty.
And the Dove broods in a tangle of bitter branches.

The Net

The first day from the weaving of the ling net
Three cod lay on the deck, gulping.
A careful gleam was put in their bellies.

The second day from the net weaving
A dogfish slapped the scuppers.
He barked at the women soundlessly.
Dog, wet or dry, is poor tooth-relish.

The third day from the net weaving
We handled a halibut on board.
The women sliced that turbulence in segments.
They wrung fierce blood in a stone jar.
(And still we tracked the gold beast into the west.)

The fourth day from the net weaving.

The fifth day from the net weaving
We gathered a mermaid into the mesh –
Njal said, a long-drowned sailor –
At least something with knuckle and rib and teeth.
Skald sullied harp with sickness.
The skull splayed streams of hair. And smiled. And sank.

The sixth day from the net weaving
A shark surged through the net.

The seventh day from the net weaving
Were bodkin, twine, snicking teeth.
The shark had laid our thousand ordered holes
In one black knot and ravel.
The second net was tougher than the first.
The eighth day from the net weaving
Herring danced in, a thousand.

Gudrun

Gudrun's song between the salt and the corn:

'A girl is thrown on a devious wheel.
The moon took my first clay.
Coldly she turned my childhood from form to form.

The maiden jar grows tall, for ice or honey.
Swans on the lake were my sisters.
Beauty my falcon thundered from cloud to wrist.
A gelding drifted across the meadow . . .
Time eased me from the moon wheel.
Time set me on a barren stone, the solstice.

A crude workaday winter vessel,
A woman is that, said my father.
Her first honey is soon drunk.
Men use her then for oil and salt and brine.

Beauty humped like a sack in the rafters.
Njal with six young skippers
Brought me down to the jetties in the fjord.

The women stank to the elbows with glut.
Thorkeld said yes to my rages, coldness, waverings.
Thy clay is unfired, said Njal.
His throat throbbed with my small honey.

He turned on me soon with thrustings of sun seed.
Thou sweet grain jar, said Njal.

Then dragon, horseback, dove, shatters of ocean!
I cling to the wheel of the sun,
My womb throbs from curve to curve.
Far in the west, say the women,
It will come to a full fragrant barley girth.'

Whales

Whales blundered across us, threshing lumps,
Blue hills, cartloads of thunder.
They trekked between the ice and the hidden shoals.

In the west the gold whale sank in welters of blood.
We killed that ghost each sunset.
At dawn our hands were red and empty.
Now the Dove faltered out of the blind fist.

We notched barbs on various sticks and staves.
We spread the deck with lashings of salt,
Made harpoonman of herdboy.
'Heave her to,' sang the ribbed strenuous oarsmen.
The Dove dipped into the first whalequakes.

The women wondered at all these tons of love.
Gudrun crouched in the doveflank.
Every whale was a bolted slaughterhouse,
A winter of work for candle-makers.
The priest of Balder balanced a ritual point.
That sea was huge with sacrifice.
The Dove lappered in gules of sunset.

One thunderer rose athwart the spear rank.
The barbs broke on his bulk.
Sky jaw from sea jaw split, gigantic laughter!
His frolicking rudder deluged the Dove.
His mild lip sieved the waves.
He balanced a fountain southward on his skull.

Our fires slept in the golden jar.

Far back, those floating feast-halls belched.
Soon the stars flashed around like stalks of corn.

II Our Lady

A Jar of Salt

Twelve women stand in the darkening doors.

> Our Lady of the Inshore,
> *Trust* and *Bountiful*
> Rock like kittiwakes under the crag.
> Lobster and creel are separated.
> The *Rose*, further out
> Uncoils a long haddock line.
> In the Pentland Firth
> A ship, three-masted, nods
> Between Norway and Ireland.
> We stretch, till shroudfall,
> A salt perpetual weave
> Through a warp of furrows.
>
> Our Lady of the Atlantic
> Remember sailors and fishermen.

The twelve women in the crofts
Light their lamps now.
The knife is beside the stone jar.
They stand in the black thresholds.
Wind and sea meet with a new noise in the west.
They have prepared their smoke
Between sunset and the first star.

CROFT WOMEN
Our Lady of Cornstalks
Our Lady of the Flail
Our Lady of Winnowing
Our Lady of Querns
Our Lady of the Oven
Blue Tabernacle
Our Lady of the Five Loaves

                    Take the ploughman home
                    from the ale-house sober.

FISHERMEN
Our Lady of the Boat
Our Lady of Oil and Salt
Our Lady of the Inshore
Our Lady of the Silver Dancers
Our Lady of Nets
Our Lady of the Atlantic
Star of the Sea

                    May cuithe and codling
                    hang in the chimney smoke.

SHEPHERDS
Our Lady of Lent
Our Lady of the Last Snow
Our Lady of Muirburn
Fold of the Agnus Dei
Our Lady of Quiet Waters
Our Lady of Daffodils
Our Lady of April

                    Guard the labour of
                    thirty-five ewes.

TINKERS
Our Lady of Vagabonds
Our Lady of Fishbone and Crust
Our Lady of Ditch Fires
(It was a long road that,

Bethlehem to Golgotha
            And you at the end Pieta, quiet chalice)
            Our Lady of Pilgrims

                                    We have this last can to
                                        sell at the doors.

            WASHER WOMEN
            Our Lady of Wind and Sun
            Our Lady of the Pool
            (As we scrub shirts for ploughmen
            Make clean our hearts, Lady)
            Clother of the Child Christ
            Preparer of linen for the unborn and the dead
            Our Lady Immaculate

                                    That these shirts be dry
                                            by dewfall.

            DEATH WATCHERS
            Our Lady of the Last Oil
            Our Lady of Silence
            Our Lady of Two Candles
            Mater Dolorosa
            Our Lady of Dark Saturday
            Stone of these stones
            Our Lady of the Garden

                                    Pray for old Sara cold
                                            as roots.

            THE CROFT AT NIGHT
            Our Lady of Dark Ploughs
            Our Lady of Furled Boats
            Our Lady of Kneeling Oxen
            (And their breath was warm on thy hand one winter)

            On an old pillow, blessing
            On the cradle, blessing
            On those laid together in love, blessing

            Our Lady of Perpetual Vigil.

Helmsman

The *Guthaland* swings in my grip.

The Bishop says, scouring salt
From paten and chalice,
'Put in under that cliff.
This voyage, pilgrims,
There's too much dice and vino.
I will say a Mass on the deck.'

And the Earl, arranging his chessmen,
'The water is sour again.
They are tired of salt beef.
Their loins are restless.
The oarsmen like olives.
They gulp that French wine like ale.
And the cabinboy with oranges
From the booths at San-Juan
Made a yellow road
All the way back to the ships.'

And Armod the Iceland poet,
'I am curious about their verse,
The formal plots,
Rose and marble and nightingale.
This is not the poetry we know,
The hawk's lonely station,
The furling, fall, unfurling,
Beauty clawed out of death.
Put me ashore at the first tavern
Among their troubadours.
I must study this rhyming.
I am anxious concerning my craft.'

Holiness, war, poetry,
One fisherman with thick shoulders.
And the oarsmen, yoked there
Like spindrift oxen,

'A queer sea, no ebb or flow.
No beer in the pubs.
Fish as small as your pinkie.
The girls dark like tinkers.
Turn the ship west, then north.
Beat the sea flat
All the way to Iceland.'

I am thinking always
'Is Gauk my mate getting lobsters
Under Rora Head?
Spring visits this coast with many roses.
Also, in May, comes our seapink.
Does Ingi, my girl, keep her body cold?'

The wind sits in the north.

And all this weighty pilgrimage,
The harp, the sword, the psalter,
I hurl at Cyprus.
The sea tears like acres of blue silk.

III Hall and Kirk

Witch

Three horsemen rode between the hills
And they dismounted at Greenhill.
Tall they stooped in at the door.
No long time then
Till Wilma came out among them, laughing.
The bible fishermen watched from the shore.
She sat behind the second dark rider.
They left the valley at noon.
And Wilma did not come back that day
Nor the next day
Nor any day at all that week.
And the dog barked lonely at Greenhill
And the girls took turns at milking her cow.
(One took the froth from her vat.)
The laird sent word
At the end of winter, to James of Reumin

That on Candlemas Friday
He should sail his dinghy to Kirkwall.
He sailed the *Lupin* to the red church.
And there at a steep place, Gallowsha,
Among tilted bottles, fists, faces
– A cold drunken wheel –
James saw the hangman put his red shirt on Wilma.

He sailed back smouldering
From the fire, the rum, the reproaches.
The dog of Greenhill
Barked in the throat of the valley.
And next morning
They launched their boat at the dawn with a wild shout,
The three unlucky fishermen.

A Reel of Seven Fishermen
(Bride, Mother, Fisherman)

Her hands put flame among the peats.
The old one took three fish from the smoke.
Cod off The Kist, drifting, an undersea song.

She sank buckets in the cold burn.
The old one broke a bannock in three.
A withershin step. A cry! A steeple of wings.

She turned quernstones, circle on circle.
The Book lay open, two white halves.
Twelve arms sought the cold dancer.

She squeezed oil in the black lamps.
The old one spread the kirkyard shirt.
Twelve feet beat on the hill, a dance.

Her hands brought fish and ale to the table.
The old one soughed, a winter thorn.
Twelve feet stood in the door, a dance.

Sea streamed like blood on the floor.
They shrieked, gull mouths.
Then bride and mother bowed to the black music.

Taxman

Seven scythes leaned at the wall.
Beard upon golden beard
The last barley load
Swayed through the yard.
The girls uncorked the ale.
Fiddle and feet moved together.
Then between stubble and heather
A horseman rode.

Sheriff of Orknay Contra Ikey Faa, Egiptian or Tinker, for Sundry Breakings of the Peace

Item: thou was drunk all Yule on peatbog whisky. *Item:* thou
kicked the dog Patrick of Burnmouth, whereby the dog
Patrick yet hirples and howls and is unable to make his
customary circle about the flock. *Item:* the bone in thy dead
fire was no rabbit bone but a rooster bone from the croft of
Reumin. *Item:* thou encountered Anna the servant lass at The
Hall, between two doors, first thy stink, then thy shadow,
then thy hand, then thy mouth, then thy ragged arms, and but
that Master Knarston, factor, came strictly upon thee, it had
gone ill with Anna's maidenhead. *Item:* that being denied ale
at Crawnest, thou wast observed to utter (as it were privily)
a black word upon the oatfield there. *Item:* that thy coat is
rightly the scarecrow's coat from Quoyness in Hoy.
The which villainies stand in clear proof.
Thy sentence: Piers the hangman for to follow thee thorrow the
Laverock of Kirkwa and sholtie-and-cart to go on before
thee and Piers for to lay about thy schamelessness the red-
stripit sark.

Shroud

Seven threads make the shroud,
The white thread,
A green corn thread,
A blue fish thread,
A red stitch, rut and rieving and wrath,

A gray thread
(All winter failing hand falleth on wheel)
The black thread,
And a thread too bright for the eye.

Grave Stone

Here lies Sigurd the fisherman
Dead of hooves

Buonaparte, the Laird, and the Volunteers

I, Harry Cruickshank, laird in Hoy
Being by your lordships bidden
To supply from my lands in Rackwick, Hoy,
For His Majesty's ships-of-war
Seven hale hearty willing seamen
Upon payment of the agreed bounty, two guineas,
Did thereupon name
      John Stewart at Greenhill, fisherman,
      James Stewart at Greenhill, crofter,
      William Mowat at Bunertoon, fisherman,
      Andrew Sinclair at Mucklehouse, fisherman,
      Thomas Thomson at Crowsnest, fisherman,
      James Robb at Scar, fisherman,
      James Leask at Reumin, crofter and fisherman
All unmarried, save for Wᵐ Mowat,
Who got wife and cow from Graemsay at the fall of the year
And James Robb, a widower –
The rest all young men in their strength.
I duly rode with officers to the valley
To give notice of impressment to the said men
But found them removed
And the old people dumb and cold as stones.
One said, they were gone fishing, very far out –
Faroe, Rockall, Sulisker.
Another, to the horse-market in Caithness.
Another, 'the trows were taen them aneath the hill' . . .
Upon the Sabbath following
I came to the kirk of Hoy secretly with four officers

Between the sermon and the last psalm.
We took John and James Stewart in the kirk door.
They were quiet enough after the minister spoke with them
(By this, they will be in Portsmouth).
It is certain, my lords,
Robb and Thomson are in the caves.
Andrew Sinclair, fisherman, Mucklehouse
Listed in Hamnavoe for the Davis Straits
On the whaler *Tavistock*
(We found his mark and name in the agent's book).
And Mowat ferried himself to Graemsay
With wife and cow
And there hacked three fingers from his right hand
And stifled the ruin with tar.
As for Leask, he is broken with troll-music.
He lies day-long in the back of the bed,
Dark hollows about his skull.
The old woman says, 'in a decline, consumption.'
She stitches away at a shroud.
But like enough, the guns being silent
And Buonaparte down,
He will make his customary furrows along the hill.
A dozen old men are left in the valley.
Last week, your lordships,
I observed two women rowing to the lobsters.
Ploughmen next April will have shrill voices.

IV Foldings

The Laird

Once it was spring with me
    Stone shield and sundial
Lily and lamb in the Lenten grass;
The ribs of crag and tree
    Resurrecting with birds;
In the mouths of passing crofter and fisher lass
Shy folded words.

Then one tall summer came
    Stone shield and sundial
The year of gun and rod and hawk;

The hills all purple flame;
    The burn supple with trout;
Candle-light, claret, kisses, witty talk,
Crinoline, flute.

Autumn, all russet, fell
    Stone shield and sundial
I wore the golden harvest beard.
I folded my people well
    In shield and fable.
Elders and councillors hung upon my word
At the long table.

Now winter shrinks the heart
    Stone shield and sundial
I'd quit this withered heraldry
To drive with Jock in his cart
    To the hill for peat,
Or seed a field, or from clutches of sea
Take a torn net.

Crofter's Death

They will leave the quiet valley,
The daylight come.
Skulls, bones have been dug
From a loaded tomb.
Seventy years burdened and sunbound, they might see in the
    kirkyard
Their honeycomb.
They will carve a name, some years
On withered stone.
The hill road will drag them back
To hunger again.
In the valley are creels for baiting,
A field to be sown.

Then Four Great Angels, Air, Water, Fire, Earth, Being Summoned, Fell from Their Eternal Circuits unto Poverty at His Single Station, to Be His Servitors

Blizzarding arcs pursue
My ploughing feet.
Through salt brimming circles
I lower my creel.
Between two querns of fire
I raise my peat.
In thundering rounds of stone
I grind my meal.

Black Furrow, Gray Furrow

From the black furrow, a fecund
Whisper of dust,
From the gray furrow, a sudden
Gleam and thrust,
Crossings of net and ploughshare,
Fishbone and crust.

A Winter Bride

The three fishermen said to Jess of The Shore
'A wave took Jock
Between The Kist and The Sneuk.
We couldn't get him, however we placed the boat.
With all that drag and clutch and swell
He has maybe one in a hundred chances.'
They left some mouthing cuithes in the door.
She had stood in this threshold, fire and innocence,
A winter bride.
Now she laid off her workaday shawl,
She put on the black.
(Girl and widow across a drowned wife
Laid wondering neck on neck.)
She took the soundless choir of fish
And a sharp knife
And went the hundred steps to the pool in the rock.

She swilled and cut
And laid psalms and blessings on her dish.

In the bay the waves pursued their indifferent dances.

Peat Cutting

And we left our beds in the dark
And we drove a cart to the hill
And we buried the jar of ale in the bog
And our small blades glittered in the dayspring
And we tore dark squares, thick pages
From the Book of Fire
And we spread them wet on the heather
And horseflies, poisonous hooks,
Stuck in our arms
And we laid off our coats
And our blades sank deep into water
And the lord of the bog, the kestrel
Paced round the sun
And at noon we leaned on our tuskars
– The cold unburied jar
Touched, like a girl, a circle of burning mouths
And the boy found a wild bees' comb
And his mouth was a sudden brightness
And the kestrel fell
And a lark flashed a needle across the west
And we spread a thousand peats
Between one summer star
And the black chaos of fire at the earth's centre.

Homage to Heddle

'Once he disputed
The Kame with an eagle,
His two lambs
Fluttering on a sea ledge. . . .

'That storm in '75
When *Swift* and *Dolphin* vanished
He beached in Lewis
Up to the thwart in haddocks . . .

'In jail twice
For drunk fighting. . . .

'Twelve bairns called him da
In Flotta and Hoy.
Three sat at his lawful table. . . .

'And he broke six rocks
Before his plough
Stitched on the bog and heather and stone of Moorfea
One green square. . . .

'He was at the whaling a winter. . . .

'An old silver man
He reads his bible now
And yawns a bit.'

New Year Stories

We call you Hoymen up
To our Hogmanay flame
From silent kirkyards – Mans
Gone over the crag face
On a flawed rope
After some scabby sheep;
Sander whose cormorant eye a blizzard sealed
At Braga rock
The day the *Nell* was cloven;
Jock with the twenty hives,
The pale plunder of the Coolags in every hoard –
(A broken comb
Would sweeten our whisky cup);
Andrew who married eight barren wives
And buried seven
And had the cold hands of a girl to close his eye;
Jeems who fiddled drunk at every hearth

In the five islands
For wedding, funeral, birth;
Tam of the Hundred Whales.
You who by nature or bad luck are dead,
This winter night again
We summon from the earth
Before the seed.
You have unyoked out of the sun and rain,
Our brutal wheel of bread,
And are lords of legend, beyond change or chance;
We are the shadows at the brimming board.
When the lamp pales
And every story is told
And the last bottle is dry,
Be off, quickly get back
To your good silence.

Ikey Crosses the Ward Hill to the Spanish Wreck

Because of the Spanish wreck I tackled the hill.
I heard of the apples,
Winekegs, mermaids, green silk bale upon bale.

My belly hollowed with hunger on the hill.
From Black Meg's patch
I plucked the loan of a curl of raw kail.

We both wore patches, me and that harvest hill.
Past kirk and croft,
Past school and smithy I went, past manse and mill.

On the black height of the hill
I lay like a god.
Far below the crofters came and went, and suffered, and did
     my will.
I wrung a rabbit and fire from the flank of the hill.
In slow dark circles
Another robber of barrows slouched, the kestrel.

Corn and nets on the downslope of the hill.
The girl at Reumin
Called off her dog, poured me a bowl of ale.

I found no silk or brandy. A bit of a sail
Covered a shape at the rock.
Round it the women set up their terrible wail.

Twins

Who finally never spoke in their place
On the side of the hill
– Small gestures did, nothing was left to say –
Old Howie and Merran his twin,
Questing about the hill all day like bees,
And he would go to the crags
Each morning, over the very face
For a clutch of eggs
(He liked a gull's egg fried among his bread)
And she to the burn with her pail
And maybe, on Mondays, rinse a tub of clothes;
First home would take the froth from the new ale,
Or turn in the press a wet white cheese,
But never a word said
– On such a tranquil wheel their time was spun –
Died on the same day.
They brought to the honeycomb bright brimming mouths.

Fiddlers at the Wedding

Lamps stared cold through the blond
Dishevelled day.
The bride cried out. We packed
Our fiddles away.

The bridegroom turned from the bride.
Guests by the score
Scattered with ploughs to the hill,
With creels to the shore.

A ditch awakening,
A bee in my hair.

Egg and honeycomb,
Cold fare.

An ox on the hill,
Gulls, ploughman, ploughshare.

A sharp wet wind
And my bum bare.

A fish-brimming corn-crammed house,
But a hard door.

Chicken, thief, and crab
Round a blink of fire.

A length of bones in the ditch,
A broken prayer.

A Warped Boat

As one would say, lighting an evening pipe
At a banked fire,
'Barley will soon be ripe.
Ale should be sweet in the mouth this year
With all that rain in May, though the seedtime was dry'. . . .
So Willag, before the *Merle* turned over
Rose from the rowlocks
And remarked to the open mouths on the shore,
'Drive old Bess, that fence-breaker, from the oats
Back to her patch of clover.
Yes, Breck can have my horse for his five goats.
And Jeannie is wrong again.
She raged by all that was holy I'd drown and die
In steepings of malt.

A fine evening it was for going to the sillocks.
But men,
It's a coarse drink at the end of a day, this salt.'

His sea boots filled, and Willag said no more.

A Jar of Honey

A woman came from every house that morning to the croft of
Scar. Slowly, like holy women, they moved through the fields.
Seven men stood at the end of the byre of Scar: five young men,
an old man, a boy. The oat fields were yellow, gulls dipped and
quarrelled over the mackerel in the bay. The men stood outside
the ceremony, unwanted and useless. One of the young men
shared the holy look of the women, but he too was outside their
ceremony. The other men did not have a thing to say to him. They
kept turning away from him. He stood there in a double isola-
tion. A woman with huge hands and a face like stone crossed the
fields, Bella of Windbreck. She walked slowly, by herself. The
door of Scar opened and shut on this priestess. Now it was noon.
The men at the end of the byre smoked their pipes, all but the
lonely one. Once the boy chased a butterfly with a shout but the
old man checked him and the boy sat down at a fissure in the
wall, watching bees oozing out and in. A girl, an acolyte, crossed
over to the burn from Scar for water. With a pure white look on
her she passed the men and returned, silent and intent, a heavy
brimming pail at each side of her. Another woman came out for
peats, her arms red from the flame. The sun dragged through the
afternoon like an ox through furrows. Suddenly the water girl
stood in the open door of Scar, her arms wild circles. 'Simon!' she
cried. 'Come now.' The young man turned his burnished face to
the house. He wouldn't move. He was afraid of the elemental
women inside there, with their water and fire, the terrible priest-
ess and her servers, swaddlers, shrouders, guardians of the gate
of birth and the gate of death. He couldn't move. The other young
men were laughing all round him now. They laid earth-coloured
hands on him. They buffeted him gently. They turned his face
towards the open door. Two of them walked with him, one at
each side, to the threshold. He went inside alone. The boy sat at
the end of the wall, gray wax at his mouth, his fingers threaded
with honey. The old man knocked out his pipe, spat, lifted six
creels from the wall, and slowly walked down to the boats.

A young man lifted a scythe from the end of the barn. He began
to whet it on a red stone.
The gate of life had been opened.
Between that and the dark gate were the fish and the fleece and
the loaf, the oil jars and the jars of salt and the jars of grain, and
the one small jar of honey.

Foldings

What they fold, what the shepherds fold,
Is this, in March
A mothering huddle.

The crofter's trade a hoarding, folding, burnishing
Of seed from snow.

What the fishermen fold is this,
A sklinter of haddocks
From the breached Atlantic banks.

What the women fold
Are torn nets, a stretch of yarn from the loom,
Sheaf after sheaf of August oats,
In the cupboard cheese and honey and ale and bread,
Shapes in the womb,
Night long as a shroud when the twelve boats
Are drifting lights in the west
And the ebb ravels itself in rock and sand.

A winter bride is ravished with plough and seed
And finds at last
The crag where mother and widow enfolded stand.

Jock

WINTER

The valley changed its patches
For one seamless coat.
Jock trudged out to find
His nine snowtranced sheep and Madrum his goat.

He dug them from bright graves
Among the Coolag hills,
All but one ewe whose bones
Are lost again in a drift of daffodils.

SPRING

First, to get to his plough,
Jock thrust aside
A lantern, a litter-and-bitch,
Twelve lobster boxes, a fiddle bow,
A gun, and a coffin half-made.
(He had spent a winter night in the ditch.
It was after the feast of the saint of ploughmen, Burns.
He was shuttled through with a pure warp of barley.
That way, he nearly died.)
He turned some sacks and found the rusted blade.
He stirred that powerful curve from its winter trance.
'So there you are, Mister Plough.
It's you and me and the mare for the hill early.
You tried to kill me, I know,
In January, you and your golden bairns.
But that's all past. I'm giving you one more chance.'

SUMMER

Who thronged the dinghy with bronze and silver each sunset?
    Jock.
Who took the coats from the sheep? Jock.
Who put Bella's Sunday hat on the scarecrow? Jock.
Who got drunk at the seven agricultural shows? Jock.
Who carted home winter fire? Jock.
Who led the bull round the twelve crofts? Jock.
(Also Jock, the day the minister called,
Was locked in the byre.)

The corn breaks, wave after wave,
On Kringnafea.
Crofts lie strewn, transfigured wrecks
In a fenceless sea.

Larks in the golden spindrift
And bees, are drowned.
Then Jock, a Canute with a scythe,
Turns the wave round.

They salvage the cargoes of summer,
The barley, the oats.
Tall women stoop among the sheaves
With bronze throats.

Funeral

Came, their eyes four puddles, the women of Park.
Came, with a flagon of whisky, Quernstones.
(And the biggest bowl was filled
And a honeycomb broken
And a pot of water hung over the red-tongued peat.)
Came the nose of the cat and quizzed the tied jaw,
Cold kissing cold.
Came the minister, a black column of words.
Came the five bairns of Bunertoon, hill dancers,
But furled their feet in the door.
Came an old one with a shroud
(And drenched the house with grief, biography, mothballs).
Came the fisherman's wife with a dish of salt
And a jar of oil.
Came the wife of Greups with circles of smoking bread.

The widow sat in his chair, a black queen.

The ox went forward, a black block, eyes bulging,
The mouth a furnace.
Tammag went forward, cursing.
The plough wavered between them.
And gulls plagued Tammag, a whirl of savage snow
On the field of the sun.
Twice the plough struck stone,
A clang like a bell
Between the burning hills and the cold sea.
Tammag clawed his shoulder. He cursed.
And the ox belched lessening flame.
Six furrows now and a bit. . . .
Suddenly Tammag heard it, low thunder
Far in the firth,
And saw blue surging hills, the whales
On trek from ocean to ocean.
They plunged, they dipped, they wallowed,
They sieved a million small fish through their teeth.
The sun stood at the hill, a black circle.
The shore erupted with men and boats,
A skirl of women,
Loud dogs, seaward asylums of gulls.
The ox stood in the seventh furrow
In a dream of grass and water.
'Tammag!' the boatmen cried. 'Tammag!'
Tammag wiped his silver face on his sleeve.
He yelled at the ox. The plough wavered.
                              They stumbled on.
They tore from the black sun
Loaf, honey-comb, fleece, ale-jar, fiddle.

V The Stone Hawk

Love Letter

To Mistress Madeline Richan, widow
At Quoy, parish of Voes, in the time of hay:
        The old woman sat in her chair, mouth agape
        At the end of April.
        There were buttercups in a jar in the window.

The floor is not a blue mirror now
And the table has flies and bits of crust on it.

Also the lamp is broken.

I have the shop at the end of the house
With sugar, tea, tobacco, paraffin
And, for whisperers, a cup of whisky.

There is a cow, a lady of butter, in the long silk grass
And seven sheep on Moorfea.

The croft girls are too young.
Nothing but giggles, lipstick and gramophone records.

Walk over the hill Friday evening.
Enter without knocking
If you see one red rose in the window.

Haddock Fishermen

Midnight. The wind yawing nor-east.
A low blunt moon.
Unquiet beside quiet wives we rest.

A spit of rain and a gull
In the open door.
The lit fire. A quick mouthful of ale.

We push the *Merle* at a sea of cold flame.
The oars drip honey.
Hook by hook uncoils under The Kame.

Our line breaks the trek of sudden thousands.
Twelve nobbled jaws,
Gray cowls, gape in our hands,

Twelve cold mouths scream without sound.
The sea is empty again.
Like tinkers the bright ones endlessly shift their ground.

We probe emptiness all the afternoon;
Unyoke; and taste
The true earth-food, beef and barley scone.

Sunset drives a butcher blade
In the day's throat.
We turn through an ebb salt and sticky as blood.

More stars than fish. Women, cats, a gull
Mewl at the rock.
The valley divides the meagre miracle.

The Laird's Falcon

The falcon on the weathered shield
    Broke from his heraldic hover
    To drift like a still question over
The fecund quarterings of the field.

Doves in that dappled countryside,
    Monotones of round gray notes,
    Took his bone circle in their throats,
Shed a mild silence, bled, and died.

All autumn, powered with vagrant blood
    (But shackled to a silken call)
    He paced above the purple hill,
His small black shadow tranced the wood.

Steadfast himself, a lord of space,
    He saw the red hulk of the sun
    Strand in the west, and white stars run
Their ordered cold chaotic race;

Till from lucidities of ice
    He settled on a storied fist,
    A stone enchantment, and was lost
In a dark hood and a sweet voice.

Five Crags
>   The five black angels of Hoy
>   That fishermen avoid –
>   The Sneuk, The Too, The Kame, Rora, The Berry.

Elder
>   Charlag who has read the prophets
>   A score of times
>   Has thumbed the salt book also, wave after wave.

Crofter-Fisherman
>   Sea-plough, fish-plough, provider
>   Make orderly furrows.
>   The herring will jostle like August corn.

Shopkeeper
>   Twine, sea stockings, still to pay
>   And Howie trading
>   Cod for rum in the ale-house.

New Boat
>   We call this boat *Pigeon*.
>   Go gentle, dove
>   Among skuas, easterlies, reefs, whalebacks.

Fishmonger
>   The fishmonger stood at the rock
>   With bits of dull silver
>   To trade for torrents of uncaught silver.

The Scarecrow in the Schoolmaster's Oats

Hail, Mister Snowman. Farewell,
Gray consumptive.

Rain. A sleeve dripping.
Broken mirrors all about me.

A thrush laid eggs in my pocket.
My April coat was one long rapture.

I push back green spume, yellow breakers,
King Canute.

One morning I handled infinite gold,
King Midas.

I do not trust Ikey the tinker.
He has a worse coat.

A Hogmanay sun the colour of whisky
Seeps through my rags.
I am – what you guess – King Barleycorn.

A Child's Calendar

No visitors in January.
A snowman smokes a cold pipe in the yard.

They stand about like ancient women,
The February hills.
They have seen many a coming and going, the hills.

In March, Moorfea is littered
With knock-kneed lambs.

Daffodils at the door in April,
Three shawled Marys.
A lark splurges in galilees of sky.

And in May
A russet stallion shoulders the hill apart.
The mares tremble.

The June bee
Bumps in the pane with a heavy bag of plunder.

Strangers swarm in July
With cameras, binoculars, bird books.

He thumped the crag in August,
A blind blue whale.

September crofts get wrecked in blond surges.
They struggle, the harvesters.
They drag loaf and ale-kirn into winter.

In October the fishmonger
Argues, pleads, threatens at the shore.

Nothing in November
But tinkers at the door, keening, with cans.

Some December midnight
Christ, lord, lie warm in our byre.
Here are stars, an ox, poverty enough.

Beachcomber

Monday I found a boot –
Rust and salt leather.
I gave it back to the sea, to dance in.

Tuesday a spar of timber worth thirty bob.
Next winter
It will be a chair, a coffin, a bed.

Wednesday a half can of Swedish spirits.
I tilted my head.
The shore was cold with mermaids and angels.

Thursday I got nothing, seaweed,
A whale bone,
Wet feet and a loud cough.

Friday I held a seaman's skull,
Sand spilling from it
The way time is told on kirkyard stones.

Saturday a barrel of sodden oranges.
A Spanish ship
Was wrecked last month at The Kame.

Sunday, for fear of the elders,
I sit on my bum.
What's heaven? A sea chest with a thousand gold coins.

Windfall

No red orchards here; the sea
    Throbbing, cold root
To salt incessant blossoming
    Burdens the net
    With gray and with white and with blue fruit.

Girl

In that small school
Learn number and word
And the ordered names.
    Then older knowledge, a kinder spell:
To lift your latch
To neighbour and tramp
Till all share
Fish, bread, and ale
At your brimming board.
    Elder and minister, what do they say?
Among the flames
Of April lust
Be cold as snow –
Let fisherman come and crofter go.
    Learn this last wisdom:
Beyond gray hair,
A winter lamp,
A leaking thatch,
You must enter the halls of the kingdom,
Persephone,
Of passionate dust.

Old Man

'Before the cuckoo puts his two notes over the burn –
> *The wings crowd south*
> *Flight by fall*
> *The birds return*

'What with rheumatics, asthma, and whisky the price it is –
> *The sap sinks*
> *Shower by spring*
> *The waters rise*

'Peerie Tam will have my plough, and my fiddle, and oars.'
> *Come, dancer, go*
> *Step by circle*
> *The reel endures.*

Roads

The road to the burn
Is pails, gossip, gray linen.

The road to the shore
Is salt and tar.

We call the track to the peats
The kestrel road.

The road to the kirk
Is a road of silences.

Ploughmen's feet
Have beaten a road to the lamp and barrel.

And the road from the shop
Is loaves, sugar, paraffin, newspapers, gossip.

Tinkers and shepherds
Have the whole round hill for a road.

Butter

What's come of my churning? The van-man, he took seven pounds, and a basket of warm eggs, for jam, sugar, tea, paraffin. I gave the tinkers a lump, to keep the black word from our byre. I put some on the damp peats, to coax a flame. I swear the cat has a yellow tongue. There was only a scrape for the fisherman's bannock, like a bit of sun on a dull day. The old cow is giving me a mad look.

The Coward

All Monday he sat by the fire, Stoney the fisherman
Loud with a hoast,*
Till Jean bought a guaranteed nostrum from the van.
In terror at the black stuff in the bottle,
When Jean was out, luring eggs from the hen,
He coughed his way to the noust†
And launched the *Belle* with a lurch and a rattle
Into a sea
Shaken with spasms as loud and green as he.
He came back late
With a score of lobsters, sillocks like stars, a skate
As wide and bright as the moon
And devil the hoast.
He felt as rich as the laird as he landed his creels.
But there, a patient Penelope on the coast,
Stood Jean with a spoon
And the phial that, warts to consumption, cured all ills.

Sabbath

On the first morning I lisped your name.
The school bell rang.
We stood at the blackboard, two unlettered pigeons.

* hoast – cough   † noust – boat shelter

The second morning
You set a scarecrow between plough and quern.
You wove a creel.
In my mother's croft I learned to smoke fish, the song of the
    wheel, brewing.

I went down to the shore to meet five boats from nine
In a lull of the storm.
You came out of the smother, a ghost with a red mouth.
That was the third morning.

The fourth morning the women put white things on me.

Between fifth morning and sixth morning, darkness,
A dozen moons that gathered to gouts of blood.
I worked the croft alone.
That was the year of the submarine.
Men sank and burned.
Women turned slowly to stone.
The sixth lamplight a stranger stood in the door,
A man from the west.
I knew that red mouth through the surge of beard.
It blew the lamp out.
Our lost sun pulsed between us.
Were rootings of good seed on a gaunt acre.

Now in the Sabbath
We mix complaint and blessing, two scripture doves.

Hill Runes

Thirst

    Horse at trough, thrush in quernstone,
    The five ploughmen
    Much taken up with pewter.

Elder

    Andrew who has read the gospel
    Two or three times
    Has quizzed the clay book also, furrow by furrow.

Smithy
>The flames of love, the hammerings, glowings,
>End one way –
>A cold nail on an anvil.

Kirkyard
>Between stone poem and skull
>April
>Touches rat, spade, daffodil.

Tractor
>The horsemen are red in the stable
>With whisky and wrath.
>The petrol-drinker is in the hills.

The Big Wind

The big wind trundled our pail, a clanging bell
Through the four crofts,
Broke the clean circles of wave and gull,
Laid the high hay in drifts,
Beat down the stones of the dead,
Drove the *Beagle* aground,
Whirled up Merran's petticoats round her head,
And set three hen-houses (cockerels raging aloft) on the
    crested Sound.

The kestrel stood unmoving over the hill.

The Drowning Brothers

The boy said (his arm a long white stone)
'The burn is a fish in a net of fences. . . .
The burn is a glancing shuttle. . . .'
A crofter turned a homing rudder.
Corn, a prodigal, stood in the door of the sun
Arrayed in harvest patches.
The crofter beached. The ripe hands of the wind
Throttled his haddocks.
He shouted the women from loom and fire.

The brother said (his thigh a struck gleam)
'The burn is a lark in a cage. The silver tongue
Yearns on and out. . . .'
The burn throbbed between hills and beach all day.
Pigeons fretted the stubble.
Women stooped to the sheaves with bronze throats.

The first boy said (half marble and half flesh)
'The tinker burn hurries from field to field.
He begs for small things.
Heather to cornstalk to seaweed he burbles gossip.
He spreads his pack at every stone,
Torrents of sapphire and lace,
Among the reeds a swatch of green silk. . . .'
An oat, a can, a straw, left the slow valley.
Ikey slouched at the stubble edge,
Banished that day with larks, rats, fishermen.

The brother said (his throat a sculpted psalm)
'The burn is our angel. He praises.
He fills our pails.
He flames in the face of the drinking beasts.
He carries the valley filth
Out to the seven brightnesses of the bay.
He has turned a key.
Quick, now, follow the cold one.
They will drag us back to their old sweat and dung. . . .'
Those hills, The Ward and Moorfea, brooded upon them,
Dark angels.
The tractor throbbed with one urgent image, bread.

Heavy with images, the statues drowned.

Fisherman's Bride

Around us a muted din
    Of fiddles and feet,
        Circlings of bread and ale.
This room we are in
    At the seaward side, is still.
        I turn a cold sheet.

Midnight. The shoal drifts
Like a host of souls unborn, along the shore.
The tide sets from the west.
His salt hand shifts
From tumults of thigh and breast
To the hard curve of an oar.

Dead Fires

At Burnmouth the door hangs from a broken hinge
And the fire is out.

The windows of Shore empty sockets
And the hearth coldness.

At Bunertoon the small drains are choked.
Thrushes sing in the chimney.

Stars shine through the roofbeams of Scar.
No flame is needed
To warm ghost and nettle and rat.

Greenhill is sunk in a new bog.
No kneeling woman
Blows red wind through squares of ancient turf.

The Moss is a tumble of stones.
That one black stone
Is the stone where the hearth fire was rooted.

In Crawnest the sunken hearth
Was an altar for priests of legend,
Old seamen from the clippers with silken beards.

The three-toed pot at the wall of Park
Is lost to woman's cunning.
A slow fire of rust eats the cold iron.

The sheep drift through Reumin all winter.
Sheep and snow
Blanch fleetingly the black stone.

From that sacred stone the children of the valley
Drifted lovewards
And out of labour to the lettered kirkyard stone.

The fire beat like a heart in each house
From the first cornerstone
Till they led through a sagging lintel the last old one.

The poor and the good fires are all quenched.
Now, cold angel, keep the valley
From the bedlam and cinders of A Black Pentecost.

VI *The Return of the Women*

Landfall

JANE

They put on pasteboard helmets and greaves. The Trojans
retired behind a high battlement (a pile of desks and
the blackboard.) The Greeks stood, a clamant wedge, in
the middle of the room. Class IVC would soon mell in the
breached wall. Helen with her blunt freckled nose sat in
the window-seat; she looked down from a high turret. An
ox-eyed Juno, I directed their comings and goings. Ulysses
took off his glasses and breathed on the left lens. Achilles
stood beside the globe of the world. *And before this day's
battle is done,* he piped, *full many a soul will be ferried
across the Styx.* Hector astride a desk brandished his ruler,
he shouted defiance. It was our contribution to the school
concert, the second day of rehearsal. Far too soon, Troy
began to burn. The classroom dappled and darkened. Fire
bowed through the door, a mad inspector. His red tongue
flickered in my face. Then he turned to interrogate the
players – forty boys and girls smouldered around him like
rag dolls. The play was over. Through curtains of ash
I came at last to the smell of the sea. Was it night? Cold
wet masses moved against a sagging wharf. I went from
one burnt element into another, till I must have been only
a spread of hair on the burnt sea. Then hands upgathered
me from the suck and drench. Oars creaked. Voices
besieged my face but no mouths moved.

Of course she's blind, said a voice. *She won't do. Let her go.* I touched the beard that kind golden words were coming out of. I said in a changed voice (for this was the meeting place of the dead beside the waters, with antique masks) *I pray you, good ferryman, have a pity of me, let me sink. I would not look again on the shadows of labour and love.* Goldenbeard held me closer to him. *Poor lass,* he said, *God help you, you won't do that. Your eyes are cinders.* His body strained and swayed above me. He smote, with other oarsmen, sounding furrows. He said, after a time, *They can generally see more than other folk, the blind.*

NATASHA

The boat is wrapped round and about in swathes and cerements of fog. The people in the stern move like ghosts. But the petrel assures me that we aren't a cargo of dead people – it spurts out of the fog, it dips and hovers, it puts a sweet askance look over the *Truelove* and her voyagers. At least, though my violin is lost in The Black Flame – and all books and statues too, I think – we won't have to live in a birdless world. Yesterday I saw a seal or a porpoise, very indistinct, on the surface (or it could have been a bottle with the world's last message in it). The petrel again – it insists *This way! This way!* The men tug hard at the oars in rising sea, spindrift salts in, sifts in, Saul the Skipper throws an oilskin over the sack of seed corn. A chasm of purple sky – one cerement is lifted from our sea shroud, then dropped again, but a few stars pulsed like boys bathing (choristers in a rockpool). The petrel again – I love these birds, the lost cold drifting sea syllables.

BIANCA

Night. Then morning again, and sea and sky one huge opaque pearl. The same day after day. This afternoon the fog lifted – we were among black islands – bone and rottenness everywhere, even on these western beaches. (Nothing for me to do but sometimes bathe the eyes of the blind schoolteacher and swab an occasional vomit from the deck. I studied vigilance and patience a long time ago.) In a few days these educated people have broken back into the narrow circle of the beasts. The antics of life are performed openly. They eat and relieve themselves and – a few of them – make love like floating dogs. Sunset. They'll soon be at it again. I was changing bandages in St Lawrence's – an old

man who had spilled a kettle over himself – when The Black
Flame burst the hospital open. It cancelled all salves and
bandages, the city was one complete scald. I will have to be
very patient, make myself a stone in the middle of these
fires. Some day they may need me. I don't know. That's
Venus, and I think up there, now, very faintly, The Plough.

SOPHIE

David chose me in the river estuary. We hadn't been in the boat a
half-hour. First thing he did was beg this bit of canvas from
The Skipper – it covers a part of us at least after dark. *That
wedge of thick blackness to starboard last night,* he says,
that was Glasgow . . . And here, he says, *is Jura with the
three breasts.* (He used to climb and sail a lot in the summer
when he was a student.) *Now Eriskay, island of music . . .
Iona of the saints . . .* Kisses, beautiful names, stars. We drift
northwards all night under this hard creaking blanket. (But
I chose him too.) I was a swan that morning. It was the final
performance, an Arts Council recital in the Seamen's
Institute, singing and flutes and dancing. Only a sprinkling
of whalers in the front seats, belching beersmells and lewd-
ness at us. Then the music guttered. Swans floated serene
into The Black Flame. I was in river oil, alone, a fluttering
clogged clamorous bird. Hard curves beat on me. I was
tangled in oars. David lifted me out of that web. Now the
sun labours up out of the mist, a gout of blood. And David
turns from me again to the harder curve of the oar.

TERESA

Sanctus said the girls in the school choir. The nuns knelt like a
flock of reverend penguins, beads looped in fingers. The
Star of the Sea gave me a sweet plaster glance. *Benedictus
qui venit in nomine Domini,* we said raggedly. Father
Mulvaney bent down and kissed the altar. The Lord had
entered Jerusalem on the ass. We strewed our bored offer-
ings in the chapel air. *Hosanna in excelsis* I said. (I always
picture the Mass like that – it is the life of Our Lord unfold-
ing.) Gloria – that was the shepherds and angels in the
stable. The Gospel was parables and miracles in Galilee; we
were there at the roadside, watching, listening, wondering.
Now *Hosanna* – the King was in the gate of the Holy City.
After that glad shout, silence. The priest murmurs his
prayers inaudibly. Soon men are going to commit their
wickedest worst crime yet, the murder of God. The bread

and wine are on the altar. In silence the Passion goes on –
Gethsemane, the kiss, the scourging, the spittle, the
mockery, the ring of thorns. Soon Christ must stumble up
his fourteen stations to Golgotha. The bell rang in the sanc-
tuary, like hammer on nail, a small sweet terrible music.
Then nothing; this boat, the strange faces, bogs and
beaches, the desolation going on and on. Father
Mulvaney's Mass did not end. Between Sanctus and conse-
cration The Black Flame came down: hosts and chalice lie
among smouldering stones. (I remember nothing.) The des-
olation goes on and on and on. We never reached the empty
tomb in the garden. Who is the saint of this sea now – I
forget – is it Columbus? No, here it is, in the missal,
Columba: 'he fished and ploughed and carved crosses on
the stone' . . . Columba, pray for us. That flushed hulk we
passed at sunset was Cape Wrath, Simon says. These black
lumps on the sea against the dawn, he says, are the
Orkneys. The missal again – here it is, Magnus: 'his skull
was breached in a furrow on a day of new fires' . . . Magnus
of Orkney, saint and virgin and martyr, have a care of the
world's last few gutterings of breath.

MARILYN

'Appleblossom' they call me. Nice in a way, I suppose, but still
I don't care a lot for it. The women give me my right name.
The Skipper calls me nothing at all. Appleblossom – it
makes me feel like one of them Japanese good-time girls.
Well, I know my skin's pink-and-white. And if my eyes
slant a bit it's quite attractive. And my small feet too. If it
comes to that, I *do* feel like an applebranch, simply burst-
ing all over with flowers whenever Conrad or David look
up from the oars. Time I had some romance, I'm fifteen.
I don't think I fancy Simon very much. Siegfried the
oarsman on the right side, he has a beautiful beard, simply
a fleece of gold from his nostrils to his throat. The Skipper,
he eyes every woman but me like a farmer in an auction
ring, even the blind woman and that old bitch of a nurse
that won't talk to a soul and her that's out with her holy
Roman beads whenever a bigger wave than usual hits us.
John the oarsman on the right side next the bow is just a
boy – a science student, they say – he grows apples in his
face whenever I so much as look at him. (I don't fancy him
much either.) Disgraceful the way David and that dancer
– stripper, most likely – carry on, trying to hide their

goings-on under a sail (as if we can't hear them going at it half the night). Conrad, he has simply the nicest way of watching the stars, Natasha, the seabirds. I like Conrad. He used to write text-books on ecology, Natasha says, whatever that is. But this is really what I'd like to happen, The Skipper just to say to me quite simply, no nonsense (and when the time came I would shake all the apples on the tree down on him till I was stark as winter), *Marilyn, I want you for my woman.*

TRUDI

What do you expect to find? I said to Saul the Skipper, (I wore his duffle in the stern last night, it was so cold.) *Better just settle,* I said, *for a foreshore with a spring of water in it,* I said, *and a cave or two under the crags. We must study the life of otters,* I said. *No Avalon or Hesperides or Tir-Nan-Og in this latitude.* He never said a word. He kept striking matches and looking at his chart in the darkness. I woke in the early morning. Crags rose sheer out of the sea, like pillars of fire. I don't think Saul had slept all night. He set his brow against every new headland as if he wanted to butt it down. Then about noon the crags dropped their swords, they turned from us, they knelt, fell, were red shoulders and knees sticking out of the water. I saw first a streak of sand, then a quiet tumult of brown and green fields. A burn flashed here and there, then ravelled itself among shore boulders, pink and blue and saffron spheroids, the heaped immaculate sculpture of the sea. The oarsmen and the women (even Jane) turned their faces to this sweet green gap. Saul pushed the tiller away from him hard and the *Truelove* circled round under hosts of white wings rising and falling about the wake of our landfall.

Houses

JANE

I'm blind but there are one or two things I can do in this new place. All morning I've been taking bits of wool from thistles and barbed wire. The place is full of sheep running half wild. Siegfried is my eyes. In some ruin or other he found a wooden wheel and a frame and treadle. *That's for spinning*, he said. *I'll find out the way myself first and then I'll teach your fingers.* Finally The Skipper showed us how it was done. So there may be a few woollen shirts for next winter. And Siegfried's going to take me to the hill when blackberries are out. I've woven a rush basket for that. There'll be jam next winter too, bitter I expect because there's no sugar. Will we find a bees' nest in July? The place Siegfried is rebuilding for us out of a ruin on the hillside, one wall is finished. Siegfried took me to the gable this morning and put my hands on the stones of the new wall and the sun was warm on the stones. *The boy*, said Siegfried, *will have the eyes that you lost in The Black Flame. I think our children will grow up happy here, in Rackwick.*

NATASHA

A host of cold voices greeted us in Rackwick – tern, skua, plover, lark, kittiwake, heron, diver, dotterel. Only the pigeons, though, come about the thresholds, looking for the old peace offering between man and dove, a crumb of bread. But till Conrad cuts our first harvest there's no bread to offer. Still the birds of God at every door insist on peace and friendship. One split the first tempest, a branch-bearer, and fell through shivering rainbows on the Ark. They tell us too, over and over – life can begin again. A hard existence though until the first harvest is cut in Rackwick. We eat boiled limpets and crabs till our guts loathe them. The wild rams run from Conrad and the other men into the hills. A northerly gale, a deluge of rain, a hidden worm might blast the acres of sown corn. But the dove goes from door to door among the seven houses always. I take this for a good sign. (Why do I love all these birds? I think they remind me of the lost music. My violin was shaped like some sweet archaic bird – yet it was very young as sounds go, three centuries perhaps – now it lies furled forever on the far side of The Black Flame, a delicate cinder. Lark and curlew, they cry on from beginning to end.) The Skipper says he will bring me a hawk from the hill.

BIANCA

Venus every night, shaking out her yellow hair in the bay. Now it isn't as bad as it was in the boat, a rampage of lust. They have paired off decently with each other, six couples. They

live in the six stone ruins and I'm alone, thank God, in
a new wooden hut beside the marsh. Conrad and the
musical woman, they have their house where the burn
empties into the sea above the sand and the multi-
coloured boulders. David and Sophie live under the little
green hill that rises half-way between the horns of the bay.
The Skipper's house is above the anchorage, looking
south. Trudi is his woman, for the moment at least – his
eyes flame everywhere like a goat before rutting time. The
young silly ones, Marilyn and John, are higher up,
towards Moorfea, near the kestrels. Siegfried with his
bright beard does nothing but get gulls' eggs. His house is
a ruckle, he has shifted a few stones, that's all. The blind
woman will have many a hungry winter with the likes of
him. Simon and Teresa, their house is at the glen where the
burn drops down, loud and heather-hidden – and what
would her priest and her nuns think of her now? Simon
fishes with The Skipper. (But when all's said and done
they're still rutting and rooting about in this place, no
better than animals.) I live alone half-way between hills
and sea – a small stretch of moss – in a hut of bleached
boards. The Skipper gathered them for me, a few one day
and a few another, whatever the sea threw up. Then off
with him, like a billy-goat, among the crofts where the
young women are.

SOPHIE

He turns from me, as soon as it's light, to the harder curve of
the plough. After he had patched up the house he roofed
the old stable and barn, to show his faith. Our green corn
is tallest of all now. The Skipper isn't pleased about that.
First David had to dig with a spade. Not a single ox had
come through The Black Flame. There was one old plough
rusting in the bog. And of course the tractor that belonged
to the first inhabitants, it was worse than useless; even the
rats and birds kept away from it; the petrol smell clings
about it, faintly, like a ghost of the last age. Well, one day
when David was among the hills didn't two horses cross
the heather towards him, very delicate and shy, shaggy
garrons, a mare with a black mane spilling into the wind
and her foal. And at last the mare came right up to him
and fitted her skull into his warm welcoming hand. And
then David led her and the snickering foal home to the
plough and empty stable. That plough leans against the

wall brighter, I swear, than The Plough in the January sky. And here's something, there's another ripeness in the world. Deep inside me a new heaviness stirs and sways, poised, the sea-begotten dancer.

TERESA

Saint Magnus, or The Skipper, or just pure luck, brought us safe ashore. The *Truelove* ended against a rock, it's true. One by one we women dropped up to our throats in the bay and walked slowly ashore, bright shivering creatures. The men followed. The Skipper held the sack of seed corn high above his head. The seven houses are roofed now, some better than others. I wouldn't care to live in Jane's hovel, but she doesn't know, she's blind, and so pleased with her Siegfried everything he does is perfect. Simon, he's learning to be a fisherman. I prayed my rosary thin all the shortening nights of spring, asking for some kind of a blessing on our bed. We must live now as if we existed in some poor pagan ballad, unparadised, Simon and I. The sun rose and set but Good Friday went on and on, the last breath guttering in the throat of God. There must have been a few women who spat and laughed and gossiped under the Cross – surely I belonged with them. And another woman stood among us, cold with grief, turned away from me, hidden. Better a thousand times to have ended in grace in The Black Flame. It was more than I could bear. Six nights ago I put my faith from me, I threw my rosary in the midden. I stood in the door then, purified. I drew breath within a crude ballad, with only a few rhymes (grave-wave-weave: thorn-mourn-corn.) Not again would the scatter of notes that was me, my identity, my selfhood, Teresa, be caught up in the transfiguring music of any Mass or Benediction. It was best that way. This morning I went down to the wooden house at the moss – Bianca confirmed what I had known for weeks – I was pregnant. I left her and her cold smiles. I climbed the hill to our house. What would I do? I would stand in the open door. I would say to Simon, *We are both hungry. There will soon be a new hunger in this house, a child, a bastard.* I stood in the door. Simon was making a creel. I could say nothing. Simon looked up. I went out again. I stood between house and byre. Simon followed me. He said, *This is good news, Teresa.* Siegfried hailed me joyfully across the valley. David cried from the burn, *Well done, Teresa.* The ballad (earth-dearth-birth) dissolved in a Gloria of fisherman and shepherd and ploughman. I stooped down in the midden. I wiped the fish-slime and dung from the bone beads. My rosary, for the Third Joyful Mystery, slipped through my fingers like corn seed, like drops of sweet water.

MARILYN

I want you for my woman, The Skipper said to me. He was up at Moorfea helping John to put mortar on the wall. *No,* I said, *I have a man, and your woman is Trudi.* John was away at the burn getting water to mix the cement. The Skipper just laughed. *You will come when I'm ready,* he said. Then when the houses were roofed and the fields sown we all went down to the moor to cut peat. *Be careful of that Billy-goat,* old Bianca said to me. The Skipper sank his spade in next to mine. He said, *You will come and live at my place the day after tomorrow . . . My house is at Moorfea,* I said, *John and I live there. John is my man. I love him.* We stayed behind to spread out the wet peats when the others went home – The Skipper, Bianca, and me. The first stars came out. Bianca shouldered her spade and went home, smiling. *I will look after you better than that fool of a boy,* said The Skipper in the darkness. He unbuttoned my shirt and probed my breasts with his hand the way a farmer will examine the first apples. Then the thing was done. *Trudi knows about this,* he said. *You will come to my place before harvest. Soon everybody here will work for me. This is the way it must be. That boy will be given his place.*

TRUDI

A host of gulls, rising and falling and screaming about his basket of fish. He's dragging the boat up, he and Simon. No peace in the man at all. He was out before first light making a fence. Now he'll eat, then sleep an hour. Then up to the hill with him to speak to the hawk. Yesterday it came down and sat on his wrist a minute, then flew into the cloud again. (He has promised the hawk to Natasha.) He took the wild ram by the horns last week – it's tethered at the end of the house. There's that bull near the Kame, he says, and a stallion somewhere in the Trowieglen. He hewed querns from an immense boulder at the beach, stone circles out of a stone sphere. He has put new strakes in the *Truelove* – they'll fish miles out in the Pentland next spring. Even our bowels is his concern. *Dung and bread are brothers*, he tells them. *Don't unbreech in the heather, save it for the furrows* . . . Then he must settle the dispute between Bianca and David of Greenhill, some patch of heather where she wants to spread her washing. He digs drains everywhere. He broods over every fish, every cornshoot, with his great eyes, to see if The Black Flame has worked some mutation. He says he made a big mistake at landfall: they should have built one large house, a Hall, not squandered their strength on the seven hovels. *I'll put all that to rights*, he says, and when The Skipper and I should be sleeping we heave up stones from the beach to make this the one dominant house in the valley. There's no rest in the man. I don't like him. But he brought us safe out of The Black Flame. He saved the seed corn. He taught the men how to fish and handle sheep. One thing I've found out, it's best to do exactly what he says; at least till our first harvest is cut.

Harvest

JANE

The baby, Siegfried tells me, has two blue eyes. His mouth is red like all mouths. Small and round and red and cold, it tugs at my warm enriched breasts. He cries often, more like the wail of a seabird than a butterfed baby. The women go and come silently. The men are a spectrum of voices among the ripening fields. Siegfried's sowing was not a success. *I will take over your ploughing next year,* said The Skipper. *Look at David's field, that's the way corn should be at this time of year. Can I trust you with sheep? I doubt it. Still you will have to be our shepherd here in Rackwick.* So Siegfried looks after the badtempered ram and the forty mild sheep that were rounded up in the Trowieglen. The spinning wheel goes for a while, then stops, then The Skipper comes to hammer in a nail or re-set the treadle. Next winter will there be coats for everybody in the valley? The child with the ploughman's legs and fisherman's arms will have the first gray coat. All the women, says Siegfried, are in different stages of pregnancy. The women are a spectrum of ripeness across the valley. The Rackwick children will be five or six years old about

the same time. Maybe then they'll want me for a teacher
again: but no history, and no poetry, and only enough
mathematics for them to count to a hundred. Beyond that,
the black circle of Mephistopheles. We broke into it. We
were burned.

NATASHA

I have the hawk. The day before harvest The Skipper came
   down from The Ward with a struggling sack. At the door
   of Burnmouth he opened the sack and set the bird on my
   wrist. Conrad was at the edge of the field, honing a scythe.
   The Skipper crossed over to Conrad. They greeted each
   other; their bodies inclined for a minute, a murmuring
   arch; then their heads swung apart and they mingled
   voices, one sweet terrible cry. Conrad flashed at The
   Skipper with his scythe and cut a ribbon of skin from his
   arm. I could do nothing, the hawk sat on my hand and
   encompassed me in a wide yellow glare. The Skipper
   struck Conrad with his fist and Conrad fell among the
   corn. The Skipper came back and took the hawk from me.
   The hawk's claw had pierced a vein in my wrist. The
   Skipper mixed some of the blood from his arm with the
   blood scattering off my knuckles like heavy red coins.
   I followed him across three fields to the Shore. Bianca, old
   mute mockery, stood in her door. Trudi kissed me in the
   threshold. Marilyn arched like a cat against the wall.
   There was a new cold room ready for me. Next day
   I helped in The Skipper's barley harvest. At the other side
   of the bay Conrad works alone in his field. The hawk sits
   in the dark of the barn. The pigeons have shifted from this
   door to Conrad's door and to David and Sophie's door
   and to the blank bolted door of Moorfea.

BIANCA

I didn't think King Goat would break his tether and rut and
   rampage as far as that! First that trash of a girl Marilyn in
   the peatbog, and now Natasha. They live, if you please, at
   The Shore now, and not a cry out of Trudi or out of John
   (the boy is simple-minded, he has the guts of a sparrow.)
   Conrad works on by himself in his field. We will see what
   we will see. The blind woman, she'll be next, I knew it.
   The Skipper has made her man the shepherd, if you please,
   Siegfried. Saul is the master here, he has one aim, to fill the
   valley with a torrent of his own goats. To him the women

are nothing but walking wombs, seed jars. The children to come will all wear his face – the fishermen, shepherds, crofters, tinkers, blacksmiths, millers, beachcombers, fiddlers. The other men are too gentle, or too stupid, or too weak, to breed the only kind of animal that can survive in this place. I know for sure now why I have sufferance here, so that whole and sound the new tribe can be brought from womb to cradle. So he comes with his animal eyes and cold charity of fish to me, a cold sybil.

SOPHIE

Sea-begotten, earth-born. I laid the baby in a corner of the field. Our barley was green yesterday. Overnight it changed colour, as if the sun was looking into a huge wind-flawed mirror. *Time for scythes*, said David. How can a dancer become a harvester in one day? My first cuttings were brief and mangled. I learned quickly from David. By noon the swathes of corn fell before me, cut clean to the bottom of the stalk. We did the Dance of Bread together, David and I. Once The Skipper came to the edge of our barley. He shouted at us but we paid no attention. I think he wanted us to work in his corn first – his field is a host of labourers and a scattering of thin stooks. Late in the afternoon I went over to the corner of the field and opened my blouse and fed the baby. David trudged on, the scythe flashing round his loins like strokes of lightning, till the last of the barley was cut. Then I brought water from the burn to the mare and her foal. Larksong above the red fires westward, a rapture of quick small hidden dancers. David carried the scythes into the barn and laid them bright beside the smouldering plough. I went to pick up the baby from the corner of the field. He wasn't there! I took my arms out of the cold burn. I stumbled a few steps towards the eagle's nest on the hill. The Skipper stood in the marsh with a bundle in his arms. I screamed at him but my legs sank in to the knees. David stood up to his thighs in the quaking earth. He held out his hands. The Skipper laughed. Then he walked surefooted through the marsh like a man on a hard road. He laid the baby beside the whetstone. *Some day*, he said, *this man will come of his own free will. And so will you, David and Sophie. I need your plough and horses.*

Corn-seed, drops of sweet water. 'Eat thy bread with joy and
drink thy wine with a merry heart.' Yes, but nothing is
said about the brutal stations from winter to the loaf and
jar that are not yet on the table – plough, furrow, seed,
harrows, the scarecrow, scythe, flail, fan, mill-stones, the
vat and the oven. We stand between scythe and flail,
bewildered. I know I can never adore again when the
Host is raised. But I think there is a kind of holiness in
coarse mortal bread too, men labour and sweat so hard
to set it on their tables. Next month there'll be a new
hunger, a child in the cradle, longed-for, loved, unhal-
lowed. Yesterday they caught no fish at all. Simon came
home with a long blue stone from the ebb. *I'm not going
to break this one up for creel-weights*, he said. *It's for you,
you like beautiful shapes.* I could have yelled at him, I was
so hungry. Then I looked at the stone and the God-Bearer
moved in it. (The last thing that had filled my eyes was
Our Lady Star of the Sea in the school chapel.) Had she
come to us through The Black Flame? I looked again. It
was only a stone. The wayward hands of the sea had
sculpted a purity. Yet there are faint chisellings that might
be eyes. Did an old mason, a hewer of querns and tomb-
stones, carve it for their first chapel? The Rackwick folk,
did they hide it under seaweed from the horsemen of
Knox? *I'm sorry about the fish*, said Simon. I looked
again. The women of Rackwick moved through the
stone, the sea-watchers, generations of them: the girls, the
young wives, the mothers, widows, the very old ones. An
endless surge of grief and patience had gone into the
stone. *It is only a stone*, said Simon. It was indeed only a
stone that the sea had washed, a tall immaculate blue
stone. *Leave it alone,* said Simon. *I want my supper.
There's enough limpets for a boiling. We put creels under
Rora. I must be up and out early.* I set the fold of stone
against the wall. I think of Our Lady, and the child, and
I pray that he will be born near that stone in the heart of
winter.

MARILYN

John was well and truly put in his place last night – plenty of
outcry at the end of the house. John had broken the blade
of the second scythe in the barley field, in the afternoon.
The stone was hidden, he said, *I couldn't help it.* The

Skipper sent him back to the house. *Go in*, he said, *you are not an earth-worker. Slowly we find our vocations. This is what you truly are, a beachcomber. Beachcombing is a mystery. There will be an initiation.* At sunset The Skipper called to Natasha and Trudi and me to come out. We left the haddocks simmering over the fire. John hung shivering like a hooked fish at the gable end; his wrists thonged to the iron bolt under the chimney head. *This man will never be a crofter, or a fisherman, or a shepherd*, said The Skipper. *I am going to initiate him into the ancient mystery of beachcombing. I am going to change him into a gull, a scavenger. Trudi*, he said, *the whip.* Trudi, cold-faced, came out of the barn with the coiled leather snake. Natasha turned her face towards the hills. *Now, gull*, said The Skipper, *go into this man.* The lash sang. The face against the stone crumpled and gasped. Lash sang, mouth gaped and gasped. Lash sang and sang, forty-eight times, but still the changing body did not admit its new state by one single cry. I had not known my John to have so much courage. From their doors the valley people watched. The Skipper stopped at last, his chest heaving. *Cut the boy down*, said Natasha, her face still towards Moorfea, *Trudi and I will see to him* . . . *No*, said The Skipper, *no one will touch him, he will stay where he is. The gull has not yet gone into him. Not yet. He must learn to be a beachcomber. This is what a beachcomber must often do, he must stand all night watching a flow and ebb. He must be patient as a bird till the sun gets up. It is not an easy thing, to be a beachcomber.* He went into the house. Natasha and Trudi and I stood about the flayed man. The sun went down. We did not speak. One by one we went to our separate beds. The Skipper came from Natasha's bed to my bed in the darkness, and parted my knees, and left again before sunrise. I stood in the door and watched him. He went naked into the sea. He swam far out and came back with a lobster, and threw it, high and thinly clashing, on the grass bank. Then he climbed up to the house and went cold and wet into Trudi's bed. This is the kind of man he is. I went out to where our first beachcomber, still clothed in the tortured flesh of man, sagged at the wall. I whispered to the skewered head. *We will eat and drink next winter.* The body was silent. During the night, though stationary, it had travelled back a great distance. *Someone must suffer*,

I said, *I couldn't help what I did. You stood between me and the sun.* With the nail of my forefinger I loosened slowly a thick dark medal that soldered his rag of shirt to his shoulders; then tore it off. A circle of new blood oozed and darkened and welled. I broke the red disc between my fingers. The sunken head rose up like a bird. The scavenger turned cold eyes on me. He shrieked, a gull in the first light.

TRUDI

We have done everything exactly as he said. Now it is Harvest Home at The Hall (what was once called Shore). On the table that I have scrubbed to its pale yellow graining lie pieces of fish and ribs of mutton. Their mouths glister with salt. No one speaks. Flame drips and drips from the fish-oil lamp: the four walls are splashed with a carnival of shadows. Their mouths are silent as a shoal of fish mouths. Quiet glimmering people, they eat meagrely in the centre of a wild flaring shadow-festival. They are imprisoned in their own night and winter and death.

It is Harvest Home (even though the crop has failed.) The corn died, and from now on Saul's people will be fishermen, and women who watch the sea. The sheaves were safely stacked under the equinox. They leaned like dancers holding each other up, three by three against the splash of sunset, tired after their light summer dancings. The morning after the equinox we all rose early to hump the sheaves into the barn. I stood first in the door – the field was pitted with rottenness – where the sheaves had stood were smears and daubings of gray treacle. *The Black Flame scorched the seed,* said Saul. *We were not to know. No one will mention the word corn again in this valley. We will turn to the sea . . .* Jane's baby died. She lifted him up one morning to feed him; the small mouth was open and stiff as a haddock's . . . *Sometimes there are whales,* said Saul. *They come into this bay, a school of whales. Every whale is a storehouse of meat and oil.* Nobody answered him. There is little talk any more. They nod here and there with their foreheads, their hands make shapes in the smoke. The fish-oil light wrenches each simple gesture into a silent threat and portent on one or other of the four walls.

It is Harvest Home; now the reason will appear. One small sack of barley was saved, enough to make one jar of ale. With

bitter care Natasha and I brooded over the malting, the
steeping, the boiling, the fermentation. Now it is ready, a
thin swill in a clay pot. Saul nods to John the beach-
comber. John rises. He takes the jar from the cupboard.
The ale glows in the vessel like a lamp that has lit the feet
of men from Babylon to Hiroshima, a merry wayfaring,
a sacred storied centuries-long procession. Now the pil-
grimage is nearly over. The sweet oil of Barleycorn is all
but spent. John brings the ceremonial jar to Saul. He
kneels, he delivers it. Saul drinks: patriarch, law-giver,
priest, keeper of seed, measurer of the west, laird. The
acolyte takes the cup from him. He brings the cup to
Siegfried. (We age quickly in this place, Siegfried's golden
beard is a badger's pelt hung from his jaws.) Bianca looks
very solemn. Siegfried drinks, inclining his face towards
Saul. *With the sun*, Natasha cries out, her mouth a savage
harp. Simon raises his sea-carbuncled hands to take the
cup from Siegfried. Bianca smiles. Teresa makes a cross
over the chalice as it passes her face, sunwards, going to
Simon. Simon raises the cup. He nods briefly to Saul. Jane
stares blankly at the blank wall. Simon drinks. Natasha
is silent. Bianca's mouth quivers. Simon sets down the
empty jar on the table. The corn lamp is out. John lifts
the jar and returns it to The Skipper. The Skipper folds
it in his hands. He stands up. He holds the cup over us.
He says,

Flung we a broad far sail,
Sought, beyond whale and star wheel
A maiden meadow. Blossomed the mew,
Salt beads on prow scattered,
Was league on league of lost landfall,
Flame of the atom behind us,
In front, green flames of ice.
In cragfolds found we haven,
After hard voyage a hidden valley,
Hills for bees to be hived,
Beasts kept, a cod-hungry boat,
A comfort of fire in the crofts.
We furled sail, set firm our feet,
Stone laid against stone,
Laboured long till ebb of light,
Hungry men round a half-made hearth.
Dreamed I that darkness
Of horse, harp, a hallowed harvest.

The Skipper opens his hands over us in a kind of bene-diction. The pot falls on the floor and breaks, a small crash and scatter. Bianca wails, she alone, a cry like a woman in hard travail. The fish people sit round the table. The lamp drips and glims and smokes. We sit quiet in the midst of an enormous jerking masquerade. In silence and frenzy the shadows feast on us. They hollow out our skulls. We have returned, uncaring, into the keeping of the Dragon.

Winterfold (1976)

Winterfold

BETHLEHEM
Angel, Innkeeper, Our Lady, Captain of Herod's Guard,
Shepherd, Magus

Gloria Gloria Gloria
FULL UP – Put that sign in the window
This is the first sorrow, that the dove should vanish
We will muster here with horse and trumpet
The last of the ewes is folded now
There it is, look, again, the scrieving star

The star, alpha to omega, spells on
Gloria in excelsis Deo
Supper the ox and the ass, I told you
The second sorrow, a crooked plough
I have an order from Herod, sealed
The sky is cold as psalms and angels tonight

Will we take our thirsts down to the alehouse?
Ill-used treasures of the old kingdoms
Et in terra pax hominibus bonae voluntatis
Not another hoof on the cobbles, surely!
The third sorrow, black seed
The despatch is marked 'most secret, urgent'

You will therefore brighten your swords
A drop of mulled ale for winter bones
The ancient scrolls dust in the jars
Laudamus te, benedicimus te
Go down. Tell the stranger 'No room'
The fourth sorrow, soldiers in a cornfield

The fifth sorrow, a starved child in a door
The security of the state is threatened
In the yard, look – a man, a loaded lass
How should we read the runes of a new kingdom?
Adoramus te, glorificamus te
What, Nazarenes? The woman exhausted?

Straw in the cowshed, that's all I can offer
The road of sorrows stops at The House of Bread
An upstart king. A rebellion plotted
We'll drink inside to a good lambing
Our road ends. The Word has been uttered
Gratias agimus tibi propter magnam gloriam tuam

Gloria Gloria Gloria
A lantern, quick. Something's happened
The last sorrow and the first joy are one
I think we know what to do with usurpers
A birth? In the byre? Whose bairn?
We give these rings and robes to a winter child

THE GOLDEN DOOR: THREE KINGS

I

I unlatched the jade door.
Worms were breeding silk,
A girl fingered a loom.
I entered the golden door
(There my throne stood, withering).
I passed through rooms
Of flowers, flagons, chessboards
And a room with a fountain.
At the top of the black spiral
A wise one said, 'Majesty,
Three nights now we have seen this planet.
The time is come
For exile, the tent in the desert.'

2

What wandered about the star streets
Last night, late?
It knocked for shelter at doors of gold, like a lost boy.
My heart was bruised with the image.
I am waiting now at sunset, again, with my charts.
I had perhaps drunk too much midnight wine.

3

When the lawmen have gone
Before the girl enters
With water and a lamp
I sit at the window.
The stars come, each after other.
'I am the bringer of Dew.'
'I am the Dove.'
'I am the Swarm of Bees.'
'I am the Grain of Dust from the Floor of Heaven.'
'I am the Emerald.'
'I am the Temple Lamp.'
I greet those faithful
Who troop to my dark window.
What should I say
To this one, intruder and stranger?
He has stood there two nights
And is silent still.
I imagine a title,
'Keeper of the Door of Corn.'
And a word, 'Come.'

YULE

Castle to forest, more wind, and the roads drifted.
We followed the map as best we could.
We came at noon to the marked tree,
A grey gnarled column.
The sergeant shouted. Our axes flashed. They bit.
We struck out pieces of bark and bole.
We laboured like men in a siege, among whirls of snow,
But root was one with berry still
In the first red seepings of sunset.
                    In the village windows, that twilight,

Tinsel stars glittered.
There were chains of coloured tissue and paper lanterns.
Under the street lamp, chaste mouths.
Then the village slept, unblessed by the winter tree.
The sky was a hushed river of light.
Flagons gleamed in firelight at the inn.
Three strangers came, burdened. They were taken inside.
'No word of this at the castle,' said Blok at midnight.
'Some childishness, star and snowman and crib,
Crippled our arms today.
In March we'll be back. The peasants will have their tree.'

THE KEEPER OF THE MIDNIGHT GATE

What are all the hillmen wanting
Around the alehouse door,
The old one carrying a new lamb?
Drink, likely, and women.
Too cold for them up on the hill
With stars snapping their silver fingers.
They've left a boy
To keep the door of the fold, I hope.

What are you? Come closer, maskers.
Melchior. Caspar. Balthazzar.
No names like that hereabout.
O thank you, sir!
Pass on, Daffodil-face, Ebony-face, Nut-face.
Go in peace
With your foreign stinks and the one clang in your sack.

No bite or blanket in that inn, Lady
Unless you're loaded.
Pass on, man. There might be a corner. I know she's done in.
His furnace mouth
Keeps the ox warm.
The publican's fire is the bleeze of gold in his till.

Yes, colonel, the following village women
As far as I know
Have been brought to bed this past week
Or are ripe to the bursting

Or may be in their sweet pains tonight –
Rachel, Tamar, Deborah,
Ruth, Esther,
Sara, Jemima, Judith.
Yes, sir –
This gate is open always for King Herod's heroic
Hooves and swords.

An angel, are you?
Mister, let me tell you
The magistrates
Want no comic-singers in this town this winter.
What are the shadows
There, at the fire's edge, with guitars?
I did not think
Angels stank and had holes in their sleeves.
All right, go through, vagrants.
Say, if you're challenged
You came in by another road.

Worms are feasting
Round the fire at the heart of the earth tonight,
Redbreast.
You can have this crumb from my sandwich.
This cold night
You'd be better in the silver cage of a merchant.

A POEM FOR *SHELTER*

Who was so rich
He owned diamonds and snowflakes and fire,
The leaf and the forest,
Herring and whale and horizon –
Who had the key to the chamber beyond the stars
And the key of the grave –
Who was sower and seed and bread
Came on a black night
To a poor hovel with a star peeking through rafters
And slept among beasts
And put a sweet cold look on kings and shepherds.

But the children of time, their rooftrees should be strong.

1 CHINAMAN

Water, first creature of the gods.
It dances in many masks.

> For a young child, milk.
> For the peasant, honey and mud.
> For lovers and poets, wine.
> For the man on his way to the block, many well-directed
>   spits.
> For an enemy, mixings of blood.
> For the Dragon-god, ichor.
> For a dead friend, a measure of eye-salt.

A courteous man is entertaining strangers
Among his goldfish and willows.
The musician sits in the pavilion door
(His flute is swathed in silk.)
An urn is brought to the table by girls.
This is the water of offered friendship.
Notice the agreeable angle of pouring,
The pure ascending columns of vapour,
The precise arrangement of finger and bowl and lip.
Birds make all about those sippers and smilers ceremonies of
    very sweet sound.

2 SMUGGLERS

Midnight. Measured musical cold sea circles.
The yawl struck suddenly!
Oars wrapped the boat in a tangled web.
The boy cried out – Smith gagged him with tarry fingers.
It was no rock, not the fearful face of Hoy.
The boat spun back from pliant timbers.
A maze of voices above us then.
Our skipper growled, 'Where's your light?'
(A lantern was to hang in the cross-trees
For half-an-hour after midnight.
In the Arctic Whaler, that had been harped on well.)
'You comm too litt,' a Dutchman said,
The words like a fankle of rusted wire.

'A sticky ebb,' said Smith
'And it's only twenty-past-twelve. Lower down
Twelve kegs rum, tobacco as much as you've got,
A horn of snuff for the laird. Have you rolls of silk?'
He drew out silver, rang it in his fist like a bell.
Now we could see green-black curves of hull,
Cropped heads hung over the side,
Even the mouth that was torturing the language.
'Fif box tea, bess China.'
With fearful patience our skipper told on his fingers
The smuggler's litany:
Silk, rum, tobacco. The florins chimed in his fist.
'Rum. Tobacco. Silk. That was the understanding.'
Smith swore to God not he nor any Orkneyman
Would risk rope or irons for women's swill.
He pleaded. He praised. He threatened.
Again the stony voice from the star-web above. 'Tea.
Noding but China tea. For silver. Fif box.'

3 AFTERNOON TEA

Drank Mrs Leask, sticking out her pinkie.
Drank Mrs Spence, having poured in a tinkle-tinkle of whisky
    (I've such a bad cold!)
Drank Mrs Halcrow, kissing her cup like a lover.
Drank Mrs Traill, and her Pekinese filthied the floor
                with bits of biscuit and chocolate.
Drank Mrs Clouston, through rocky jaws.
Drank Mrs Heddle, her mouth dodging a sliver of lemon.
Drank Bella the tea wife, who then read
    engagements, letters, trips and love in every circling clay
    hollow.

April the Sixteenth

What did they bring to the saint?
The shepherds a fleece.
That winter many lambs were born in the snow.

What did the dark ones bring?
To Magnus the tinkers have brought
A new bright can. Their hammers beat all night.

What have they brought to the saint?
A fishless fisherman
Spread his torn net at the wall of the church.

And the farm boys offered
A sweetness, gaiety, chasteness
Of hymning mouths.

The women came to their martyr
With woven things
And salt butter for the poor of the island.

And the poor of the island
Came with their hungers,
Then went hovelwards with crossed hands over the hill.

Fiddlers at the Harvest Home

Quarry
Hewings in the groin of the earth
    A stone for a threshold
    A stone for a hearth
    A stone for a chisel to flash at in the kirkyard
    A stone to sharpen a scythe
    Two heavy rounds for the mill
    A niche for butter and fish, to keep them cold

Corn
The green and the yellow upstarts
    A wind dancer
    Keeper of the secrets of dust and sun and seed
    Spume at the scarecrow's thigh
    The oat for the oven
    Malt for the kirn
    A crust kirk-broken
    A brightness across the jaw of the winter mouse

Sheep
Drifters across a hill and seashore
    A smouldering ram
    Tilt of sharn-and-fog for the shearer
    The horn at the crag
    The scripture fleece
    The ewe among red tatters of snow
    The daffodils' friend (the lamb)
    Giver of coats to the cold ones at the shore

Fish
Silent seekers through wave and wrack
    A cod for the kirk
    A cod for the laird
    A cod for the boat
    One for three green plates in a croft
    One for peatsmoke
    A head for a wind-blue hand at the door
    And bones for needles, livers for a winter lamp

Dance
Islanders come to their stillness
    From the dance of plough and flail
    And the fling of the net
    And waverings round the lamp and barrel
    And the fire-dance on the hill
    And sheer stone sea-egg seeking
    And the midnight reel of seed and soul
    At last near the kirk
    The music is cut on stone ramshackle pages

Wheels
Wheels that hallow ghost and bone –
    From turning wood, a skein
    From thunder of stones, meal
    From the reeling kirn, butter and cheese
    From lessening oil rings, a winter flame
    From creel-broken circles, the lobster
    At midnight, the tryst of seed with soul
    The sun-wheel turns
    Stone to dust to corn to bread to breath

Kestrel Roseleaf Chalice
Twelfth Century Norse Lyrics

1
The Accomplishments of an Earl

Chessboard, tiltyard, trout-stream
Know my sweet passes.
Old writings are no mystery to me
Nor any modern book.
Ski across winterfold flashes.
Deep curves I make with arrow and oar.
I know the twelve notes of a harp.
At the red forge
My clamorous shadow is sometimes rooted.

Earl Rognvald Kolson

2
Merchant Ship

Five weeks our keel lay choked
In Grimsby mudflats.
Lugworm and silt, a foul gray honey.
Unfurl, white sail
Eastwards, over the loose waves,
A fishing skua
To the hard rock of Bergen.

Earl Rognvald Kolson

3
The Westray Monks

Sixteen walkers about the church,
Heads bare as stone,
Long striders, deep-voiced, rough-handed.
'Brother wind, gentle sister raindrops' –
That's what they call this black whirl of storm.
They haven't a sword between them.
Here they come, in procession,
Demure and harmless as girls.

Earl Rognvald Kolson

4
The Burning of a Welsh Village

Brits, did you order cheap kindling?
We poured flame through your walls this morning
Till the sun was a cinder.
Stay in the wood, farmers.
We took our pay in advance,
Silver coins from a niche here and there.
Sweyn was your coalman.
Cracked hearthstone, charred rooftree.
No flint, bellows, or fireside talk next winter.

Eric the Icelander

5
A Shipwreck In Shetland

Help and *Arrow,* those slender seekers,
Scatter to a hundred boards.
Women may weep for that
But the poets
Are glad of shipwrecks many a winter night.
The sailors, shamed,
Will ravel their sea-skills with a tougher thread.

*

I've swallowed mouthfuls of sea.
They gladdened me more
Than the best wine or mead.
The sea sings like a girl over my half-drowned feet.
With shivering mouth
I draw the hammered snake-ring from my finger.
I pledge myself to Our Lady of the Waves.

*

In a princely coat, stiff with runes and dragons,
I leapt from the wreck.
Cold now, sea-insulted,
I shiver at a Shetland fire.
With tattered sealskin
The women cancel my nakedness.

*

Asa the Servant-girl's Song
D-don't d-dare laugh at me,
N-N-Norsemen.
I want a s-seat at the f-f-fire.
Ice in my b-bones!
I f-fell in a well in the f-fog.
It was water to sweeten your ale.
M-make way, easterling!
That th-thick arm, if you were to wrap it round me,
Might make my teeth quiet.

*

Einar, laird, though at your board
You give room to no stranger
Unless the chief stranger come, the Earl,
Yet set out horns
And ring your hearth with benches.
Tonight I am riding
To visit your unpopular house.

Earl Rognvald Kolson

*

The Earl in a fisherman's coat
stumbles on seawet rocks, and
a woman mocks him

'If you fall on land, crab-killer
How will you fare in a rowdy sea-reel?' ...
Cacklings from the crag above.
Fisherman, up with your cowl.
Show that hag
A sea lord, commander of ships.

Earl Rognvald Kolson

6
Duel in a Tapestry

Two figures, one a dwarf
Burdened with hump and sword,
A sewn glittering toad,
The other a skipper horizon-eyed –
In this lordly web
They dance, fixed and futureless.

Will hunchback pierce hero?
A witch's question.
The swords cross, quiet as fish, in the linen.

Earl Rognvald Kolson

7
The Earl attacked by a Madman

Verse is a golden ring, a gathered silence.
Nobility a cloak, quartered.
Heroism a rune, cold cuttings on stone.
Today in the claw of frenzy
I fluttered, a naked soul.
Masks and songs were no longer a comfort to me.

Earl Rognvald Kolson

8
Crusaders

Storm bends mast like a frantic bowman.
We've salt in our mouths.
To starboard, the loop and curve of the Humber,
And Anglia, a low coast.
Hug the fire, clodhopper.
Ride home, councillor
On measured stone-ringing hooves.

Armod Earlsskald

9
The Strait of Gibraltar

Three happy days I remember,
The hunt on the mountain,
Then ale and talk
Beside a fire in the castle
- Not those hogsheads of salt
Splashing our shields!
The Earl spurs the ship,
A gray stallion
Between Europe and Africa.

Oddi Little

Ermengarde of Narbonne

Your hair, lady
Is long, a bright waterfall.
You move through the warriors
Rich and tall as starlight.
What can I give
For the cup and kisses brought to my mouth?
Nothing.
This red hand, a death-dealer.

Earl Rognvald Kolson

*

Farewell to Narbonne

A gale of beauty – like rosepetals
My breath scattered.
Throw, voyagers, now
A last farewell to Ermengarde.
(The cut-throats on the rowing bench
As well as Armod
Had one wild dream,
To toss and snore in her bed.)
O heart-broken poet –
That gold-and-ivory forehead!

Armod Earlsskald

*

Love Song

The summer mouth of Ermengarde
Commands two things –
A sea of saga-stuff, wreckage, gold,
As far as Jordan,
And later, at leaf-fall,
On patched homing wings
A sun-dark hero.

Earl Rognvald Kolson

*

Love and War

White as snow
White as silver
The lady,
A beauty all whiteness,
A kindness
Red as wine.
Another redness, fire
About the castle
A sharp whiteness, swords.

                                    Earl Rognvald Kolson

11
Instruction to Birds

Between this snow
And the lucent solstice
Compel the sunwheel,
Seek the balance
Of light and winter,
Rose and skull
In seeded islands.
Furl, crosswings, there.
Find in a door
A girl with skeins
And a wooden wheel.
Say to the cold one
'Lady, your lover
Left the scarred skippers,
Eager he entered
The querns of war,
Sigmund's shield
To castle came earliest.'
Sweet throats
At an April threshold.

                                    Sigmund Fish-hook

In praise of Audun, the first
warrior to board the African ship

Audun the Red
Was the earliest reaper
In this harvest.
Black sheaves
Fell on the dromond.
Flame-bearded Audun
Was complete gules.
Erling's Audun
Through fire and blood
Bound his red harvest.

Earl Rognvald Kolson

13
Poet on Watch

Night. Sheets of salt.
Armod on ship-watch.
A wash and heave of lights from the island.
The lads of Crete
Toss in hot tumbled linen.
This skald on watch,
Cold, burning, unkissed.

Armod Earlsskald

14
Elegy for Thorbjorn Black, Poet

Lift him, sailors
Thorbjorn with the black beard.
Bear gently, poets
The harp of Thorbjorn.
Carry with candles
The king's friend
Down to the crypt of the kirk.
Requiem aeternam da ei
Southern stones
Pile over Thorbjorn Black a bright howe.

Oddi Little

15
Jerusalem

We stand here, shriven,
A hundred warmen lustred with penance,
In each hand
Assoiled from murders, whoredoms, thievings now
A leaf of palm.
Footsteps, free and fated, turn
To the fourteen redemptive lingerings
And the hill marked ‡ with this sign.

Earl Rognvald Kolson

16
A Mass at Sea

We left our shares to rust
On a northern hill,
Exchanged oxen for green and blue tramplers!
Poet, peasant, priest,
One ark of pilgrims
Out of the dragon sea, a seeking
Into the lucencies of Christ.
(Salt furrows we make
Under your headlands, Byzantium.)
Sin darkens the grain-hoard.
We have branded their coasts with rage and lust,
The old dragon-breath.
No end of sorrow, soultroth, still.
Kyrie, Christe, Kyrie eleison
The Golden Harvester
Seeks orient, our swineherd mouths.

Earl Rognvald Kolson

The Desertion of the Women and Seals

Howie gave sentence of slaughter
    To the fifty seals on the skerry.
        For a month now the inland lasses,
    Bella, Jemima, Mary
And Hundaskaill's cold beautiful daughter
            – It was said, because of his hard grudging fist –

Denied their kisses.
  A month he watched the drift of seals in the
    west.

A clean gale out of the sunset
    Would cancel scent and sound
        But make those creatures vivid upon the floods.
    'Maybe,' thought Howie, 'a pound
Or thirty shillings, for powder and shot' . . . .
        He would change the flock to bag and slipper
          and brooch –
        Entrancing gauds –
          And gather the spendthrift girls back to his
            couch.

That sunset, shrug after shrug,
    The seals abandoned the shore.
        Across the sacrificial rock
    Drifted a delicate smirr,
Tresses of haar, a fleece of fog.
        It scarfed in one cold weave the selkie-flight.
    Then, rook by rook,
        Round Howie's impotence drew in the night.

Vikings:
Three Harp-Songs

BJORN THE SHETLANDER SAILS TO LARGS 1263

I am a farmer from Yell in Shetland.
Bjorn my mother called me.
I grew among seals and clouds and birds and women.
The men came home in the ships for harvest
With wounds on them and bits of silver.
One year my father did not come home.
The sea has him, off Lindisfarne.
I learned drinking and love that winter.
I can handle horse or boat,
Useful crafts for a man to know,
And am thought to be a good chess-player
And passable on the harp.
Next year, if I live that long

My beard will have a fine golden curl to it.
Perhaps Thora will love me then.
I have never been further south than Whalsay.
Is it true, what the vikings say –
Wine-skins, brothels, black faces south of Spain
And kirks colder than sea-caves?
This is good, to have seen fifteen summers.
Tomorrow with Paul and Sverr my brothers
I sail for Scotland.
A thousand sea-borne swords, a golden mask.

THE NEW SKIPPER

Arn, Thorvald, Sven, Paul, Grettir, Harald
The *Sea Wolf* is out of the shed, new tar on her hull.
The rollers are under the keel.
The women have put ale, salt meat, and bread on board.
As soon as the wave runs clean from Birsay
We will leave the Orkneys behind us,
The scarred hills and the creeled sounds,
And tonight we will anchor at the mouth of a Scottish river.
Our voyage lies east this year.
We have heard of such towns – Aberdeen, Grimsby, London,
And the merchants who live in tall houses.
The churches have had enough of our swords
And the girls who weave their words into curse or spell.
Our voyage does not lie west this spring
Among holiness and drifts of rain.
There are few chalices left in those islands.
It is time the merchants knew about us.
We will be back in time for the corn harvest.
You women, see that the scythes are sharp and the barns
     swept,
And the ale thick with honey.
We are tired of broken coast-lines.
This summer we deal in wool and useful currency.
They are not too beautiful, the girls in the east.

Remarking, 'It is not to my taste
To wheeze on a white pillow
Nor to toil gravewards on a stick, murdered slowly
By avarice, envy, lust,'
Einar ran where the swords fell thickest.

An Irish axe
Struck the right shoulder of Sweyn the skald.
'In future,' said Sweyn,
'I will write my poems with the left hand.
I will sup a sinister broth.'

Near the end of the battle
Rolf returned to the ship, downcast.
'Gudrun,' he said, 'is a proud woman.
She will not bed with boys.
Hard wounds I sought
For thigh and chest and forehead today.
All I have got
Is a broken tooth, an eye blue as an oyster,
And my pinkie scratched.
From now on, Gudrun,
I will court less particular girls.'

The Escape of the Hart

(for S.C.)

Suddenly, on the hill, pursuit and flight!
Taut bows, a hound across the dawn, the stag's
Enormous leap to pacify the arrow.
Love,
Let the white beast move in power this evening across the
      hunter's hill, breaking through
All tangled desires, dancing wounds, to a secret water.

Cold it was in the corrie that morning,
A harsh rain. We drew the prince
Round by the eyrie, the thunders of new water.
The Saxons lay in the next glen.

We signed our bread with holy crosses. Then,
Red on the moor, through shrouds and prisms of fog, we saw
    the hunters
Issue like beads of blood.
God keep our prince, our beautiful stag, from such danger
    again!
He looked at them with a cold eye.
Then rain let down its silver enchanted walls.

The Sea:
Four Elegies

THE SEA

The word 'sea' is small and easily uttered.
They utter it lightly who know least about it.
A vast ancient terror is locked in the name
Like energy in an atom.
Sailors, explorers, fishermen know this.
Women who stand on headlands, they know it.
The maritime tribes knew it well.
Their artists strove at harp and loom
To cover the terror with beautiful names.
The sea is the Great Sweet Mother.
She is the Swan's Path.
She is the Whale's Acre.
She is the Garden of White Roses.
She is the Keeper of Horses.
(The Loom also, the Harp with a thousand voices.)
She is the Giver of Salt and Pearls.
The Vikings, her closest children, hated the sea.
She summoned them, twice a year, from plough and lovebed.
They called her, with cold mouths, the Widow Maker.

THE DOOR OF WATER

Think of death, how it has many doors.
A child enters the Dove Door
And leaves a small wonderment behind him.
For soldiers and airmen there is the Door of Fire.
Most of us, with inadequate heart or lung or artery

Disappear through the simple Door of the Skull.
There is the Door of the Sheaf: the granary is beyond.
The very old enter, stooping,
Harvesters under a load of tranquil sorrows.
For islanders, the Door of Water.
Beyond a lintel carved with beautiful names
The sea yields to the bone, at last, a meaning.

THE LOST

One stumbled on a grey hill, very steep.
One drank deeply, and found himself at a carousel of angels.
One whispered in the secretest cell of salt.
One (young) exchanged many untasted Aprils for a brief ecstasy.
One who had turned hundreds from the door of The Salt
    Mother knocked on her window that night, alone.
One wrote 'amen' on a spindrift page.
Were they offered for all seareft – piracy, pain of fish, the
    black and gold cargoes?
A storm-ripened one went swiftly that March among
Sea-scythes, flails, winnowings.
After the third wave, the sea-querns had him.
The Atlantic was veined all summer with slow pure glitters.

A DROWNING

I am the unborn who go my ways at
        once to the dark door: to drowning,
        rot, fire, the choked heart, the
        choked brain, the choked bowel, the
        stroke of God: but one door is ajar
        always for the people who live in
        islands.
I am the child among sand and rockpools.
I am the boy who lays two lobsters on
        a poor threshold.
I am the young man who comes out of the
        storm, a ghost with a red mouth.
I am the father whose sperm tastes of
        the sea.
Should an old man weary the people at
        last with legends of shipwreck?

The waters opened last night. I
entered. The grey door shut
behind me.

Unpopular Fisherman

They've carried a seven-foot coffin
Down to the shore.
In Quoylay, look for no net-reft
Or rapes any more.

(Who is it dead? A man
With a shortage of friends.
God send us more grief when we
Come to our ends.

Is it the laird? That great one
With five or six fawners
Might reach his long porphyry home
– But who'd be the mourners?

Is it Ezra the tinker? Not him.
There'll be pipers to blow,
Fist-fights and reels and whisky
The day he's laid low.

Is it Swart who gives the short measure
For the ale and the rum?
That one could stretch the length of his counter, unmourned
Till kingdom come.

What unpopular man is dead?
The slow feet pass
Among the tombs. . . . *As for a man, his days
Are brief as grass*.)

The cold tumultuous hands they fold
In the lee of the kirk
For seven winters were at the plundering westwards
Of herring and shark.

Look for no lawless cradles in Quoylay more.
Wholesome the fights
With no more gouging, blasphemy, broken bottles
On Saturday nights.

Eynhallow: Crofter and Monastery

I rent and till a patch of dirt
Not much bigger than my coat.
I keep a cow and twelve swine
And some sheep and a boat.
                    Drudgings, stone

The name of my wife is Hild.
Hild has a bitter tongue.
She makes passable butter and ale.
Her mouth brims and brims with bairnsong.
                    Driftings, stone

What's winter? A thousand stars,
Shrinkings of snow, an empty pail.
All summer I go, a drenched ox
Between the plough and the flail.
                    Drudgings, stone

I say a prayer when I remember.
When the bishop comes to bless his flock
I tell my sins and give him a fish.
Once I saw a sealwoman on a rock.
                    Driftings, stone

Twelve bald heads have come to this island.
They divide the day with Terce and Laud.
Herring are 'the little silver brothers'.
Like dust-of-gold they sift each clod.
                    Dancings, stone

Deor
(from the Old English)

Weland that famous swordsmith
Endured the gull and the wave.
He blew his fists in winter,
He looked for a foreign grave.
He trudged about the headlands,
A cripple and a slave.
                    That sorrow withered, so may this

Beadohild wept when death
Cold on her brothers was snowing.
And sorrow grew. No gown
Could hide from public showing
The glebe of her body rich
From Weland's reckless sowing.
                    That sorrow withered, so may this

The stranger paused. He marvelled
At a heart-rooted pain.
The thorn ran deep, the bud
Spread a crimson stain.
He would not pluck it, for fear
The rose scattered like rain.
                    That sorrow withered, so may this

Earmonric the tyrant
Sat like a wolf by the wall.
Secret mouths round the board
Drank to the beast's fall.
He licked long lazy chops.
The ale grew bitter as gall.
                    That sorrow withered, so may this

Deor the poet's my name.
I enchanted the leaves of June
Till Heorrend Honeythroat came
And warbled me out of tune,
And sang my fields away,
And shaped a purer rune.
                    All sorrows wither, so may this

1

At the door marked with the sign Bordel
I was expensively entertained.
For that rich hour I hobble on a stick.

At the door marked Poet
I never sat with such a dull spiteful creature.
Yet harp can cancel crippledom.

When I come to the door marked Death
It will be sorrow to me
I had not been carried through it, a small white wordless statue.

2

She was a very luxurious lady.
She rotted my leg.

This man made street-stones jade and diamond.
I did not like him.

An old ploughman, that's what I'd like to be, near my death,
Ignorant of ode and perfume.

3

I still get angry at the loss of five gold pieces
And my boyhood
And my ability to dance, to that madam.

'I am poor. Nobody understands genius.
What are you wanting here?'
After the stings and blunderings, honey.

Death is a stroke of fire
Or a slow withering.
Some say, a circling magnificence like the ocean.

4

'I charge more than most
Because my love
Will make you a lord or a beggar.'
That's what the witch said
And I naked among the webs of silk.

'One poem, price one silver denarius.
Then off with you.
My shirt is torn. Look. I must see to it.'
That's what the enchanter said
One morning, among privy noises.

Death, lord, my inheritance is squandered
Among courtesans and artists.
Never a thought I gave to you
Until now, when I stand at your door
Without greeting or a proper gift.

5

The address given was Peacock House.
I came to Full Moon House.
Each girl had an ivory box, for gifts.
In one room a silver mirror.
Toothlessness, scant hairs, peered back at me.

Also by mistake I called on the wrong poet
For instruction in verse-craft.
The man could explain nothing.
He took the fee. He sent me home early.
He is said to be the best poet in all that long street.

I hope, when I am summoned by death
That – sick and one-legged as I am –
Once more I will be directed to the wrong door.

6

If Sandra would open her blue robe,
Nothing more. There is nothing
I would ask or desire from the gods.

If Sator would recite The Hill Song
I would seek, a ghost,
That same day, the marble.

She showed the silk under the silk.
He uttered 'plough-to-oven', a spell.
Why have I lived another half-century?

7

With a golden key I opened a door
On a bowl of dead rose-leaves.

In a house of withered webbed stone
The harp is hidden.

Be patient now, near the end –
Fold hands.
Bid the stone enter.
                    Love and Beauty,
One old April, cut epitaphs.

Sea Widow

1
SILENCE

Did I plead with you to keep from that rock
Where the *Merle* lost strake and mast?
I have dreamed of the white bone under a wheeling flock.
I said, 'On that skerry he'll be cast
This fog or that gale –
A kind story will be over at last.
It is not good for a man to plunder the horizons and bounds of the whale.'

But I said nothing. Love ebbed and flowed. We kept the feast and the fast.
Last night my father came with the funeral ale.

2

LOST LOVERS

What if I had turned to greet the tall stranger
With kindness on his face, on the road?
There was one mouth that trembled with desire and danger.
Another suggested a clover ditch for the drift of his seed.
A merchant promised whiteness, a ring, a proper blessing in
   the precincts of God.
That man was grey and gentle and rich.

I was carried to a door marked with salt, and with tar and
   weed.

3

WHAT THE FISHERMAN SAID

There is no bread like the crust and fragrance
From your hands.

A fisherman dreads a witchlook
On the road to his boat.
Stand well behind me, girl, and always.

Leave that old man
And three thankless brothers.
There are women whose love at last is all for cats.

Spin out of me
Into yourself, the stuff of life, secretly.
Weave it on a sweet loom.

I have not relished ale-house talk
Nor my pipe
With its flame-flowers and smoke and spit,
Nor even Sigurd's fiddle
Since the first kiss among seaweed.
Next morning I woke richer than laird or merchant.

There is nothing to the snow and daffodils and larkrise of you.

Sealed with the brightness of your mouth
How will it be for me now
In the dangerous house of the sea-girls?

Why was this study not ardently taught
Among the globes and inkpots?
Love is better than numbers, seaports, battles.

I will build you a house with my hands,
A stored cupboard,
Undying hearth-flames, a door open to friend and stranger.

I wished once I had not met you.
Sea generations are too long.
It is a net I have folded in your womb.

From strange earth and stones,
A kirkyard on another shore with different names
You came through wind and cornstalks
For the mixing of dust,
For two names to be carved on one stone.
I did not think then
You might lie under it lonely
And I shells, salt, seaweed.
I have put a black streak of tar
Through the ignorant name on the hull
And painted yours there, in red.
Old men, going past, look wicked and young.

4
WEDDING RING

Gold to enclose two lives for ever. There were maybe four
Good rounds, perfect returnings, in that one year,
Four circles of grace.
The rest were pub-stoked lurchings, blood on his face,
Back to my healing or raging hand –
A trudging up from the beach with broken gear,
Or from the merchant's with meagre silver
For his baskets of shifting bronze.
He was lost three days, at the fair, with tinker and miller.
And once
I left him, stone-eared to all his implorings,

His vowing and swearing,
And stayed a month at my father's place.
Four precious restorings
Made all those tatters of time the bridal coat
And sweeter with every wearing.
He left all, house and woman and boat
For a wave that trundled him on past time and space.
The bed, where each day's devious circle closed, is seedless
    and lonely.
They unweave him, mackerel and gull.
I know the man only
In flecks of salt and grains of sand,
And when through the drifting pools of a child's face
Looks back the skull.

Stations of the Cross

I FROM STONE TO THORN

Condemnation
    The winter jar of honey and grain
    Is a Lenten urn.

Cross
    Lord, it is time. Take our yoke
    And sunwards turn.

First Fall
    To drudge in furrows till you drop
    Is to be born.

Mother of God
    Out of the mild mothering hill
    And the chaste burn.

Simon
    God-begun, the barley rack
    By man is borne.

Veronica
    Foldings of women. Your harrow sweat
    Darkens her yarn.

Second Fall
    Sower-and-Seed, one flesh, you fling
    From stone to thorn.

Women of Jerusalem
    You are bound for the Kingdom of Death. The enfolded
    Women mourn.

Third Fall
    Scythes are sharpened to bring you down,
    King Barleycorn.

The Stripping
    Flails creak. Golden coat
    From kernel is torn.

Crucifixion
    The fruitful stones thunder around,
    Quern on quern.

Death
    The last black hunger rages through you
    With hoof and horn.

Pietà
    Mother, fold him from those furrows,
    Your broken bairn.

Sepulchre
    Shepherd, angel, king are kneeling, look,
    In the door of the barn.

2 PILATE

Cool water over my fingers flowing.

The upstart

Had ruined a night and a morning for me.
I thrust that stone face from my door.

I was told later he measured his length
Between the cupid and the rose bush.
The gardener told me that later, laughing.

And that a woman hung upon him like a fountain.

What is it to me, who helps this 'king'
Or strikes him down?
I reduced majesty to a driven shadow.

Another woman stood between him and the sun,
A tree, sifting light and shadow across his face.

Outside the tavern
It was down with him once more, knees and elbows,
Four holes in the dust.

More women then, a gale of them,
His face like a scald
And they moving about him, a tumult of shadows and
        breezes.

He clung close to the curve of the world.

The king had gone out in a purple coat.
Now the king
Wore only rags of flesh about the bone.

(I examined cornstalks in the store at Joppa
And discovered a black kernel.

Of the seven vats shipped from Rhodes
Two had leaked in the hold,
One fell from the sling and was broken.)

And tell this Arimathean
He can do what he likes with the less-than-shadow.

No more today. That business is over. Pass the seal.

3   THE STONE CROSS

At dawn Havard sighted a hill in Ulster.
'A point to west,' said the helmsman. 'There the hive is.
There the barren kingdom of drones.'

We sailed past cave and cormorant and curragh.
We anchored under a stone cross at noon.

Creatures came down to meet us
With stony heads, voices like insects, raised hands.

They murmured, 'Mother', 'Sancta Maria', 'Our Lady'
But that hostess was not to be seen.

Brother Simon drew me from sea to rock.
He made a cross of gray air between us.

It was a household of men only.
A boy offered to wipe salt from our foreheads.

'Havard, it is time to make a start now.'
Havard flashed his axe in the face of a brother.

Then women began to screech from the crag above,
Gaelic keenings and cursings.

A dozen eunuchs fell beside the porch.
The boy made a dove of his two hands.

We entered a cave of wax and perfumes.
Mund took a silver cup from a niche.

Cold tinklings like nails
Took us to nothing – a crust, a red splash.

Soon that hive was all smoke and stickiness.

We brought a fair cargo down to the *Skua*.
The abbot had called that treasure 'moth-food'.

Sunset. Sharing of spoils. A harp-stroke.
Soon I drifted into the stone of sleep.

4 SEA VILLAGE: SHETLAND

There he rides now. Look. The laird.
A brace of grouse to the Manse.
One hand on the rein long and white and scented.

Every boat in the voe his, and the gear.
He fixes the price of the catch.
But a certain fisherman has laid his own keel.

The store? That's his too. After dark
It's a shebeen, with a crock
Of peatsmoke whisky. A man can drink till he falls.

The fisherman's mother bides here, a good woman.
Every tramp, with her, is a prince.
It's her boy, Ollie Manson, that's building the boat.

The whole parish forbidden to help him.
But Simon left his threshing
And brought hammer and rivets down to the rock.

And Vera, when he humped over the tarpot
Came with a jar from the burn.
His face flashed once in the gray water.

A black lamp in a window there. Look.
A good skipper once,
All but ruined with aquavit and rum.

The five widows of the *Hopeful*
In this one threshold,
Rock-gathered, like stormbirds, head into wind.

Socialist books, that was the start of it.
I blame the dominie.
Paine and Blatchford, they'll bring him down.

It'll end with lawmen and prison.
They'll burn the thatch,
The mother will sit under a bare roof-tree.

No need to tell you, with the clang and reek,
Who's shuttered here.
The blacksmith hammering nails for the Hall.

That's it now, on the noust, the *Equality*.
'The yawl is finished!'
The yawl is finished. More than a yawl is finished.

L. Smith, Joiner. Always a coffin on hand.
Never a smile on Lowrie
But when a window goes blind in some croft.

Up there, among the cornfields, the kirk
Cold as a sunk creel.
On a Sabbath, sea voices shake the stone.

5   CARPENTER

'Workman, what will you make on the bench today?'
I was going to hammer a crib for Mary.

I went into a multitude of green shadows, early.
I came to the marked tree at last.

I struck the root with my axe.
It groaned in the dust.

Mary came over the fields to call me to dinner –
One glance among trembling branches.

The woodman dragged it into the village,
A length of gnarls and knots. A bad bargain.

Could it yield, perhaps,
A wheel for spinning of coarse yarn?

(It looked ancient enough, that tree, to have carried the seed
Of Adam's Fall.)

I could drag out of the thrawn-ness, I suppose,
A board
Or wash-tub or shelf or churn, for the village women
– Never a crib for Mary's boy.

I let it lie
Among the adzes and squares, in a dazzle of sawdust, all
     morning.

I lopped, later, boughs and branches and bark.

Then a centurion came
And ordered, in the governor's name, a gallows.

I sent him elsewhere.
That's all it's good for, though, a tree of death.

Mary stood in the door, curling cold hands like leaves
Round the fruit of her womb.

'Hurry,' she said. 'Let the saw sing,
Soon it will be time for the cradle to rock my boy.'

6 A JOYFUL MYSTERY

He had left the tree, the ass, the apple basket.

We turned our faces back to the town.
One man had seen a boy traded for silver,
Gone on with camels then.

A boy had stood at a stone with bruised knees.

Boy after boy, blithe lissom corn-high faces,
Never the lonely sun-look.

We got to Simon's yard at noon.
He had lingered there.
On had danced, playing shepherds, reeds at his mouth.

At Veronica's he had asked for a basin.
She showed us the towel,
A splotch of happy dust and blood at the centre.

Three beggars sat with locked tongues
In the next village.
A stick wrote in the dust.

Women at a bleach-green stretched long fingers.
An hour since, city-bound
Young hair indeed had streamed past.

We circled, slowly, a foot-print in dew.

A cloud,
Red tatters, the drained heart of the day.

Star scatter (grains of dead salt). I laid
Skull beside breathing skull.

We took our skulls at dawn to the Dove Gate.
The market-place a tumult of ghosts and skulls.

Skulls traded, mimed, looked out of windows, smiled.
Ghosts came and flickered and went.

We drew, hollow-eyed, at noon, to the temple.
Doctors of law read tombstones
Under dew and drift of apple blossom.

7   THE HOUSE

In such granite rock
How shall a house be built? Let them see to it.

After the rains, men dug to the hard rock.
The carpenter strove with the roof-tree.

A scaffolding fell.
Three drunk labourers were given their books.

She who was to grace the finished house,
Baker of loaves, keeper of the loom,
She stood in a web of rafters.

The work languished. Another mason was sent for,
A man of solid reputation.

One hot day a girl took a jar of ale to the site.

Thunder in August wrenched an iron lattice,
A sudden brilliance out of the banked gray and purple.

Masons laid a lintel, a cold stone.
Women stood here and there.
They gossiped. They nodded. They said, 'House of sorrow'.

Before harvest labourers climbed down from the eaves.

A diviner went in a slow dance.
Rock was struck to a tumult of bright circles.

Dazzle – first snow – on planed and sanded pine.
At the time of crocuses
Carpenters put the last nail in the staircase.

Painters, tilers, men with snibs and latches –
Ladders and planks and buckets borne away.
The architect's voice from the balcony, 'It is finished'.

The woman came again with daffodils.
She set a jar on the sill.

And still the house echoed like a tomb
Till the village women arrived with gifts.
They stayed to eat the cakes from the new-lit hearth.

8 CREATOR

He is the Grain of Dust and the Raindrop.

He is Leaf and Forest and Fall.

'Where wert thou, angel, when I came to this stone?'

He is the Pitcher at the fountain.

He is the Winter Tree dragged by a peasant.

He is Flax and Wheel and Fold of linen.

'It was my hands and knees fashioned the earth;
                    suffering I lay upon
                    chaos; then galaxies
                    grew from my fingers'.

He is the Street where the Daughters of Music
                    foregather.

'I beheld again, marvelling, the atoms that
                    compose the worm'.

He is Adam undone by the loom.

He is Three Nails, least fruit of the Forge.

He is the Black Diamond at the centre of time,
                            burnt out now.

He is the Hollow in the Rock.

He is the Seed locked in the House of Dust.

9 KINGDOM OF DUST

This the inheritance – slaves and exhausted earth,
A botched kingdom.

Three years he went, therefore, dropping seed
In drained dunged plough-broken glebes.

For that usurpation
He was brought before the seven corrupt stewarts.

'Let him,' they said, 'be given to the heaviest millstones.'

The dust of his eye, blood-crusted
Turned from the immaculate dust that had cloistered him.

The shoulder was broken
That had fashioned from dust shoulders of ploughman and
    blacksmith.

He put the red mud of his face in a crumpled mirror.

The turning earth scraped at his hands, knees, eyes.

He had fashioned from dust mouths for the daughters of
    music.
'Lament well, stone wombs, now.'

The sun, turning, uttered more burning grains.

He suffered himself to become, on a hill,
Starker than seed or star.

His dust was stirred with nails, thorns, vinegar, spearthrust,
All sharpness.

He hung, the Man of Dust, a whisper
In the noonday of nothing.

They gave his dust back to that purest of urns.

Then they locked their king in a cave
Far from the turning querns of earth and sun.

10 THE LESSER MYSTERIES OF ART

Rood
The lesser mysteries rooted also
      in that first garden,
    apple-fraught, with pure rinsings.

Harp
He at a stone, head upon strings,
      summoning
    to a sweet circle the seven red beasts.

Lamp
Last seed of the sun, hoarded
      for sunlessness, ice,
    beastbreathing cave of winter.

Image
A prince lost
      in a maze of corrupt mirrors
    and Fold of Light, unmoving.

Ballad
Reveller at the door – grey mouth
      uttering ocean spells,
    sea-skull on brideboard set.

Mask
Among flutes and statues
      a vestal unwinds
    scarlet web from skull.

Dance
Golden mask into grave –
        twice now, dandled, thistledown's
    frail dust drag.

Symbol
It outlasts roses,
        statues,
    even the grief of women.

Legend
Listen, in a mud-kissing mouth
        the six-day story –
    star, tree, fish, bird, beast.

Loom
Into the seamless coat-of-songs,
        through sereness, starkness,
    the shuttle drifts.

Jar
Midnight, and the last red circle breached.
        A jar, upset
    in first seepings of light.

Rune
Obliterator
        of a thousand questing mouths,
    and sevenfold silence still.

Talent
The minted circle, gift
        of the lavish god
    withered soon, and the hand a bone.

Stone
Are not long loved,
        remembered, even decipherable,
    your purest deepest cuttings.

Flung from the fowler's fist
Ride now, lonely hawk

Through the hungers of the morning sky.
Shoulder the sun now. Take

Light about you, aloof and silent, now swivel,
Stumble on a step of air, trek

Into the heart of a cloud – folded awhile – then out
Like ore from a cleft, flaming, break!

(The fowler leans on a stile,
Foot-bound, face-bright,
And lets out, on swirling air-streams, lure and hook.)

The sky repeats your curves of talon and beak.

Halt now. Hover. Let your golden eye
Flame on that tussock below, a single stalk,

A windless twitch. Descend. Query. Then in a scythe swing
Scatter the delvers and spinners. Reach down. Lock

One guttering life in your claw. Engorge,
Engut, all but a flake

Of feather and slivers of bone. Be crested then among
    creatures,
Lord of the fast, the sacrifice, the wake!

(The fowler's spell
Will drift into you soon, a sweet ache,

A delight and a doom, a summons
To a bleak black

Rafter in a barn, almost forgotten then
Under that yearned-for yoke

Your brief lordship of cloud and rock.)

Those humps and hollows are jars too, stranger.
  This is for Jude, the fig-merchant.
  Bespoke, this cluster of white curves.

'Jude requires a jar for his new arbour.'
  But hump-and-hollow surely, never
  A 'fountain for thirst of angels'. . . .

What was brutish mud in a pit, last thaw,
  Rose, slow and lissom,
  Into the wheel of the sun.

Never before such coldness from my kiln.
  It is dust in the sign of oblation.

Today the removal from workshop to villa.
  Some yokel will bear it
  On mule-back, among fig spittings.

Any unlustered hand might sully it.
  The palm of a girl, poised delicately
  For love, mothering, death. I think, even that.

What questing ghost between dewfall and dawn
  Came, summoned, to the threshold of clay?

(Here they troop now, the village trollops,
  All clattering, to the well,
  Thick clay shouldering thick clay.
  They linger always, silent, about the miracle.)

Do not speak about fall, or flaw, or the flow of time.
  The drift and cling of a butterfly
  Might start a fissure.

It should endure in a secret niche in the temple
  Its fragile centuries.

Foreign hooves will whirl about it, some April.
  It will be five shards on a hill.
  And the ghost exiled from the circle of its peace.

The dream, the wheel, the dancing mud, the kiln.
    It issued from these, an amphora.
    My hands beat, obedient
    To the harpings of planet and atom.
    Bide then, angel of the jar, beyond all breakings.

Tilt it. This jar will be dealing wisdom and beauty still
    When the last Caesar is urned.

No. The vulgar wealth that commissioned the work
    Will reserve it for dust of roses.
    It will stand on a sunless shelf.
    'Adam made this, in the Street of Potters, one winter.
    It did not stand well among our silks and silver.
    Here, in the cellar,
    It keeps cold the wine for wake and wedding.'

Portrait of Orkney (1981)

Horse

The horse at the shore
Casks of red apples, skull, a barrel of rum

The horse in the field
Plough, ploughman, gulls, a furrow, a cornstalk

The horse in the peatbog
Twelve baskets of dark fire

The horse at the pier
Letters, bread, paraffin, one passenger, papers

The horse at the Show
Ribbons, raffia, high bright hooves

The horse in the meadow
A stallion, a russet gale, between two hills

The horse at the burn
Quenching a long flame in the throat

Voyages (1983)

Seal Island Anthology, 1875

Market Day
    He came back from the town
    With news
    Of fighting in Russia
    And red things like tatties (apples)
    And sixpenny spectacles –
    His eyes were big as an ox.

Minister
    Polish twelve boots.
    Run
    To the well for water
    To splash faces in:
    Kirstag has seen
    The boat rowing from Rousay,
    A black column in it.

Fishing Boats in Fog
    Rob's boat is in, blinded,
    A thin catch.
    The *Teeack* had nothing. (Mist, sun-pearl.)
    Rob, did you see Tam and Mansie?
    What ghost is this
    Driven by insane pewter swirls?

Widower
    Old Stephen three winters now
    Has spoken to none
    But his cat
    And the spider at the back of his bed
    And himself
    And to a stone in the kirkyard
    With thirteen names
     (The last cut sharp and deep).

Croft Wife
    Make ale. Make
    Butter, cheese, bread (small suns).
    Make
    Every summer the nine-fold rounding
    Moon shape.
    Make fire. Make a star
    In the frozen well.

Dead Faces
    When I saw the first star-coldness
    I was a child.
    I have seen faces the sea has eaten
    And pain-clenched faces
    And faces like flowers, gathered.
    I have seen the face of a dead man
    Who still
    Laughs, bargains, boasts, at the pier.

Rain
    A gray hoof whirled at the sun, splinterings
    Of blue and yellow and orange.
    I felt
    Corn cells, underfoot, gorging.
    A trout
    Flashed from the salt into brief sweetness.

Blacksmith
    As the wild bees
    Forge
    Sweetness under a stone
    As roots in darkness
    Hammer up
    Clusters of the may-flower

    Since the lass of Clett
    Was here
    With her father's plough to patch
    I go with sun pieces
    Between forge and wincing anvil.

Letter

Dear Parents, at last
    You hear from me.
        The day
I went to Kirkwall for feeing
        A kind-spoken sailor
Asked me to broach a bottle in his cabin.
    I woke among wastes of sea.
I am well. I write this
    At a table of black gold-ringed hands.

Wisdom

Say, 'I have seen the migrant sail dwindling west.'
Say, 'Golden hand among fallen stalks.'
Say, 'We ate seaweed and limpets one spring.'
Say, 'I have closed ten eyes, or a dozen eyes.'
Say, 'The laird gets younger and greedier.'
Say, 'They increase, the things beyond utterance.'
Then it's time
To leave dark lamp and folded breath
And row old into the dayspring.

American

Sander is home from gold-mines and railroads
Twanging
Music from the root of his nose.

Gossip about a Girl

'She goes like the burdened bee' . . .
'The slut. The shame' . . .
'She has the face of a bairn that keeps a bird in the cage of
    her hands' . . .
'The moon wheel turns. The ninth round knits with the
    wheel of the sun, as burn is meshed into ocean' . . .
'She goes, in secret, migrant to cranny' . . .
'That my hidden silver (it rots) might be hers' . . .

Nocturne

The candle draught-flung. I hit
The shadow
At the pane with my pillow.
I hit it with nails and feet.
I hit the stranger

(That smelt like Willie of Gorse)
Again and again
With the rose of my mouth.

Pig Sticker
The sweet pigling
Squandered
His life in shower on shower of roses.

The bairns
Put drained faces against the wall.

He washed, later
In gray water, the last beast-petal off.

Snow
The young men went
            Here and there, secret
    At star-time.
            Black swirls – a sudden
Blanket of snow!
        And the blank
            At dawn, a maze
                Of silvery tell-tale trystings.

Ploughing Match
If you come tonight
Fisherman
Take the track from the shore.
The hill road
Is reeling with malt-red ploughboys.

Clock
We had the sun, stars, shadows.
Today
In Greta's house, a box
Of numbers and wheels
And cleek-cleek, click-clock, that insect
Eating time at the wall.

Scarecrow
A stick and tatter
I lean into the sun's loom.

Envy

I wish I was Andrew
Standing
With a bright shivering ring
Beside that tall whiteness
In the hushed barn
Tonight
When the minister urges the gold circlet from fingers
        to finger.

I would rather be Andrew
Than the laird
With a sideboard of silver plate
And silk hangings
And his seat in the parliament.

I would rather be
That ploughman
Than Lord Raglan on his stone snorting horse
Or Victoria stamped on a thousand coins.

Cat (to Dave Brock)

Swingler came in soft slippers.
My trout was needles
Before the knife could flash at the silver belly.

Swingler, pirate, with one patched eye
Unlocked
My golden cube of butter.

Swingler, exile, sits at my fire
All the six nights
The moon locks herself in her crystal cave.

My peats rage red on the winter stone.
Swingler sings.

The Laird's Garden

Idle summer out (sang the bee)
There are no jars
In a cupboard of the House of Winter
For drifters and dandlers and dreamers.

Plunder the sun (mocked the butterfly)
Smoulder. Save. Scheme.
Mask-and-Glove take all, at last.

See the gowned ladies and tulips going (said the bee)
See, in the kirkyard
The swirls of scented dust.

The queen and her ingot-hoard (said the butterfly)
Where are they
When the Ice King
Walks through the garden in his ancient armour?

Gravestone
Suddenly a stone chirped
Bella's goodness,
Faithfulness,
Fruitfulness,
The numbers
Of Bella's beginning and end.
It sang like a harp, the stone!

James-William of Ness
Put a shilling
In the dusty palm of the carver,
Fifty years since.
Wind, snow, sun grainings.

The stone's a whisper now.
Soon
The stone will be silence.

Aurora
The Arctic girl is out tonight.
(Come to the doors.)
She dances
In a coat of yellow and green patches.
She bends
Over the gate of the stars.

What is she, a tinker lass?
Does she carry flashing cans
From the quarry fires?

[199

I think
She's a princess in a silk gown.
She holds (turning)
A bowl of green cut crystal.

Come to the doors!
She is walking about in the north, the winter witch.

Snow and Thaw
The first snowflake we called
'silver moth'.

We hailed the hill next morning –
Moby Dick!

Sun on sea,
blue silver blinding
mirrors.

The thaw, it was like an old filthy tramp
that had slept
in a ditch in downpours.

Mulled Ale
The circus in Hamnavoe –
Is that a fact,
A man swallowing fire,
A clown with patched cheeks?
You should see my Jock
After he's stuck the red-hot poker
Five or six times in the ale pot.

Lessons
Chants the young schoolmaster
'First arithmetic . . .
'Now spelling . . .
'Now dates, kings and battles . . .
A butterfly loiters past the pane.
Sam has a burning punished hand
Because of a wind-flung flower and a cloud.

'Now geography . . .
Book-bent heads. The first Arctic bird
Crosses the window between ice and roses.

I stood at ten doors in that island.

In the first door
I was shown the tooth of the dog.

In the second door
A stinking fish was put in my hand.

Senseless unprofitable babbling
In the third door.

A fiddle like a tortured cat
In the fourth door.

In the fifth door
A skull wrapped in a shawl, whisperings.

Sixth door, seventh door, eighth door
Barred.
I stood, a cancelled man, in the rain.

Twilight in the ninth door,
A star, a kiss.

When I come to the last door,
Take me, earth, soon
From their grain-gold sea-silvered hands.

Bird in the Lighted Hall

The old poet to his lute:
'Bright door, black door,
Beak-and-wing hurtling through,
This is life.
(Childhood lucent as dew,
The opening rose of love,
Labour at plough and oar,
The yellow leaf,
The last blank of snow.)
Hail and farewell. Too soon
The song is mute,

The spirit free and flown.
But you, ivory bird, cry on and on
To guest and ghost
From the first stone
To the sag and fall of the roof.'

Magi

(To Katia and Dominique)

JUNE 24: This day Karlson, Balth and I left the ship *Thor* secretly,
and rowed in a small boat to one of a hundred islands. Sand
burned, sun poured unbearable gold upon us.

JUNE 27: The map was plain in the mind of Balth. He drew it with
his toe in the sand, and put an X where was the treasure. We have
been to two islands. There is no word of the place.

JULY 1: Black and brown faces flee from our guns. But the forest is
full of eyes. The water low in the skins. The night flies have bored
me, arm and thigh.

AUGUST 18: How long we have lain in this village, in a hut, I do not
know. The fever has branded us, all three. The ruined eyes of an
old black man watched our shivering bones. Insects and honey he
put in our mouths.

AUGUST 20: Karlson was first on his feet. He staggered like a drunk
man. The old man laughed.

SEPTEMBER 29: Balth has left us, two days ago. Balth has taken the
map that was in his mind. *They are a burden to me.* Did Balth say
that? Yet he was a good companion. May he find the silver, may it
sweeten his age. We are free and lost, Karlson and I.

OCTOBER 8: With Karlson and me, the only desire is to find a port
with ships. Black hands point. *There, there the sails, beyond two
rivers and a forest . . .*

NOVEMBER 21: One night lately was full of shapes of terror. Sleeping
then, after sunset, I dreamed I was a child in Orkney, and I owned
the whole world, corn and buttercup and rockpool, and the men
and women and animals put looks of love on me and on each other.
Then to awake to the scarred face of Karlson, and mosqui-
toes, and smoke of a volcano, and a hidden mockery of parrots.

DECEMBER 1: The nights have been cold. Even the smaller peaks
wear snow capes. In the port, one Spanish ship. A poster on the
harbour-master's door: concerning absconded sailors, a reward, 3
familiar names. We drank the harbour-master's rum.

DECEMBER 8: We have nothing. We have no skill to catch wild crea-
tures for the fire. The few rags on us are shameful compared to
the comely nakedness of the savages. This is what the gold
seekers have come to, penury and sickness.

DECEMBER 15: We saw Balth this day, talking with some brown men
in a village. Their faces opened with white flashes. They chewed
sticks. Balth gathered us into the company. *We are near the place,*
he said. *The old map was useless. I have spoken with the Indians.*
A black boy marked the dust with a star. Balth gave cuts of
tobacco to the village men. *I knew we would come together here,*
he said. *Perhaps tomorrow night, perhaps in nine nights or ten. It
is worth the broken feet, a small betrayal.*

Letters to the River

1

I am expecting a caller tonight.
Do not take river smells to my door.

I send this scroll by an old man.
He does this and that for a small coin.
He cannot read.
Do not say a harsh word to the old man.

The old man's daughter stitches my masks.
Either she has put a flower in the window
Or a gray unlit candle.
(The cold wax for nights I do not dance)

2

I have never been better off.
I have three coats, large butterflies, across the bed.
I have a purse with a silk cord.
Gifts are left at my door.
A poet I have never seen
Is, they say, praising me in the villages.
And the children imitate my dances.

3

I see a horseman coming between the gardens.
I wonder how things are with you?
Are you catching a fish or two off the island?
A river fish has been left at my door.
Did you come by last night?
If so, I thank you. Gifts come like autumn leafage in the
     doorway.

I cut the fish into fine pieces.
The slices are drying in the wind.
I will set them on a plate tonight, for my guest,
In a circle of blossoms.
Perhaps I will think of you eating alone.
The little white cat
Has already devoured the eyes and the tail.

My fingers stink. I will dip them in scented water.
I will put a flower in a cup
As soon as the first star is out. Then
Men will carry me on poles to the theatre.

4

Is this not good news?

A man came up-river in a skiff.
I stood among the reeds.
He said, 'I will tell what I have seen.'
He pushed with his oar into midstream
Going urgently down-river, then.

I wondered, between two moons
About the boatman and his words.
Now I have a letter.
A horseman brought it on a stick.

The lord is to come upstream
Next week, in a barge.

'Talk of your comeliness has made me young again.'

I have written many letters to you.
The old man
Takes back no letter from your hand.

The old man says, 'The second letter
Did not make him weep
But there were old tear-stains on his face.
The fourth letter, perhaps the fifth
Made him laugh.
(Not river laughter, more like a masker.)
Your last letter
He put behind the nets, unread.

Once he gave me a cup of wine.
He said, *Drink, man*
To a river girl of two summers ago.'

6

I am leaving this house soon.
I will live in a villa.
The garden is a mile outside the city.
I am to have two servants.
A boy gets silver to go errands.
You will not be seeing the old man any more.
The old man
Is ashes in a pot, a quiet ghost in the garden, wandering.

I am learning to ride a horse.
Bathing me, combing my hair, dressing me
The two women call me 'lady'.
I can pour wine now without spilling a drop,
I can write a dozen words on silk.
I am forgetting the river language.

Perhaps my horse will stop near the jetties.
I always look at the boats
As I pass on my way to the city.

7

It was told me, 'A fisherman
Was taken two days ago from the river.'

My heart was a hive of questions.
Did the nets entangle you?
Perhaps there is water in your lungs.
Will your sister come?
Will your sister nurse you among the nets?
Perhaps he is dead.
He has gone perhaps with blue hands and a crab-eaten face
into the fire.

Now, at last, a letter. 'I thank you.
I only suffered a cold in the throat.
No, I will not come
To live with the butterflies in your garden.
I am uncaring and cold
Whoever enters your fine door or leaves it.'

Why do I still think in the evenings
Of the river and the river smell and river words?

Sonnet: Hamnavoe Market

No school today! We drove in our gig to the town.
Grand-da bought us each a coloured balloon.
Mine was yellow, it hung high as the moon.
A cheapjack urged. Swingboats went up and down.

Coconuts, ice-cream, apples, ginger beer
Routed the five bright shillings in my pocket.
I won a bird-on-a-stick and a diamond locket.
The Blind Fiddler, the broken-nosed boxers were there.

The booths huddled like mushrooms along the pier.
I ogled a goldfish in its crystal cell.
Round every reeling corner came a drunk.

The sun whirled a golden hoof. It lingered. It fell
On a nest of flares. I yawned. Old Madge our mare
Homed through a night black as a bottle of ink.

(to Dennis O'Driscoll)

On the third morning
We came to the whale acre.
No whales, the net
Surged with a galaxy of herring.
The raven, uncaged,
Fluttered over hidden islands.

On the eighth morning
A buttercup braid
Came down to meet us at a shore.
Her name was Gudrun.
A bluebell eye
Led us to hall and husband,
Harp, alehorn, fine flowers of flame.

No man, flame-fettered, finds fame
Or lockfast gold.
On the twentieth morning
We dared the dark whirls,
Furious looms of sea.
There *Hawkwing* left us,
Whether
Broken in the salt shuttles
Or set on private pillage westward
We have not known.

We had small luck
With the holy crosses, the halls
Of Gaelic chiefs.
All were empty, all
Bore the famous brand marks.
Our fathers
Had been that way before.
Our fathers have left
Fine stories, burnt stones.
We sat hungry
Between a loch and a mountain
On the hundredth morning, under
The fourth moon.

Ragna, I write this
From an Irish village.
Are you still in the world,
I wonder
With your loom and querns and cheese-mould?
I am a gray humped man.
I had to learn new speech long ago.
I tend horses in a field.
After ten thousand mornings
Of rain, frost, larksong
How should I find a way back
To the waterfront of Trondheim?

Sally : A Pastoral

(to Charles Causley)

1

Three harvest days she wasn't at school.
Sally was ill!
Now
I hear from the stooks a summons, a challenge, a call.
There's the brighter sweep of her brow
Among the broken gold of the hill!

2

'Sally,
You'll be in trouble, you're late for school.'
She listened, loitered, lingered.
Silent, she ebbed and eddied and flowed.
She fingered
Gray blobs of wool
From a twang and reverberation of barbed wire,
The truant, Sally.
Larks rained round her, out of a cloud
An unlearned shower.

Sally and I fought.
I got
An eye like a plum.
I have from her
Three strands of sunbright hair
Between my bleeding fingers and thumb.

4

From the top of the Ward
A turning head can see
The ring of the whole earth, with the western sunset smoulder.
Hallward he rides, the laird.
In the heather, the first stirrings of midge and moth.
The yawls, with their shifting silver, are in from the sea.
(I have laid three fish at her door.)
Now the west is a jet and crimson bar.
The wind blows colder.
There's none under the first star
But Sally and me.
Earth wrecks on a reef of stars, and drowns us both.

5

Sally, bride
Glides like a swan
Into the psalming kirk.
The wedding guests have all gone in.
I turn, alone, outside
As the ox plods to its winter work.

Stars: A Christmas Patchwork

Innkeeper
    I know you, Tomas the shepherd-boy.
    A skin of wine, is it?
    Tell them, no wine skins for hillmen. This ledger
    Is crammed with their debts.
    Take that cold face
    Up among the cold stars.
    Tell them, a new lamb

Might broach a barrel.
The rabble again –
Taxmen, yokels, tarts, soldiers.

Not another knock!

Census Official
    Names and occupations in order.
        Isaac, tribe of David, fisherman
        Saul, tribe of David, goat-herd
        Joshua, tribe of David, baker
            (It's Caesar Augustus
            Wants your names, not me.
            Soon as I see
            The last of your mules and drums,
            It's the bright lights for me, pronto.
            Make your star on the parchment.)
        Jacob, lineage of David, brick-maker.

Soldier
    No Miriam. I'm a soldier. It's midnight. The sentry
    Locks the gate at midnight.
    The colonel said,
    Sharpen your swords, I want
    Each eye cold as a star
    Before the wakening of birds and children.

First King
    Fix on one star, at last,
    Any star
    In the circling star blizzard.
    That star will take you
    Whithersoever,
    Death and Birth and Love.

Herod
    Tramps, dogs, children with palms, recognize Herod,
    The skull with the sun-crown.
    Kings would know a king, if the king
    Wore a leper cloth.
    I gaze, blind, through a golden mask.
    Look for star-troubled strangers.
    Under the merchant masks

They are kings and king-seekers.
Bring me word
Where the masquers unload their bales.

Bedtime Story, Bethlehem
There was this old Chinaman
(Once on a star time)
A king yellow as a goldfish.
He lived in a crystal palace.
And one day came knocking on his door
An Ebony king.
And next noon came knocking
An Ivory king.
The three kings kissed. They crossed.
They saddled mules. Their faces flushed with sunset.
And then –
Wheest, the bairn's asleep.

Second King
A lantern at the gate, red as an apple.
A village, clay houses.
A lamp in every niche.
We went on slowly, seeking
The inn.
(Sweet the wine bowl, bread, bason of water
After such brandings of sun and sand.)
At the inn
One candleflame in a bottle, athwart
A tumult of flushed mouths.
In our chamber
A star like a nail was the only light.

Priest
Folded it is now, the dove,
Furled, star-folded.
Endless rain falls, the black floods are rising still.
What hand
Will take the branch from the dove's beak?

Third King
We stand, three vagrants, at the last door.
A black fist
Lingers, a star, on withered wood.

Shepherd
'No wine.' He wouldn't part with a skin or a bottle.
It was closing time.
'Come tomorrow,' the porter said.
('Bring a lamb,' said he.)
'The innkeeper's out of his wits
With stars, soldiers, taxmen, foreigners, hill folk.'

Vinland

1

Wet shirt, breeches, kamiks
For a week
And a loud cough.
No blink of fire still
On the bleak
Unbroken circles of sea,
No singing throats
Between ship and shore.

2

The hungry raven
Astir in the basket. This
Is good, the bird
Eager
To be twelve masts up, turning!
That black hunger
Is smelling (we think)
Seeds and worms in the blank west.

3

Salt in the mouth,
The rage
Of north wind at morning,
Sodden crust,
Cold kissings of rain.
This unease
Is better than my Ragna at the hearth.

This heals heart,
On a blank stone westwards to cut
Such runes –
ICELANDERS
HUNTED THE GOLDEN WHALE
BEYOND HESPER

5

Too late for the rudder's turning
Back into history,
The old worn web,
King, lawman, merchant, serf.
The prow breaks thin ice
Into a new time.

6

He that can cup in the ear
Spidersong, dewfall
(Six weeks I hear only
Salt monotony)
Has heard, ahead,
Sea fingers fringing shore foam.

7

They will say next winter
At Greenland fires
'Leif Ericson went
The fool's voyage'.
A man will sing to a harp
'Heroes
Venture for more than bits of gold'.
An old woman will say
To girls at candle time
'It is that slut, the sea
Always
That has their hearts'.

Lighting Candles in Midwinter

Saint Lucy, see
Seven bright leaves in the winter tree

Seven diamonds shine
In the deepest darkest mine

Seven fish go, a glimmering shoal
Under the ice of the North Pole

Sweet St Lucy, be kind
To us poor and wintered and blind.

The Star to Every Wandering Barque
(for a 25th Wedding Anniversary)

Wave above wave – westward that night
The sea was a broken stair

In a house of menace, and never beacon or bell
To tell us where we were –

Near the great whirls, or close
To crag or reef or shallow (God knows where).

Above, thick-woven cloud. Beneath
The skull-strewn dragon lair.

How long, how late, since the ship
Had cleared the harbour bar

We made no reckoning soon. Our skipper plied
Ship-wit, sea-care.

(Will the heart keep tryst?
Does the dove, branch-burdened, quest through the perilous air?)

Precious the cargo,
Urgent the hunger that drew it from shore to shore.

Deep in the hold
The jars of love we bore.

All who trade in that freightage
Dread the devourings of time, and salt, and tare.

How could we have doubted?
Like a lantern in a barn door,

Like the roof-furled familiar dove,
Upon our voyage hung the homing star.

Orkneymen at Clontarf, AD 1014

What are you doing here, Finn?
(I ask myself that.)
Today, Good Friday, the ox in Stronsay
Tears sweet grass
Beside an idle plough, the women
Go between kirk and bread-board.
Panis angelicus sing
The priest and the boys.

Sigurd is the name of our earl.
His mother the witch
Wove our black banner.
That raven croaks above the host.
Whoever bears the bird of victory
Drinks tonight in dark halls.
Now Sigurd alone
Offers the raven to a sackcloth sun.

'If you go to Ireland,' she said
'Speak to the holy men
With their prayers and candles,
Not to the little kings
Offering bits of battle silver.'
That's what my mother said, in Westray.
I'm young. What do I want with a psalter?
The silver pieces
Will buy an ox for next ploughtime.

I forget the name of the saint
That saved my grandfather
Under a burning wall of Paris one summer.
Whatever your name, white one

I am grandson
To old Olaf, that you kept from torrents of lead and tar
One day in the Seine.
I intend to light a candle to you.

I bought the horse in Dublin.
Seven times
It reared against horn and shield-wall.
Now that it's hide and bone, that nag,
And tatters of blood
I am walking back to the town.
At the river mouth
The proud Minch-trampler is moored.

Coming to Ireland
We stopped first at Barra.
A cold week, snow in the ale.
Coming to Ireland
About some royal mix-up or other
We stopped at Man.
I devoted an April day to bright edges.
Coming to Ireland
We have stopped at a noisy fairground, Clontarf.
The revellers
Go and come in red masks and patches.

When they said, *Rolf is dead*
Under a hoof
I said, 'Fare on, Rolf.
It goes well with you, friend.
Flesh-unfastened,
A swift swallowflight soon
To the Hall of Heroes.'
Then I turned and gave release
To three Irish axemen.

We drank thick ale in Galloway.
Brave boasting there –
Battles, blood, wall-breaching, booty.
Now the glory is come
There is no ditch anywhere
I would not creep into,
Sharing a mushroom with tramp and slut.

Sven swore, in Hoy, he would never
Come into Ireland.
'A place of enchantment, Ireland.'
Yet he sang with us at the rowing-bench
Down the broken coastline of Scotland.
Here
A white star has broken on Sven's brow.

In Rousay this sunset
Under Scabra
Men will be lifting lobsters.
A girl at a rockpool
Is shaking out yellow hair.
If I do not get back from this battle
Tell the brewer at Kierfea
We have found a quieter alehouse,
Free drink, no hangovers.

William and Mareon Clark

I

THE OPENING OF THE TAVERN: 1596

Johnsmas. The noon light clear and hard,
   He bade Mareon, his ship-shape wife
     Unlatch the new oak door.
No lingering man or beast in the yard.
     Not a foot crossed the sanded floor
   To chair and flagon, platter and knife.
       A barrel seethed in one corner, the best March ale.
       Five hams hung, cured in winter smoke.
From the kitchen, a fragrance and crispness of bread.
Beyond, clean bolsters and blankets spread.
       A house of keeping it was for far-come folk,
   With turf and driftwood to feed the welcoming flame.
   Four days of silence. Nobody came.
     Then William said, 'Goodwife, I see
       Bad counsel I had from lawyer and shipman and earl
       Anent the lease of this inn
Here on a barren spit of shore.
       We will flourish here like the winter whin.
It's road and tinker rags for you and me' . . .

The next day (sea lash, gull whirl, gale)
      They saw a Frenchman anchor and furl
    From the outer Atlantic roar.
  William and Mareon endured an anxious silence.
      Knockings and strange shouts soon at the gale-fast door.
     A brig blunders bayward, anchors and furls
  Behind the two sheep islands.
Mareon's hand brims over with bread and ale,
   With gold of honey-jar, pinkness of hams.
       What sea-gray faces now – Balticmen? Danes?
      The table strewn with strange-carved coins.
  A dark boy asks, with voluptuous palms
    (Making shapes) about girls.

2

THE FIGHT BETWEEN SVEN AND PEDRO IN WILLIAM CLARK'S ALE HOUSE: 1599

Fierce music of two mouths
(Hamnavoe, winter) twixt barrel and candles.
Sven: 'Rat in the hold! Dry-rot!'
Pedro: 'Ice man!'
A Spanish sailor. A Swede.
William Clark: 'Mareon, wine to that table.'
An arm aureoled with light.
A dark hand, otter quick.
William: 'Now, gentlemen, I beg. . . .'
Concerning the fist of Sven,
It described a wide fruitless arc.
Concerning the Spanish table,
It held pots of various capacity
Before the bright rush of music, pewter to stone.
William: 'Mareon, the truncheon, quick!'
The hand of Pedro flashed twice,
A piece of sunlight fell from the beard of Sven.
Mick (Irishman): 'They'll do bloody murder. Hooray!'
Mareon's mouth was a mute hand-plucked harp.
Foot of Sven, fist of Pedro,
Flight and flash and fall of the knife.
Mixed European music, rune with rondel.
The drawn truncheon: fulcrum: point of stillness.
William: 'I now declare this war over.'
Pedro uncoils an olive hand.

Sven thrusts out a gull-bright hand.
William: 'Mareon, two glasses rum
For storm-shook haven-fast seamen.'
Pedro has kissed the beard of Sven.
In Clark's inn, white music of concord soon.

SICKNESS

William, the skull
No mistake. I counted thrice. The brewster in
    Stenness delivered *six*, not seven barrels ale.

William, the worm and the skull
Provided for. First winter here I sent for the
    lawyer. 'You won't starve, Mareon.' Quill
    and parchment and wax. The will.

William, the shroud, the worm and the skull
The sun. (Take off that crushed root and spider!)
    Breckness wind in the face. That restores me.
    Flood in the Sound – curve and brake and splash of a gull.

William, hands crossed, the shroud, the worm and the skull
Has she blown out the lamp? set traps? locked door and till?

*William, the dark one, hands crossed, the shroud, the worm
    and the skull*
We all go under the hill.

*William, the weeping, the dark one, hands crossed,
    the shroud, the worm and the skull.*
I repent me of (heartily) world-wickedness, my
    part in such, all things done ill.

*William, the burning blood, the weeping, the dark one,
    hands crossed, the shroud, the worm and the skull.*
It does well.

Four hundred years since you both
Went, sundered, into the dark,
Hearts and hearthstone cold,
    William and Mareon Clark.

Search for a stone in the kirkyard –
Nothing. Never a mark.
No one knows where your bones lie,
    William and Mareon Clark.

Even the inn you built
To hustle about the work
Of welcome and keeping, is vanished,
    William and Mareon Clark.

Your door stood open wide
From the rising of the lark
To the pole of night, to all men,
    William and Mareon Clark.

You gathered about your fires
The crew of the wintered barque
From Bergen, or Brest, or Lubeck,
    William and Mareon Clark.

Did Rome and Geneva strive
For the helm of the storm-tossed kirk
Even in this quiet haven,
    William and Mareon Clark?

Tired, you'd put out the lamp,
Cover the fire, and hark!
A scatter of hooves on the cobbles,
    William and Mareon Clark.

You did not live to see
On the steep dyked westward park
The merchants' houses rising,
    William and Mareon Clark;

Tall houses hewn from granite,
Piers on the tidal mark,
Yawl and cobble noust-gathered,
    William and Mareon Clark.

Your first eyes never saw
Boys from the crofts embark
For the Davis Straits and the whale-fling,
    William and Mareon Clark.

Nor saw them come back in August,
Sovereigns sewn in each sark,
Salt men urgent for barley,
    William and Mareon Clark.

Eighteenth-century wars,
The herring shoal and the shark
Dowered that shore with silver,
    William and Mareon Clark.

Eighteenth-century wars,
Doubloon and kroner and mark
Made later taverners rich,
    William and Mareon Clark.

Graham and Gow and Millie –
You never drew the cork
For hero, pirate, spaewife,
    William and Mareon Clark.

Nothing. You cannot hear us.
Two names, quilled and stark
On a lawyer's parchment, ghostings –
    William and Mareon Clark.

Forgive this deluge of words,
First townsfolk, wherever you ark.
I have cut you dove-marks on stone –
    WILLIAM and MAREON CLARK.

Countryman

Come soon. Break from the pure ring of silence,
A swaddled wail

You venture
With jotter and book and pencil to school

An ox man, you turn
Black pages on the hill

Make your vow
To the long white sweetness under blessing and bell

A full harvest,
Utterings of gold at the mill

Old yarns, old malt, near the hearthstone,
A breaking of ice at the well

Be silent, story, soon.
You did not take long to tell

The Wreck of the Archangel (1989)

The Wreck of the *Archangel*

Who saw a rudderless hulk, broken loom of cordage
That nightfall? None. In the dregs of sun
    Westraymen had drawn high the yawls.
    They fed their byred lantern-lit cows.

Indoors, women tended the different flames
Of lamp and hearth. The old ones chanted again
    Mighty tempests of foretime.
    The children tumbled gently into sleep.

Then, under the lamentation of the great sea harp,
Frailty of splintering wood, scattered cries,
    The Atlantic, full-flooded, plucking
    And pealing on the vibrant crag.

Clifftop and shore thronged soon with lanterns,
The ebb strewn with spars and with drowned
    Foreign faces, but no breached cargo,
    Wine casks or baled Baltic furs.

And all lost, all drowned, a pitiful strewment,
Emigrants set forth to root poor lives
    On a free and fruitful shore,
    Skipper and crew with seaflock scattered.

(No, but spars and planks enough to keep
An island in roofbeams, tables, coffins, doors
    A century long – a quarry of wood.
    The jaw of sea at hull gnawing all night.)

A man listens. This can't be! – One thin cry
Between wavecrash and circling wolves of wind,
    And there, in the lantern pool
    A child's face, a dwindling, in seaweed tassels,

One only glimmer. The man turns from a sure quenching.
Probe and quest in the rich ebb. A girl
　　　Lifts the lost cry from the sea whelm.
　　　It breathes, cradled, at a kindled

Hearth, a thin cold flame. He endured there
The seventy ploughtimes, creeltimes,
　　　Harvests of fish and corn,
　　　His feet in thrall always
　　　To the bounteous terrible harp.

Orkney: The Whale Islands

Sharp spindrift struck
At prow's turning.
Then the helmsman,
'Either whales to starboard
Or this storm
Is thrusting us at Thule,
Neighbour to bergs, beneath
The boreal star'.
Sunset. We furled ship
In a wide sea-loch.
Star-harrows
Went over our thin sleep.
Dawn. A rainbow crumbled
Over Orc, 'whale islands'.
Then the skipper, 'The whales
Will yield this folk
Corn and fleeces and honey'.
And the poet,
'Harp of whalebone, shake
Golden words from my mouth'.

Voyage
The Months

　　They have drawn and dragged a keel, down wet stones,
glim of a star on one stone.
　　Dark water. Ropes glittered with night frost. The

ship lingered, languid as snowflakes.
    Wheel of wind upon waters! – the carved
head snorting – plungers unseen, the crystal hooves!
    They drew to a voe. Came down the jetty a girl with
daffodils, wine in a jar, bread new from flames.
    The sun, morning by morning, a fountain. Faces opening,
flushed with northfire.
    Tell us, what is the cargo? The helmsman had a stone
ear.
    They came to an island where dwelt, it seemed, only
the young: honeycombs, harps and dances, apples. They
felt their urgent witherings.
    Sharp beads from the bow, cut silver swathes.
    Fish, gray fruit of the shaken tree, fell into hooks,
hands, the knife, the fire in the well of pinewood and
stone, the purged mouths.
    Sea-jarl – the hall of a sea-jarl, washings in sweet
water, a fire, autumn beef and ale, welcomings, there
they warmed and worded them well.
    Yet now, said the skipper, *my skull is the hour glass
with few grains. No oar-fold, no sail-furl, but
forth-faring.*
    In the deepest web of winter they wrecked on a
shore. They dragged bales from the salt siege.

Fishermen in Winter

Such sudden storm and drifts
    We could see nothing, the boat
        Fluttering in a net
        Of reefs and crags.

The islands, blind whales
    Blundered about us. We heard
        The surge and plunge
        And the keening, all around.

Farm women had set stone lamps
    In the ledges that night.
        The village lamplighter,
        He had not thrown

Over the village his glimmering net.
The skipper glimpsed one star
– Soon quenched –
But it beckoned to

A poor island with one croft.
We moored *Fulmar*. We took
Up to the croft door
Two fish from the basket.

Saul Scarth
A prose poem

A man walked one morning from his croft to the well
above the shore, a yoke of empty buckets at his shoulder:
Saul Scarth. It was a fine summer morning. He was seen
by seven people going to the well, but he did not return
that day or ever to the house where an old woman waited
at the hearth with a dry kettle. The flames lessened.
The hearth was a cold cave at last. A star shone in the
window.

THE NEIGHBOUR

I saw Saul. And I saw there was
a small boat in the Sound. Further
out, three furled masts, America-poised,
America-pointed. I saw that Saul opened
a purse, and beckoned. The man at the
tiller raised his hand. I covered my
eyes from the smuggling. They won't
drag me to the law-court in Kirkwall,
to be a witness.

THE TINKER

He'll be gone through the gray
door of the wind. He must have
drunk the moon bottle, that bright
unchancy stuff, to the last black
drop. I've gone myself a thousand
times through the silver doors of the

rain. No lowering of Saul down into the
earth door. He's unlatched the horizon,
he's in places further than Longhope or
Leith.

THE KELP BURNER

I remember thinking, 'Here he comes,
Saul.' Then I turned to the burning
tangles. I looked again. His face was
flashing above the reflections in the
well. I stirred the kelp. I saw a shape
struggling in webs of smoke.

THE MERCHANT FROM THE NEXT ISLAND

Saul S.:
2 ozs. tobacco snuff powder, 3d., for the old mother.
One pair sea stockings, 1s.
A golden love ring, one guinea.
One half sack barley seed, 2s.5 1/2d.
(Enter in ledger, in red, 'bad debt')

SWEETHEART

I watched from the window. Then I
did not watch. We had had quarrels
the night before. I had bled his face.
That terrible temper! I'll keep my fingers
gentle as daisies. Saul, why did you not bring back
your cheek for a cure of kisses?

MOTHER

So I sat at the smoulder in the hearth
all morning waiting for water to make a
pot of tea. A man came in I didn't know.
He said, 'Mother, here I am with coins
for the herbwife, shrouder, beadle, undertaker' . . .
I had not seen that man before. He left, laughing.
The fire sank. My mouth is dry. That creature
of mine isn't back from the well yet.

Scarth gone. The whaling boats, I expect. Or
pressed for a man-o-war.
A golden hand less, next harvest. In the
snow, bowls of broth from the Hall
kitchen to that old sour mouth.

Island School

A boy leaves a small house
  Of sea light. He leaves
    The sea smells, creel
    And limpet and cod.

The boy walks between steep
  Stone houses, echoing
    Gull cries, the all-around
    Choirs of the sea,

Ship noises, shop noises, clamours
  Of bellman and milkcart.
    The boy comes at last
    To a tower with a tall desk

And a globe and a blackboard
  And a stern chalk-
    smelling lady. A bell
    Nods and summons.

A girl comes, cornlight
  In the eyes, smelling
    Of peat and cows
    And the rich midden.

Running she comes, late,
  Reeling in under the last
    Bronze brimmings. She sits
    Among twenty whispers.

Hard rowing it was, set north. Then, six sailors
Wading ashore, flashed bronze coins
    Under a round tower
    Thick with eyes and arrows.

Was no exchange of bread or beef,
No mixing of Latin with Celtic.
    We filled six skins
    From a silver wavering stream

Under the steepest crag. We left
One coin, that the barbarians might consider
    Our *pax Romana*, petitioning soon
    For columns, laurels, law-book.

North still, the navigator muttering
Of whirlpool and whale and the winter
    Hangings of fire. There
    Beyond the utmost headland,

The helmsman called, 'whale islands'
And we saw, through gray whirls, the Orkneys.
    Then oars rose from the waves
    Heavy, as the sea had been honey

And sailors cried out, a tumult of millstones
Fell on the prow. Then, the light
    Thickening, we cast anchor
    Near the mouth of a small river.

Dawn flashed from the silver orb
Further on, where forbidden fires smouldered.
    The slaves dragged oars
    Through ash and charred skulls.

1 The ship of Earl Magnus, going to Egilsay for a peace tryst,
is struck by a great wave in a calm sea

'Steer the ship into this one steep wave.
But nothing matters more.
We have brought unwanted cargo, a jar of peace' . . .
Bailing pans flashed.
The comber struck the hull, and scattered the
          oarsmen, and flawed the jar.

2 Magnus foretells his death on Egilsay

Sailor, your heart is a stone bowl,
The wine gone sour.
A thistle will thrust daggers through that clay
On the trysted shore.

3 The sorrows of Magnus in the island of the church

If your good angel stands in a door
With a song of greeting, be sure
His dark brother is biding, silent, inside.
Today a long black coat stands at the pier.
The welcomer
Folds, with his cup of keeping, at a cold fire.

4 Magnus passes a night in the church, and a Mass is said for
him in the morning

So cold it is in the kirk
So dark this April night, in cell and choir
His hands dovetail
Like the one stone that locks an arch
To hold his shaken spirit still.
So cold it is, so dark.
Then, soon, the opening rose of dawn.
Calix sanguinis mei
One hand unfolds like a bird
And makes, at matin-time, a cross in the air.

5 *Magnus comes out of the church and stands
among his enemies*

Ite: the voyage is over.
The skipper steps out of the stone ship
With a blank bill-of-lading.
A daffodil keeps a crumb of snow.
A lark
Soaks the 'isle-of-the-kirk' in a shower of lyrics.
He offers his clay to wheel and kiln once more.
Below, a ploughman
Follows, with a drift of gulls, his dithering share.

6 *The cook Lifolf is summoned by Earl Hakon to execute
Earl Magnus in a stony place*

Lifolf the cook had killed a lamb
And a brace of pigeons.
A shore-stone flowered with flames.
Lifolf gave the stewpot a stir.
Eight hawk-masks stood on the hill.
'Lifolf,' they sang, 'here's better butchering –
Come up, come up!' . . .
'The lords get hungry after a hunt,' said Lifolf.
He washed his hands in the burn.
He went in a slow dance
Up to the blank stone in the barren moor.

7 *Invocation of the blind and the infirm at the tomb of
Magnus*

Saint Magnus, keep for us a jar of light
Beyond sun and star.

St Magnus Day in the Island

Now the door is opened. Now the bell
    peals thrice to summon the people.
They are there, outside, a disorder of voices,
    a babble.
'Enter silently and in order.'
Came first the brothers of Peter, seven fishermen,
    with a net, smelling of strong

salt, the silver scales in their beards.
    Seven from *Fulmar* and *Otter*.
The bell rang.
Came the miller deaf from the thunder of great stones,
    and his dusty boy.
A peal, again. (I think the island trembled from
    end to end with the joy of that bell.)
They are not long down from the hill, the shepherds,
    from dragging ewes from the blizzard, folding
    new lambs from the east wind, breaking ice
    on the stiff burn. Summer will be a golden
    time for the shepherds. (No, daffodils
    wither also.) The old shepherd leaves his
    crook at the door.
Now the bell is a trembling silence. But the boys
    have begun their psalming.
I do not know how many poor people came into the
    church. There were many humble ones, they
    kept well back, they wished to lose themselves
    in the shadows. The boy with the
    censer threw sweetness about them.
Open, everlasting gates, sang the choristers.
All outside make way for the laird, keeper of corn
    and peathill and jetsam, lord of the longship.
    The deacon sets him not far from the very poor.
    (All are grass and flowers of grass.)
A cloud covers the sun. The window darkens. The
    candles are suddenly bright. The young
    voices go on.
Welcome to the women in their gray shawls: who most
    endure, and have the silence of stones under
    sun and rain, but cry each upon other at a
    time of tempest and grief, stone upon stone
    shaken and huddled and harshly singing and
    each more precious than onyx or ruby. They
    are given honoured place. The lady Thora
    (the mother) is among them, neither the first
    nor the last. And one a daffodil breaking
    the bud, a child. And one with ashes about
    the mouth.
Is the bishop here? William, *senex*, will enter soon
    from the vestry.
The man of iron enters, dark from forge and anvil,
    smelling of soot and burnt water, strong

from the tolling of his black bell, and his
    boy with him bearing horse-shoes.
The master of choristers turns a page, voices flutter
    like flames draught-flung. And resume,
    Who is the Lord of Hosts?
Now the boatbuilders, men of the adze and nails and
    the powerful keel, the caulkers, they that
    curve the oars and make straight the mast,
    they that send out seahorses to trample the
    waves – the makers too of the little boats,
    fish-seekers, that wither soon and break
    upon rocks or are swallowed quick by the
    Atlantic. They come, with cunning hands,
    into the stone ship.
The doors must soon be closed. The doorkeeper holds
    his place. Is there not room for sty-keeper
    and beachcomber, the tinkers, and them that
    rifle the rockpools for dulse and whelk?
There is room for all. They come in, one by one – a
    knee seeks the floor, they rejoice with a
    cross in the air like a shield going before
    them.
Now a silence. Now there is silence, but for a jostle
    and jargon outside – wherefore the doorkeeper
    sets finger to mouth. The ploughmen. They
    were late unyoking – the new field was stonier
    than they had thought – late they were stowing
    the ploughs in the lee of the barn. They come
    in, one by one, the earth-workers, with the
    sign of the earth: plough, and seed-sack, and
    harrows, sickle and flail and winnowing fan.
    The grieve from the Bu with a loaf and a
    stone-jar, he is there.
Small cry of a bell at the altar.
The bishop comes in, with boys in white all about him.
    The bread and the wine are set on the altar.
Dominus pascit me, sing the boys from the hill in the
    choir.

Pilgrimage

The ship of Earl Rognvald, first of fifteen,
Gold-encrusted, left Orkney in autumn.
    Storm-beset in Biscay, they harboured
    In Spain; after Yule

Burned Godfrey's castle, and made
Twelfth Night masque with villagers.
    In a French garden the earl
    Lingered long with lyric and rose;

Endured salt of betrayal; burned
A tall-masted Moslem dromond, but lost
    Her molten gold to lobsters.
    Thorbjorn the Black, poet,

Perished in Acre, ashes after
The fever-flame, silent always under
    A sunbright howe.
    'We will come soon

To ivory and gold of Byzantium' . . .
The sailors stand now, bearing palms
    At the door of this kirk,
    The Holy Sepulchre in Jerusalem.

The Jars

    A house on the mist-shrouded moor! –
the ghost of a house

    Over the lintel this carving
HOUSE OF WOMEN

    Not a woman stirred, outside
or in

    He knocked. No-one answered.
He pushed open the door

It was dark and cold inside
the house

He opened a cupboard. In the
cupboard was a small clay
jar with markings on it

He tasted the stuff in the jar:
finest of honey! His flesh
glowed with lost suns and
blossoms. He sipped again

Now the window was black
as tar

He stooped. He stroked with
blind hands the shape of a bed.
He covered himself with coarse
weave

He slept at once

The man woke. The window
was gray. He took down the jar
to taste more honey

The single jar stood on the shelf –
the shape of it had changed, and it
was of coarser clay

He opened it. It was crammed
with salt.

(The man heard, somewhere in
the house, a small cry)

He went through the rooms
of the house in search of a
child. The house was empty still

He returned to the room with
the cupboard and jar. He said,
Young one, whoever you are, you
won't starve because of me –
There will be fish for the salting

He came to a room where
the hearth was cold and the
lamp empty

On a stone of the wall was
carved the shape of a fish

He looked at the rune so long
that it seemed to pass into him
and become part of him

In another room, hidden, a
girl was singing

The man said, *Lost and*
darkling creature, I will bring
you oil and driftwood
always

The song guttered out. It
stopped. It faltered into
low cries of pain

&

The man wandered again
through the rooms of the house

He saw his reflection in a
pane. Furrows in the face,
a mesh of gray through his
black beard

A poor house, he said.
There should be a bowl
on the sill, daffodils
or roses or heather, to say
what time of year it is – yes –

to spill some beauty into a
bleak place. This jar is all,
it seems

He took the jar from the shelf.
An earth smell came out of it –
it was half full of flailed corn.
His hands that held the jar were
twisted with a summer of pain

Through the corridors of the
house a contented cry came. It
must (he thought) be a woman over
new loaves and ale, well pleased,
arms and face fire-flushed

Lost one in this house, he
said, *there will always be*
cornstalks – I will see to it

He scratched an ear-of-corn
on a stone beside the stone
with the carved fish

He lay down on the bed.
He was as weary as if he
had toiled, sunrise to
sunset, in a harvest field

He lay under a green and
a gold wave

His dream was about the
one jar that flowed always
from shape to shape, and
was ripeness, keeping, care,
sorrow, delight

The man woke. He knew now
that he was old

A thin-spun silver flowed over
the blanket. His hands were like
shreds of net, or winter roots

Seven women of different
ages stood about his bed. They
all, from first to last, had the
same fleeting look: the lost
girl at the horse fair

One by one, beginning with
the youngest, they bent over
and kissed him

The mid-most woman smelt
of roses and sunlight. Her
mouth had the wild honey
taste

The oldest one dropped
tears on his face

Then the seven women
covered their faces and
went out of the room

∽

He slept on into the starred
ebb of winter

∽

He opened his eyes

A young man was
standing in the open door. He
carried a jar on his
shoulder

The young man greeted
him – then he turned
and went out into the
sun

The man said, *That is*
my son. He is carrying
away the dust of my
death

Poems for Kenna (1988)

1 The Prince in the Heather

'He is safe in Paris.
He circles among high-spoken ladies.
Long fingers touch the harpsichord.'

'No. I saw him last week
On the flank of Schiehallion
Laughing
Up near the snowline, with laughing friends.'

'There was no such prince.
The mountain people
Dreamed for half a century, then woke among ruins.'

'How can a young man delicately bred
Eat coarse bannocks
And lie at night under rain and stars?
The terror, wakening, of gold and betrayal!'

'I was on that shore, hidden,
When the foreign ship let down a rope
Into his tinker-dark hands.'

'Because of that Stuart
I stand useless with one arm
At the nets
Or when the harvesters heave through their golden sea.'

'No dream, no disgrace.
I was with Charlie
When we broke the lock of the tower,
But drowned soon
In Saxon blood and steel, on the stone stair.'

'She that we stormed the fortress for,
Alba,
She will be a crone from this day forward,
Her lovely Gaelic
Lost in whiskers and toothlessness.'

So I, bard at Strathnaver, heard
From poet after poet
In deserted chapel and hall, and in fireless huts
All down the glens, that summer,
Going on to a strange shore, summoned.
Battles, betrayals, dynasties.
What salves for their ancient pain?
The swords and the harps lay broken.
'I have word of a well of loveliness in the west.
Its overspillings
Will brighten our mouths for the new music.'

My silver coin flashed in the sun.
The boatman at the rock
Shook the gull from the rowlock.
– 'I will ferry you to Coll, man.'

2 Sailing to Papay

Prow set for Greenland, a westerly
Weeks-long, a graybeard gale
    Drove *Skarf* at Iceland,
    A bleak shore, behind it

A burning mountain. One farm all night
Thrummed with harpsong and saga
    But a hard mouth at dawn
    Bargained for cheese and eggs.

The gale northerly then, a hag
Spitting hail, herded *Skarf*
    Among Faroese yoles, rowlock-deep
    In drifts of salmon.

Cold we challenged across the Sound,
Banter with bargaining, the Faroemen
    Squeezed one silver coin
    From our hoard, for seven sea-heroes.

'Now,' said the skipper, 'you won't be seeing
The Greenland girls, nor yet gathering
    Vinland grapes. Fate
    Flings our keel at Shetland.'

Fame-lust, beyond glebe or gold,
Had launched us on that ocean
    Not to be arguing at sunset
    The price of a barrel

Of sour ale, and smoked mutton, with
A surge of Shetland women on a shore.
    We held south, we ran past
    Islands thin as plates.

On the Island of the Celtic Priests
Beyond, I at the helm saw
    On a seal-flecked shore
    A girl of such brightness

The king's tax-hoard in a Bergen vault
Held not such a torrent of gold.
    The twenty young oarsmen
    Followed my cry and flung finger.

3 A Writer's Day

GULLS
It was a long day in his field
Turning furrows like pages.
He strove towards a sign, the cornstalk.

THE INN
At noon he went to the inn.
Voices, smoke, shadows. He sifted
One heavy hard gleam from the gossip.

FISHERMAN
A fisherman came in, gale tangled,
With a basket of haddocks.
He struck a fish-shape in the stone of his mind.

CHILD
He met a child from the school, dawdling.
The wind
Strung gold across her quiet face.

GRAVEDIGGER
In the kirkyard, a spade
Knocked on the earth door.
In a croft, on the far side of the hill, a long silence waited.

SUNSET
His seaward window smouldered, black and red.
Would a poem come with the first star?
Lamplight fell on two white pages.

STRANGER
The latch lifted. A stranger came in
So beautiful
She seemed to be a woman from the sea.

4 A Carol for Kenna

Many a wanderer this day-wane walks
A winter world; with luck
    Under first stars, might find
    A hovel (the hearth long black,

A crack through the stone cupboard.) That one
Will have the raftered owl for room-mate,
    A cat's shadow shifting
    Along the garden ruckle

That once kept kale, tatties,
Fuchsia, rosebush, butterflies,
    Bees, echoes of laughter,
    Lost children, all gone

Into the last darkness and silence,
Intensities deeper than snow.
    Listen. New stones
    Are being quarried and set

This very day for love and birth
And for laughter and welcoming
    Round an unmade hearth-fire.
    This sunset, near the solstice,

Lost a little between two images
I offer praise in a winter poem
    For a very dear friend
    Who has come from Pacific suns
    To sit, a guest, at my fire.

Interrogation

How was the journey, man?
Darkness. A trudge in sun and wind and rain. Now, again,
    shadows.

What holds the line that curves upon itself, end to
    beginning? Can you tell?
A grave centre.

Lissomness stoops to dust. Plough and fiddle are
    dust. Children are tall distant dust. Love is
    dust of roses. Vanitas, grainings.
I honour the jar and the grains in the round jar.

Here's your door. Wait. Listen. Silence deeper than snow.
I accept the solstice.

What then, afterwards?
No more. The circle is closed.

The dance of clay goes on. You are not a memory any
    more among your waters and cornfields and skies.
    What then?
The millstone is quiet; then turns.

You are lost, man, among the atoms and planets.
I am content to be here beside a broken kirk
    where the poor have been fed.

The Scottish Bestiary (1986)

Moth

The moth travels from pane to pane, in August
Wherever a lamp is set.

There's old Sammy playing his fiddle,
Such a rant
The sweet plea of the moth at the pane is lost.

In the next croft
Three children are reading their school books.
He thuds on the pane.
They are lost in labyrinths: seaports, poetry, algebra.

Travel on, moth.
The wife is out in the byre, milking.
A fire-drowsed dog
Growls at the birring in the window.

Will nobody help a lost moth?
All he wants
Is a rag to chew, best of all
The golden rag in the lamp.

The moon is too far away.
In the next three crofts:
Ploughmen were drinking ale from a cog
And an old woman was knitting a sock
And a twisted couple
Were counting pieces of silver out of a sock
On to a scrubbed table.
They looked scared at the moth's delicate knock.

Ah, the fisherman is mending a creel in his shed
In a circle of light.
The moth enters on a sea-draught.
Ecstacy of flame
Hurls him to the floor, scorched.
And the fisherman says,
'Night-fly,
I wish the skate were as keen to come on my hook.'

The moth woke to ashes, dawn, a cold lamp.

᷈

Lobster

What are you doing here
Samurai
In the west, in the sunset streams of the west?

How you lord it over those peasants,
The whelks
The mussels and the shrimps and scallops.

There you clank, in dark blue armour
Along the ocean floor,
With the shadows flowing over you,
Haddock, mackerel,
And the sun the shadow of a big yellow whale.

Nothing stands in your way, swashbuckler.

The orchards where you wander
Drop sufficient plunder,
Mercenary in the dark blue coat of mail.

Be content, be content far out
With the tides' bounty,
Going from smithy to smithy, in your season
For an ampler riveting.

Fold your big thumbs,
Under the trembling silver-blue scales of the moon.

᷈

Nothing still: the west empty.
The sail useless in this north-westerly.
Sea too rough for the oars.
The raven in the wicker cage, he rages more than the seamen.
The seamen have their cheese and beer.
(For the raven, no food.
That raven hated us, through his bars).
Sun went down, russet.
'A good sign,' said the skipper,
But like all of us could hardly speak
For the shaking of his teeth.
We were cold men, from spindrift and hail showers.
A few stars came out
And they had the faces of children.
The young seamen slept.
I lay cold all night. The raven did not sleep.
The helmsman did not sleep.
Yet there is land in the west: Orcades, Alba, Ireland.
Raven screamed with hunger at dawn.
He screamed, seeing our oatcakes and beer.
Then sudden the wind swung nor-east,
The sail drank the nor-east
And *Seeker* went like a stallion over the gray field
        of the sea white-flowered.
He whose mouth was full of dooms
Pictured us galloping
Over the roaring edge of the world.
The young sailors, cheerful with the wind,
Laughed, and wind laughed,
And laughter of sea lay all about us.
(The starved raven, he laughed not.)
'Now let the raven go free.'
The boy unlatched the raven's cage
Cautiously, lest the raven have his eye.
But no, all thin as he was,
The raven leapt at the sun, and wheeled
High, and higher, and flung
His hollow eye round the horizon's ring,
And fluttered no bigger than a fly
Westward. Like a black arrow
The raven sped then into the empty west.
Then was our skipper glad.

Then he flung his arm about this shoulder and that.
'There is land there.
Our friend Raven has smelt worms and carrion.
Raven will be there first.
Seamen, keep your axes well honed.
There is land for us in the west,
Islands, fertile straths, mountains for goat pasture,
Fiords full of fish.
Boy, you shall have a sweetheart in Alba.'
One day still we followed the raven.
Then the helmsman pointed to a hill.

Whale

He has broken his boreal bounds, the whale.
Sea seethes about him
Like cauldron on cauldron of ale!

The rinsed eye of the whale
Sees, through spindrift and smother
A watchful wind-drinking sail.

A snow-cloud lours on the whale.
The armoured hide
Rebounds with volleys of sleet and ice and hail.

He pastures deep down, the whale.
The dreaming plankton,
Over his delicate lip they drift and spill.

He must breathe bright air, the whale.
He surges up,
A sudden fountain flowers from his skull.

What bothers him now, the whale?
A boat-ful of men.
He scatters them with a lazy sweep of the tail.

A harpoon has struck the whale.
And the barb quickens.
The iron enters him slowly, cell by cell.

Go to the lee of the berg, wounded whale!
The eye dims, and the foundry heart is still.
He welters in blood.
The eye dims, and the foundry heart is still.

         ∾

Eagle
The Child Stolen from the Harvest-field

An eagle, circling high.
The swaddled child
Lay in the bronze
Shadow of a barley stook.
The mother,
Bronze-throated, bent and gathered and bound.
The eagle
Hovered, stooped, threshed.
The child hung
Hooked in talons, dragged
Up blue steps of sky
To a burning nest
In a crag of Coolag hill.

The harvest mother
Followed. She changed
Burnish for blue wind,
Bleeding hands. She
Lifted the boy like an egg
From the broken
Circles of beak and claw and scream.
She brought him down
To her nest of crib and milk.
She kissed him.
She lit the lamp.
She rocked the cradle. She sang.

Old grand-da muttered
Through the gray
Spittle and smoke of his pipe,
'Better for the boy, maybe
That freedom of rock and cloud,
A guest
In the house of the king of birds –

Not what must come,
Ten thousand brutish days
Yoked with clay and sea-slime.'

∽

Henry Moore: Woman Seated in the Underground

How many thousands of years she has travelled
To come to this place.

Above, burning wind
Broken stone and water.

She has sat in Troy and Carthage and Warsaw.
She has endured ice and sun.
She sits, pure from those weatherings.

Is she waiting for the hunters and soldiers to come home?

Does she hear
The laughter of lost children?

She breaks the long vigil
With spinning, baking, gossip, welcomes and farewells.
    In April she will set daffodils in a jar.

Fires, shaking of cornerstones!
Nineteen-forty. This is her longest winter.

London is burning and breaking above her.
Persephone, wait on your throne.

The Old Actor in Athens

I masqued kings and wore a tinsel crown.
Next play, I was the cunning one
Who scrawled the plan of a labyrinth on a skin
And laid stone upon stone
And prisoned there a thing half-beast, half-man,
Till the hero came with the skein.
I was Achilles above a streaming mane

And thunder of hooves on the plain
When Hector, maggot-blown,
Hither and thither, this way and that, was thrown,
Great Priam's son.
The Trojan walls were thronged with the soon-to-be-slain.
Scullion and spinner and queen
Wove from mouth to mouth the ancient keen.
The lips of Helen made a thin cold line.
Orpheus I was, the hell gate clashing behind, alone
In the wind and the rain,
Alone, after the music, with his pain.
(The crowd throws gold and flowers. The masker grows vain.)
Another masque. A ship cleaves the main,
Old sailors young with salt and boasting and wine,
Ulysses I, we lean,
Discoverers yet, into a sea unknown,
Out to the cold gray streams where the sun goes down.
And I was the king that pierced his eyes with a pin.
(Gray in the beard. The voice gets cracked and thin.
For masker and dancer soon
Only a random handclap, a silver coin.
Yes, but our mimes, every now and again
Distil to one
Pure lucent drop of benison
The fogs that rot the heart with each breath drawn
Until men seal the urn;
They honour the seven coats about the bone.)
At last I was one in a rabble, some street scene,
A drunken clown.
They put on me the mask of a keeper of swine.
The manager said, 'If you want to stay on,
Sweep up the empty grape-skins with broom and pan
When the curtain's down
And the crowd goes off to the wine shops in the town' . . .
So, a dog's day is done
Who once was Midas on a golden throne.

'Throw a mite to the old mimic-man'.

John Barleycorn

I stirred in a cell deep underground
Blind, no taste or smell, no touch, no sound.

One day I slid the bar from the door.
I poked a pale nose into the air.

What was to be seen?
My hair and hands in the sun were green.

I saluted a canty old creature –
Mister Scarecrow, a stick and a tatter.

I was very poor, but then
I could dance to the pipe of the wind, the thrummings of rain.

The lark with its fluttering sky-weary breast
Was often my guest.

One morning I brightly awoke –
I was wearing a prince's yellow cloak!

I thought my dancing days would never be done
Under the sun.

A mud-coloured knave with a crooked knife
Stood before me, he threatened my life.

He severed me from my root.
He bound me hand and foot.

He beat the flesh from my bones.
In a double circle he trapped me, thundering stones.

O bitter hurt,
The graining and ooze of the heart!

'Can you sink, John, can you float?'
He scattered my dust in a seething vat.

The torturer
Finished his work with the red sign of fire.

In furrows born,
Forever I flush the winters of men with wassails of corn.

Greenpeace

The small kings bargain and feud and fight.
Among them, unhindered
Pass the wandering priest and the bard.
I seek, I sing the goodness of this land, said the poet,
More lovely to me than a sweetheart.
The Kings of Pictland
Gave passage to his harp up the broken waters
    of the west –
How, being briefly troubled, it returns to purity,
Always the blood and the rust
Are washed by sea and mist and rains.
The kind mother
Cleanses her children from cornsweats and
    slime of fish . . .
Therefore this bard
Left the beautiful village of Glasgow.
He passed the Inversnaid torrent,
And he lingered at a beach in Barra,
And at Iona knelt awhile
For the purifying of his harp with meditation
    and psalms.
In winter, among the mountains,
The harp rejoiced in the whiteness and coldness
    of snow.
He sat, one week of westerly gale
At fishermen's fires.
He gave them a song for Minch herring, a cluster,
    a soundless silver bell.
Northwards, in Orkney, men piled
A longship with arrows and axes
For venturing (but it was murder, burning, pillage
As far as Man and Scilly.)
The seamen stopped their lading. Poets are welcome,
They remind men of the great circle of silence
Where the saga sails forever.

A peaceful ship gave him passage
Through the Pentland Firth, the bow
Thrusting the strenuous waters this way and that.
He saw under a Caithness crag
A fisherman hanging salmon nets to take, at dawn,
Glitterings of sun and wind.
Later, at a market, at Dee-mouth,
Silver of mackerel exchanged for silver mintings.
There, among barrels,
Hungerer struck harp, a fish was given.

∾

What bard now to strike
The rock of elegy
For sea, the lost mother?
(The harp is flown,
Carved ship-with-mariners
A museum stone.)
Skua, whale, herring
Litter a rotted shoreline.

Cover mouth till the bell is struck.
Our veins run still
With salt and questing of ocean,
Eyes to unlock horizon,
New lucencies, new landfalls.
Poets of machine and atom,
A last bird at a tidemark
Announces the death of the sea.

Follow the harp, songless one.
Find the bride
Asleep, in lost Atlantis, beside the fountains of waters.

Desert Sleepers

Dawn opened, a rose
Upon three travellers asleep.

The moon
Drifted from them, a worn
Washed shell.
            They slept.

The well
Beside the palm, a deep
Pearl glimmer.

They had come far.
They slept out
The seven flashing mirrors of the sun.

One woke. Twilight
Silently
Battered a bronze nail (a star)
In the west.

The dreamers awoke. A new wind
Lifted
The red petals from their eyes.

Rackwick: A Child's Scrapbook

The valley was a green jar,
        corn crammed

The green bowl
        brimmed with milk, honey, fish-oil

Once, the green jar
        tilted at sixteen hungry doors

Sealed in the jar now
        dust of old laughter and grief

They say, the jar flawed
        with heaviness of coins

Long fallen, the jar – shards
        half hidden in rushes

Hills tell old stories. Cliffs
    are poets with harps

Brightnesses broached –
    Shoal, peatbog, sheaves

Waver west, fish, with moon and stars.
    The sun's a cornstalk

      *

'Every day,' says the sea,
    'I count shell and wrack'

Stone in the burn
    counts millions of urgent waterdrops

The burn numbers
    roots, clouds, trout

'In my pocket,' says the cloud,
    'a thousand silver coins'

The rose
    spills incense and cold curls, a candle

Worm shares with lark
    charlock, broken gold

      *

'Soon now,' sang the peat,
    'I'll wear a red and yellow dress'

Welcome, eagle. That bird
    is home after a hundred years

      *

Buttercup, iris, clover
    idle in troops at the sun's door

Cornstalk cries, 'I'm the heir,
    first child of the sun-king!'

The shy worm, 'I toil
    in a cellar of the king's castle'

    *

Thugs are abroad with knives in July
    – clegs!

Yes, bandits too with rows of knives in their mouths
    – rats!

Midges in millions, at sundown, tapping
    cellars of blood

Mouse, clever thief
    unlocking stone to get to butter and candles

'No rose this,' sang
    the bee on the rusted barb

Has a lark
    slept in a bed of nettles, ever?

I wonder, does the butterfly
    say *hullo* to the spider?

Listen – *plop*! – a trout
    has been gossiping with a cornstalk

Oh, bee
    to die in the heart of that rose . . .

The Island of the Children

A man with a silver beard wrote an invitation
To a boy or a girl from every country on earth
To a picnic on his island.
They came, one after the other, one morning.
They were all delighted with the black boy
Because he was black as ebony,
And with the Chinese girl
Because she was yellow as starlight

And with the Eskimo boy
Because he was plump and smelt of ice and whales
And with the Greek girl
Because she was honey-coloured
And her words and her breath were like honey too.
The Arab boy
Ran through the fields with the Jewish girl
And their voices mingling
Were like one ancient wise harp of praise.
A girl from Siberia and a boy from Arizona
Had great wonderment
Describing 'bear' and 'cactus' to one another.
The hundred and fifty children
Delighted in all the animals round them
And the fish and the birds and insects.
It seemed that day would never end
Till the old enchanter
Who had lured them to his island
Sang, 'The sun's down!
Time to go home, to get on in the world and be wise' . . .

                *

The hundred and fifty children
Woke up in scattered beds.
A long long time had passed.
They found themselves the rulers of their countries,
White-haired, grave, and honoured.
They made important speeches
About 'freedom', 'progress', and 'peace'.
From time to time they spoke to each other
Across long distances, coldly.
They set spies to spy on all the others.
They had maps with shifting frontiers.
They revolved those globes often.
At last a silver-haired President
Discovered the Island of the Children on his map.
His heart sang like a lark that dawn.
But it was too late.
A thousand missiles were hurtling here and there.

'Look out, he's coming.
The black horseman is coming!'
Children run down from the hill,
Wild flowers spill
From their hair and hands.
Down the net-spread sands
The fishermen push out errandless boats.
Only the goats
Are content on the hill, and the cows
Shift their slow jaws.
Ploughman the furrow has fled, shepherd the fold.
The laird double-locks his chest of plate and gold.
He's off to his town abode
Quicker than lover or highwayman ever rode,
His wife up behind.
They pass dunghill and dump like scented wind.
Doors are barred, windows shuttered.
'What's all the fuss?' one old man muttered.
'To a gray fire-sider
He's a good friend, that jet-black rider.
Sooner he comes, the better.'
Girls at the bench of cheese and butter
In the great farm
Run here and there in whirls of alarm,
Apple-bright girls
Driven by a shadow to shrieks and skirls.
The calm birds angle and circle and go.
The jaunty scarecrow
Cares not a jot
For the whirling hoof of the stallion of jet.
The preaching man droops here and there,
All DOOM and BEWARE.
A tinker boy
Sprawls in a ditch to see the black horseman go by.
'*The black horseman is coming!*'
Stones of the hidden hamlet echo the hooves' drumming.
The sun goes dark.
It falters and falls from the blue, the light-drained lark.

Miss Instone said, 'Children, you were all at the Fair
yesterday, I'm sure. Out slates! Out slate pencils! Write a
composition on the following – My Day at the Fair . . .'

Twelve slate pencils squeaked and squealed on slate like mice
in a barn.

Willie rubbed honey-of-sleep out of his eyes. He wrote.

I went to the Horse Fair.
I sat in the cart beside old Da.
In Dounby
We left Daffodil in the Smithfield yard.
A policeman was holding on to a man that could hardly stand.
Old Da gave me a penny and a farthing.
Old Da went into the inn.
I bought a bottle of stone ginger at an old wife's tent.
I saw hundreds and hundreds of people.
I saw Skatehorn the tramp.
Mr Sweyn went on with a long stick and a deer-stalker
And the women curtsied in his wake.
I saw Old Da in the crowd at last,
His face was like a barn lantern.
We stood and watched the tug-o'-war.
What red faces, bulging eyes, what staggerings!
It came on to wind and rain.
The whisky tent
Blew out like a ship in a gale.
Old Da had dealings with the blacksmith,
Nails and a new plough.
The blacksmith wrote numbers and words in a ledger, after he
    had licked a small blunt pencil.
The blacksmith
Took a bottle and two glasses from a stone shelf.
He gave me sixpence!
We went home in the cart, Daffodil
Danced all the way.
She struck many stars from a stone.
The fiddler! – I nearly forgot the fiddler.
The whole Fair
Seemed to go round his fiddle. I saw
A coal-black man stretched on a board of nails.

Three farmers,
Quoys and Graygarth and Longbreck,
Seemed like they had red patches sewn on their faces, coming
    out of the whisky tent.
Daffodil
Whinnied at the stars, 'What are you,
Nails or mayflowers?'
The moon was a skull.
Then the moon was bees and honey.
I woke up.
Old Da carried me out of the cart to our fire.

*'Spelling and punctuation need special attention,' said Miss
Instone. 'Few of you, it seems, had a really enjoyable day.'*

Sprinkling of water on eleven slates, rag rubbings, sighs.

*Willie spat on his slate and wiped out that day with the sleeve
    of his gray jersey.*

Stone (1987)

Flower of the Stone

Flower of the stone,
    Fire on a hearth.

Flower of the stone,
    A jar of honey.

Flower of the stone,
    A jar of oats.

Flower of the stone,
    Fulmar, unfurling.

Flower of the stone,
    Butterfly, thistledown, bee.

Flower of the stone,
    A name, two dates, cut deep.

The tall shore dust,
   Fish seekers, drift
      Among the heavy flowers.

Seascape: The Camera at the Shore

In the rockpool a child dips (shrilling)
Fingers, toes.

Below the widest ebb it opens,
The lost sea rose.

Then, drowning rose and reef and rockpool
The west inflows . . .

The Atlantic pulse beats twice a day
In cold gray throes.

Shy in a rock-caught crumb of earth
One seapink shows.

Scotland, scattered saw-teeth, melts like petals
In the thin haze.

Lucent as a prism for days, this shore, until
A westerly blows.

Then stones slither and shift, they rattle and cry,
They break and bruise.

Shells are scattered. Caves like organs peal
Threnody, praise.

Tangles lie heaped in thousands, thrust and thrown
From the thunder and blaze!

Silence again. Along the tidemark wavelets
Work thin white lace.

Among that hoard and squander, with her lens
Gunnie goes.

Tell us then, skipper, about the islands. Were there people?
Men with Ploughs and Boats
(fruitful curving Wood), Women
with Fire and Water, Children,
Giants in a stone circle.

Were there trees?
No trees. Wind cut too sharp from
North and east. There were Stones.

Cities?
The smallest City, a stone cluster,
at the heart of the city a stone
Kirk. The Kirk seemed a Ship.
Earth-rooted, it sought (red) the
Gold of sunrise

Were there fruits?
Little black Globes in coarse
stone-scattered Grass that
stained the Mouth.

Animals?
Horses, Whales, Oxen, Goats,
Swine, Bees, Eagles, Fish.

Were there dragons? Did you hear the music of that folk?
Fiddles. I saw a Dragon carved on
a stone.

Were there stones?
Everywhere, like Flowers. Stones
of great beauty, Wave-blown.

Stone and Star

The stone that sinks a creel
The stone that whets a scythe
The stone
That locks a bridge over the burn

The stone that keeps milk cold
The ordered stones that stand between hearth and a winter
    storm
The carved stone over the nest of skulls
The stone that children
Enchant to flower, ship, castle
The stone sea-vested twice a day
The stone the beachcomber
Strikes a match on to light his pipe
Between a crag and a stormfall,
A tall stone in a field
Strayed reveller from the circling Brodgar dance,
The seapink stone
The stone the Ice Giant dragged out of Norway
The stone, Hesper,
That kisses a darkling ebbtide stone.

Shore Songs

The crab said, 'I'm locked in this pool
Until the Atlantic
Rolls back, and turns the blue key.'

The seapink said, 'I stand awhile
On a bare rock.
All summer I breathe salt and sun, then I die.'

The shell
To the child's shell-cold ear gives back
The innumerable choirs of the sea.

A driven ship in a gale,
A reef, a wreck.
'Here I lie, a piece of that kiss ever since,' the stone sang
    secretly.

Building the Croft House

We took the first basket
Near the Old Man,
We climbed, loaded. We crossed Moorfea.
We set down the stones.

This we did, we two
A hundred days
Between boat launch and butter making.

Peat-cutting, stone-getting, stone-dressing, stone-setting.
That summer
A dream of stone, fish, corn.

We carried up stones
In June, when the grass was tall and bee-thronged.
A gable looked out over the bay.

Flashing scythes, falling corn.
The doorstep set.
We drank ale from a stone jar.

Hearth-stone, water niche, lintel.
Small stones sang from the chiselled querns.
I can't work wood.
I had to give silver for roof-beams, door, table.

We carried the last load
Two days before the wedding.

The day after the first snow
Sam the ox stood in the byre. He chewed. He wondered.

Time a Stone

Storm and sea loss and sorrow is all
An old mouth at a rock

Tomorrow's wave will cover that boy and his yawl
An old mouth at a rock

Trust only the sweet clean water in the well
An old mouth at a rock

Let other girls wake to the black sea yell
An old mouth at a rock

Once I was lissom and sweet and tall
An old mouth at a rock

Fishermen hung sea silver at my wall
An old mouth at a rock

One lingered, fishless. My blood beat like a bell
An old mouth at a rock

I lit a lamp at a secret sill
An old mouth at a rock

A kiss is a cruel spell
An old mouth at a rock

A summer of kisses, then all goes ill
An old mouth at a rock

On the rosetree scents and petals sicken, they fall
An old mouth at a rock

Strength and goodness go under the hill
An old mouth at a rock

No songs but from the mouth of a child or a shell
An old mouth at a rock

And time a stone, and the feet of the dancers still
An old mouth at a rock

The Masque

Cometh one in a green coat, he follows broken earth.
Rainbow coats follow, children. They dance in sun and pools.
Cometh a blue coat with a fish sewn on it.
Cometh a gray one, a spinner.
She labours

To cover a thing brighter than sun
Till the dust of seventy summers
Devours weft and stitch . . . Silence again: brightness, a bone.
Cometh the one in black, with a black flute.
All dance together.
The one in a green coat
Makes the sign of breaking, of beckoning, then of peace.
The masque
Was before dust or harp. It moved
With the first movement of stone and water.

A Stone Calendar

JANUARY
    The icy stone –
        a fortress in Siberia

FEBRUARY
    Hall of prisms:
        rain, haar, spindrift

MARCH
    Silence: a stone cell.
        Around,
    Shell choirs, abrim

APRIL
    The sun temple, two lochs,
        dance of sixty stones

MAY
    The stone: brief
        Inn of a butterfly.

JUNE
    Sea-pink, fish-girl,
        a vigil at a sea wall

JULY
    Bee blunders from stone to flower,
        heavy, harping
            to the golden city

AUGUST
Whetstone, quern, kiln –
three harvest stones

SEPTEMBER
One small shadow
drifts to the door of the stone

OCTOBER
A star hangs, a lantern
at the stone's lintel

NOVEMBER
A host of shadows
clusters
about the House-of-the-Dead

DECEMBER
Silver key, snowflake, star-wrought.
Three sea kings
seek the House-of-Bread.

Mile Stone

How many miles to the kirk of Magnus?
Fifteen
And to the circle of Brodgar stones?
Four

And to the sea valley in Hoy?
Six,
As the seagull flies

And to the village where the Irish soldier
Built his inn? . . . Seven

How many miles to that other place, the Inn of Night?
Ask a blank stone in the kirkyard

The mile stone
Has opened a wise mouth a many a year
To horseman and traveller

How many miles to the lost children?
The stone
Cries in a daffodil surge, with spindrift of dew

Song of the Stone

Said stone to buttercup,
'Dance till you're yellow rags, then die.'

Said stone to seagull,
'A broken egg, a chalky skull in a niche of a crag,
Not long, not long.'

The stone spoke to the man going with a plough.
'A mouthful of bread and ale,
Then the long sleep, under snow.'

Sang stone to star,
'Burn, cold candle. I wear after rain the swarming colours of
    day.'

Said stone to raindrop,
'Don't run.
We're for the mill, you and I, to grind bread.'

Stone in hourglass
Whirls, sighs, sinks upon silence.

In Memoriam I. K.

That one should leave The Green Wood suddenly
    In the good comrade-time of youth,
    And clothed in the first coat of truth
Set out alone on an uncharted sea:

Who'll ever know what star
    Summoned him, what mysterious shell
    Locked in his ear that music and that spell,
And what grave ship was waiting for him there?

The greenwood empties soon of leaf and song.
>Truth turns to pain. Our coats grow sere.
>Barren the comings and goings on this shore.
He anchors off The Island of the Young.

The Silent Girl from Shetland
A Prose Poem

At the year's beginning I too made a beginning, to pilgrim to Orkney.

But I am a poor man that has no boat of my own. But I have a hardworking wife that spins wool and knits beautiful things.

And we have a poor dumb girl.

There was much storm that month.

The wool my wife spun in February looked gray in the white dazzlement of snow coming in at our open door.

And I took my score of sheep into shelter but two died in the blizzard.

The dumb girl wept without sound about the bright graves of the two sheep, in February.

In March, in the village of Scalloway, my wife got a shilling for the scarves and stockings she had knitted.

How the wind blew in mid-March! Fishing boats were hauled high up the nousts.

Gulls followed my ox and plough. The silent girl clapped her hands, for another furrow done.

We kept a bowl in a niche, to gather the coins for the voyage to Orkney.

My wife sold a hundred eggs to a sailor on the shore. The Dutchman gave her a shilling and a few herring.

A blackbird sat on the girl's forefinger, and sang and sang, for her alone it seemed.

Now there was a scattering of shillings in the bowl.

The dumb girl made the bowl sing and ring between her hands.

At her table my wife made fine round cheeses, and rounds of butter yellow as the moon.

All that work was for the pilgrimage.

In the month of June the sea trembled with blueness and light. The first of the barley was green in my rig.

My wife went here and there to the big houses, with knitted things and with eggs and cheese and butter.

When the blackbird sang to the daughter, 'What's all this stir and labour for? Why all the shillings?' the girl would laugh without sound and point south.

A wandering friar touched the girl's mouth, and went on.

The spinning wheel sang in the open door, morning to night. And my wife sang a song as the wheel turned.

The fishermen rowed home from the east with full baskets of silver fish. Boat after boat sailed in from the 'haaf' in the east.

All the women watched from the shore.

But the daughter was looking south.

August: month of the sickled corn.

The wife left her wheel and wool and bowl of shillings to glean corn in a score of crofts, first one, then another.

She of the locked mouth was often up at the chapel that month. She knelt by a lighted candle.

'A passage to Orkney?' said the skipper. 'In midwinter? Now, in the gray winds of September, is a good time for sailing. There will be storms in December, for sure. I can't guarantee you a passage at that dark time.'

The wife sold him a jersey for cold sea-nights.

'I could take you next week,' said the skipper, 'if this wind keeps.'

The girl shook her head. She counted twelve on her fingers: December.

Shillings lay in the bowl like a little heavy drift of snow.

I shut the ox and the two cows in the byre.

The girl filled the cruisie with oil and lit it, at sunset.

All were shadows in the croft, but for the shine on her soundless face.

In the month of souls, November, we visited the graves round the little church.

And I threshed oats in the barn after sunset.

The girl stood near the rock where the fishermen drowned six winters before. She wept without sound.

Darkness when we sailed from Shetland, in a still darkling sea.

Then the brief flame of noon.

Darkness when we came to Birsay, and were set ashore by the light of one lantern.

A feast of candles inside the kirk, seven red candles round the tomb of the martyr.

'It's good,' said the monk, 'that you have come this winter. Soon the bones of Saint Magnus are to be carried to Kirkwall.'

The dumb lass stayed by the tomb all night.

The monks sang, low and grave, in the choir.

Christus natus est, cried the girl at midnight. *Christ is born*.

Christus natus est, sang the joyful monks.

Four Poems for Edwin Muir

1 FIFTEENTH OF MAY, 1887

A hundred Springs ago, the winter-byred
Beasts blundered at the sun
    And the fields of Folly
    Were littered with new lambs,

And a first sleepy bee began to bend
Marigold and mayflower for the barren
    Treasure of their cups,
    And the unyoked horse

Hurled out of servitude, a surge
Of hooves above the ocean thunders.
    Between equinox and solstice
    Torrents of boreal light,

The black ploughland a thin plash of green,
Scarecrow-kept. Now James Muir, farmer,
   Stands awkward beside his glebe, imagining
   Far on, the miracle of loaves.

I expect, somewhere in Orkney that day
A soul slipped down to a boat
   And the ebb bore a death into dawnlight . . .
   Tide turns now. See, the women –

Country welcomers round a wondering cry –
Are setting the new voyager in his crib.
   Far off, far off, against the headland
   Time surges, cries, celebrates.

2 THE LOST CHILD

They looked for him among the cornstalks.
He was not there.

In the field where the horses roamed
No sign of the child
Though one great plough-horse raised his head, listening.

Down at the shore
The limpet gatherers hadn't seen him.

'I think he'll be holding
An egg or a butterfly in his hand.'

He stoops to the bees and the clover.
A pure bead
Gathers, then falls forever through his thought.

I saw a boy chasing a small boy,
Their boots hidden
In little clouds of sun-dust.
The bronze of the school bell
Trembled around, like sword on shield.

That boy
Will trance a ship to the rim of the sea
Till his mother calls him.

Someone went in at the door of the green hill.
There the harp is,
Carved in stone among skulls and bronze helmets.
That rune will unlock
Time's labyrinth, door after door
To the tree and the apple.

3 THE COAT

In a croft door a boy puts on a coat
With a fish sewn on it
And a daffodil
And a great horse with a whirling hoof
And a quartered sun
And cornsheaves
And a high lonely hawk
And a seal on a rock –
The hem all stars and spindrift

The island women cover their heads on the shore

The boy in his coat of creatures, a Joseph
Journeys
Between the fifth and the sixth day
He lingers outside a tower

A gate opens. Seven iron masks
Consider the green coat.

4 CORMACK THE SAILOR

('My mother's name was Elizabeth Cormack . . . There is in
Deerness a ruined chapel which was built in the eighth or ninth
century by an Irish priest called Cormack the Sailor, who was
later canonised . . . Whether the names are connected over that
great stretch of time in that small corner no one can say; but it
is conceivable, for in Orkney families have lived in the same
place for many hundreds of years, and I like to think that some
people in the parish, myself among them, may have a saint
among their ancestors, since some of the Irish priests were not
celibate'. Edwin Muir, *An Autobiography*.)

Listen to Cormac the sailor.
He is bent over a harp. He sings.

'When I see the cloud on the hill
I give praise to God.

When I see the sun on the many waters
The round ocean
And the quiet circle of the well
And in the rushing burn
I give praise to God.

I travelled in a ship from Ireland.
I stood in the warehouses
And discussed cargoes and bills-of-lading.
I entered houses
Where there was music, dancing, and verse.
Those things entranced me. Now
The lamp and the jar are lost in light,
I give praise to God.

In middle-Europe I woke from long sleep.
This harp stood at the wall.
Who left it there, an angel?
I give praise to God.

I have known praise and blame.
I have sat at the fire of a good woman
And have eaten her bread.
I have sat, darkling, in a place of bone.
I sailed back over the ocean.
Near a spring of clear water, my childhood,
Continually now *Laus Deo* I sing

When I hear thunder, or raindrops
I give praise to God.
I am an old man now, in a hood.
My fingers are twisted
And I have small taste for wine or fish
But more and more urgently
As days and months and seasons pass
As I see my skull in a stone that shines after rain
·O clear and pure as larks in a blue morning
I sing, *Deo gratias.*

Autumn Equinox

If you say, 'I am light'
I answer, 'Darkness'.
If you say, 'I tended the rose bush'
I reply, 'Frost flowers'.
If you say, 'A girl is reading a letter with parted lips',
I see a widow on the roads.
She knocks at a door. She has candles and needles to sell.

'A bird carries a burning seed
Into the blizzard.'

'The loom of time
Casts, this sunset, the year's third coat, harvest'.

We are sisters of a golden king.
We have travelled
One from the pole, one from the burning wheel
To a tryst on a doorstep.
I will light the lamp now in the west window.
You set the sun, as always, broken flames on the hearth.
We bide together one night, gladly, in the House of Man.
We go again, at sunrise,
One to the ice, one to the cage of fire.

The Long Hall

The skald tuned his harp. The riff-raff
   Lounged between the barrel
   And the hearth (the Earl
     That winter night

Sat with the Bishop, a golden
   Cup between them, a loaf
   Tasting of honey, flames
     Eating the spitted ox).

Harp sang the swallowflight
   Through the lighted hall,
   A small troubling
     Between two dark doors.

Barnmen came in. Fishermen
Shifted into the shadows.
A kitchen girl carried
A plate of bones

To the hungry hound. A keg
Was broached. Outside
Children went by, chanting
Of snowflakes and apples.

Solstice

The winter tribute. It is time to go with the islands' tribute
At the end of November
We set the keel for Norway, a lantern in the stern.
And had fair passage. And anchored in the fiord.
I knocked at the lodge of the castle.
A long gargoyle face – *The king is sick.*
A princess said, in the hall,
Winter will be long – there is no heir – What are we but
    ice-maidens after today?
There entered the king's room soon
The seven with hoods over their faces.
Eat below with the horsemen, I was told.
'The treasurer?' The treasurer could not be lured from the
    hoard, as if locked gold was the king's breath and blood.
A black bell shivered, once, in the tower.
The horsemen diced with blue fingers in the stable.
A girl put cinders in her hair.
The hooded seven
Stood round the last candle. One stooped in the chapel,
    holding back his hood, in a rush of gray breath he
    quenched the flame.
They went down,
They carried torches and the sword with runes on it, to a ship.
The soul of the king will set out northwards, alone, at midnight.
Peasants and fishermen
Stood, red and black, at the edge of the circle of burning.
In the shadows, unmoving, the very poor.
The Orkney ship was five days out of the harbour.
Where should I leave
The gold and the poem and the jar I had carried from the west?

They Came to an Inn

They came to an inn
And they reined in the horses
Sat down with crusts and beer

They came to a river
And they reined in the horses
A ferryman stood with a lantern

They came to a garden
And they reined in the horses
A hand bled in a rosebush

They came to a smithy
And they reined in the horses
Three nails and a long lance

They came to a mountain
And they reined in the horses
Shepherds broke ice in the pass

They came to a palace
And they reined in the horses
The eyes of the king were thorns

They came to a fair
And they reined in the horses
They bargained for gold and a jar and a web of silk

They came to a prison
And they reined in the horses
The chains rang out like bells

They came to an island
And they reined in the horses
Storm-watchers stood on the shore

And they came to a chapel

Epiphany Poem

The red king
>Came to a great water. He said,
>>*Here the journey ends.*
>>*No keel or skipper on this shore.*

The yellow king
>Halted under a hill. He said,
>>*Turn the camels round.*
>>*Beyond, ice summits only.*

The black king
>Knocked on a city gate. He said,
>>*All roads stop here.*
>>*These are gravestones, no inn.*

The three kings
>Met under a dry star.
>>There, at midnight,
>>The star began its singing.

The three kings
>Suffered salt, snow, skulls.
>>They suffered the silence
>>Before the first word.

The Twelve Days of Christmas: Tinker Talk

I saw the four shepherds, black
In the sun's ruin.
Four star-cut shadows, soon.

Folk going to Kirkwall to pay the tax,
Cart after cart.
We trailed behind, packs clanging.

I stood awhile at the shore.
Three ships
Quested by needle and hidden star.

Fire on the quarry-stone rooted,
A winter rose.
Butterflies of snow everywhere, a gray whirl.

Our donkey danders
Up small roads
To poor crofts. We offer cheap enchantments.

We chew limpets. Their peat smoke
Cures the sea silver.
A scatter, struck gold, over barn floors.

The islands white whales in the snow.
The rook on the branch
Had black thorns in his throat.

I thought I heard a night cry, a bairn
Poorer than me.
A white dream, surely.

In the street of Kirkwall
Talk of troubles.
Soldiers in the slush, kestrel-headed.

I saw the shepherds. One
Folded a shivering lamb.
They lingered at the door of the inn.

The sun was a shuttered hovel
Last time we passed.
Look now, new bright roofbeams!

We took pans and mirrors to Hamnavoe.
Three foreign skippers,
The pier heaped with bonded cargoes.

Desert Rose

No one will praise your beauty, the poet said –
You must live and die alone.

Three travellers out of the morning rode.
They lingered. They stirred my incense. They journeyed on.

No shower or shade –
I suffered all day the barren gold of the sun.

A star lifted its head
And seemed to murmur to me alone,

All beyond time are made,
Star and poem, cornstalk and stone.

Now to the House-of-Bread
I guide three hungry gold-burdened men.

Midnight, the star throng, shed
Dew in my cup like wine.

Dance of the Months
A Christmas Card

January comes with his ice-crown.
February spilling thaw and snowdrops.
March, bursting loud cheeks!
Then April, with a troop of lambs and daffodils.
May, keeper of peat-hill and cuithe-stream.
June, covering the night fire in the north.
July, tall and blue as lupins.
August with the cut cornstalks.
September, dusting cobwebs from the lamp.
October, good witch, with apples and nuts.
November, host to shades and hallows.
December with snowflake and star.

In the inn of December, a fire,
A loaf, a bottle of wine.
Travellers, rich and poor, are on the roads.

The Last Gate

'Stop, travellers. The way goes no further.
Stop. Beyond this moor the tracks of wolf and of
    creatures that have no name.

Stop. Do you not hear the sea roaring under the
    broken cliff ledge?
I charge all travellers, that they should return
    to their lamps and flowers and cups.
No gold nor seal nor gun turns this sentry.
Stop. A few have gone into the blackness by other
    ways. No word of them has come back, ever.
Stop, friends. I stand before you in consideration
    of a duty owed between blood and
    stars: a sign of preservation.'

The keeper of the gate heard, coming on, the chatter
    and the hooves of a new company.

Then a word was proffered, a sign, at sunset.
The keeper unlatched the gate.
They went through with their creaking beasts, all three.

On one side, the burnt ocean.
On one, a desert of vitrified cities.
In front, a mountain with steps cut in the highest ice.

Far on, they saw what one took to be a star,
Or a man with a lantern,
The man who is sent out to guide travellers to an
    inn.

A Winter King

'Now,' said the sea king
'Freight the death ship
With jar and tapestry and gold.
I must sail alone, very far.
It is time for a new saga to be told.'

The king was bronze-bearded, not sick or meek-mouthed
    or old.
On the hull a bird had been cut,
Branch-beaked, a long gray wing.

Fishermen loosed the rope.
They sent the ship down the rollers with a darkling shout
Under the voyager's star.

The red king said to the boy, 'You're too small
To shift such baggage.
Here, buy an apple or a bird.'

The yellow king said, 'Icicles
Hang like gray nails from the lintel, boy.'

The black king said, 'In my castle
The women would clothe you in blue silk.
Your cold face
Would be a star among the gold and ebony.'

The boy said, 'Here they come now,
The hill shepherds.
A rough lot. At midnight
They always come down for their jar of wine.'

The boy blew notes from his pipe.
Shepherds and kings followed the carol.

Carol: Kings and Shepherds

'Here's the place,' said the kings
    And the black one set on the sill a rose.

'At last, at last,' said the kings
    And the yellow one played, inside, his flute.

'Open the box', said the kings
    And the red one poured a torrent of gold.

        Then a troop of shepherds came.

The shepherd boy was cold as a root
And the old one like a thorn was cold
And the five shearers stood blue as ice.

        The shepherds brought to the place a winter lamb.

Christmas Poem

We are folded all
In a green fable
And we fare
From early
Plough-and-daffodil sun
Through a revel
Of wind-tossed oats and barley
Past sickle and flail
To harvest home,
The circles of bread and ale
At the long table.
It is told, the story –
We and earth and sun and corn are one.

Now kings and shepherds have come.
A wintered hovel
Hides a glory
Whiter than snowflake or silver or star.

A Winter Tale

In an island, no one escapes the sea.
Spume and gull everywhere.
The sea beats at the end of every road.

I think I will not stay long here.
'I am looking for this house' . . .
Across the boat
The ferryman shook his head at me.

Three old women mumbled
As if I had come
To burn the roofs over their heads.

A boy listened, above the waves' thunder and blaze.
His finger pointed
But drooped soon like a flower in a jam-jar.

The blacksmith
Had never heard of that house.
The beadle turned the pages of an old book
And shook his head.

The schoolmaster listened gravely.
The laird
Would not so much as open his door.

And the sea! Lamentation
Of sea at the North Head, in the darkness.
If the westerly slackens
It may be (said the ferryman) he will loosen the rope.

The innkeeper had one room,
Very expensive.
'We don't expect tourists at this time of year.'

By midnight, I had stood at every door
In the island but one,
And it a shelter for sheep.

House of Winter

At last, the house of winter. Find
On the sill
Intricate ice jewellery, a snowflake.

Open one dark door. Wind-flung,
A golden moth! Soon
A candle flame, tranquil and tall.

It is a bitter house. On the step
Birds starve.
The sign over the door is warped
   and faded.

Inside one chamber, see
A bare thorn.
Wait. A bud breaks. It is a white rose.

We think, in the heart of the house
A table is set
With a wine jar and broken bread.

The Child in the Snow

'Listen. Somewhere outside, a footfall' . . .
    A snowflake on the pane.

'I have heard it again, the low knocking' . . .
    The fall of a frozen bird.
    It is the sift of ash in the hearth.
    It is the sound a star makes on the
        longest night of the year, a silver harp-stroke.
    No one is out on a night like this.
    You heard a mouse between the walls,
    Or a lamb in the high fold, trembling.
    Turn over. Let your brain
    Brim with a winter hoard of dreams.

'At midnight I dreamed
Of a thin lost child in the snow.'

Snowman

Chime of ice chains between
Sky and freezing burn.
Swans on the loch are crystal
Sculptings.
Three children rend the new white
Flowing silk.
(Splinters of glass scatter from their mouths!)

In radiant tatters they robe
The Winter King.

Feast of Candles

Here a candle was set, for a cure on the hill
And there a candle, a shy flame, for a cradled
      one at the shore
And there now, a candle, swiftly set, the flame
      draught-flung: for a sailor in
      Ireland
A candle, laving pure flame on a face: and
      the mouth moved with a name and
      names, and a sorrow
Such a procession of flowers-of-flame, in winter
One by one, out of the bitter black night, under
      the stars
And an old woman, sifting names of else forgotten
      dead, with a bleak blown candle
And girls from the big farm, leaving their empty
      mirth outside, each girl a candle-
      bearer, and there children-brides-
      mothers-deathfolders-mourners
      (those five girls) beautifully
      lighted about the eyes and the
      hushed mouths
And after, a shepherd, shielding his flame, whispering
      'Saint Agnes'
Then fishermen from the boat *Fulmar*, each
      lighting his candle from the
      boat's lantern
And a candle set, as if the laird's face was
      kissed by an angel, the man's
      rock-hard face, and the mouth
      unlocked with a prayer
And another flame of candle that seemed to go
      out and gulped for life and
      folded wings like a summer
      butterfly: and that was the
      hen-wife and her candle
(And the monk gathered the folds of his cloak
      together at the altar and bent
      and prayed between two tall
      set-apart candles: in Latin
      whispers and a boy replied,
      hesitant with the Latin syllables,
      in country whispers)

And a flame set, and a flame set, and a flame
          set . . .
Then was the cry heard down at the shore
And there were whispers, 'The skipper'
For the ship *Olaf* would weigh that night for
          Trondheim, with news of Magnus
          and the light at his tomb beyond
          sun or stars or candles
Yet a dozen candles would be lit for that voyage,
          and brought from keel to kirk, for
          a blessing on the voyage
And there again a candle set, Bjorn the ploughman
          seeking good furrows to follow his
          oxen and plough
And a candle set, the flame borne by the earl's
          poet purer than words he would ever
          strike, but he had no sorrow for that:
          who shall say whom wax-and-
          wick-and-petal was set there for, a
          lady or a light to welcome the spring,
          or a drop to be lost in the ocean of
          the first and last Light
Then two children from the hill, one crying for his
          candle was out, but the other rekindled
          it, and the tallow rooted in warm
          dribblings
(And the altar-boy turned a page for the priest)
And a wave of lights, with sea breath, broke
          upon the door. And that was
          the sailors . . .
Then the priest, in the stone ship, turned and
          blessed that feast of candles on
          Candlemas night.

1

Now it's Spring, there's not that much to do.
Daffodils open, then tulips
(The roses very doubtful this year.)
The blackbirds open their throats.
The masons have finished the tomb, and gone away.

2

Soldiers go past, a bronze column.
Trouble in the city.
Always trouble, in street and hill, these days.
The quietest place is my garden.

3

I worry about the rosebush.
Has the worm gotten in?
The worm eats the coat of white roses, often,
To a rigging of rags, a scarecrow.
Ten summers ago, it all but died.

4

Nightingales sang all last night.
I hardly slept.
Joseph came with my wages, a silver piece, in the morning.
Then a rout of children
Pleading, at noon, for olive leaves.

5

Crowds going past, surging, lingering, herded by soldiers,
Among them one,
A young man carrying his tree of death.
(I dare not look at that.
I nip the tainted buds from the rosebush.)

Joseph at my door at sunset. *Hurry, man!*
Bring jars of oil. Bring
A web of linen.
It is not my business
Who is to be the guest in the hollow rock.

7

A woman crying beside the fountain.
The last stars.
Two of those fishermen, I think,
Hesitant at the gate, watchful.
I should send those folk about their business.
A dove furls in my dead tree
At gray of dawn.
And now the tree is clusters of light and incense!

The Flute in the Garden

(to Judith)

January
    The flute sang
    Silently
    in the ear of a snowman

February
    A little white blossom
    unfurled
    through a stop in the flute

March
    The flute
    was washed in a wave of new green grass

April
    A daffodil danced in the wind, a splash of sun
    over
    the sleeping flute

May
> Small lyrics
> – daisy, buttercup, clover –
> covered the mouth of the flute

June
> Blackbird cocked a head at the flute, then
> trilled, questioned

July
> In the rosebush over
> the flute
> roses whirled, a white ballet

August
> A honeybee
> blundered across the silent flute
> – sweetness!

September
> Fall light, leaves,
> on
> Orpheus asleep in those chambers

October
> Waken the flute with a gift of apples,
> girl

November
> Can the flute
> follow her in to the fires and the lamp?

December
> Flute-song,
> star in the solstice tree

Tryst on Egilsay (1989)

The great drama at the heart of the Orkney story is the meeting on Easter Monday 1117 of the two earls of Orkney – cousins – Magnus Erlendson and Hakon Paulson. What had been planned as a peace-meeting ended in the execution of Earl Magnus; the events that led up to it have the power and inevitability of Greek tragedy. The murdered earl soon became St Magnus the Martyr; the murderer became one of the greatest and justest of the Orkney earls. 'So shines a good deed in a naughty world'.

The story of Magnus and Hakon is magnificently told in *The Orkneyinga Saga,* written down in Iceland about AD 1300.

This seven-fold poem celebrates the events of that April day as seen by some of the people on the island.

EARL HAKON

I reason with Norway, 'Here are the two earls
In the great hall of Orkney.
The stone hawk over the door is withered.
I pass from room to disordered room.
I wait for a dove-sign from the lord Magnus.'

I walked on the hill of the farmers.
Ploughs broken, sickles rust-eaten,
Rats at the seed sack in the barn.

I came to the yard of the shipwrights.
The peaceful strakes for fishing-boats
Are gone to the swelling hull of a longship.
One shipwright spoke with masons and a priest.

I came to the chamber of the women.
The daughters of music had twisted mouths.
Some sewed an altar cloth.
One woman stood apart, and wept.

In the chamber of the skippers
They traced viking routes on a chart.
A few discussed, in secret, a *stone ship*.

Then, in the chapel, this cry
That they may take the wings of the morning . . .

Magnus housed long, in a seagirt cell, westwards.

This can never be good, a cloven earldom,
Bad governance, the folk
Fallen into faction, insolence, orisons.
I too would have a sheaf carved on the lintel.
Therefore to Egilsay we have sailed,
The prows of my eight ships beaked like falcons.

HELMSMAN

Off Scilly I first swung an oar
Going then to Africa for gold, a boy.

I am not that old now
But I've been as far as Greenland.
Ice gnawed at the hull with green teeth.

I think there may be land further west.
Only the eye of the sun sees it.
An Icelander, Leif
Plucked grapes on that shore.
The old sailors in Shetland say
Leif had too much of his own treading
The day he stained his mouth with Vinland juice.

I went with Swedes down a river in Russia.
The domes of Byzantium! My eyes dazzled.
There were too many Norskies in that town.
Their axes a hedge about the Emperor.

What am I doing, rowing gentry
Through a sea of glass *ad insulam ecclesiae?*
Yes, I have smatterings of Latin
As well as French, Scots, Spanish.
I like best the Greek words for *sea*.

Phew! that wave made a tangled web of the oars.

I didn't know Finn and Hold, those lairds,
Cared all that much about kirks.
What, there? Sea bell on a hidden rock?
Swing the prow of *Dove* a point to west.
It's the bell of the little kirk,
A slow small joy over the black and gray furrows.

THE KILLERS

Now they go down, laughing, to the shore.
Now they shout for food, for ale clamour.
But truly this face and that, gray-masked.

Yea, and the fire gray embers, the pots
With raw meat on the bone and cold dregs.

Lifolf would not cook that day, Lifolf
Walked under the crag with red hands
And never cook wore such a coat,
Sewn gold and scarlet from throat to hem
And seven buttons of carved ivory.

Then Sigurd blew strong breath on the embers
But the fire died on the stones.
Would they break down a door for kindling?
The sport and the laughter
Were dead in them suddenly like the fire.
And one said, 'The peasant will need his door in winter.'

One said, 'Every man drinks his own cup of death.
Whatever road he takes, forest or firth
Or mountain path or moor scratchy with whins,
At the end of the road is the cup brimming with shadows.
He must hold over his gray mouth
The inverted cup to the uttermost black drop.'
In the church the Mass of the dead is sung.

The earl said, 'Go now in order into the ship.'

The earl that had drunk the cup said nothing.
A day and a night, nothing.
Nor priest nor peasants came about that silence.
With the evening star, the soul began its singing.

THE DEATH OF MAGNUS

What's this? I'm bidden to a great feast?
But here I stand, lost
On a dark moor, and I can hardly move
For the heavy coat-of-state on my shoulders.

Men pass me on the moor. They wear masks
Of wolf and of raven.
They *seem* to pass me, then come about,
They stand in a yelping circle.
They are the ones appointed, I think,
To bring the earl to the feast.

How have I, of all men, deserved a feast?
The islands are in trouble.
Fire in the thatch, blood on the shore,
Their tables and cupboards empty,
Weeping at every doorstep.
And I who am set over this people
Bidden to bring them with me to the banquet.

The women go by with clay pots to the spring.
Where is the golden bowl?

A man stands before you, Magnus.
He is poor. He's in tears.
The axe shakes in his hands.
The spring morning is very cold.
Put your coat-of-state about him, Magnus.

Quick – let the silver cord be loosed.

The dark waters rise up into my soul.
Here's your ship of death, Magnus.
Those bright ones? They ferry you over to the Feast.

Sun wakes me. I go into the cold kirk.
I light candles, set out wine and bread.
A boy might come, sticky-eyed.
Now I am another, vested, with clean hands.

Otherwise, Petrus, this is a poor place.
One might come, grumbling – some old man
Had the last hunger on him.
One might come – 'Thord, ploughman,
And Gerd my lass are bespoke.
And the dowry, one ox.'
I must set seal, unbreakable, to that pledge.

One might come. In April Erling
Hammered a new cradle.
Now the bairn's on board. Let three water drops
Signify the great deluge
That bore, brimming, the ark and all creation.
But that the seven gifts in my keeping
Put the beauty of heaven on this people,
I'd be better dusting parchments in Trondheim.

One came, at sunset. 'Sir, two fine ships
Are anchored off the ness.'

Another, 'A lord, cold, is knelt in the kirk.'

Let the bishop see to the lords of Orkney.
That one golden bird
Should brush this poor island and drop
A splendid plume, is a throw of chance.
If the man is there when I light the Mass candles
He'll have greeting like any cleaver of the clay.

THE MEN OF EGILSAY

All morning on the sea, cold, with creels.
And not one lobster.
Home now, and the fire out, and not a hunk of bread
On table, or cupboard, or griddle.
I'll knock that Sigrid black and blue. I will.

The plough stottering after the ox since dawn,
I stottering after the plough.
The house empty and cold as a cave.
Not one baked sillock* to eat. Oh, my good Ragna!
I'll tell you where they are, the women.
They're all in the kirk, kneeling.
Don't bide indoors. The lords of Orkney are here.
They're throwing silver about them like rain.
Forget the fish and the bannocks.
Enough shillings to drink the ale house dry.

The lords walk in order to the moor.
Their speech is like old carved stones.

One of the lords sat in the kirk all night . . .

Why should the lords choose Egilsay
For their corn dance? Why not?
We have just ploughed and seeded the furrows.
A third of our barley is for their longships,
A third for Bergen, the king's granary there.
In a masque there's always a death,
Always a hero, always a clown, and women keening.

Look – the shape of Ingi against the sunset!
And Thora, Sigrid, Ragna, Sunniva, Maurya.
Return to us, Magnus, laden with cornstalks.

THE TWO TINKERS

'If I had their seven silver cups
I'd be richer than the king in Bergen.'
– A drag and a clang like chains on you always.
'But if I had two silver cups
We wouldn't be poor all winter.'
– No sleep for you under the stars
For fear Slok the thief
Might have the cups from under your skull.

'The priest is lifting – look – the silver cup.'

* sillock – young coalfish

– All the world can drink from that cup,
The two tinkers that we are,
And the lord Magnus with the heavy folds about him
And Aud the skipper
And the fisherman with a bunch of herring
And the wife with a loaf from the fire.
The priest drinks for all, high and low.

'If I had four silver cups, or five, or six,
It would mean this:
A great hall and a fire in every room,
And a garden with an oak and a falcon,
And a ship in the west,
All the people kissing the dust as we ride past.'

– What are a thousand silver cups
And you a dead man
And no thirst or quenching in you at all –
A clay pitcher fallen on a stone?

On they went, one April day, through an island.
Mugs – best tin – three for a penny.

Foresterhill (1992)

In the spring and early summer of 1990 I was a patient at Foresterhill, the Aberdeen Royal Infirmary. To pass the time, I worked on a sequence of poems, imagining a medieval monastic beginning for Foresterhill.

I was trying to express some gratitude, too, to the surgeons, doctors, and nursing staff.

I finished the draft of the sequence at Balfour Hospital in Orkney, before coming home.

Cutting Down Trees
    In a clearing of trees
        (Cut down twenty trees)
    Here let it be built, the hut
            Near a well, with a hearthstone.
        We can spare two brothers
        One with healing in his hands
        One with a psalter interleaved with herbs.
    It may be, the sick man
    That fled from stones into the heart of the forest
        Will seek the fire
        And will be there still when morning sifts through the
                branches.

Pirates
    The pirates drifted between Benahie and the woods,
    The sea bandits
    That put knives in this net and that
    And prowled under the castle roots,
    Lewis-men or Danes.
    Farmers drove cattle into byres,
    Set a night watch on a fold here and there,
    The provost had a drum sounded at the Don-mouth.

    The wolf-man, trapper
    Saw their prints
    And fire marks in twenty places in the forest
    And a trail of blood.

'Yes,' said the brother in the hospice door
'A foreigner with a sea wound on him,
And we put oil and leaves on his thigh.'

Architect
Macher, architect, built merchants' houses.
Last month, a villa at Dee-mouth for a skipper's widow,
Five crowns in purse for that work.
Soon, in farms, the fever-fire.
This mason, master of the granite hewing, squaring, last
      pure chiselling, cold star glitters,
'There must be a cool place, infirmaria,
Pines that have lately known snow
Where they bide till the roses of sickness wither.'
See, this drawing on a hide: *Macher made this* inscribed.

Wreck
A stack near Colliston of the yawls.
The *Schwartz,* Lubeck, wrecked there,
Cargo, Rhenish, heavy wax at the bungs,
      for chamberlains at Holy Rood, twenty-one casks.

One sailor in the hospice, salt-scarred.
With leaves, distillations of herbs restored
He might yet stretch a sail beyond Kiel.

Lowlanders
This one broke an ankle in a furrow.
This one lost teeth fighting.
A rash huntsman,
This one took the boar's fang, at Insch.
Another hand poisoned with salmon hooks.

Knife, lint, essences from phial and phial.
We give them back to wind and sun.

Is there war in the mountains westward?
We heard of Saxon horsemen
At Tummel, the heads turned north.
We have seen ploughboys
At barn-gables, singing war songs,
Women urging, women
Dragging the fools back by their coat-tails.

The stockmen drive herds west and north.

At Foresters' Hill is no provision
For a festival of wounds.

Healer

Gift of wholeness, blossoming, the dance
Of air, stone, rain.

I think of Eck, his blundering
With pen and scroll – such blots – in the library.
No, he could not wash a floor
But the bucket was upset.
The voice of Eck a crow at Matins and Vespers.
Weed the herb garden, Eck. Weeds only
Infested the plot.
We must send Eck back soon
To his father and the fishing boat at Catterline.

In the diversity of gifts, for Eck
Nothing, a stone on his palm.

At Foresters' Hill, our infirmary there
Eck found rare roots in the burn
We hadn't known before.
Virtue flowed from Eck's fingers
Into abcess and lesion.
The lepers cry, 'We'll have Eck for bandaging, brothers.'

So we may see, dear people
Blessings may break from stone, who knows how.

Fee

A horseman going in and out of the trees,
He ties bridle to branch.

A purse from the tapestry coat,
Spanish leather.
A gold coin, drop of sunsweat
Offered to the doorkeeper.
For healing of my father, last harvest
Who died however in the first snow.

How should Eck know
The fee from a hard round of butter, a frozen honey-splash?

The infirmarian:

Your honour, that treasure may not rot the fabric of our
    house
– And may your sire
Have inherited riches beyond price – grant us at Foresterhill
    rather
The rock with watersprings under it,
A field where Mags and Moondrift our cows
May yield us gold of butter and mead
For restoration of sick guests.

Pilgrim
  'Who went quickly among the trees
  Disturbing that blackbird?'

  Finnbar stopped here at sunset
  Finnbar from Pluscarden
  Going on to Walsingham, Compostella.
  We put bandages on his feet,
  A crust in his bowl.

  Finnbar has sat so long
  In the scriptorium
  How will his white feet endure
  The Pyrenees and the Alps?

Castellan
  A man from Dunnotar stopped at our gate
  Going from salmon runs in the Spey,
  Drops from his net and hooks, like gray blood.

  'Cough, ague, bone-break, fever –
  Why do you waste your days
  On death-farers?
  Let them take their bruisings
  To the swart door of the skull.
  Your mercies
  Deny a clean surge, the dance in the teeming estuaries.'

  The castellan, laughing
  Put five fish on the doorkeeper's plate.

Lux Perpetua
Three axemen from the woodyard. They mark
A tree here and there. Snow
Comes shivering from black branches.
A drawing on a scroll.

    A face beside a dead candle, cold.
    It is not good
    To hurry him in at the earth door.
    Let him lie three nights
    In this stark cell
    Glister of oil on eyes and mouth
    The hands folded
    New candles lighting head and feet
    And the chanting *Lux perpetua*

The builders will build in this clearing
A waiting room for the poor soul
Before it whispers for entrance at the door of purification.

Beeman
We have Alisdore with us, master of the bees.

    Alisdore from Echt tired of a wife
    Trading his golden combs
    At the haberdasher's for ribbons,
    Saying to a cadger
    'A sun-oozing box for seven salt herring.'
    She might feed the pig honey, that woman.
    There's a stickiness
    In the cups, on chair and on blanket.
    One old May
    She had a sweetness, that lass, no hive could match.

    Alisdore brought a swarm from Echt
    And built hives in a clearing
    Thick heather blossom on three sides.

    Village folk hoarse in the throat
    Tilt faces to a gold-dripping spoon.

A Scroll
Sun faileth not
    Pouring our cornstalks and honey
        From the golden jar.

Moon never fails, the shifting silver of the plate
    A-jostle with fish.

Stars not fail, that fleece and cargoes
    Be ushered home under Hesper.

    *

The lantern at our gatepost will soon be out.
The candles over our beds of suffering, they will be cold
    wax in time.
The refectory fire a smoke-blackened stone.

    *

A holy man had written:
Prayers, charities, alms, blessings
These be the little flames
Outlasting diamond and emerald and the star-in-the-granite.

Homily

We go into distances, near or far, each man to his own
    bourne.

In childhood, all is green and good,
Trees, horses, stones, stars, flowers.
                (There is only the garden,
                  never gate or a road
                  beyond the garden.)

There comes a call in the night, in youth, a summons
                  purer than music,
                deeper than truth itself.
We go out into wind and a few stars.

In the morning we are on a desolate road
(Where is the woman, keeper of fire, the children,
The house on its firm rock, the flock on the hill?
There and not there: shadows.)

The voice is all delight to us still
In the first lingering flakes of age.

The sun sets on our labouring urgency.
We hurry to find an inn
With fire and bottle, fish and bread.

It thickens to black snow.
Breath, heart are snagged with nets of blizzard.
But there is no lamp of welcome at midnight.

Cry of a torrent under a broken bridge, far on.
What will the dayspring show?

Look for no company of goodly folk
No fellow pilgrims on that road.
Loneliness is all
And the bitter fruit of the selfhood of each man –
Shame, regret, fear, sorrow, rage.

We are beyond the last scars of snow
And there the fires begin.

                    *

We brothers put ourselves here, at the door
And in the choir, with music
And at the board with a few loaves
And at the beds with candles
And one on the road outside, at midnight, with a lantern

Should a soul go past bereft and weeping.

Water Casks
Rain after drought – it gargled
All a night in pipe and water barrels.

What did the downpours sing?

'A barrel for the kirn and the still . . .
One for washing wounds . . .
One for the herb-yard when a wind blows the dust . . .
One for the horse, he curls black lips at the end of the
     twelfth furrow, he slurps on the brigstone, he strikes
          out galaxies with the hoof, the eye rolls like a
               thunderball . . .
One for Fergus, may he make the flagstones to shine in the
          chapel . . .
One to mirror in a meniscus the young ice of the moon,
     the star wheel, rose of dawn, before we come and make
          a disturbance with bucket and bowl . . .
One for small jars to mingle with the altar wine . . .

    'Another clearing, higher up?
    Cut down fifty trees!'

    The forester at his door, red in the face.
    Downturned faces of three brothers.

    'Would you drive the deer from the forest?
    What will they say, the burghers?
    What will Dunnotar say
    If the stag climbs into Lochnagar?

    Would you have no chanting in the dells next spring,
    Blackbird and linnet?
    Have the little black pigs of the forest done you harm?
    Must the charcoal men starve?'

    The woodman shuts his door against them.

    The woodman went up with a honed axe in winter.
    Snow fell shattering from boughs in fifty sudden dazzlements.

Cattle Thieves
    Rievers were out before sundown. Rievers
    Were out. Rievers from Mearns or westward
    Astride shaggy colts
    Poured down the hill, wild shadows
    And turned and were off
    Driving cattle from Kirkton and Tarty
    And the night full of rage, laughter, urging.
    What will we do with one thief
    Thrown from horseback, his leg askew?

    The bailiff twisted straw, looked for a tree.

    We sent Nechtan with a lantern.
    He carried the lad, a sack of pain, into dawnlight.

    Seven weeks on, we think
    The boy will go gravewards rolling like a tipsy sailor
            through streets in Arbroath,
    A stranger always to horses and horned cattle.

Comings and Goings

Where do you go from here, traveller?
    Ruddy in the cheek again, I go seeking a harvest fee
      in Echt.

Do you go on far, traveller?
    To Catterline, with a cart to buy fish, now the fever has
      left me.

You will leave us so soon, traveller?
    Yes, I can hammer nails again in the boatyard in Torry,
      bright and true and ringing.

A bleak day to cross the hill, traveller.
    A shepherd with an eye-patch sees but half the
      ewe-graving snow.

We are not innkeepers, traveller, and charge board.
    Take this silver, Charon will have his due soon.

You must bide with us longer, seaman.
    Cargo me with oil and bread, father, against the
      troubling of the bar at sunset.

What do you seek at this door, traveller?
    The word is, you have good leaves for toothache.

Returns

There is no compulsion, those
Who've been made whole
Can chop logs beyond the burn.

Our garden has plenty of roots and stones
For hands renewed
If hands and hearts are willing, only.

An old patient can call in cow to byre.

If a man has ten gold pieces
He might leave one (scripturally)
That would build a new chamber of wholeness among the trees
If the forester is agreeable.

It is sufficient
To say *Ave* and *Gloria* in the hospice chapel.

Brodgar Poems (1992)

The poem sees the work on this Neolithic stone circle as lasting two or three generations at least. 'She who threw marigolds over you . . . is a crone now with cindery breath . . .'

It may have been a meeting-place, a temple, a hymn to the sun and the stars.

Even as a civilisation is being established, its history is beginning to crumble. Strange boats from time to time sailed along the horizon, going north and west, threatening the precarious settlements.

But a circle has no beginning or end. The symbol holds. People in AD 2000 are essentially the same as the stone-breakers and horizon-breakers of 3000 BC.

The Third Stone
> The third pit is dug. Stone
> Sips the brim of darkness.
> The stone tree
> Will have tonight its star-leaves.

The Fifth Stone
> Hunter, don't give all your strength to the wild boar.
> A stone waits in Vestrafiold.

The Eighth Stone
> Disturb the roots, let the worm
> Seek a new stair.
> I hear shouting between the hills.

The Ninth Stone
> After this snow, the ninth stone.

The Eleventh Stone
> They say, never such loveliness between the lochs
> As that girl.
> In the pause between two stones
> She became a swan.
> She flew from us into sunset and stars.

The Thirteenth Stone
 We have heard, men
 Who have no knowledge of stones
 Are in ships.
 Save us, stone, from the harps in the west.

The Fourteenth Stone
 We said to the children,
 'At last the stones
 Will be like the first little rose, that opens beside the burn.'
 'It will be like a spider's web
 With the dew on it.'
 Those children
 Were at the dragging of the fourteenth stone.

The Seventeenth Stone
 They go, the old crones
 Plucking heather
 To thatch the huts before winter.
 'Swan', they called one.
 'Daffodil', one, once.
 (The old men laugh)
 'Dew of morning.'
 'Butterfly.'
 A new stone watches them.
 They stoop, here and there, snatching.

The Nineteenth Stone
 The girls hold buttercups under their chins.
 'You will make the best cheeses.'
 A cow cries to be milked.
 The girls turn,
 They shower the newest stone with buttercups.

The Twentieth Stone
 Today, the young men, a score
 Levered from Vestrafiold
 The tallest stone, a star-raker.
 Ale-skins were dry
 Before the arrival of the stone-dresser.

The Twenty-third Stone
 Those ships on the horizon
 Are made of trees.

The bog has eaten our forest.
What are our curraghs but thin water flies?
Stones, one more than last winter,
Guard us from the foreign ships.

The Twenty-fourth Stone: Thunder

Hammer on the hills,
Black stammer!
The cloud, a fistful of flashes,
Cut a stone forehead.
The stones, against the purple sky,
Danced.
After the thunder, sun.
One stone has a red wound.

The Twenty-sixth Stone

The man from the shipwreck said
'We have seen stone clusters
Far south, in Lewis, Wessex, Brittany.'
That seaman
Withered soon in the circle of the hills.

The Twenty-seventh Stone

Sunset, midsummer. Who
Reads the riddle,
The dance, the torches of celebration?
None.
Corn whispers, wonders, urges. *Ah, gold kiss.*

The Twenty-eighth Stone

Curlew-cry
Across a clean stone face.
The old stones have lichen beards.

The Thirtieth Stone

Hill in the west, Mother
Vestrafiold,
We thank you for one more child, this strong guardian.

The Thirty-first Stone

Fish-net, fleece wheel, quern, milk-kirn,
Hollow of wet clay
Standing all night in a nest of flame,
Be this new stone a friend to all.

The Thirty-second Stone
   She who threw marigolds over you, stone,
   A child,
   She is a crone now with cindery breath.
   You, stone,
   Two younger stones curve beyond you.

The Thirty-third Stone
   Lift from us the curse of time,
   Birth, blossoming, cinder breath.
   A beautiful stone
   Is walking today across the hill
   Under a splurge of larks.

The Thirty-fourth Stone: The Pipes
   This new stone is acquainted with pipe music
   Grave and pure –
   Not shrieks from a split grassblade.

The Thirty-seventh Stone
   It may be, the stones are attentive
   To first cry and last cry,
   The thunder
   In the heart of a young man in April.
   Release us, stone,
   From the three anguishes.

The Fortieth Stone
   This stone walked through the hills
   Between cornstalk and fish.
   What, the men groaned and bled
   Clearing a way for the stone?
   One skull, in truth,
   Has been laid bare by the eagles.
   I tell you, the men danced.
   They stretched their mouths with praise, laughter.

The Forty-first Stone
   That yellow row of skulls on the shelf
   Saw one ship only.
   The shrunken mouths at the aleskin,
   They counted seven.

Men from the sea
Took a hundred fleeces
At Skaill, the year of the fortieth stone.

The Forty-second Stone
Thunder among the hills.
   'The wild Kierfiold horses?'
   'Waves against Yesnaby?'
Twenty men left at sunrise
With rollers, oxen, ropes, a jar of ale.

The Forty-third Stone
'The new stone, broken and dressed
It could be a house
For falconer and first child.'
The chatterer beside the small sun on the hearth,
That ignorance,
We drove out into the stars and snow.

The Forty-fifth Stone
What broke from the cloud? Rain, sun, the hawk.
A stone walks under a cloud slowly.

The Fiftieth Stone: Plague and Pillage
And if the pustules, the fevers
Fired
This people again, like dry heather
Or if a foreign sailor
Stood in every door, some dawn
And the circle not closed ...
Fowlers, fishers, farmers
Have not been quarrymen
Now, seven years.
In Vestrafiold a stone waits, half-hewn.

The Fifty-second Stone
Look, a small boy with hook and limpet shell
Lying in the reeds.
The swan does not care.
The tall stone, if it cares, has care
Beyond the span of our caring.
Take seaweed from the boy's mouth.

Corpus Christi (Uncollected 1993)

1

How could I know what time was?
    A boy too young
To go out in 'Sion' or 'Jericho' with lines.

But I baited lines and mended nets.
    In the morning they sailed out
    And came back at sunset
Heavy with heave and slither of silver
    Or with a few thin sklinters.

Then the gutting, the booth at the shore,
    Women and cats,
    The weighing and the bargaining.

And Peter nodding over his beer-pot,
    Fingers all salt and blood,
    Too tired to break his crust.

'Next year, boy, you'll sail with us . . .'

Time draws a brutal circle
    About all trades and livings of men.

One night this stranger
    Sat at the fire with our fishermen.

2

I know this about time and vintners.

It needs a summer of sun and rain
    For ripening of grapes
A hundred wounded feet at the tubs,
Cooperage, storage, strewment of leaven

The listening a winter ear, to grape songs,
      Filling of casks, bottles, skins
Before the inn-keeper
Drives to the gate with his cart.
I know when time is a dancing circle.

I was a boy at the wedding
With the fishermen and Joshua and the good woman,
When the steward whispered to the bridegroom at midnight
      'The cask is empty'.

3

You might well ask, country folk,
      What were fishermen doing
Wandering among the hills,
Village and mill, smithy, sheepfold,

The sea scars silvering on their hands
Following Joshua
      In a kind of a slow dance

As if they heard another music
      Than weddings or harvest home.

'Get back to your nets and boats!' . . .
      'The harvester needs sickle-men!' . . .

The loveliness of the Word
      Compelled tributes, fish and wine and bread
      From grudging cupboards.

4

I was there, a boy
      Little better than truant or tinker
      Far from our sea sounds

When shepherds, ploughmen, women
      Washed across the hill, five thousand

Hungry for God, and fed like angels
   With heavenly beauty and truth

But I hungered, under the first star
(Such are the ebbs and emptyings of time)
      For a long loaded table,

When this other boy comes to Peter with his basket.

5

HOC EST ENIM CORPUS MEUM
HIC EST CALIX SANGUINIS MEI

      The net-mender was too young
      To be in the high room that night

But I was at the gate
When the treasurer left for the city by a secret door

And the mother of sorrows
      Stood outside, under a tree, alone.

6

And I was at the last hill
      When he was notched with five wounds

I stayed to watch (unregarded)
      When Corpus Christi
Was unhooked from the black wave
And wrapped, dripping, in the death net

When bread bakers and fishermen
Came and lingered at dawn
      Beside the stone of time's ending.

I am an old man now. Every morning
    I send out five fishing boats.

I know this about time,
It has set me on a distant shore.
    It has given us history,
Not the circles of ceremony all men ought to rejoice in.

Today, in a western island, at least
    On a summer morning
    I can kneel at the Mass of Corpus Christi.

14 June 1993

Following a Lark (1996)

Following a Lark
A Country Boy Goes to School

1

There he is, first lark this year
        Loud, between
That raincloud and the sun, lost
Up there, a long sky run, what peltings of song!
        (Six times 6, 36. Six times 7, 42
        Six times eight is . . .)
Oh, Mr Ferguson, have mercy at arithmetic time
        On peedie Tom o' the Glebe.

2

There's Gyre's ewe has 2 lambs.
        Snow on the ridge still.
How many more days do I have to take
This peat under my oxter
        For the school fire?
(James the Sixth, Charles the First . . . Who then?)
Oh, Mr Ferguson, I swear
        I knew all the Stewarts last night.

3

Yes, Mistress Wylie, we're all fine.
        A pandrop! Oh, thank you.
I must hurry, Mistress Wylie,
        Old Ferguson
Gets right mad if a boy's late.
I was late twice last week.
        Do you know this, Mistress Wylie,
The capital of Finland is Helsingfors . . .
        Yes, I'll tell Grannie
You have four fat geese this summer.

4

When I get to the top of the brae
I'll see the kirk, the school, the shop,
    Smithy and inn and boatyard.
I wish I was that tinker boy
Going on over the hill, the wind in his rags.

Look, the schoolyard's like a throng of bees.

5

I wish Willie Thomson
    Would take me on his creel-boat!
'Tom, there's been six generations of Corstons
    Working the Glebe,
And I doubt there'll never be fish-scales
On your hands, or salt in your boots . . .'

(Sixteen ounces, one pound. Fourteen pounds, one stone.)
A sack of corn's a hundredweight.
    I think a whale must be bigger than a ton.

6

Jimmo Spence, he told me
    Where the lark's nest is.
    Beside a stone in his father's oatfield,
    The high granite corner.

('I wandered lonely as a cloud . . .' Oh where? What then?)

I could go up by the sheep track
    Now the scholars are in their pen
And *Scallop* and *Mayflower* are taking the flood
    And the woman of Fea
Is pinning her washing to the wind.

I could wait for the flutter of the lark coming down.

7

The school bell! Oh, my heart's
Pounding louder than any bell.

A quarter of a mile to run.
My bare feet
Have broken three daffodils in the field.

Heart thunderings, last tremor of the bell
And the lark wing-folded.

'Late again, Master Thomas Corston of Glebe farm.
Enter, sir. With the greatest interest
      We all await your explanation
Of a third morning's dereliction.'

A Boy in a Snow Shower

Said the first snowflake
No, I'm not a shilling,
I go quicker than a white butterfly in summer.

Said the second snowflake
Be patient, boy.
Seize me, I'm a drop of water on the end of your finger.

The third snowflake said,
A star?
No, I've drifted down out of that big blue-black cloud.

And the fourth snowflake,
Ah good, the road
Is hard as flint, it tolls like iron under your boots.

And the fifth snowflake,
Go inside, boy,
Fetch your scarf, a bonnet, the sledge.

The sixth snowflake sang,
I'm a city of sixes,
Crystal hexagons, a hushed sextet.

And the trillionth snowflake,
All ends with me –
I and my brother Fire, we end all.

Maeshowe: Midwinter

Equinox to Hallowmas, darkness
    falls like the leaves. The
    tree of the sun is stark.

On the loom of winter, shadows
    gather in a web; then the
    shuttle of St Lucy makes a
    pause; a dark weave
    fills the loom.

The blackness is solid as a
    stone that locks a tomb.
    No star shines there.

Then begins the true ceremony of
    the sun, when the one
    last fleeting solstice flame
    is caught up by a
    midnight candle.

Children sing under a street
    lamp, their voices like
    leaves of light.

Gray's Pier

I lay on Gray's pier, a boy
And I caught a score of sillocks* one morning

I laboured there, all one summer
And we built the *Swan*

A June day I brought to my door
Jessie-Ann, she in white

I sang the Barleycorn ballad
Between a Hogmanay star and New Year snow

sillocks: young coalfish

The *Swan* haddock-heavy from the west –
Women, cats, gulls!

I saw from the sea window
The March fires on Orphir

I followed, me in black
Jessie-Ann to the kirkyard

I smoke my pipe on Gray's pier now
And listen to the Atlantic

One Summer in Gairsay Isle

1 *Ivor*

The wings, leaning south, this April morning,
The beat of a sail, the lessening cry of the helmsman.
I that left my good arm in Ireland,
That assault on the keep,
Now I am going up from the shore
To study, all summer, corn-growth
And have my two ears washed
With women's words, all summer
(Ragna kneels, silent, at a rockpool)
And see all summer
Old men and boys rowing to creels.
All summer I must keep cows from the oatfield.
I can still fling a falcon on the gale.

Those who come back for harvest,
The ghosts who do not come back
At Lindisfarne fallen, or under a cliff in Brittany,
I am at ease with them.
I can drink with the living
And hear praise of the lost sailors, in winter.
I will not be despised
When the ship is furled in the shed like a golden bird
And the women fold themselves
In a decent silence, among looms and cheese moulds.

All but I will go out then with sickles.
Ragna will follow, bending and binding.

2 *The Girl*

That young broken Ivor,
I will go to his hut.
In the morning I'll lay and light his fire.

The hurt in his eye
On the hill, at the peat-bank,
Along the boat-cluttered shore!

The women of Gairsay
Bake, brew, weave for him.
They leave (unthanked) the offerings at his door.

I am not too ugly a girl,
I long to put honey in his mouth,
I would draw a comb through the blown corn of his hair.

Hild and Thora, those girls
Scatter the sweet looks all about him.
He curls his lip like a cur.

He will say the good word to one creature only,
His hawk hung
In torrents of high blue air.

3 *The Old Woman in the Kirk*

Here I am again with my few candles
Lady.
Let the corn have gentle falls
Of sun and wind and rain.
Let my old Thord bring in a few lobsters from under Scabra.

Ploughmen and shepherds
Are in the south again, in Sweyn's longship.
Let them not
Be washing their hands in too much gold and fire.

I pray, let the winter
Lie not too heavy on me and old Thord.
There is nothing so fine
As your face, Lady, above the seven small flames.

Saint Magnus will bid you often
Be good to his folk in the cold islands.
I am lighting a candle now
For one-armed Ivor and for Ragna
Married today by the Eynhallow monk.

The Journey

The spirit summons out of chaos
Galaxies
And sun moon stars
Then a tree with an apple and a bird,
A river with a fish,
A place of grass for lions and gazelles.

At last a man, a woman, a son and a daughter

All danced together,
The planets, mountains, forests, waters, islands, beasts, folk.

God said,
'All things I leave in your hands, man,
For praise and profit
But never leave the dance.'

In the end the man turned from the music.
He studied numbers.
He forged a key to open the golden door of the sun.

Let a path be made now by his children
From his ruined house, under
The apple tree, under
The broken scroll of the stars.
Let him set out, with the girl before him, guiding him.
(He is blind from the sun-probing)
His hand a withered leaf.

'On the far side of the hill
A boy will come with a lantern.
He will take us to the inn, father' . . .
A table was set with bread and bottle and lamp.
He danced there, old man, on sun-scarred feet.

Crossing the Alps
Macbeth King of Scotland and
Thorfinn Sigurdson Earl of Orkney

What should I say to Pope Clement?
   I do not know what I shall say
      Till the confession screen
Is there between us. Will it matter

If the Bishop of Rome doesn't understand
   My Gaelic, nor I his Latin?
      In truth, cousin, I hardly
Understand your Danish, but for

The courtesy and kindness that
   Flashes between us now and then
      Brighter than the high snows
We have ridden through since morning.

What should I say? I have killed a king.
   But in every court, from
      Scotland to India, powerful men
Stalk still like wolves in the forest

And Macbeth is marked in his turn
   For knife or poisoned cup.
      Besides, that king was weak
And the ordering of such beasts

Calls for puissance in sceptre and crown.
   The hands of the princes
      Frail as garden flowers.
Moreover, a nation needs a queen,

A strong mother to succour innocence.
   Sir, when I left Inverness, Gruath
      Walked many nights with a candle.
We will light heavenly candles for her

In the hundred churches of Rome.
   I have moreover this sack of pence
      To throw to the wayside poor.
Cousin, we have come to such friendship

On those perilous snow passes
   I know you will prevail on those
      Norwegian wolf-ships,
The men from the bays, Vikings, away

From our settled Scottish coasts, now
   I am threatened from south
      By the Saxons, from west
By the savages from Lewis and Argyll,

And your tables will never lack
   Salmon and Speyside usque
      Nor Ingibiorg your countess
Go without our cairngorms and silver.

Was there not Babel, the thousand
   Tongues? There's an angel
      Carries a heart's true sorrow
From penitent tongue to priestly ear

Urgent as the pleading of David's harp
   And the answer falls
      Purer than dew, silent
As manna in the desert. Look, cousin,

A gap of blue between the mountains.
   The groom goads the mule no more.
      Shall we halt beside this torrent?
The road winds down to orchards and vineyards.

To a Hamnavoe Poet of 2093

Language unstable as sand, but poets
    Strike on hard rock, carving
    Rune and hieroglyph, to celebrate
        Breath's sweet brevity.

Swan-path, whale-acre. Do you honour
    The sea with good images?
    We wear the sea like a coat,
        We have salt for marrow.

I hoard, before time's waste
    Old country images: plough-horse,
    Skylark, grass-growth,
        Corn-surge, dewfall, anvil;

Rain-trail from hill to hill, a hushing;
    Mayburn a penny whistle
    Lilting from Croval, lingering
        (Tinker-boy) under my window;

Creel-scattering gales; Thor's
    Hammer, studdering,* on Hoy.
    Do your folk laugh and cry
        With the gentle ups-and-downs

Not so different, I think
    From talk in Skarabrae doors,
    Celtic shepherds at Gurness,
        Sweyn's boatmen off Gairsay?

The masque unchanging, the maskers
    Wear different motley.
    'Ox' is 'tractor' now
        On the green surge of Fea.

So, image maimed more and more
    On the grid of numbers
    Folk must not forget
        The marks on the rock.

* studdering: reverberating

Keep vigil. The tongues flow yet
        To rhythms of sea and hill.
        Deeper than stone, guard
                The pure source, silence.

Anne Bevan, Sculptor
Hills, Woolcraft, Stone

'Good' said God as he made the
    wind, the sea, the fire, the
    folded hills

'Good' said the shepherd as he
    fleeced his flock

'Good' said the wife at the hearthstone
    spinning wool on her wheel

'Good' said the weaver as the shuttle
    clacked

'Good' said the housewife as she
    folded blankets in a basket, fresh
    from sun and wind

'Good' said the quarryman as he
    hewed a great stone from
    the mountain

'Good' said the sculptor as she
    made her sculpture

            *

To make things is to do well

        *

And to do things in harmony, all
    trades and images cohering, is
    to catch time and form in their
    flight, until all cry *Gloria*

328]   **A New Child: ECL**
      11 June 1993

   i

Wait a while, small voyager
   On the shore, with seapinks and shells.

The boat
   Will take a few summers to build
That you must make your voyage in.

   ii

You will learn the names.
That golden light is 'sun' – 'moon'
   The silver light
That grows and dwindles.

And the beautiful small splinters
   That wet the stones, 'rain'.

   iii

There is a voyage to make,
   A chart to read,
But not yet, not yet.
   'Daisies' spill from your fingers.
   The night daisies are 'stars'.

   iv

The keel is laid, the strakes
   Will be set, in time.
A tree is growing
   That will be a tall mast.

All about you, meantime
The music of humanity,
   The dance of creation
Scored on the chart of the voyage.

   v

The stories, legends, poems
Will be woven to make your sail.

You may hear the beautiful tale of Magnus
  Who took salt on his lip.
Your good angel
  Will be with you on that shore.

vi

Soon, the voyage of EMMA
  To Tir-Nan-Og and beyond.

vii

Star of the Sea, shine on her voyage.

**A Rainy Johnsmas
23 June: The Hill Fire**

JEREMIAH, FISHERMAN

Heavy showers for a week,
Wind nor-east
In the light lengthening.

    Not a star.

I think it's the old dinghy, *Simon*, for axe and fire.
She's been a hen-house now, twenty years.

MAISIE OF QUOYS

What does an old done wife
  Want with a cradle?

Two grown sons, five married daughters
  In Selskay, Canada, Hamnavoe.
Grandbairns along hill and shore
  Come and go like birds.

Take axe to crib, Maisie
  For the longest-day fire.

The bonny burn songs
  Lost, this June, with cloud slurpings.

MINISTER

The new minister says
    'No paganism from now on.
    Johnsmas, that's papish.
    I'm sure the Baptist never saw fire
Other than the desert sun
And maybe the small invisible flame
    He roasted locusts on . . . '

But Rev Murdo Keith
    Made no move to stop us
When we went with sacks of red peat,
    A bucket of tar, past the Manse.

Cover the kindling with a patched sail –
    Three days of rain now.

MAGGIE, SPINSTER

Fire! I want to see no more fires for ever
After the ale-fire and bread-fire
    I slaved over,
Beer a month, bannocks a week,

To keep the dance in the dancers
On the top of Fea,
The boys leaping like goats,
Flames washing the soles of their flying feet.

Four drenched bairns at the door
'Maggie, have you a few sticks, if you please, for the fire?'

SCHOOL-MASTER

Gifts of the crowned sun,
    Horses, bee-hives, bread
(We think fish
    Circle and surge with the moon
And fish-oil fills the winter lamps.)

No lamp in the crofts on Johnsmas Eve.

The scarecrow in Maggie's field
    Has a dark dripping sleeve.

St John the Baptist, you stood in the Jordan.
Purest water fell from your hands.
Bless our fire tonight. Bless
    The demptions* of rain.

Creator of sun, moon, stars
He stood with John among river rainbows.
    He later walked among hills
And dried his coat at fires
And read by a small lamp at midnight.

The Light of the World
    Broke bread with fisher folk.

The poor folk of an island
    Honour you, St John.
Tomorrow's the brightest day of the year.

What's a raindrop or two in the long grass?
    A lucent trembling orb.

MANSIE'S WIFE

This Johnsmas Eve
    Fewer dancers than last year.
A hundred fewer on the hill-top
    Since Mansie, the oldest dancer
    (He threw down cap and stick
And hobbled, ale-flown,
    A sunward step or two)
Was dandled, a bairn,
In flame shadows and sunset.

The two fiddlers went home
    Drenched, early.

The young laird says, 'Another rain-storm
And their corn will be green mush!'

    *

---

* demptions: heavy rain-showers

The Johnsmas Fire
Was never lit on Fea again.

Black Thorbjorn

'In Acre, sickness broke out in the ship's company, and many men of
note died, including Thorbjorn the Black, Iceland poet'
                                        Orkneyinga Saga

1

The best poets live in Iceland.
I have a farm there.
It is a long house – cows
Winter in one end.
          At the other end, barn and kiln.
I have been known to scythe hayfields.
          I've put a ring in a bull's nose.
          But men say, behind their hands
          'Thorbjorn with the black beard
Is the worst farmer in Broadfirth'.

2

I said to my father,
          'The wife you are bringing here for me
          Let her be good with horses.
          She must have strong shoulders
To row the boat to the salmon.
I expect good goat cheeses,
          Ale that comes brisk from the keg
To marry with honey' . . .

I must give my strength
          To the welding of rune and kenning.

Lo, with the dowry (a hundred silver pieces)
Has come this mingy creature
          With wheel and coloured wools.

3

A ship from the Baltic,
      Two French priests, a Flemish deacon
      Wine, tapestries for the cathedral.

Their word is, Rognvald of Orkney
      Will be Jerusalem-faring, come spring.

Rognvald of Orkney, poet, earl, skipper
      Wants poets for five ships.
He'll get cut-throats, roof-burners,
      Icon-breakers, drouths*
(But generally those Orkney seamen
Can set a sail to drink wind
      From the edges of a storm.)

4

It is a fortunate thing, I have here
      At the farm Oykell
      A good cattle-man, a passable shepherd,
Two butter and cheese girls

And a rheumaticky uncle
That still has a way with crab-creels,

      Or Thorbjorn the poet
Would be a beggar in his own farm

Distracted from the difficult craft of verse
      By this butterfly of a bride.

5

I took two dowry mintings. I passed
      A week in a Reykjavik tavern
      Mostly drunk, with Ubi, Oddi, Arni,
      Poets from the fjords.

We sang, boasted, quarrelled.
      Ubi's harp a tangle of oak and wires at midnight.

* drouths: drunkards

'Good skalds are voyagers,
    Drinkers of gale and battle' . . .

'No, but the storm of images
Draws the mind beyond Rus or Markland
    Though the poet
Never leaves circle of lamplight' . . .

Then this sleaze of a taverner,
    'Thorbjorn, sir, the two silver pence
    Were exhausted
With the last clash of your ale-cups,

And Oddi, glacier poet
Has broken a valuable carved horn'.

6

I said to my butterfly
    'Let your brothers come! Let
The graybeard come, the father, a rascal
Tore fields from twelve poor men
    To build a long hall at Eshaness.
In Thorbjorn's farm
    A wife must be early at cheeseboard,
    Beehive, spinning wheel, hearthstone,
Not dimpling daylong upon needles and coloured wools,
Not destroying the silence
    Skald or monk must wear about him always'.

7

Ragnhild, butterfly, out and off
    Across glacier, across
The burning mountain. But back
    Before the first snow. 'Thorbjorn,
I intend to be now a thrifty wife.
I can make a pot of ox-broth.
Look, Thorbjorn, the reddened arms
    From baking, steeping clothes!'

By then, my sea-chest was roped.
Ubi, Oddi, Arni
      Stood shuffling at the byre wall,
Harps on shoulders.
      Bishop with crozier on the shore stones.
Sail fluttered at *Raven*'s mast.

The milk girls wept in the byre door.

'My Ragnhild, you have done well.
    I will bring you
    A bolt of red silk from Paris.
I will pray for my farm-wife
    In the kirks of Byzantium.
Ragnhild, honey-bee, expect your wordman
In five years, or six, or whenever'.

Winter and Summer

1

The old scant-silver King,
Ice axes
Have hewn him down.

      Give him to the ocean.
      Lay in the ship his long bones.

The death ship burns, south-west horizon, early afternoon.

2

The world's winter.
      Twelve old folk
Have followed their king
But into an earth-wave, a howe.*

But you, old crofter-fisherman
Sit at your smouldering peats awhile.
      Ponder time. Be patient.

* howe: burial mound

3

So the Norse skalds: an end
      In ice and fire, Earth

A bitter drop in an ocean of numbers,
Lost note in a music beyond understanding.

4

Ploughmen break furrows
      But for more graves.

There are no fires
      When fishermen's throats
      Are blocked with salt, westward.

5

Fountains of light, never. Flamings
      Of the last fire, drifted
      Flakes of snowdrop, crocus, rose.

6

The drowned King
Left the stone wreck at midnight. He stood
      Knee-deep in daffodils.

Soon tongues of fire
      Made poets of all the fishers and ploughmen.

7

Midsummer. The ascended King
      Stores the island
With honey and green corn.

Fiddles, a dance on the hill,
      A midnight fire.

And the ship veers
      Towards the islands shaped like loaves.

A Calendar of Kings

They endured a season
Of ice and silver swans.

Delicately the horses
Grazed among snowdrops.

They traded for fish, wind
Fell upon crested waters.

Along their track
Daffodils lit a thousand tapers.

They slept among dews.
A dawn lark broke their dream.

For them, at solstice
The chalice of the sun spilled over.

Their star was lost.
They rode between burnished hills.

A fiddle at a fair
Compelled the feet of harvesters.

A glim on their darkling road.
The star! It was their star.

In a sea village
Children brought apples to the horses.

They lit fires
By the carved stones of the dead.

A midwinter inn.
Here they unload the treasures.

Winter: An Island Boy

A snowflake
Came like a white butterfly on his nose.

His mother's bucket
Was blue splashings at the well.

And grandpa
Was notching hooks like stars on his lines
Down at the noust.*

The school locked for Yule
– Time was a bird with white wings.

A swan on the loch
Bent its head like a flower.

He was lost on the hill till sundown
In a dream of snow.

Hunger and lamplight
Led the wanderer home.

A black peat, stirred
Unsheathed claws like a cat
On the purring hearth.

One white star
Walked slow across the pane.

St Peter and St Paul

I

Here where I write poems,
Three generations ago
A clerk
Wrote invoices in a ledger, concerning
        Consignments of 'Old Orkney' whisky.
He headed each letter
Stromness Distillery, June the 29th, 1900

* *noust: boat shelter*

The boats were in from the west.
    The seven fishermen
Had sold their haddocks along the street,
    Threepence a pound,
Weighing the fish on brass hand-scales.
The calendar
Behind Billy Clouston's bar counter
    Is ringed June 29.
Flett's ale is twopence the schooner
    To the scaled and salted fishermen.

3

An old blind man
Sits on a bench on a pier in the sun.
    He has thumbed his bible
Cover to cover, more than once
And he knows Peter
    Better than the famous whalers of his youth,
And Paul blinded with glory
On a road a bit like the road to Kirkwall
    (Not the drifting webs
    That dimmed his sea-wrinkled eyes)
But this summer day he doesn't see
    Today is the Feast of Peter and Paul.

4

Mrs Ross, postmistress
    Date-stamps her little flock of letters
'Stromness, 29 June 1900'.
    A postman – my father maybe –
Will take them in a sealed bag
    Down to the mail-boat 'St Ola'.

And the birds will fly
    To Birsay, Edinburgh, St Johns, Sydney.

And Mrs Ross ponders letters with exotic stamps:
    'San Pedro', 'Sao Paulo'.

5

'This on the haddock's gills'
  Says Sinclair, fisherman, to a tourist
Sketching his boat and pier
Is Peter's fingerprints'.

But Peter's fingerprint on the living silver
Is too small for the water-colour.

  And Paul is a sea-echo only
To a far-travelled wealthy amateur artist.

6

Captain Halcro, skipper,
  Takes snuff, tells the minister
  Yes, indeed, he knows the waters
  St Paul sailed over, the rock
Paul shipwrecked on, in Malta.

Captain James Halcro
Has a very fine house behind the ramshackle town.
  He dines frequently
With Mr Rae at Clestrain and Mr Thom, Sheriff.

At each month's end
He visits Peter Halcro, fisherman,
  At the door they were born in, twins
Sixty-two years ago.

A pound. 'For twine, not rum, man . . .'

7

The kirk an old fisherman
  Will be buried from today
Is called St Peter's.

The globe-girdling ocean,
St Paul's waves peal forever
  On the beach below the kirkyard.

And tomorrow is the Feast of Peter and Paul.

The Old Wife and the Hill Folk

What were they that passed my door?
        A shower
    Hid them from me.
    A few shapes only in the cloud I could see

At the end of the road, as they went
        Slow and bent
    On up the hill
    Past the fold, into the last of the outspill

And whisper of rain. They were
        The tinker
    And his bairns and pony
    Loaded with kettles, going on to their stony

Hollow from the Hamnavoe Fair.
        Oh, I fear
    The fated folk
    Who'll stand round my bed soon with cinders
        and a glimmering wick.

Lux Perpetua

A star for a cradle

Sun for plough and net

A fire for old stories

A candle for the dead

     *

Lux perpetua
By such glimmers we seek you.

Five Christmas Stars

1 *Spinning Wheel*

The wheel utters a long gray line.
    An old woman
    Is turning her wheel at the fire.

The sun goes behind the hill.
    She lights her lamp.
    The wool lies in a drift on the floor.

Some winter morning
    She'll waken to a web of whitest wool
    Hung over the tall straw chair

For a bridal or a christening
    Or for a shrouding at harvest.

2 *Bairn Song*

What does Dapple say in the byre?

Dapple says
    'They give me turnips and hay by lantern-light.
    Last summer
    God gave me grass and clover,
    Sun, wind, a blue sky, a green hill, dew in the morning
    And I gave them milk butter cheese.'

That's what Dapple's saying,
Bairn
In the byre on Yule morning.

3 *Stars and Fish*

The sky shoal is out tonight,
    Stars in a surge!

Two fish on a blue plate
Suffice
For one croft, for the great world-hunger.

'How shall we know
The sun
Won't grow weaker and frailer yet
Till he's the dead King
With hair frail as snowflakes
And a star locked in his eye?' . . .

In the croft ben-room
A bairn sleeps
Through a night of storm and star-gifts.

5 *Star*

No more fishing till after Yule.
Haddock
      Will glimmer silent through cold gray halls.
The tractor is locked in the barn
With a sack of seed.

The hill humps like a white whale.

The glim of one star
      On a shore boulder, where the ebb begins.

Homage to Burns

1 *Hebridean*

'A book of poems is it?'
      Said the old man in Uist.
'When was it ever known
Songs between boards like caged birds?

Tell me more about this Burns –
      Has the wild rose
      Spilled over his hand ever, like heart's-blood?

The oppressor and the hypocrite,
Has he driven them, with bitter laughter, out of the glen?

Has he run his eye along ploughshare
     And broacher of blood, those edges?

But poetry should be given on the wind, like a lark or a
     falcon'.

2 *Minister*

Rev Wm Clouston of Stromness:
One box books
From McCriven, booksellers, in the Canongate of Edinburgh.

The carter goes away with his fee.

Mr Clouston: 'Pope's *Iliad*,
Not a patch, I warrant, on the far-horizoned Greek,
But worthy the perusal.
Blair. Rousseau. Shenstone.
What, here? *Poems and Songs Mainly in the Scottish
     Dialect . . .*

Yes, Jane, the snuff-horn.
And light, if you please, that lamp on the table.

3 *Skipper*

What, Simpson, what's that they're singing below?
What – repeat, please –
'A man's a man for a' that' . . .
There will be none of that Jacobinry on this ship.
Tell them, find better words.
A man
May be king or beggar, Simpson,
It's better so, every man
Locked in his place in the great music of society.
It was thus from the beginning of things.

A man's a man for a' that
On this ship a man is a sailor
And Simpson, I am the skipper.

Lermontov. Byron. Burns.
The poets
Drop fruits from the great tree of poetry,
Lemon, pineapple, pear
And the roots locked in the hearts of men.
The Scotsmen,
Their poems are the wild sweet berries that purple the tongue.

Adieu for evermore, my dear . . .

Even here, in Petersburg
As the coach comes to take Nadia away.

5 *Sugar Planter*

'To Robt Burns, Mauchline, Ayrshire, Scotland –'

There's no such place as Scotland more,
Write, 'North Britain'.

Has written poems, has he?

Rest assured, Mr Burns will write no poems in Jamaica,
Mr Robert Burns
Will be too taken up with account books, ledgers.
Here the black slaves do the singing.

Proceed 'Dear Sir,
We are in receipt of your letter of application of 16th ult' . . .

6 *Professor*

Was at the professor's last night, was he,
The rustic bard?
I thought Professor Blackie
Might open his door to worthier guests.

Here is one professor of law
Will not be entertaining
The wild warbler from the west.

89.

Mr MacAndrew, listen.
The cloak of poetry is ancient and rich and jewel-encrusted.
It is not to be hung on a scarecrow between
The plough and the sickle.

7 *A Looker into the Seeds of Time*

In the starswarm is a world
In that world is a country
In that country is a mountain
In that mountain is a quarry
In that quarry is a stone
On that stone is a name

    The stone lacks chisel yet
    That quarry is unbroken yet
    The mountain has no root yet
    The country is the floor of a lake
    The world is a wheel of dust and fire,
    It turns
    Through chaos, blackness, silence.

      Now read the rune of the stone
      ROBERT BURNS POET

The Lords of Hell and the Word
A Poem for Burns Day

I

Stop every bard, poet, versifier,
    Tragedian, laureate, balladman.
Too many have slipped through
    To stand always in the choirs of Light.

Sift them, dust by ash.
    There should be no song in the urn.
The reports came in, in thousands.
    Only a whisper now and then,
      A sigh through the skull
Lost soon among root and rut.

346]

Sir, a sailor lost,
    No dust songs, salt in his throat.
    His last Atlantic cry
A call to a girl on the far shore,
    A shout between two waves.

Is this a poem?

We may have lost that faceless one,
    He crossed over with such a vivid mouth.

3

Frail lamps of clay, the Light is in them.
    Jars of clay, they keep
A handful of the threshed winnowed grain.
Clay flutes, their flawed chambers echo
    The original Word.

So, for all their droopings to dust,
    Our lordly Lie is never complete.

We have uttered winter on earth, centuries long.
    A ploughman
Seeks, in his barn, with a lantern
    A warped plough,
His flesh, graining to sure dust
Transfigured with hopeful harvest dances.

How, in such brutish clay
    To set our subtle black sentence . . .

4

We have our eyes, lord
    On a young farmer
With a liking for fiddles and girls
    And verses in chapbooks.
    He rhymes in a ledger in his father's attic.

We know his kind well.
Seedsmen's bills, worm in the corn,
    Taxman in May and November
Tear the strings from the mouth, soon enough.

Leave the Ayrshire rustic
    To the rusts and rots of a few winters.

5

Lord, a young man in Vienna
    Slipped by us two days ago.
    We saw pauper clods
Thudding down on the coffin.

Another boy has come
    To another attic in Vienna.
A dark-browed leveller: Beethoven.

Block his hearing. Choke
    The pure runnels of song – strike
    The music-man deaf!

6

Question every caller, every long silence
    At the kirkyard gate.
If the mouth
Has uttered bitterness at the end,
    Denial, hate, hunger
    For more goods, gear, gold
Near the tollgate of death
    The man is ours, poet or pauper or pilgrim
And the seamless Song poorer by a tatter.

Sir, the bards are few on earth now.
Since that German engraver
    Cut Gothic letters on wood-blocks
Maggots
    Scrithe* by millions in the corpse of Language.

* scrithe: proliferate

Sir, the farmer you said, *Ignore him*
    He stood against his troubles,
Debt, poverty, defamation,
    Blaze of flattery, a last painful
    Stooping to dust,

And the harp of his mouth
    Stronger, winter by winter.

Against such radiance in the clay
    Our lanterns were black.

We have lost the farmer-poet, I think.

We will try diminishment now
    With couthy quotes, skirlings, haggis suppers.

February

I

How will he be remembered
    The old king, Winter?
In offices, barracks, libraries the whisper 'In this reign
    Evil walks through the land,
Children hollow, the face of age is stark, fishermen
Challenge the impossible west,
His tax-men trench
    The last corn sacks, a wolf
Slinks through the city square at moonrise.'

So the best minds conspired
By candle-light, behind locked doors.

'We know the tyrant has gone up now
    To his highest castle, beside eagles.'

II

To the eagle-watching king, in the high battlement
Have ridden six doctors
Besides the one trusted royal physician,
Breathers on the ruddiness in cinders,
      Bringers of the poppy,
One to still for an hour the shifting bone-rack.

Majesty shows itself, thrice in the day
Lest the fowlers and foresters
And the folk in the high snow village say
      'Is this true, that our king is sick?'
      'No. For we saw him on his horse this morning, up near
         the torrent'.

III

The old laureate wrote on his page –
'This king will be remembered for cruelty and coldness,
For stern performance, which is love.

Did the tax-man trouble the sack of seed corn?

The thrush throbbed on a snow bough
The root will raise a green fountain
Through the ruined tree of kings.

Logs are brought to winter fires,
Ice is broken at the well.

The king lies in the frosts and fires of time
That a poor peasant
Might bring betimes a sickle to cornstalks.'

IV

Rumour is, the enemy is in movement again, in the south,
In the forest, among bird marshes.
It was said, a few tribes of bandits only.

A flag, trumpets, soldiers with skis and guns
      Would uproot the outlaws.
The column has not come home yet.
One, a deserter, was seized
Drinking wine that tasted of tar

In a sea tavern.
'They carried branches', said the man before he was shot.
          'Their guns were wreathed in flowers,
          We fled from the sun on their foreheads.
          They unlocked the frozen waterfall . . .'

The veterans have received notice, the heroes
Of November and December.
So it is rumoured. It will take more than leaves
To overcome our guardsmen.

V

The old king has trouble in sleeping, now.
He has asked the chancellor's boy
          To read the Iceland stories,
Njal, Grettir, the Vinlanders,
          Men who hoarded light like silver
Between the two darknesses

The better to relish ale and wolf meat
          At the Feast of Solstice.
(One sits at the high seat, hooded, a stranger)
Silver rings are given to guest and stranger.

'Sire, here are urgent missives from the fortress . . .'

'Sire, the chaplain has come with missal and oil . . .'

VI

The seal of the master-shipwright, broken
          'Sire, the carpenters fitted the last strake yesterday,
          A bronze battering.
          The figurehead has its inlay of ore,
          Its golden look will burn the horizon haar.
          Sire, the Trondheim carvers
          Have rimmed the hull with tree runes.
          Women sat all winter
          At the weaving of the one broad sail.
          The mead jars are shipped now, sufficiency of loaves.
          Thwarts are of the best oak,
          The mast a single pine from the snow-line.
          Lacketh not anything now
          But loosened ropes, the dripping anchor

That majesty might stand with helmsman soon, looking
to westward,
To Hesper, away from this shore of exile'.

VII

The grand-daughter of the king
Lights her lamp late in the afternoon now.
A month ago
The yellow circle was thrown early
On her page, on her sewing-frame.

In a little glass on the high sill
The gardener has set fresh snowdrops.

She knows that her reign will not be long.

When the first star looks through her window
Then she will seek out the old king
Up and around and along the labyrinth.
She will put her mouth
To the quiet flung storm of his beard.

Daffodil Time

I DAFFODILS

Ho, Mistress Daffodil, said Ikey (tinker)
Where have you been all winter?
There was snow in the ditches last night
And here you are.
Did you light your lamp in that blizzard?

When Ikey came back
Next day, with his pack, from windy Njalsay
The yellow hosts
Were cheering and dancing all the way to the inn.

That idle brute of a man of hers
– Jean's phrase –
Has gone to the garden shed this morning
Instead of to the *Arctic Whaler*.
And Jock has scraped
Rust and cobwebs off a spade
And there he stands, idle ale-man, in the sun
Leaning on the spade, eyeing
That square of sodden sand and clay.

After his broth and fish
He asks Jean for half-a-crown.
'For drink? Nothing doing' . . .
'For seed tatties from the village shop, woman.'

3 STONE

The stone that wore darkness like the minister's coat
All winter,
Where the crow furled, where
Snow lingered longest –
    Look, now, sunrise
    Is tilting its jar of light over the world
    And now, this noon,
    A random splash has hit the winter stone.

4 SCHOOL

In the island school
The children's heads
Are like green sheaths that will open soon.

And one of the seven shadows
Has left Mr McSween's face.

A lark glitters out song along the lift of the hill
And the bird
Is louder today than the chanted
Multiplication table.

And the globe of the world
In the dark corner, has a splash of light.

And Mr McSween says, like
A solemn song, 'This
Afternoon the Easter holiday begins
But now, again – and better this time – the three times
      table' . . .

And twenty-one faces
Open like daffodils.

5 MONASTERY

Monkerhouse, is this it,
The ruin among the tombstones
Where once
The sanctuary light glowed like a ruby
And the sanctus bell
Beckoned, from winter, corn folk and fish folk?

Hoy Sound
Swallowed the good stones long ago.

Four and a half centuries
   the angels' hour-glass
Are but a whisper of time between
Good Friday and Easter morning.

The sea will give up its dead
The rock will break into cornstalks
The drowned bell will cry:
     Laudate dominum in sanctuario.

6 THE RUIN

Scollie, Baltic merchant, he built the house,
Clean new stone,
A garden with roses and hives.

When does a house begin to rot?
After the blessing
Flies out like a bird, then
The strongest house is open to worm and rot.

Smiley, lawyer, lived here. Eunson,
Grocer and smuggler,
Stewart, a poor dominie
    (For three generations
      Not a child laughed in the long hall),
Smith the carter,
Ronaldson with trauchled* wife and twelve bairns,
All kept by the poor fund.

That grand house,
It's like a skull for thirty years now.

Strangers – who? – have bought the ruin.
I saw, last Sabbath,
A new rooftree inside the walls.

7 SPRING BLIZZARD

An April northerly. I sit
In the lee of the crag
Tarring my yole†, *Charity*.

Another flake flurry – old Bessie Millie
Plucking her hens. I sit
In the lee of a rock
    Tarring this yole, *Charity*.

Spring: The Kids of Feaquoy Farm

I

And one day after school
    The lamp stood gray on the dresser
      That had lit all teatimes since October.

---

trauchled: bedraggled   †*yole: fishing-boat*

Willie dug his horn spoon in his egg.
      Strange he thought it, the dead lamp
      But he said nothing.

A leaf of light
      Opened in the branches of his blood.

2

Saturday. Maggie astray on the hill.
      What's the faltering light
Beside Peg the old ewe?
      One knock-kneed lamb.
And they'd marked old Peg
      For one last fleece,
      For a few smoked scrag-ends and chops.

3

The island hill was scarved in smoke,
      The cleansing muirburn.
Tom found a first daisy beside a stone.
      Was the rooted granite
      Guarding the fragile earth-flame,
      Or had the daisy
A message from the dead to the stubborn rock?

      That night
The burning hill Fea washed out the stars.

4

A shroud of darkness from north.
'Lambing snow,' says an old farmer.

Anna could see
Neither Bu nor boats nor the next croft
      Through the dark surges.
Flakes clung to the window of Feaquoy,
      A thousand glimmering moths.

A blue sky chasm soon!
There, on the island loch,
      Twelve dingy swans.

The tractor up to the axle in a drift.

And father in from the byre
With cheeks like turnip lanterns.

5

Miss Simpson, teacher
Has a jar of daffodils on her desk.
Wilma brought the tight buds, drooping.
They open, flower by flower.
That stern stone face
Is lit, between history and sums.

6

Old Merran's score of Rhode Islands
Are never done laying!
Here's another orb glowing in her hand.

Tomorrow (Saturday)
Wilma and Maggie, Willie and Anna and Tom
Will come with pace*-egg baskets
To plunder (pleading) her hoard.

7

On Easter Day, the journey is over,
The fourteen
Stations of the death-faring.

A boy in white is lighting the paschal candle.
The lilies lie in the chapel window.

The old priest, entering
Is robed in white.

The people kneel, like a new wave breaking.
(But that wave, four centuries since, was drawn back
Into the loom of ocean, a glittering thread.)

pace: Easter

Seven women at the seven gates of the city.
    One has scales on her arms from the fish market,
    One fire-flushed from the kneaded oats and the oven,
    One an old woman, the eyes broken webs,
    One comes running, water spilling from the jar on her
        shoulder,
    Veronica plucks a shred of wool from her mouth.
    One has issued
    From a place of silver and silk and mirrors,
    A child is there, splashed with buttercups, dew,
        dawnlight.

They sing *Magnificat*. They sing *Ave Maria*.
Their mouths are dark soon with *Dies Irae*.

    *

A cry from the city square, 'He is fallen' . . .
        'His shoulder is bruised' . . .
Then trumpet, wheel, a scatter of hooves.

    *

    The women have left the seven gates of the city.
    They stand here and there, among crowds
    On the Road of Thorns, that goes on up the hill.
    On one side a field of green corn and a vineyard.
    On one side fishnets drying in the wind.

    The Man will come soon, carrying the dead tree.

Stations of the Cross: Veronica

Close your linen-shop, Veronica.
Who buys and sells
    The day a death-sentence is given?

This young man
I saw among the palms and shouting children!
    He must carry the dead tree.

He is not riding an ass today.
He is on his face, in swirls of hot dust.

A woman says his name
Like a mother that calls her child in from play.

He can't bear that baulk further.
A countryman slopes the burden across his shoulder.

I'm a quiet woman. But I took
A napkin I wove this morning
        To the blood, thorns, dust, sweat, on his face.

The centurion thrust me back. Six soldiers
Dragged him again to his feet.

There is weeping along the road.
The town women
Think of their sons, all the Sorrows of Man.

I would (but for the guardsmen)
Gather him up from the hot stones.

I would
Weave for such a one a coat of great beauty.

God created trees
For birdsong and fruit, not for this.

Tell me, sir – I can't read –
What is the writing on the tree?
        THE KING OF THE JEWS

Now the mother folds him home.
The child has never
Come back to such a sleep at evening, out of the country
        fields.

Go home now, Veronica, to your looms.
In a field outside the city
        See, a sower is burying seed in a furrow.

The cold Roman eye, hand on seal.
Vale. Take the thief away.

'You carry your own tree, Jimmy . . .'
Another gallowsbird behind.
One ahead, burdened, a bruised brightness.

I've carried millstones, wine-vats, a mast.
That one was a carpenter.
His knees buckle under the heavy baulk.

My mother, poor woman, is dead.
His mother is here. Poor woman. Poor woman.

Look, Simon's come into town
With an ox to sell.
They've laid another yoke on Simon.

Veronica, seamstress. No napkin ever
Soaked up such blood and sweat.

I stagger but I don't fall.
The sneak-thief plods like a mule.
The bright one, he's down again.

Those women! Miriam, Judith, Esther
Go home, sing over your cradles.
Sing among looms and pots.

Below, cornfields and vineyards.
A third time, fallen,
He tastes golden dust.

The soldiers won't bother, I think,
Haggling over my coat.
No scarecrow would wear a rag like that.

Silence – curses – from cross and cross.
From the mid-ark
A dove wings out into the blackest storm.

Thrust of lance into heart-root.
The soldiers are coming with mallets
To break the legs of the thieves.

The eyes of the mother
Drown all the world in pity and love.
The hammer beats on my knee.

That the hands of such a woman
Fold me gravewards,
Bear me and all men in her folds of light.

Easter in an Island

1 PACE EGGS

They cross the hill with their little baskets
To farm after farm
And the farm wife sets a warm egg in every basket.

The dog barks at the troop of children
From the end of the barn.

And maybe there's one old wife
Who shuts her door against them.

And Lisa takes them in to her fire
Out of the cold wind
And butters a bannock for them, with rhubarb jam.

And the cock rears high on the barn roof.
He rings out rage or triumph.

2 CHOCOLATE EGGS

'What'll they think of next?'
Says Tom at the village shop
To the sweetie traveller from Dundee –
        '*Chocolate eggs*' . . .

And the traveller in the bowler hat
Writes in his order book,
'One score chocolate Easter eggs
For Thomas Yule, merchant, Selskay.'
Then Bella Smith came in for a stone of sugar
For the spring brewing.

3 MUIRBURN

On the hill three young men with heather torches
At the muirburn.
Drifts of smoke over heather and peat-bog.
After sunset
The hill is scarred red with fires.

And the three men at the inn
Washing the muirburn soot out of their throats.

4 SPRING-CLEANING

What's wrong with the women?
Out! Get Out! they rage at their men.

They're on their knees with bucket and clout
Till the stone floor
Shines like blue mirrors.
And the chaff beds are beaten outside till stour*
Darkens the sun,
And their panes glitter like stars.
(There's been a mighty rout of spiders.)

Even the cat has left this madhouse
And sits, tail lashing, on the planticru wall.

At tea-time, it's as if the first wind of time
Had blown through every house.

Schoolgirls, in troops,
Drift home, spilling first daisies.

* stour: dust

No ordinary cookies, today;
Richan the baker
Has shaken a pot of spice into the dough
And every blob of dough
He crosses with strips of damp pastry.

'There!' says Richan the baker.
'Let the hearth-women try to do that –
Them and their mud-tasting bannocks' . . .
And he blows up the bakehouse fire.

Jimmy the apprentice
Carries a smoking basket of hot-cross buns
Out to the grocery van.

6 SATURDAY

The *Beagle, Skarfie, Trust,* fishing boats
Had no longing for the West
On Good Friday.
Today's a fine day for the haddocks, too
But the twelve fishermen
Sit on the rock, smoking their pipes.

Tomorrow is Sabbath.

Come Monday morning, we'll hear
Their blue-gray shouts along the shore,
Shriek of keel upon stone,
The sails yearning westward into a sea-growl
Before the lark is up.

7 GRAVEDIGGER

There's no other way. Flaws, gravedigger,
Has been in the kirkyard all day
Making a grave for the tinker
Who died a quarry-death.

The end of the road, he says
With every spadeful of clay.

It comes to us all, puffing his pipe
To the sculpted marble over the laird's wife,
To the blue sea-stone for the fisherman's boy.
    (They ended the journey last month)

The wonder of it, the wonder,
Turning a skull with his spade.
Lark song spatters a hundred gravestones.

In at the gate come seven men
And one is wound in the long silence.

A Landlady in Emmaus

I was just thinking, 'I hope Tom and Ed
Haven't got themselves in the jail' –
I knew they'd been going to the meetings
And when they could find the time
They'd been following this preacher through the villages,
Driving here and there in their van –
When there came Tom's knock at the door
(I know Tom's knock, it's different
From the soldiers' or the taxman's knock).
I tell you, I *was* glad . . .

Now the preacher's dead, him
That put such disturbance on the countryside,
And took Tom from forge and anvil
And Ed from his sheep, days on end,
Maybe they'll settle down now,
Get married, and put a little by
For a house and a garden, and be good citizens
Like they were meant to be.
I was never tired of telling them that.
That's what I thought, when I heard the news on the radio.

I like Tom and Ed, they've been boarders two years
At this establishment, but since the preacher
Came to the city they've been in their rooms

One night in seven, if that.
And they're not what they were, I don't know how
But they're different, more cheerful and careless
And they never come home drunk
And they'll stop to talk to a child or a bird in the dust
And once I saw them with the blind man
Whose eyes (they say) are full of light now.
Well, I thought, going to them meetings
Is better than being with the football hooligans.

Then the newspaper headlines – TERRORIST LEADER
    ARRESTED,
The road-blocks, the blackout, identity cards,
Soldiers everywhere, the city in turmoil,
One day all flags and songs, the next
Black with guns, loudspeakers, lamentation,
And men scattered to the caves and the bitter shores.
Then trial and sentence, and the execution on the hillside
– It was all on TV, with theologians and politicians
Telling us what it all meant –
It was then I worried most about my lodgers.
'They're only hangers-on at best,' I thought,
'The authorities won't worry about the likes of them' . . .
Still, you never know, in a time of troubles
The guilty go free, the innocent are caught in the net.

I set a supper that night for *three*, not two,
A bottle of wine and a new loaf,
Just what Tom and Ed always liked
After a long day of sun and dust,
One from the smithy, one from the sheepfold.
I didn't like it, a stranger
They'd given a lift to on the dark road.
You never know who's a spy or informer
Nowadays, and the man's head was hooded
And the one candle (there was a power-cut too)
Hollowed his face, and lit
Only the strong beautiful mouth.
Tom said, 'You're welcome. Break the bread.'
The words of blessing
Came like the first and the last music.
He stretched out a wounded hand

To the loaf on the plate.
The cowl fell back. I saw then
The crusted ore and rubies at the temple.

Trinity
Sailing to Greenland

Cargo
Stowed trees into *Blue Swan*, three days
At Hamnavoe, brought thence
From Man and Tummel
    Shipwrights in Iceland
Might make keels of, powerful ocean curves,
    Stout rooftrees in plenty
      For craftsman and carver.

Less trees in that island
    Leif told us – cook and lookout –
    Than in Hoy, Papay, even.

Wood is weighed against thick silver.

Fiddler
Shetlanders offered us dried fish.
    'Take Lowrie, fiddler
For cheer on the bleak ocean' . . .

We knew, before Torshavn
    The boy Lowrie to be an apprentice music-man
Bundled from Yell
For wool-reft, creel-reft, night-goer
    Among the shore houses.

Oarsmen blocked ears against a screeching.
    Thorfinn had that boy
    More at the bailing-can than fiddle.

Whalemeat
We had to guard our cargo seven nights
    In Faroe, such hunger was
    For oak, sycamore, larch.

Gorges rose against raw whalemeat,
Throats rasped from that ale.

Ballad-making in a long barn.
    Lowrie returned with a hundred verses,
The bird at his shoulder
    Shrieked farewells to Mykines.

Monkfish
Blue Swan had sailed Rinansay down
    Three days after Easter.

Leif shaded eyes east and west
    For wolf ships, Vikings.

Sven and Rolf released monkfish jaws
From bone hooks, a hundred.

We gave heads and tails of monkfish
    To a ship of Irish monks.
They gave us a blessing
Cleaner and brighter than a jumping salmon.

Trond, helmsman, asked for a strong curse
On the demon in Lowrie's fiddle.

Vale
In Reykjavik we had bitter news.
    Three ships from Norway
Had held east from Iceland
At Pentecost, the holds empty
    By half a Norwegian forest.

Our skipper: 'Icelandic trick
    To get the timber for next to nothing,
        For a cartload of ewe-cheese heavy as stone' . . .
We held west. Lowrie
Made a tune 'Farewell to Iceland'.

368]   *Floes*
The easterly storm, two floes
    We sailed between, ice jaws
Would have cracked our ship like a nut,
Rudder broken, Bui from Rousay
    Licked by a green sea-tongue, lost.

First sun-glitters. Quiet waters.

Then Sven, 'Bergs are far south this spring.
    Better we should point prow
At Vinland, rim of the golden bowl'.

Angel bird
We heard Mass with Greenlanders
In the bishop's kirk, two days
    After good trading for bear skins, walrus tusks.
Much eagerness for the Scottish timber.

We covered the ale casks.
    This had been told us,
Greenlanders, after drink, roamed like wolves.

On Trinity Sunday, between
Boys singing *Sanctus* and *Benedictus*
    Lowrie made an interlude.
    The old bishop said,
'That boy's bird-shaped box,
Surely an angel lives in it'.

Crusaders in Orkahowe

Norwegians wintered in Orkney in 1151, before the great
northern crusade under Earl Rognvald II of Orkney (1151–4).
They carved runes in the burial chamber Maeshowe, called by
them Orkahowe.

1

Ghosts guard here a great treasure, men say.
    The Orkahowe ghosts
Drove some men mad, they

Shelterers from a blizzard.
Guardians of the gold,
        Have the hoard keys ready for certain seamen.
We are coming today to see you.

2

Prise up a roof slab. Look,
        Morning sun
Falls like a sword through stone-dust.
Lower the ropes,
        A knot here and there, hand holds.
        We have lit three torches,
Frail flung flames outside in sun and wind.

3

What, Rolf, you can't stay?
        Rolf bleats like a goat on Orkahowe.
        I'd clean forgot. I owe
The Appiehouse farmer in this parish
        For three cheeses his wife made me
At Lammas-time last . . .
        Other business is of high importance
To a man with a gray face and shaking hands.

4

Who's to go in first? Who
        Will climb down into this grave?
Ingibiorg's boyfriend, will you
        Kiss the cheek of the ghosts?
        (No redness on their mouths)
Hermund is putting
        A biting edge on the last axe.
        Well, we are pilgrims, Jerusalem-bound.
See how the ghosts will shrink
When I write JERUSALEM on the wall.

5

I'm tired of salt, fish guts, tar, gulls.
        Since Trondheim
I've slept in a sack on deck.
I have no skill in writing runes

              But I will hold a torch for Ragn
Who cuts pure and deep,
       Far from the flung spray off Unst.

    6

Thin skull, a ruckle
       Of long thin bones.
How long, lady, since your eye sockets
Brimmed with light?
Milk lass and weaving lass
       Stood higher than you, lady
       The day your loveliness
       Was laid in this stone bed.
Be glad, poor ghost.
Ragn intends to write a stone poem for you.

    7

Maybe it was last winter
       Thieves took gold from the finger bones.
We are too late, brothers.
But I think it was a thousand winters ago
       Men with small imagination
Deprived poor sailors of silver.
Today we are writing axe-poems
       Longer-lasting than any yellow ore.

The Laird and the Three Women

Clay curves shining from my plough
Says Tom the ploughboy

I must harrow a hill, come sun, come snow
Says Tom the servant

My fingers let the good seed flow
Says Tom the tenant

Now the first brairds* green and grow
Says Tom the crofter

                    * brairds: first shoots of a crop

Gold winds round the scarecrow blow
Says Tom the horseman

I own whatever I reap and mow
Says Tom of the Glebe

My tranced harvesters come and go
Says Tom the corn-man

Ale and bread in my big barn stow
Says Tom the laird

*

Star and icicle pierce me through
Says Tom, bewintered

*

Time to light him a candle now
Say the three women

A Poem for _Shelter_

Who has set his house among the stars?
Who has made his dwellingplace the
            dawn, and the western glory
            where the sun goes down?
Who has instructed the eagle to
            establish his place on a
            mountain ledge near the snow
And the little mouse in a cell safe from
            hawk and ploughshare?
The albatross dwells in the house of
            blizzard and spindrift,
            south of Cape Horn, he
            'sleeps on his own wings'.
What has The Word chosen, to be his
            house among men?
A byre, shared with winter creatures
But that was to set at naught
            princes' palaces and the
            pyramids of dead
            jewelled pharaohs.

The true inheritors of earth are
    the people
Who desire to live in simple houses
Not too close together but enough
    for neighbourliness
Where a family may sit at peace
    under its own rooftree.

There is enough stone in Alps, Urals,
    Himalayas
To quarry a million cornerstones.
But always, in winter, under
    stars like thorns
The wanderers wait, the breakers of icicles,
    the homeless ones.

Saturday: A Boy in Hamnavoe

Penny
The Saturday penny
    Sang a small boy in Hamnavoe
What sweetness can I buy
To glue my teeth
    Between two sea breaths?
    I could buy
A sherbet dab from Janetta Sinclair
Or a Guilio Fuggacia ice-cream slider.

Sweeties
He went among shop windows,
    A small sweetaholic.
The new Mars Bars taste like heaven
But they cost twopence
Twopence for Rachel Smith's claggam* too.

Chocolate and Lemonade
A bottle of lemonade
    Is only for picnics at The Tender Tables
With ginger snaps, abernethy biscuits.
I'd do a lot for a bar of Cadbury's

claggam: home-made toffee

Or Fry's chocolate cream.
Why do such bits of heaven
  Have to cost *two* pence?

Cinema
A penny doesn't go far
  When it costs fourpence
To sit in the cave of shifting shadows
With Tom Mix or Charlie Chaplin.
  The 'Wizard' on Tuesday –
*Two*pence again – that everlasting barrier.

Olive Oil
An old gentle-tongued lady
  At a close end:
'Georgie, will you get a bottle of olive oil
From the chemist?
My man needs olive oil for his stomach.
  And here's a shilling for going.'

Silver Star
A shilling! I held a star
  On my finger-ends.
Not a bird flew faster
  From chemist's to close-end with olive oil
  Than the boy dying of sweet-lack.
  She was no old woman, she
Was an angel, and her man
– So rusty inside! – had the gentlest of smiles.

Debauch
All that Saturday a debauch
  Of bon-bons, butternuts, Gowans's
American Cream Soda,
Ice-cream to make the teeth shiver,
  A liquorice stick, slab of Highland Cream.
Why aren't you eating your good mince and tatties? . . .
  Languor at evening
Under the shifting cinema shafts,
Wallace Beery, a hoodlum, on Death Row.

Attie Campbell
1900–1967

Where do you wander now, old friend?
Where do you drink?
Few inns better than Hamnavoe bar,
Few better stories, I think.
Is there a star
Stirred with laughter that has no end

A million light-years beyond the Milky Way
Where Villon and Burns,
Falstaff and slant-eyed Li Po
Order their nectar by turns
(No 'Time, gents' there, no drinker has to pay)
And words immortal gather head and flow?

For that far glim you'd crank your aged car,
But that the faint bell-cry
Of tide changing in Hoy Sound,
The corn surges that salve the deep plough-wound,
Would draw you home to where you are
At Warbeth, among the dead who do not die.

Agricultural Show: Dounby

We are the old men. Days scatter,
Husks on a threshing floor.
    Shall we look on the black
    Or on the bright solstice again,

Or go in at darkling Barleycorn doors
Or surprise April through the green gate?
    Time gathers to a fullness; then
    He's wise who turns gravely,

Raises a hand in thanks for the story
And leaves in peace under the first star.
    We linger it out. Better men
    Have gone when the sun stood over the hill.

We would linger it out, earthbound
Till ice-blades shred us to scarecrows.
    We would plead with winter,
    Barn bound, for one more furrow-time.

Too late, too late. The last stook
Is long in the yard. Light tarnishes.
    To wish back the sun
    Sets ice on a child's lips,

Some farmer's son – He's there, look,
Outside the gate of a 'fair field
    Full of folk', the festive
    Dance of the nine parishes.

Turn at the gate. Bless his urgency,
This new word in the story of Orc.
    Bless the supplanter.
    Lay sunset lingerings on

That hill of blond surges, they hallow
Tomorrow's harvester. And see,
    The horse we banished from our hills
    Drifts delicately to his handful of grass.

Pomona Inn, Finstown, Orkney
(founded by John Finn, Peninsular veteran)

I'm tired of Spain and musket and cannonball,
Said Finn the soldier

I'll be like Napoleon and go to a lonely isle,
Said Irish Finn

I journeyed to 'the islands of the whale',
Said Finn the soldier

What work for a veteran soldier on Heddle Hill?
Said Irish Finn

Ploughmen, I think, like a jar or two of ale,
Said Finn the soldier

And here there's no shebeen to sip or swill,
Said Irish Finn

No place to go when their wives scold and shrill,
Said Finn the soldier

I'll have a word with the man that keeps the mill,
Said Irish Finn

To sell me some sacks of malt, his overspill,
Said Finn the soldier

To where I'll build an ale-house, wall by wall
Said Irish Finn

And there in peace travellers may drink their fill
Said Finn the soldier

Twixt fire and lamp and barrel and rattling till,
Said Irish Finn

Lovers may linger long when love goes ill,
Said Finn the soldier

And mourners warm them from the kirkyard chill,
Said Irish Finn

I'll be your good host, come you when you will,
Said Finn the soldier

I've beaten the cannon to pewter mugs – all's well,
Sang Finn the landlord.

Robert Rendall
Orkney Poet

You have been here, before your latest birth,
    (Cheeks, at the pan-pipes, apple-red and round!)
Followed your wooden plough through Attic earth,
    And pulled your lobsters from a wine-dark sound.

Now for a flicker of time you walk once more
   In other islands, under geese-gray skies,
And note, on Birsay hill and Birsay shore,
   The year's glad cycle out of ancient eyes.

O happy grove of poetry! where the soul
   Is never sundered from the laughing blood,
But sweetly bound, harmonious and whole
   In covenant with animal and god.

But I came here unheralded, and meet
Masquers and shadows mingling in the street.

One Star in the West

To have got so far, alone
Almost to the seventieth stone
      Is a wonder.
      There was thunder

A few miles back, a storm-shaken
Hill and sea, the bridge broken
      (The bright fluent
      Burn a bruised torrent.)

But all cleared, larks were singing
Again, the April rain ringing
      Across the sown hills,
      Among the daffodils.

The road winds uphill, but
A wonder will be to sit
      On the stone at last –
      One star in the west.

A Work for Poets

To have carved on the days of our vanity
A sun
A ship
A star
A cornstalk

Also a few marks
From an ancient forgotten time
A child may read

That not far from the stone
A well
Might open for wayfarers

Here is a work for poets –
Carve the runes
Then be content with silence

Water (1996)

1

Find, said the intruder, *your*
            place of lustration.
I rose from my father's door.
(Birth binds breath to glebe
            and quern, till cess of hunger.)
A skipper enrolled me, vagrant.
Five winters yoked to oarlock
            in the ship 'Wolf',
Cold seas over the shipmen,
Was spindrift in the bread broken.
Put ashore, in Torshavn, again
            that stranger.
I showed silver wrung from my sea
            sweat.
Good water, he said, *the highway*
Where men fish and trade, and
            consult charts.
Your place is otherwhere.

2

In Denmark, I dug a well.
I planted a tree beside the well.
I built a house
And I led Ingerth, a bride, to
            the door.
Was music in the long room
            that day.
I rode weekly to the ships and
            the market.
Water did not fail in our source.
Among waterfront merchants, the
            drift of faces,
Came the face like a star.
I mentioned wife and child, the
            cornfield, the well.

The spade broke a core of
      sweetness,
My hands gloved in light
Raising the pitcher . . .
That is good water also (he said)
The well you are seeking is not
      here.

3

Surely I will tell the destroyer
      of peace
How I sat under an ice mountain
Set there, in exile, with others
      after knives and
      wounds in Trondheim.
Five, seeking assoilment
On the green tongue of a glacier,
Acquainted with wolf and
      walrus and arctic skua.
The rage
Burned down in me there, and
      down
Till was left a small ring of
      heart-wax.
Seven years I atoned for the
      killing at the sea-front.
I and the ness-gangers, the
      young careless ones, once
Falconer, broker, shipwright.
They left, one after other.
I waited, after the seven
      winters in Greenland,
      very far north
For scroll and pardon.
Seven winterlong burials of the sun,
Seven sun prowlings (all summer)
      through the sky,
A cold heart-eating lion.
Friends of salmon, caribou
      and walrus,

A drifting folk
Fed me at their fires, they taught
       me (smiling) secret by
       secret
The twenty-one intricate signs
       for 'snow' –
Breath and bread it was to
       them, the ice.
I sought continually
The one syllable that might
       lock purity in the
       ultimate crystal . . .
The guardian, then, in a blizzard
You have met the masks –
       snowflake, berg, glacier.
Element and essence are
       further on.

4

The convocation of old men. One
Had drained a marsh,
A Swedish lakeside, for ploughs
       and scythes and
       barns (twenty.)
One had stood where sea
       gargles in a river's throat
       with nets
And a scale for pearls and
       salmon.
One, under the sign of sheaves,
Enchanted the rain torrent
Into murmurous barrels, barley
       prisons
Where merriment of ancients is set free.
I looked from my cup, heart-struck.
The friend stood at the tavern door,
       Not here, man. Not those.

Doorkeeper. They call this old
    man 'Brother Doorkeeper.'
Mornings, I stand at the door.
Out of today's dawn a child came,
    a ploughman, a woman
    with a shawl.
They dipped fingers in the
    hollow stone.
Thrice shaken, the shining inside the
    stone.

For the Islands I Sing (1997)

To Sylvia Wishart

Salt in the wind, and corn.
Your green valley
Lies tilted to the shifting Atlantic gleam.

Vacant now,
It waits, an overturned grain jar,
Abandoned in the world's flight from poverty, silence, sanctity.

When will people return again to Rackwick?
I see a thousand cities broken,
Science
Hounded like Cain through the marches of atom and planet,

And quiet people
Returning north with ox and net and plough.
They will offer it again to the light, a chalice.

Lullaby for Lucy

Let all plants and creatures of the valley now
Unite,
Calling a new
Young one to join the celebration.

Rowan and lamb and waters salt and sweet
Entreat the
New child to the brimming
Dance of the valley,
A pledge and a promise.
Lonely they were long, the creatures of Rackwick, till
Lucy came among them, all brightness and light.

Stella Cartwright (for her birthday – 15 May 1982)

So, once in the 50s
There was this crazy chap, high among clouds,
Edinburgh-bound.
Laurel-seeking he was, out of Orkney,
Long and salt his throat
Among the stanzas that starred the howffs of Rose Street.

Could he not bide forever in that beautiful city?
A sweet girl, one day,
Rose, a star, to greet him.
To him, she spoke sweeter than rain among roses in summer,

While poets like columns of salt stood
Round the oaken Abbotsford bar.
I, now
Going among the gray houses and piers of Stromness,
Hear that voice made of roses and rain still; and see
Through storm-clouds, the remembered star.

Stained Glass Windows (1998)

Saint Laurence

See, the mother is kindling a lamp, child
    To light you to bed,
She is covering the fire on the hearth
    Look, where she bakes her loaves.

You woke early, boy, and a net of stars
    Hung in the north.
A banked-up fire under the hill.
    Then the sun walked, like a king
    Up the fourteen steps of the sky.
Oxen stood in the field,
    You seized a golden horn.

The graves are cold, martyrs' tombs
In a deep labyrinth
    Hidden from the kind sun.
You with the burning beard, in that place of skulls
    Saw a mosaic, the Sacred Heart
In a nest of flames, unconsumed.

How beautiful, the little streets
    Where vendors roast chestnuts
On braziers fed with charred coals.
Boys bring small birds for roasting.
    In the temple of Jupiter
    Sconces light acolytes' hands
And scoop shadows in an old face.

Six soldiers came about you
    So close, they seemed like friends
Welcoming a far traveller.
They seemed like beggars
    Tugging at the sleeve of a rich senator.
Then one spat – the spit
    Hissed into your red beard.

'What, Laurence, the farmer
Must have roasted an ox on a spit
   For a winter feast.
We have heard this, meat
Comes in tender flakes, fat-dropping
   From a gridiron sweetly set
On smoking faggots, with a bellows snoring.'
   So the captain at the city gate . . .
The people clapped their soot-black hands.

The corrupt flames, the cleansing flames,
   Purgatory pure and pitiless.
   Having shed our tatters,
The red coat was put on you there
   At the gate of The Golden City.

Song for Saint Andrew's Day

1

Where were you, man
   The night your brother sat, mocked
Among the soldiers and the servant girls?

I think Andrew was going like an otter
By secret paths, shoreward
   Away from the terrible city
   Out there, on an outcrop
Shaped like a skull.

Go home along the coast.
   Hide behind boat, rock, bothy.
   Be intent on the leap of a dolphin.
Go north, still
   Till lake water washes your feet.

2

It is impossible
   To wash words
   Carved in the stone of the heart,
Images cut deep there,

Two fish on a hillside,
The donkey, branches of olive and palm,
Wine casks at Cana.

3

Fishermen with hands burned
   From rasp of rope and rowlock
Out on the lake,
Who is the man in the last light,
   At the fire-glimmer, on shore stones
   Poaching fish in a pot?

It is the man they hooked
   On the dead tree.

4

Go, Andrew, take the fish image
   To Rome and the cities,
The star, the fish, the sun, the loaf: sacred images
They will make of you at last
A winter man,
   Tongueless, eyeless, no ear
Hearkening the shifts of tide, wind, shoal.

5

The April fisherman,
   Rivet-gnarls on hands and feet
Where will he go now with his gladness?

The world is wide, to cast nets in.
   The Holy Spirit
Fills his coat like a sail.

He speaks to fishermen on the Alpine lakes,
He lingers by Belgian rivers.
They listen, rough Breton fishermen,
   Minglings of sea-wit, laughter, gull-talk.

6

'Where are you taking me, Spiritus Sanctus?
    On this cold ocean
I have seen the grandsons of Jonah's whale,
    Gannet and bonxie,
The small fish in silver armour, 'herring'.
Where are we bound, ruthless dove?

7

Well, I am content. This place will do
    With sinners, saints, mostly
Gray minglings, like fish in a barrow.
Alba, Pictland, Scotia,
    The beach strewn with curraghs and sea-gear.

They are bringing stones now
    To be a house of Christ.
    I, Andrew, fisherman-doorkeeper
At home here, in a gray November end.

Saint Magnus

So, there was this knock at my door near the end of the night.
    I thought, 'Kurt the old man of Quoy is dying at last. Or, Brunna's child will be born at sunrise.'
I lit the candle. I took the bar from the door. A darkling stranger stood there.
He had the high-born chant. 'Mother, may I sit at your fire? Cold it was all night in the kirk. I want to sit at a croft fire for a while.'
The lord smelled of holy water, and sweat, and the salt of sorrow.
I pointed to the straw chair and the fire. I knelt. I blew the embers into a rage of flames.
I was shaken with rage against this lord. I whispered, 'Valt my son is dead. He went to your wars. He drowned in the sea at Sumburgh.'
The man said, 'The salt is over my mouth also.'
I said, 'Old Jon is dead because of you. Rents, taxes. He laboured harder than his ox. The last harvest broke him.'

He said, 'They have sharpened a scythe for me. I am near the
   mill and the millstones.'
I said, 'Here is not your place, sir. Go wherever you like.
   There are one or two stars still to light you through this
   island, to see what your wars have brought about.'
He said, 'You are an old woman. But you seem like a bride
   on the day before the wedding feast, flustered
   a bit with the ceremony to come . . . I will leave you now.
   Remember me in your morning prayer.'
I said, 'I get a smell of the ashes of death from you. I know
   that cinder. I have shrouded a hundred, men and
   women and bairns. I am happy to smell the ashes of
   the end on the breath of a war-bringer. Death was a
   friend to old Jon. I think Valt in your warship was not
   so pleased with his last mouthful of salt. Death is a
   thing of terror to the young and the rich and the great.'
He said, 'Remember me also when you light your candle to
   old Jon and young Valt.'
I said, 'Well, if death comes to you here in Egilsay, I will lay
   you out decently before the day is done, so your
   mother will sail here and look into the stillness of your
   face, and so come away again.'
He said, 'It will be for me a skull like a felled ox, a welter of
   blood and smashed bone. Even the rooks will stay far
   from it.'
The first light came in at the open door. The man's face was
   gray as a drained comb. I thought, 'This is a man that
   smelt of essence of roses yesterday and ate honey
   bread and had this and that spice in his French wine.
   He reeks like a shambles now. There is yet a kind of
   justice in heaven and on earth.'
I said, 'You will die today, I see that, like any hard-driven
   harvest ox or like a salt-throttled fisherman. I will put
   on a pot of ale for you to drink now. You must have a
   bannock with a bit of cheese and fish. A man
   shouldn't crawl to his end but stand up straight and
   look Death in the eye.'
We laughed together, like a harvester and a gleaner among
   the last sheaves.
His highness said, 'I thank you for your good cheer, mother.'
He made a cross with his hand upon the board.

We broke croft bread together.
   It seemed that all the barley and meadowsweet and clover
   ever grown in Egilsay had come on the morning wind
   into my croft.
The lord of the Orkney glebes said, *Deo Gratias.*
He said, 'There is a square of brightness on your floor. It
   grows. The flagstone is warm. It is a sweet thing for
   the eye to behold the sun on a morning in April.'
Then on the doorstep Earl Magnus of Orkney kissed me on
   my withered apple of a cheek, a thing Valt never did
   for fear of fishermen's mockery, and old Jon did only
   when he was merry with ale at harvest home and Yule.
And here a fisherman passed on to the shore with his lines
   and there a ploughman was yoking his ox.
This death-farer fared on first to the kirk: to the Breaking of
   the Bread there, the first and the last Bread.

Soon there was a great stirring and shouting at the hidden end
   of Egilsay, and a smell of fires and stewing and
   grilling and a breached ale-barrel on the wind of
   morning.
'Magnus . . . Magnus . . . Magnus,' yelled the hidden hunters.
   'Where are you hiding now, Magnus? Are you in a
   cave, Magnus? You can't bide forever in the kirk,
   Magnus. Come out soon, Magnus. Stand in the sun.
   Today, Magnus, we are all to sit down to a great feast.'
I threw the crusts that were left to my half-dozen hens.

Northern Lights (1999)

A Ballad of Gow the Pirate

One tree in the garden, Mister
William Gow, merchant in Hamnavoe.
Water the apple-tree, John.
The boy hides among summer leaves.

One tree in the school, Mister
Clouston, dominie: his desk.
'Navis' – ship – decline that, boy.
Ocean branched, many streams, through Gow.

One tree off Sicily, Monsieur
Ferneau, master: his keel.
The arms-chest key, keep it, John.
Smoke, flame, a ball in the Frenchman's skull.

One tree in the Bailey, Mister
Justice Bigwig there: his bench.
Gallows, chains, tar at Wapping.
Night, tree of stars, over Marshalsea.

A bare tree at Thames-side, Mister
Jack Ketch, gallowsman.
Fiddles, broadsheets, bottles of gin.
The boy bites on the salt apple.

A January Day: Burns

They've blown our coats about, those wandering
Westerlies, since Hogmanay; now and then
    Gesturing to the Pole, and then
    Small artilleries of hail

Stotter on the skylight, and once
North-seeking still, the noon darkened
    With a broken snow-cloud,
    A too deep dazzlement, then.

Masques of the January moon –
Ice sliver, silver gondola, crystal
    Cygnet, till the queen
    Holds the complete orb.

The pauper sun ventures a few steps
Further, east and west, at day's
    Rising and setting – another masquer
    With a gold coin in his rags.

Ancient bard, I too went a few steps
From flames and books to find again
    Under that clatter-tongue of weathers
    The lovely task of winter.

There, under a skeleton sycamore
– above the sea – a cluster of snowdrops,
    Children of snow and sun
    Who must die before the lark sings.

I thought of the immortal
January makar, created (it seems)
    To hammer out winter's worst
    For hansel of delight to a dour folk.

January the Twenty-fifth

I

The old men said the name Robbie Burns
    As if he'd farmed
Very recently, in Cairston or Stenness or Hoy.

What a man, what a man! they said
    Shaking their heads, smiling.
    What a man for the drink!
What a man for the lasses!

It was of utmost importance
    That Robbie was a poor man
Like themselves: a toil-bent farmer.

There might be a Barleycorn pause
    Between a quote and a stave of song.
The women, they never seemed
    To give a moment's thought to that poet.

II

The Hamnavoe kids groaned inwardly. There
    On their open books
Was a new poem nailed to the page
    To A Mouse:
    'To be learned by heart,' said the teacher.

Words like thistles and thorns
They ploughed through the winter language
    And pity ran for cover
    This way and this, and entered
A few small cold wondering hearts.

III

They moved in the schoolroom
    Among heroic images,
The Bruce at Bannockburn under the shouting castles.

Mary Queen of Scots
    Inside that English castle
    First in her black gown, then the red,
    Then block and axe and blood.

Bonny Prince Charlie at Holyrood, dancing –
    On the rainlashed moor
    Turning a horse's head into the west –
    An old broken king at the brandy bottle
    In a foreign castle.

Now this ploughman shaken with song and love
    Among stones and furrows.

IV

There was another hero, more marvellous even
  Than Bruce or Burns.

He too died in the glory of the field
  Young and beautiful
  John Thomson, goalkeeper of Celtic.
For the boys of Hamnavoe
Football was war, was magic and chant.
A star glittered and went out.

V

At last, into one council house
  A wonder was brought:
  A wireless set, with wet battery and dry battery.

Better than Henry Hall's dance-band
Better than *Murder in the Red Barn*
Better than Toytown and Larry the Lamb
  Was that January torrent of sound, teatime to bedtime.
  'Bonny Mary o' Argyle', 'Tam o' Shanter'
  A heuch of pipes,
  A trenching of haggis, reek of whisky,
  The lass in the cornrigs, the lady
  In the Potter-row.
  In Dumfries, a debt-ridden deathbed,
  The Allowa' cottage with snowflakes seeking in.

VI

Not one of the fishermen
Not a single sailor, or farmer
  With sea-light in his eyes

Thought it strange, on 25 January,
  That Burns hardly mentions the sea.
'The wan moon sets beyond the white wave
And time is setting with me – Oh' . . . Only that

All was forgiven the great lover
   Of lasses, cornstalks, liberty
    In the Hamnavoe doorways of herringscales
      And salt fish.

VII

A tinker leaned on the Smithfield bar,
In Dounby (Hamnavoe
   Had no pubs in the time of the kids of fable).

Is Burns still alive? said the tinker.
The tavern was shaken with mockery and mirth
And maybe the tinker went back,
   Ashamed, to the fire in the quarry.

There was no need, wanderer.
   Stand a moment
   There, on the brae: under the white star.

John Rae and Sir John Franklin

Sir John Franklin's two ships, *Erebus* and *Terror*, left Stromness
in 1845 on Arctic exploration, and were never seen again . . .
   John Rae was in every way a remarkable man. He had been
born in 1813 at the Hall of Clestrain, near Stromness. In his
boyhood, as he lingered at the corners of the Stromness piers and
heard the yarns of the old sailor men, his imagination had been
quickened by stories of the great white spaces of the north-west.
As soon as he became a doctor in Edinburgh he signed on as ship
surgeon aboard the Hudson's Bay Company vessel *Princes of
Wales*, sailing to Moose Factory. Thereafter his fate was bound
up for ever with the unexplored regions of Canada's frozen north.
   The highlight of his career was when he discovered the fate of
Sir John Franklin's lost expedition. It was then that Rae's name, for
a few weeks, was on the lips of all Britishers. The people of
Stromness were the last folk in Europe to see Franklin's ships sailing
west. It is a rather curious coincidence that John Rae, a man born
within sight of Stromness, should be the man to discover from the
native Indians and Esquimaux how Franklin and his men died.

I

'The purpose of which voyage shall be: to discover a north-west
  passage by sea betwixt the oceans, for the furtherance of trade
  and the enhancement of her majesty's empire'.

South-east wind, overcast, out of Gravesend. Bearing north,
  between dawn and the Longstone light.

The Forth. Two men committed to the courts for drunkenness.
  A seaman missing. Another taken from the stews.

Our mother the sea, receive us. Who bears, nourishes, chastises.
  The cold gray mother.

The Orkneys. A pilot: fierce whiskers, rum, pipe-spittle.
  Upthrust of Hoy, blue shoulders. Herring boats. Cairston,
  a wide bay. Hamnavoe and 38 howffs.

'Dear one, the only comfort I have in this bare place is to write
  to you and so I comfort myself and long for you. I carry
  your dear gift of linen in my sea-chest.'

The White Horse Inn. A whale-man turned away from our
  questions.

And north and west. Congregation of waters, a lamentation
  and a gossiping, unfathomed endless utterances, sisterhood
  of the sea. The North Atlantic.

The green heart of icebergs. Green and black undersea fires. The
  ice roared. Gray shuffling packs, the ice moved in behind us.

Here a man is as nature intended. Naked he goes among mirrors
  of ice. Furled to the eyes, but naked, among prisms and
  mirrors. He walks on a solid sea. Ice is everything.
  – A man eats ice.

'Gentlemen, nothing remains for us, in these unfortunate
  unlooked-for circumstances, but to leave the ship and trek
  south. There are communities of Esquimaux all down the
  coast. Take your guns and powder. Be of a good heart . . .'

Spalding died. Gregor can walk no further. (Leave him now.)
  Trewick saw a piece of Cornwall in the snow: a spire,
  rosebushes. We left Simpson to the bears. One knelt, a flash
  in the hand, turned away: had white and red stuff in his
  mouth afterwards.

Alone, on wrapped feet. Emerald, onyx, garnet burn. This is an
  enchanted city. I go through the street of the jewellers. A
  diamond blazes.

II

John Rae and his Orkneymen discover the fate of the Franklin
Expedition, 1850

        West and north. No people for six days,
        Then a Russian.
        He spoke with eyes and hands.
        The great captain had found a way through. No doubt
        The captain sat in high honour
        Either at the court of the Mongols, or in Siam.
        He chewed an offered cut of tobacco.
        There was nothing to the east (he said) –
        A broken green river, an ice-mill.
        A wild goose that night
        Rained down fat into the flames.

        One morning the snow lay, a knife
        Across Folster's face.
        Head blanketed, he stumbled after.
        A gun, north or west,
        Shattered the huge crystal. Feathers, blood
        Drifted on snow.
        An Eskimo boy, a shadow
        Passed the fire. And returned, closer,
        Then left. At midnight
        The sky was blue and green fountains of crystal.

        The Eskimo boy was suddenly there, smiling.
        He had something to show.
        In his own time, after a hundred smiles.
        Bread-eaters? Two ships, ice-bound?
        He had no knowledge (smiling).

Had heard of the 'gray troop of ghosts'.
Then from his wolf-coat offered
A blue ribbon (Order of Hanover)
Coins, a silver fork crested 'J.F.'

In the village, no information.
We must first sit at a fish-board
Lit with smiles.
All left, smiling, soon, but an old one.
In the House of Ice (he said)
Iron and oak are frail flowers, bone
Is subtle and lasting.
Our elements came kindly about the strangers.
Birds, fish offered help.
They could not understand. The greeting
Withered in the air.
They could not reply, *Come goose.*
Come, caribou. Come, wolf. Come snow-bird.
They were ghosts before death,
One after another, drifting
In bright and dark circles, untrysted.
We watched, just under the horizon.

They smiled. We faced south.
(I had put a knife in sea boils,
Drawn twelve teeth,
Given hot whisky for belly-ache and cough.)
Down the white ringing map
We strode on to trees and trains,
To ordered stones
Where is no pure tryst of the creatures.
The same Indian woman
In Mackenzie's store, chewing tobacco,
Asked, stone-faced, had we found the heroes?

Guns, here and there, before hunger,
Shattered the crystal.
Birds, twitching, thudded on snow.
Corrigal said at the last fire,
'In Hamnavoe, tonight
Oatmeal and whisky in the White Horse.
I see a fisherman's wife
Waiting at a draughty close-end.
She is taken with bitter sea-thoughts.'

Snow: From a Hospital

Best leave the paper blank.
If you must write,
Imitate old smiling Chinamen.
They scribbled on silk,
Three arrows in a corner (trees),
A broken diagonal
And February's dyke is full.

This is the snow for me –
My bronchial tree loaded and loud
With the white birds of winter.

They come from Venus, Orion, Betelgeuse,
Such unearthly cargoes!
Now wrecked here,
The innumerable shining bales are too much.
What can we do with such delicacy?
Our coarse eyes long for grass, stone, puddle.

Winds like the hands of Penelope
Forever weave
Web after web of snow.
When will Odysseus come, the golden hero?
After the ploughman, sower, harvester.

This snow is like time in its youth.
Against that light
Tinkers are blacker and fiercer,
Birds hungrier,

What so bright as apples and stars and children!
But the swan is jealous.
She pushes her dingy breast over the loch
To find some blue.

How clumsy and endearing he is,
The snowman,
A flocculent teddy bear.
But I tell you, friends,
He's not what he seems to be.
This February
His claws tore my chest open.

The First Daffodil: A Tinker Wife

Dead grass whispers under my feet.
I am going from croft to farm
   With my pack – needles, cotton reels,
   Tin mugs, cheap hankies.

I am going past dog-barkings,
Mockery of a bairn, a tree
   Of starlings shaken like a bell.
   Sometimes a farm lass

Buys a trinket, often enough
I'm given the hard door, but
   A kind one here and there
   Pours me a mug of tea.

(I can tell their fortunes too. A few
Suffer a heartfall when I frown.)
   Dead dry grass between the crofts
   Of Quoy and Seatter,

But last month my boots squelched mud
Along that track. On Greenay side
   Boys are lighting fires
   – the muirburn – to clean the hill

Of winter's dregs. Sit in the ditch,
Old woman, sit in the ditch.
   Strike match into pipe. Another flame
   In the wind, over there, a March daffodil.

The Harrowing of Hell

He went down the first step.
His lantern shone like the morning star.
Down and round he went
Clothed in his five wounds.

Solomon whose coat was like daffodils
Came out of the shadows.
He kissed Wisdom there, on the second step.

The boy whose mouth had been filled with harp-songs,
The shepherd king
Gave, on the third step, his purest cry.
   At the root of the Tree of Man, an urn
   With dust of apple-blossom

Joseph, harvest-dreamer, counsellor of pharaohs
Stood on the fourth step.
He blessed the lingering Bread of Life.

He who had wrestled with an angel,
The third of the chosen,
Hailed the King of Angels on the fifth step.

Abel with his flute and fleeces
Who bore the first wound
Came to the sixth step with his pastorals.

On the seventh step down
The tall primal dust
Turned with a cry from digging and delving.

   Tomorrow the Son of Man will walk in a garden
   Through drifts of apple-blossom.

St Magnus

What road did you come, traveller
To this place?

At the first station
I had a white coat put on me, a silver ring.

I went with a psalter
Through the rage of a sea battle.

I ruled in turbulent islands,
Hakon my cousin and I.
We smoked pirates out of caves in Shetland.

There was this chessboard between
Red earl and black earl –
   Ruined crofts, breached boats,
   A people with gaunt faces.

Between Magnus and Hakon
How should dove wings fly out
And a hawk furl on a mailed fist?

I passed last night
In the kirk here in Egilsay.
   At dawn, an old priest said mass.

Now I have come to the last station,
This stone seems better to me
   Than my carved chair in Birsay.

A red martyr coat?
   Domine, non sum dignus

The butcher, Lifolf
Has come up, weeping, from the stewpots.
His axe is the key
For the unlocking of the door into light.

Song for St Magnus: 16 April

I

Keeper of the red stone, remember well
   Sufferers today, those
   Who are to cross the dark firth,
   People in hospitals,
   In hospices, eventide lingerers,
Children who look at daffodils
   (Both with the dew on) each
   To break today in spring tempest.

Consider, Magnus, the fishermen
   From Noup Head to Rora,
   Those with a hundred creels,
The old man with two creels behind the Holms,
   Consider a stranger at the shore
Who is in need of ferrying.

III

An Icelander wrote on his skin
   Death is darkness
   Death is the cold skull
   Death is the bitter journey all men take
   Into silence, nothingness . . .
The skald wrote. Music
   Moved across the parchment.

The dancer fared on to the stone.

IV

What you suffer at the stone, it has all
Been fore-suffered.
   We sit in an assize of shadows. Evil
Must be atoned for.
Whispers, beyond ear-reach
   Load us with shame and terror.

Heroic one, comfort us, you
   Who have uncovered your head.

V

Magnus, friend, have a keeping
   Of the shepherd on the hill
   Whose ewes are having difficult birth
In the last snow.
Bestow peace to ploughmen in stony fields.

Be present at the fires
   Of women in Bosnia and Somalia
   Kneading dough smaller than fists.

Remember the Easter feast
   Your mother prepared in Holm
   You could not come to,
   Being finished with shadows.

The murderer came. He drank ale there, in Holm. He wept.

VI

Magnus, pray for priests
   In this time of hate
   (Never such hate and anger over the earth).

May they light candles at their altars
This day and all days
   Till history is steeped in light.

It was a cold night, your vigil
   In the kirk in Egilsay.

At dawn an old priest lit the paschal candle:
   Introibo ad altare Dei

VII

Never so many strangers at Orkney's doors
   'We need peace' . . .
   'We are sent here about the business of government' . . .
   'Our quest: silence and healing' . . .

The old ways are worn out
We turn our hands to work on other looms.

Our ancestors
   Beat down the doors of Pict and Celt,
The people of Magnus
   Broke the first curraghs,
   Choked sacred wells,
   Filled barn and byre with flames.

Magnus, give welcome to strangers.
   Their children
   Will sing with new voices, in April,
   The words from the Iceland parchment.

So he, turning the pages of the lost man's
   Ledgers, hoping to catch in some phrase
   The flawed fated thread
      That ruined a whole fabric

Found nothing, in notebook and notebook
   But cargoes sent out and received,
   Seamen's wages, price of cord,
      List of shipwright's repairs

And how a southwesterly had wrenched
   Copestones from his pier – what Sabbath
   Coins he had put in the plate,
      How this spring the rheumatics

Had set a clamp on one knee,
   How the merchants had relinquished a Dutch
   Cargo of rum and tobacco,
      The word going from counter to cabin

That excise officers, an entire posse
   Lay crouched by midnight rocks . . .
   (The eyes of the seeker, sore now
      With scrolled Hanoverian

'*f*' and '*s*'). No word of threatened
   Bankruptcy, law's lour, blackmail, the blacker
   Root nourished at some
      Ancestral foetid source,

To show how a sober Hamnavoe merchant
   Suddenly slipped mooring, shook off
   Store, kirk, council chamber,
      This well-kept desk and diary.

Then this: 'Girls passed my door in troops
   For the Ward, at sunrise, for to touch
   May dew to their faces
      That by such beguilement

They might get them good husbands,
    And amongst them one . . .' Pen faltered
In mid-sentence, but resumed
    Next morning: 'Three baskets

Duck eggs received from Hoy, one shilling
    And fourpence halfpenny . . .' He thought,
Turning the last blank pages
    How a dry stick

Must have quickened that May morning
    And dared not disclose the madness
But launched out secretly, at sunrise
    Under a star, to bury the rose
    In salt chasms beyond Hoy.

Hamnavoe: The First Village

The settlers' farm at Breckness built, the builders
Are summoned to the ale-drinking in the long hall.
    Arn tells one, *You are to be shepherd*
    One, *You must see to the horses . . .*

All behaved well on the voyage, says Arn.
Now we must wait till winter to discover
    If bread and cheese are good on this glebe,
    If turf of Orkney will warm like our mountain logs.

Tonight the best barrel is to be broached,
Sea-brought ale, I bid you then
    Wash salt from your throats,
    Rid your teeth of sawdust.

They tilt horns, fire-fast, fleece their mouths.
A few call for stories. The farmer,
    You, Lief, will see to the sty . . .
    Your task, Sven, to drain that field for the plough.

Girls come in with buckets of ale
Slurping on flagstones (wet star-splashes!)
    And Arn to Rudi (oarsman)
    Get shore stones tomorrow for a winter byre.

Now Nord, that had held helm on shipboard
Will sing, but Rann the grieve
   Stills the harp, till each seafarer
   Is fitted with his ox-coat.

A sheet of ale hangs in the air, it lingers
Across faces of ploughman and goosegirl.
   Not long then to fierce kin-combing,
   Flung fists, blood, bench-breaking,

Girls screaming, women stone-faced.
Then Arn to Nord, *Brawlers, ale-berserkers*
   Will not yoke here in Breckness.
   Go, Nord, take your slut and your song with you.

Ten Norskies follow Nord through the mussel-blue night,
Lovers of song and sea, three miles over the ridge
   To the voe with two islets
   And a granite hill behind,

A good place for boat-furl and curing of fish.
Women come also, with pot and lamp and loom,
   One girl – I know this – most beautiful,
   Her hair in the morning broken honeycombs.

They have three boats, *Skarf, Gannet, Skua*
Fishing west, beyond Breckness, at plough-time.
   Fishermen call to hill-combers
   Bondmen! Dung-spreaders! Dumb oxen!

Look, the free fishermen of Hamnavoe
Strike your mud eyes with dazzle of herring.
   We sail through the Sound. Soon
   Beyond Hoy, we are to dredge up pearls.

The Wandering Fiddler

In the island of tall corn
A spit of rain in my face,
A rabbit for my pot.

Down at the shore
Lobster boat, cod boat.
They hung a crooked fish on my finger.

A thick red wife
Stood in the open door
Between me and the apples, the tobacco and the jam.

The farmer set his dogs on me,
A black-and-white storm!
But his lass broke an oatcake, butter and drops of honey.

I shared a roof
With one old sheep,
A bird, spiders, a rat, a broken plough.

I unsheathe my fiddle
At the August Fair.
I strike the islanders to the heart.

My cap rings –
Copper and silver and one gold piece.
They take their wounds home under the stars.

Myself and a sailor
Drank whisky in the tent.
That man told me a hundred lies.

Skara Brae: A Time of Drought

The stones hot. Sere grass. The dead ewe
   A bag of stinking bones.
     Big salt round,
Where have you hidden the black clouds?

Girls went to the secret place
   Every girl with a jar
     Their hands clean.
A string of shells at each wrist.

How long till the word came back?
   A month the girls were gone, then all
      Water-changed.
We knew them by their shell signs.

A hawk sat, fierce and gray, on the rock,
   Furled, sun-fallen,
      The cloud cleaver.
The curl of a claw on a limpet.

One was a swan, the white bird,
   Shaking sea from webs, burying
      Her neck deep.
She trod the sand, oyster-beaked.

Nervous deer, hill dweller
   Do you remember your snow?
      Hesitant,
One hoof gentle on a scallop, lifted?

Butterfly, flower of the wind,
   Drinker of dew and nectar,
      Lights on the lip
Of a grottie, flower of the ocean.

The sow came, wisest of creatures
   Snortling, it scraped in a midden
      Orts and roots,
It turned a shell like a great thunder-drop.

A horn cried. The girls tore the masks.
   They danced. They brought the elders.
      To a bruised rock,
Five jars filling with gray blood from the rock.

I

Images grow slower on the worn loom.

    Lucent rain-bubbles
    Burst on the pools of his balcony
    And a sparrow
    Eyes from the rusted railing
    Bits of bread an old man scatters.

A blue sky patch – a scoured
    Silver coin eastward –
    A golden stone at noon.

No need for other pictures.

II

A burden: weaver, quarryman, poet.

    His house is crammed with books and manuscripts,
    Pictures, jars, music,
    One stone hollow heavy with coins.
    Better a bare cell in Eynhallow
    And a heart at peace.

III

Bairn-coat to shroud, the journey

    Near the end of the road
    The wind of before and after

Begins to shake the tatters of a man's life.

IV

'If only I was this sunset
Dear friend
Beside your fire, talking, proving
    The depth of your ale-mug . . .'

The quern of too many autumns
    Sifts dust of April into the urn.

All things indeed come from the hand of God
   But the random stone
   Is not thrid with our pain.

V

Think rather: the stone
Ruins in sun and rain –
   Not ruins, it runs out
   Centuries long, fruitful or barren dust.

A wild stalk in a dry place
   Lifts into light.

A thousand winters on, somewhere
   A pilgrim mouth
   Will taste, thankfully or brutishly, the bread.

VI

This is true. Not wisdom or wealth can redeem
The green coat, childhood.

Truth is, an old man comes
Led by a cold hand
To a hovel without a hearth-stone
   Empty cup, bare board.

On a wet morning, in an island
   An old man breaks a crust
   For a sparrow on a rusted railing.

VII

In the white theatre, autumn by autumn
A masquer takes needles to a torn coat

And the man must go out again
   Into deepening winter.

There is no skill or enchantment
   To make the old coat green.
There can be at best, now
A flung or fated pattern of patches.

Stars pierce like nails, after harvest.

Near a hallowed stone
The sparrow also builds her nest
   Introibo ad altare Dei

   Who giveth joy to my youth.

The Joiners' Yard: 1886

The yard above the sea
Is a well of light
This August afternoon, filled with mint
And stars of ox-eye.
Here the joiners worked
A century ago,
The journeymen and apprentices.
And the foreman
Stood at the gate, thumbing
The pages of an order-book.
A yell! A boy
Has hit his thumb with a hammer.
The apprentices titter.
The foreman trances the yard with a black glower.

All week
They've made tables, chairs, a cradle.
The stone floor
Is thick with blond shavings.
Planes whisper, hammers thud.
A dinghy drifts to the slipway.
A fisherman calls,
'She needs a new starboard plank,
Soon, before the winter.'

The edge of the pier is lined with gulls.
A bee
Blunders about with its bag of gold.

Then a woman, black-shawled, whispering.
The foreman is solemn.
'I must go and measure a bairn for a coffin.'

The sun flashes off the blue silk of the harbour.

Two journeymen
Begin to cut the boards for a small voyager.
She waits under a garret window, cold,
For sunset
For the one star of voyaging.
Now the foreman's gone
Apprentices
Shower the stone-girt yard with nails and shavings.
They shout.
The gulls rise in swirls about the yard.

All lie now under a green wave in the west.

Sunday in Selskay Isle

I

The anvil doesn't ring today.
    The black creels are stacked high.
The village shop is shuttered.
Selskay the island
Floats on a blue Sabbath silence.

There: the kirk door is open.
    The solemn beadle, Tammo
    Looks along the two roads.
There: the solemn bell
    Gives a first cry.

II

The horse gallops in the Glebe field
    As if the sixth day
Had not been uttered yet.
    Beadle pulls rope,
    Bell summons.

The elders in black suits
Put horse and sheep behind them
　　Making for the kirk.
Girls droop like flowers, following.
Gravely they dance into the seventh day.

III

Across the Sabbath of peace
　　The third bell psalms.

In the Manse the minister's wife
Brushes crumbs and hairs
　　From the minister's collar.
Reverend Hector MacSween
　　Gathers up the leaves of his sermon.

IV

Laird breakfasts late. Laird
– James Traill esquire of Selskay –
Has sipped port, he has
　　Played whist beyond midnight
With the Kirkwall magistrate
　　And the excise officer
And with the young Mrs Traill.

The hall chapel is locked.
The Episcopal rector
　　Can't cross for matins every Sunday.

What will he have with his toast,
Honey or marmalade?
　　The fourth bell stroke
Floats like the tongue of a small angel
　　Over the loch to the hall.

V

'Think shame!' cries Lizzie Ann
　　To the swine-snores under the blanket.
'All the hen-money
　　Poured down your drunken throat' . . .
'High time,' she cries
　　'The shutters were up at that inn.'

Lizzie Ann passed the innkeeper
    (Mr Archibald Fettes)
Tying flies to fluent rods. Her fire-words
Die on the fifth bell-tremble.

VI

Mr Frame, schoolmaster
    Drinks coffee in the schoolhouse.
He will go for a walk, later, through the empty island.

No, Mr Frame is not an atheist
    (He tells this farmer, that fisherman)
But, 'the divine is everywhere
In Nature, in books and music.
    I worship in Greenfields Kirk.'

The sixth bell-song
    Is no more to Mr Frame
(How long will they be able to keep
A clever young man like Mr Frame
    In a primitive island like Selskay?)
Than the chime of his spoon
    Against his empty coffee cup.

VII

Now the road is solemn with folk
Moving out of the death-ending darg of a week
    To Sabbath and resurrection
Drawn by the seventh summons
    In the small stone steeple.

The Tinker Wife

Three things have worked her that indignity,
Travelling the roads with her ferocious man,
Until she seems a moving wind-warped tree –
Rope's end, and heather rut, and porter can.

Yet old men swear that when her budded breasts
Flowered from her maidenhood, her glances shed
On market, wayside weddings, harvest feasts,
A grace that might have driven the preacher mad.

And year by year after her breasts were dry
That tinker wife would call for whisky and pipe
And bid old Ezra fiddle a gay snatch,
And dream she offered him again her ripe
Virginal flesh in some predestined ditch
Where youth ended in a cold desolate cry.

The Kirk and the Ship

The master mason said
'Sail to the island of Eday
And quarry blocks of yellow stone.'

Others drove oxen to the Head of Holland
Where sandstone is red.
The lark's skein
About and about the April hill was thrown.

They did that work, the labouring Orkneymen.

Masons from Durham, strange speakers,
Squared the blocks rough-hewn.
They chiselled their marks, setting stone on stone.

And the Kirkwall villagers
Paused, and shook wondering heads, and went on.

And the kirk grew, like a lovely ship
Freighted with psalm and ceremony, blissward blown.

*

He that ordered the minster
Fluttered in a frailer ship
Across the Mediterranean
With pauses for dalliance, siege, piracy
But always, Jerusalem-drawn.

*

Pillars soared up, red as fire or blood.
And in one they laid
Their martyr, Magnus: his breached bellchambered bone.

Weather Forecasts

Seven old fishermen
Sit on the sea wall in the sun.
A storm, a week away,
Frets their blood.
They smoke pipes. They reckon
A few baskets of cod between now
And the purple chasms westward.

I sit in my rocker
Watching 'the fronts' on a glimmering screen.

Lamp

The lamp is needful in spring, still,
Though the jar of daffodils
Outsplendours lamplight and hearthflames.

In summer, only near midnight
Is match struck to wick.
A moth, maybe, troubles the rag of flame.

Harvest. The lamp in the window
Summons the scythe-men.
A school-book lies on the sill, two yellow halves.

In December the lamp's a jewel,
The hearth ingots and incense.
A cold star travels across the pane.

All Souls

'There are more Hamnavoe
    folk in the kirkyard
Than there are walking the
    Hamnavoe street' –
My father used to say that,
    and I a child.
Death was a door
    that never had opened,
I had no dread of the skull
    beyond
Nor of ghosts that troubled
    some of the living.

Today a throng of good
    ghosts visit me,
Coming at the bellstroke of
    the prayer *de mortuis*
A host so numerous I
    can't name them all.
Name seven, as the
    second sun of November
    comes cold in at the
    window
And a November cloud
Rattles first hailstones on
    bereft gardens.
Name Peter Esson, tailor,
    presiding from his bench
Over sailors' nightly anthologies,
    stories
Rooted in Shanghai,
    Rio, all ports between,
And Peter stitching a
    Sabbath suit for some
    farmer.

Name Attie Campbell, whose
    every utterance
Brimmed the ears of beermen
    with joy
As his mug brimmed with
    tawny Barleycorn fleeces.
Bring Edwin Muir:
    he in age with the chalice of childlight still.
Bring John Folster, fisherman
    who gathered haddocks
    and lobsters
From the thunder-bruised
    Atlantic
Into his frail boat, then
    read his books by
    lamplight,
A lonely gentle pier-dweller.
Summon John Shearer, teacher,
    kinder to his stumbling
    pupils
Than to those who moved
    dextrously
Through the labyrinth of his
    little lab.
Come Peter Leith, farmer,
    turning the leaves of
    books
As familiarly as furrows
In a farm, generations-old, above a loch.
Sing an unknown brother,
    whose bead of light went out
Before the first star.

How many crowd today
    at the kirkyard gate!
Such fragrances filled Hamnavoe's
    closes and piers!
Seventy-year-old tongue
    of dust
Say a blessing now, once more
    in early November.

Mary Jane Mackay, died 3
　　November 1967.
At her name's telling,
　a light breaks
　still
On older Hamnavoe
　　faces.
In this year's flower-time
She'd have garnered
　　a hundred summers.

Two Maeshowe Poems

Circle of light and darkness, be our sign.
We move in shadows.
Brodgar* has burned on the moor a dance of sun.

Ring of quern and plough, contain
Our tumults of blood.
The stars' chaos is caught in a strict rein.

Wheel of life and death, remove
The sweet warm breath.
Ingibiorg flowers in stone, all beauty and love.

Round of sun and snow and seed,
Out of those skulls
Breaks the first green shoot, the full ear, then the bread.

　　　　*

The first island poems
Cuttings in stone
Among the tombs of very ancient dead,
Young men's lyrics　　　　·
Struck with chisels among thronging ghosts
INGIBIORG IS THE LOVELIEST GIRL
HERMUND WITH A HARD AXE CARVED RUNES
A GREAT TREASURE IS BURIED NEARBY
JERUSALEM-FARERS BROKE IN HERE
DRAGON, GUARD THE BONES AND THE VERSES

* Brodgar – a Neolithic stone circle comparable to Stonehenge

The young seamen climbed out of Maeshowe,
Their nostrils wide to the salt wind.

Carol

First, the making of sun and moon and stars.
Then: sea girdling the seven continents.
A green fountain, a tree, shaken with wind
   and sun and rain – and green
   seas, prairies.
The lion burns, the lark is a sweetness
   lost in light, lamb and horse
   converse at ease with ant and elephant, a
   salmon climbs the loud ladder of
   a mountain torrent. They go
   their separate ways in a wind of morning.
At last, a garden in the wilderness, well
   watered, a house of branches:
   there stand in the door a man
   and a girl and a child, under
   the apple blossom.

History has cancelled that music. History
   has brought these ruins,
   confusion in the elements, disaster
   to the blood and dust of man.
In the darkest time, we bring
   candle and carol to the door of
   a byre.

New Year's Day: 1920s

On New Year's Day
My father took us to visit the Museum
Just across from the derelict
'Old Orkney' distillery.

There Mrs Lyon, curator, received us.

And we had our Sunday suits on.
And we had just eaten
The one and only roast beef dinner of the year.
And, there, among the furled birds in glass cases
The Golden Eagle stared out.

Then there was the world-famous fossil, 'Homosteus Milleri',
Hugh Miller, geologist,
Had found in his west-shore wanderings.
My father said his name with reverence:
'A self-taught man, Hugh Miller,
A stonemason.
A whole book he wrote about this fossil,
The Asterolapis of Stromness.'
To me it was just a black mark on a stone.

And there, tall in a corner, the first clock in Hamnavoe,
The brass face beaten like a boxer's.

And there, the model ships,
Their wings yearning towards Diemen's Land or Boston,
Their masters boys
From pierhead and close and croft.

And there, a congress of stone smiling Buddhas.

The chief thing we wanted to see
Was the wooden idol from Borneo, hideously
Carved and dyed, a dancer.

Betty Corrigall

The girl buried in the moor

Child
  in the blue scarf of wind
    begin to dance

Girl
  in the yellow coat of sun
    ripeness is here

Woman
   in the gray sheet of water
      steep your griefs
Queen
   lie robed from looms of earth
      Persephone

The Thresher

In a winter barn, surly Thord
Hung the lantern at a rafter. He swung his flail
   At an oatsheaf. The grains
   Scattered, golden rain, from the straw.

Then the farmer, Finn of the Hill
(That had measured his fields in darkness
   Till Magnus Martyr
   Took from his skull the blind stones

South in Birsay; he joyfully then beheld
Seapink and tern and star
   And fields plough-combed
   And the faces of children)

Came soon to the barn door, calling
'Thord, friend, now is St Magnus Eve.
   Put down that flail,
   No man labours this hallowed time,

Come in to the fire and the ale-cup.'
And Thord, dappled with flame and shadow
   Said, 'Not till today
   Have you thought I laboured too long here.'

And, the shadow of Bergfinn
Gone from the star-crammed door
   Thord struck ripeness on ripeness
   From the bare broken stalks

And his strenuous shadow
Jerked across the granary wall
    Like a mad dancer
    In a place of incense and whispers.

Voices from the farm, 'Thord, Thord,
The Magnus ale is poured for you.
    Come in, Thord, soon, or
    We'll froth our beards from your jug.'

But Thord laboured to the last sheaf.
Then he snuffed the lantern,
    Closed the barn door, went up like a troll
    To the fire and the long bench

And his throat throbbed thankless
With the seethe and the gold of summer.
    Then a madness threshed
    Through Thord like a roost in tempest

And he flung between fire and firkins
And fell, foam-lipped, till ploughmen
    Brought bonds, as a mad bull
    Is chained to a byre wall.

Then Finn of the Hill, farmer,
'Saint Magnus, show mercy
    To Thord my servant, as once
    You implored lucency

On my swart skull sockets.
Then your shrine will be richer
    By half a silver mark, after
    I sail Thord to Orkney

For a three-night vigil, by starlight
And candlelight, soon.'
    The women slewed their heads
    Like birds, all the way, in a storm.

The prayer, a palm-branch, fell on that passion.
Then had Thord the peace
    A glebeman knows, at a glebe edge
    Blessed by pieties of plough and flail.

. . . And left Alba and the wrathful rocks,
Suffered, between Alba and Orc, sore belabourment of sea.

Every beach along the west
Had its stone house and wattle huts
And young horses
That sieved wind through their manes, on a hill
And a woman at well or rockpool.
On one headland, an arch and a bell.
The last island, that also had its coat of barley patches.

Fish, brief brightnesses in the nets
Sweetened mariners' mouths.
We held our sail, a hollow, under wringings of black cloud.
In Shetland, watcher and watcher on every verge,
Boats furled between crag and crag
Wherever a last wave sang among pebbles.
Then, at sunset, drew to a black rock.

'Vementry, black hill in the sea,
We are to gather stones
For a hall, barn, loft of gray pigeons.
We have not forgotten
Mattocks, and the heavy seed-sack.
We will put nets cunningly woven
Here and there under your cliffs.
Will you set your free hawk on the fist of this boy?
Hide us from the voe dwellers
Until we set our tower of strong stone.
You will not lack for fires next winter.
Your fluent heather
Will make caisies for the women, Vementry.
It may be, next summer,
We will have speech with the men in the next valley,
A bartering of well-cured fish for an ox and goats.
Marigold fields on the far shore,
Blue groundmist of squill,
First seapinks in clefts of rock.
Vementry, we will honour you with beehives.'

The helmsman is putting his mouth to the sand now.
'Waken from your long sleep, island.

In the time of our children's children
You will wear a green coat, Vementry,
A young beautiful isle in the throng of islands.'

Ode to Adam Christie

Dark visitors at your door, in starlight.
They would speak only with you, Adam.
Only you can read the word on the summons.

You are sentenced to stand among flames,
Adam Christie.
'Let him thole his torment life-long in a place of stone' . . .

The iron ship is waiting.
You will not see cornfield or fishing boat more.

You sit under a high barred window,
Adam Christie,
Visited by butterfly, bird, star, rose petal, cloud.
And now your mind is quiet.
You thank God for many beautiful things.

I think, one night an angel came to your cell –
Adam, sing.

You woke, prisoner, your tongue touched with the coal.
You sang your days, and our days
On the blank of a thrown-away cigarette packet
And on a warped tea chest
And on a heap of brigstones, striking with six-inch nail.

Beautiful your script among the scattered trash of time.

Then, Adam Christie, you died,
Aged eighty, far from Cunningsburgh.

Ignorant hammers broke your stone poems.
Moths came with the moon,

Their mouths went here and there at the manuscripts.
Did the angel bend, did he gather and sift the work?
Did the adamant mouth
Cry, *Well done, Adam Christie . . .?*

Adam Christie, we don't know much
Moving in these opacities,
Only that sometimes, after cosmic fires
Lies, clear and shadowless, the crystal.

Thomas Leisk, Factor, at his Ledger in the Haa of Grobsness

Item: 3 score geese in sacks for Scallowa market . . .
  I am old, beard lost its blackness.
  I dream this, a poor lass may be lady at my Haa.
  I have power to part her Peter from his yole.

Item: 12 sacks barley to his lordship, the rent . . .
  Cometh not wisdom with silver hairs?
  Their love, a bird-cry on the waters, lost.
  Would not his salt eat into the apple of her?

Item: A heifer for 2 kegs Hollands . . .
  A many a lass clustered my youth.
  I know, a sea lantern spans the hill.
  Yea, but my sovereigns are surer glitterers.

Item: 5 baulks timber for a new barn . . .
  Full harvest it is for me now.
  May she not lift the silver cup to my mouth?
  Salt covers the mouth of many a fisherman.

Item: Eviction of a father from his holding . . .
  I am frown and fist to his lordship, here.
  The lass turned from me at sheaf-binding.
  The boy makes mock of me at ale bothies.

Item: Order a stone from Lowrie, stonecutter.
  Man knoweth not the day or the hour.
  She has stood at the kirk door in white?
  Yea, and cometh the white coat to all, at last.

In early winter, in Orkney, I took up the scarred 'Orfeo' manuscript once more and unwove and wove, and ended with a kind of masque that, if music and design were put upon it, might keep some of its ancient power.

Orfeo: A Masque

I

Orfeo and the boat *Dayspring*
    And six fishermen off Foula.

The uncoiled line, baited, wandering deep.
Orfeo and the fiddle and empty fathoms.
        Play a reel, man.

The hauled lines, burgeoning hooks,
Twenty score cod,
        Bare barb, a red bead on the fiddler's finger.

Row home, fishermen, flushed with sunset.
Your women wait
        With knives and plates on the shore.

No smoke from one chimney. Orfeo,
    He of the winged blithe wooden bird,
Brideless and bairnless, unbeholden, bides alone.

He slimes a flagstone with seven fish.
Glance of a gray-eyed girl through the door.
New flame in the hearth, a fish in the pot,
    The board set with butter and salt.

The lass goes away, unthanked, under a star.

Orfeo dreams of cornfields, a hill of sheep,
The fiddle folded forever at a farm wall,
    A corn bride.

II

Orfeo at the farm door, with a string of fish.
        '*A sea gift, for Maurya your lass . . .*'

'She's summoned to tend the lady in the Hall of Scalloway, *With silver combs, and silks,
And servings on a silver plate . . .'

*[429

The gray-eyed lass in the lee of the barn
    She listens, lingers.
Orfeo under a net of stars, silent,
    Shut out from fire and farm.

His house is not dark. A girl's hand
Has put the fish-oil lowe in his lamp in the window.

III

Dayspring, the fishermen, the lines let down,
Long lingering furlongs, black, off Unst,
    An empty sea.

The sun bleeds like a whale in the west.
    A rage of women at the shore,
    Sullenness of men.

Orfeo's been all day among fields with his fiddle,
Aware of the lift
    And long liltings of a laverock.
He listens to the green corn growing.

He goes home.
    A gift of new bread is on his board, smoking:
The neighbour lass
    Has not lingered, the gray-eyed one.

IV

Orfeo at the door of the Hall, with an oyster,
A glimmer, cloistered,
    In two storm-gray valves.

He beats. The door
    Is oak, iron-studded.
    His knuckles bleed.

'A gift for Maurya, servant to the lady here,
A sea pearl.'

Dance of laird and ladies,
          A thin cold chime of virginals.

Storm rattles the shutters. Honeyed bread
Is brought, and wine, to a long table.
    Ladies flow through mirrors,
In lamplight, lissom and lovely.

Maurya draws a silver comb
    Through the long hair of the laird's lady.

A hound howls in the kennel.
    A thief! A spy! Pirates!

V

Orfeo in the ale-house: lamp and barrel:
    The luckless crew,
Beards of fishermen, barley-foam fleeced.

Orfeo thrusts the fiddle in his bright beard.
          At midnight
    The heavy feet begin to dance.
Questing, flashing, the bow upon snarling strings.
Shawls at the star-filled door, shrieking!

Gray eyes under a carved lintel,
At Scalloway Castle, alone,
    She weeps, that watcher.

Sixern and ale-sodden six, in the east,
    In swart snarling sea,
And the lift like layers and foldings of lead.

A sudden reef, a knife
    In the boat's long belly,
Six cries, a scatter, soon salted and sunk and silent.

VI

Orfeo on the shore at sunset,
He wanders and watches still
    Under the broken net of stars,
And the fiddle a folded bird at the bothy wall.

The lass at the rockpool, with hot aquavit in a cup.
The clay grows cold,
Clay and spirit grow cold on the rock.
Clay by clay, a scatter of six, sunk fifty fathoms
And the blood
Cold and silent as shells soon.

VII

What is the white shape laid
By gardener and groom
At the pillared gate of the Hall?
It is Maurya consumed to cinders and shadows.

The corpse is taken by four crofters,
It is borne over the moor to the barn.

It is borne, soon, by six brothers to the kirkyard.
It is drowned in earth, in a wave of clay.

The gravedigger's spade is bright when the last clod
Is turned and tramped on.

VIII

Who stands in the ale-house, with tinker
And smuggler and poacher
And gangrel and beachcomber,
Till ale flushes faces and feet
And they shout for music?

Orfeo.

But Orfeo is sick of that fiddle
And the thousand wrongs it has wrought,
The scattered sea dead,
The snowcold folded hands under the mort-cloth.

Who stands at the door of the inn in a black coat?
    A horseman, with news.
Who stands between the corn, throat-high,
    And the fisherless shore,
And waits till the ale-house empties
And the kirkyard brims with shadows?

Guardian. Giver. The gray-eyed sea girl.

IX

Midnight. The dim of summer.
    The unfurled fiddle, a song at the rock:

'Let her go. Let her bend to the scattered corn stalks.
Let her hand
    Shine along knife and fish at the rockpools.
She is beautiful among the daughters of Voe.
    The time is short.'

The rock opens. The fiddle
    Flies in at the fissure.
It sings to the Dark King
With the gold cup in his hand.

The fiddle pleads. The Dark King listens.
The daughter of music
    Death-maiden, Maurya, covers her ears.
The fiddle urges. It wheels,
    A death dance, seven circles.

The Dark King says:

'You man, out there,
Set your face homeward now,
    Maurya will follow.

'You will see her bent and sour and ugly, going graveward
    In a slow broken dance.
    So be it.
Now turn your feet, go home.
She will come
    With marigold, squill, first wild roses.'

X

Maurya stirs – kindled wax and wick –
   A glimmer now
From the clot of shadows at the heart of the rock,
   Death bride.

Orfeo prepares his mouth
   For a surge of kisses (no song),
As many as the drops from a splintering wave,
As grains from the flail,
   A golden shower.

The fiddle flies out into dawn-light.
It lies, trembling, on Orfeo's shoulder,
   In the light and lift of his hand.
Orfeo throws it down, the bird of dancing,
   His dower and delight.

Orfeo turns to take the corn-bride.

She wanes, frail flame,
   Drowned in torrents of noon.
The doors of the rock roll shut
   With a stammer like thunder.

XI

Orfeo sits on the rock, in winter, in snow.
A fell of white hair
   Flows from his face.

A lass finds him, a breaker of ice at the well.
The girl leads the stranger
   Out of their legend
To a house with clock and calendar,
An almanac, births and deaths
   On the blank page of a bible.

Orfeo sits in the poorhouse with twisted hands,
   A nuisance to the strict nurses.

'See what it's brought you to, all that dancing and ale-mugs!'

'Shift your feet, I must sweep the hearth . . .'

'What fiddle? We broke an old fiddle in winter to
Light a fire . . .'

'What lass, Maurya?
Never a woman of that name in this parish,
We've searched blank stones in the kirkyard . . .'

'Have you pennies put by for a coffin?
Well, there's parish and poor fund. You must lie
With the paupers.'

He is torn to death, slowly,
By the tongues of the women of Voe.

XII

At last Orfeo was a length of clay on trestles.

A girl came to cover his face,
Last look of the leal gray eyes.

The girl kissed him. The dead mouth
Smelt of marigold, primrose, squill.

XIII

THORFINN RAGNARSON – FIDDLER
Chirped chisel on stone.

The stone sang among silent choirs,
The dead in the kirkyard of Voe.

It sang through a thousand suns and snowfalls.
After three hundred summers
The stone was a blank page in the book of the dead.

The Ballad of Betty Mouat

Old kind Betty Mouat
Setting out to Lerwick, to the shop there
With knitted shawls, stockings, bonnets.

Patient Betty with the crippled foot
In the *Columbine*'s cabin,
Wind and seamen shouting above.

Wondering Betty,
In the creaking boat, in the up-and-down sea
Under a broken mast.

Benighted Betty, in a sea cell,
With a biscuit to chew,
With a text or two for comfort.

Betty, a ghost holds the wheel now.
The skipper,
He is one with starfish and spindrift.
Women wail from sea-banks far back.

Brave Betty Mouat, she remembers
Other voyages, God-charted,
Noah with the raven and the dove,
Jonah in the whale's belly.

Ships search in wide circles, they batter
Ramsheads into the tempest.
Nothing – a gray waste, with cold fringes.

Betty wets her mouth with milk.
She thinks of New Jerusalem, no more sea.
'I aye liked tidemark and rockpools.'
Betty dreams. Ocean is a cloth
Sewn with whale, herring, lobster, jellyfish, sailor, whitemaa,
    limpet, star
Hung on a wall in New Jerusalem,
Just like the tapestry
On Mr Bruce's hall in Sumburgh,
An undulant splendour, mothless immortal fabric.

Beautiful scriptured old woman, Betty Mouat,
Not a ghost kept the helm,
An angel herded *Columbine* through those wolf packs of ocean.
Norwegian fjord-folk
Find you, fold and fire and feed you, you with the basket
    Clover-sweet still.

Yule Candle

'Mary Mother, we women of Voe
Bring one small flame from many peat-flames to a long
   Gray column of beeswax
For you, this Yule night.'

The children stand about that light in the sill,
A winter petal, pure-mouthed.

A lass kneels in the lantern-dappled byre.

The bride of last winter sits by a cradle.
The boatman's boy hangs on a wave of sleep, the candle
   His mast-lamp.

A widow's sun-cakes lie on the hearthstone.
Her hands are folded
Except to shore up wax in the weeping candle.

An old one says, 'This heart-fire
Will be cinders soon.'
The blessing laves her, bone and winter breath.

Then all those women:
Star of the Sea, shine for the fishermen of Voe.

Travellers (2001)

The Green Gate

So Mansie came to the green gate.
A hooded man
Asked Mansie for the password.
Mansie said, 'Password? I came here
Because the road
Stops here (it seems) and I always give a greeting
At an open door, going past.
I have nothing in my hand. I'm sorry.
Seventy years with plough and boat
And never a gift!'
The grave voice said, 'Not a name worth carving in marble,
But go in, man. Go in.
Such as it is, you have a story to tell
Different from the memoirs of statesman or poet,
And always
Simplicity is something.'
Mansie went in, clothed with his days
And sat down
At a table with six quiet strangers.
There was food and drink on the board,
From hand to hand a weave of good courtesy
On a loom of silence.
Then a child said to Mansie,
'The face of the man at the gate,
I saw it,
And it was brighter than the sun.'
Their tongues were unlocked at the table then.
Far into the night
They told, one after another, their stories:
Pure as root or shell or star.
Listening, Mansie considered
His days of clay and sweat and sea-slime,
And he shook his head.
But when he stood by the fire at last
His mouth was a harp. His mouth was a struck harp.

The labyrinth: an old blind man in the centre of it with a
      crystal key.
The labyrinth: towers, vennels, cellars.
The labyrinth: a wilderness of dark doors, with one bright
      lintel here and there.
  Bright lock by bright lock he turns the crystal key.
At every door, a rag of time falls from him.
   Through ghetto, shambles, graveyard he goes.
   The brightness spills out, spills out before him.
   He brings the poem to the hidden bestiary.
The labyrinth. The labyrinth.
He stands, a young man, at a threshold of unbearable
      brightness.

      *

The child plays, in his island, his eyes filled with the sun.
Far back, the beast lies in a pool of darkness.
The child goes among the sun-bright ruined stones of the
      labyrinth.
  (The epic is over. The lyrical echoes have not yet begun.)
A little ship sails its horizon forever, freighted with bales and
      barrels of the sun.
Below, his father opens the door of a simple field to the golden
      guest, the sun.

Modigliani: The Little Peasant

What's he thinking of, sitting there?
He's thinking of a girl,
She who makes cheese and butter in the next farm.

I think he's waiting for the horsemen
To come from the stables.
They're to take him for a pint or two at the inn.

Is he remembering the circus
That passed through, in April,
An elephant, clowns, a drummer?

I think he's been cutting barley all day.
His eyes are sore
With sun, scythe-flashings, corn dust.
Tomorrow, the setting up of stooks.

No: when (he wonders)
Will the farmer's wife call him indoors
For broth and bread?
His nostrils are stretched with kitchen smells.

We stand before him in the gallery now,
Thousands of ghosts.
The Little Peasant welcomes us from the country of forever.

Tolstoy

He sits at an oak desk,
    The old lordly peasant,
There is fire about his heart.
In the crucible of his heart
    The ore is troubled.

He swings a scythe,
    In a field, with serfs,
Count Leo Tolstoy,
    In the sweat of his brow
    He scatters the gold of a summer.

He is home from the wars,
    Sword over hearthstone set.
Now the greatest war
Is there for a transmutation (this alchemy?)
    Bald Hills, Natasha, Borodino.

Truth is a clear star.
    Men root among husks and roots.
Clear and simple, the star.
    Tolstoy lay on the rack of age,
The star on his forehead.

The heroes of history
    Perish in their fires,
        Caesar, Napoleon, Genghis Khan.
Time, a wind, mingles their dust
With dust of falcons and flowers.

Look, the crucible is cold,
Look, the manuscript
    Sifts pages across the great oak table,
The sheaves are in the barn.
A book is heavy with jewels and icons.

Norman MacCaig

Milne's Bar, Rose Street, Edinburgh –
A Saturday afternoon in 1956.

Sitting here and there about the unlovely tables,
Sydney Goodsir Smith, Tom Scott, Norman MacCaig,
    Robert Garioch, George Campbell Hay, Alexander Scott
And other bards
Whose lyrics, scratched on the backs of envelopes,
Would never fly into books.

A cry on the steps, 'Chris, he's here!'
And the bards rise to greet their king, Hugh MacDiarmid,
Just off the Biggar bus.

(This Orkney bard sits alone.
    He is too shy – as yet – to visit the bards' table.
Enough to look at them, with longing.
Their words have flown out of books
    To sit, singing, on the branches of his blood.)

And now, a few days since,
The last of those poets is dead,
MacCaig, he with the head of a Gaelic chieftain
And the courtesy,
His tongue an edged and glittering dirk
Against whatever is ill made, unworthy.

May the mountains
Gather about him now, in peace, always.

Old Woman

None has seen tears from this face
But the mother
And a sharp-tongued teacher
And one ploughman
And a young sea widow
And my bairn in the cradle

But for rain and spindrift
A worn dry stone.

Elegy for a Child

This second door stood open only a short while.
Now close it gently.
The ghost has gathered its few belongings into a bag.
It has gone through the garden gate.
It has turned its back on the fire, the roses, the stories.

Fragrance from lintel and threshold –
Fragrance of bread –
Fragrance of sharing, after a good word uttered –
Fragrance of laughter too young for mockery.

Have you seen a disturbance in the blue wind
Between the cold hearth and the moor?
The brief flesh
About the bone, brighter than a cornfield
And the ghost beyond dew and snowflakes bright.

(For a short time it is lost – it weeps –
It does not know where to go.
Ears are too gross for its grief and questionings.)

Shut the door gently upon women's weeping.
Twelve hands
Light him in at the door of his first mother.

In Memoriam John L. Broom
28 July 1992

John Broom, an old friend of the poet, was a librarian by
profession, also a Unitarian minister, film buff, and biographer
of John MacLean, the Clydeside Socialist.

In sorrow the bread and salt are eaten.
From first cry to last sinking under wounds like a hunted
            beast,
The circuit is sorrowful.
The man who owns veins of gold
No different from the eater of crusts.

The feast and the dance
Are more beautiful
For that road of thorns and stones.

Somewhere, to all men and women
The summons is coming to a feast, with music and the only
            bread and wine.
    – It is a furrow you follow.

Yesterday we gave the dust of a friend to the wind.
And afterwards
Between a black cliff and the sea
A rosebush was planted.

Mhari

Mhari Brown (1891–1967) was the poet's mother.

1

'Go down. Good fishing (lobster, haddock)
   Off Strathy, in the salt streams.
You starve here, in these glens.
   Factor, minister, will speak to those with boat-wit
   In Durness, Scrabster, Wick . . .'

They had not seen sea before.
   To the bleak rocks they came,
Vassals of an English duke.

In hovels above the rocks, starved a summer
Till son and nephew got a measure of sea-wit
   Struggling in skinflint drowning tides.

There, sixth of nine children,
   Mhari spoke the ancient Gaelic
   Till the English schoolmaster came
   To cleanse their tongues of that music.

2

Look: a boy of that clan on the sea-edge
Has prospered in Wick,
   Climbed from 'boots' to own hotels
In Orkney, Caithness, Shetland;
Forgets not his blood,
The Sutherland croft lass, and others.
   Mhari, there she is, gray-faced from the Firth
On the *Ola* gangway,
   A parcel of belongings in her Celtic hand.
The gruff hotel-boss: he stands,
Look, with strict impatient hands
   In the door of his big new hotel.

3

Fiddles, melodion, a Town Hall dance,
    Fishermen, country boys, clerks.
Is this sinful?
Is cleaning hotel-rooms on Sabbath sinful?
    The Free Presbyterian rock
    Keeps ancient springs of laughter

And she laughs with the joky postman
    (Waxed moustache, stylised wit)

And round they circle, this time a waltz.

But a kiss, under the streetlamp?
    Sinful, dangerous. 'I won't
    Walk out with that man again . . .'

4

Midsummer. The wedding feast –
    Cheese, lobster, cake, whisky
    In Strathy, small scatter of Celtic crofts.

Tinkers came through the dusk,
    One had a fiddle.
    The parish danced till dawn.

The bridegroom, he was drowning
    In a sea of lovely Gaelic;
And woke, his mouth cold
With dew of the wild white rose.

5

Gentleness, poverty, six children
    (One died) in stone houses
Along Hamnavoe, at close and pier.

A cupboard sparse but never empty,
Oatcakes and bannocks on a smoking griddle,
    The Monday washing
Flaunting, damp flags, in a walled garden,

The paraffin lamp on the winter table,

Jar of bluebells on a sun-touched sill,

And a wordless song moving
   Through the house, upstairs, downstairs,

At the creeled pier, in the bee-thronged garden.

She thanked, out of an ancient courtesy,
   All visitors for calling.

6

No woman but lips many times
   The dark chalice,
Parents, husband, children, friends.

A comely sorrow, the mouth tranquil:
   Thy will be done.

The first dark petal fell,
Then others, a cluster of shadows,
   Flower of oblivion
    About her gentle turning away.

7

On a winter night, from the Hamnavoe God-acre,
   There, the Strathy Light!
Between, rampant hooves and manes,
   The Pentland Firth.
   The dead lie, rank on rank,
   Facing the sunrise.

Wintered roots coil
   For upsurge, the arms of a girl
   Overbrimming, the new light.

Today, June the fourth, 1993
Mhari – her death month November –
   Had been one hundred and two.

    *

To Sister Margaret at Sacred Heart Convent on St Magnus Day 1992

St Magnus Day 1992

Outside my window daffodils
Dance in the north wind.
In another garden
A blackbird
Clothes, before leaves, a tree in song.

It is Saint Magnus Day.

But for that company of heroes
But for those
Whose blood purified the roots and sources
The daffodils
Would be a measurable disturbance of earth and air today,
That blackbird
A graph on a cold grid of sound.

But the poor still dance (thank God).
Because of the saints
We, a throng out of winter,
Dance now in coats brighter than Solomon.

Saint Magnus Day

'She's making for the open ocean, that ship,
A scatter of oars
Between here and Rousay.'

'Them and their axes and loot.
This ox, Sam,
He won't have the yoke put on him.
He was awkward last year too.
More of this, Mister Ox,
You'll be pies on the hearth, next winter.'

'What's the priest doing down at the shore?
And that flock of hens, the women?'

'I took that many stones out of the heather
I could build a hut.
Only the laird would charge a rent for such a wilderness.
I tell you this, men,
We're going to have some wrestle with the new ground.'

'Stand still, you brute! Look
At this plough.
More than one spider's wintered here.
Look, a rat's tooth in the share.'

'I told that woman to be here with the ale-skin.
Look, Ragna, says I,
We begin the ploughing at noon.
And there she is, the slut,
Gawping at a longship going past.'

'I don't see shields along the hull.'

'What we need is new strong ploughs,
Curves of Scottish oak.
Then the laird might get his rent on time
If he gave us strong wood
And had less tapestries and goblets
On shipboard, from Dublin, for his lady in Rousay.'

'The candles are lighted in the kirk.
Is there a death in some house?'

'The ship, she's nudging the tide,
Egilsay-bound.
That's it, the bishop's on board.
Oh, how they'll smirk
And curtsy and hand-kiss, our women, soon.'

'All I know is, if we don't put ploughs to the hill
There'll be no bread in winter,
Not a jug of hot ale
When we come in with blue hands from the lobsters.'

'No harvest home. No fiddle, no dancing.'

'Look at that hawk
Up near the sun, slewed north.
A big wind
And he hasn't stirred for eight gatherings
And shatterings of sea.'

'Up, Sam. Up, ox. Kick him.
Sam, you should be glad.
You've been in that dungeon of a byre all winter.
Sun and sweet grass now, Sam.
Sam, think of cornstalks.'

'Simon, you have the thickest shoulders,
Pick up the plough.'

'A man has left the ship.
Look! A man in the sea, his mouth brimming.'

The Doors of Death

The earl rode past my door, the saddle
    Studded garnet and gold.
The gravedigger held a skull. Ploughmen
Struck the glebe into furrows.

A pilgrim passed my door. He held
    A silver fare in his fingers.
Last ice along the ditches.

A poor man passed my door. He wore
    The mask of man's hunger.

    I am Death. No hearth in my house.

    A poor man sat at my board.
He broke the bread into blessings.

    A pilgrim stood at my thwart. Prow-
Shape, dove-shape, share. A wave
    Traversed him, silvering.

Who takes plough to the lord's glebe?
Lord or labourer,
It is man sets out on the long road
To the Inn of the Cornstalk.

Earl Rognvald Kolson of Orkney to an Itinerant Builder of Churches

To Master Roger at Durham, builder of kirks,
It is no clerk or scrivener
Seals this letter. I am an earl,
Commander of ships, poet,

A man skilled at ordering sounds and silences
On a winter harp. I pull in nets
With my fishermen, I delight
In smithy flames, hammerings, hot iron.

All good labour – plough and oar and peat bank – dances
To original music. I urge now
A famous maker of stone poems
To meet me in a place of silence.

I say to a skipper, 'Take this letter
To King Olaf in Norway,
Unfurl a sail, be swift and sure
As a dove through spindrift.'

And he stows the sealed parchment
In a leather bag, old shipman,
Against salt encrustings . . .
Maker of scattered stone ships,

I do not know where skipper or horseman
Will find you, you and your workmen
Are forever on the roads
Going with your carts, scaffoldings,

Plummets, compasses, ladders, wedges,
Mortar-boards, hammers, chisels
(No rest till all get thrown,
Worn out, on the far shore of time).

You do not build town houses
   For merchants, however much gold
      They ring on your bench,
Nor barns, nor lodges, battlements,

But kirks only, *Ad Majorem Dei Gloriam.*
   This morning a thing was told me,
      You and your carts are encamped
About a stone hull in Durham.

A great kirk for the bishop there
   Soars as high as the rooks, I hear.
      The last stone will be locked in
Before the wrecking storms of Yule.

Shipwright in stone, I have purchased
   Three acres of land near Kirkvoe,
      A village in the Orcades
And I've had it long in my mind –

Rather, an angel winged in with it –
   To build a red minster there
      In memory of a murdered uncle.
What! I can hear you growl,

Earl or beggar, this man is a fool –
   I am not a carver of tombstones.
      But if I say, this murdered one
Is Saint Magnus the Martyr

By whose broken skull blind men
   Behold the sweetness of sun again,
      Cripples and mourners dance
To poetry,

And I that whirled away youth
   At ski-slope, tavern, tilt-yard
      Stand in a place of silence.
(The honeycomb is in the rotting lion.)

I have a headland of lavish sandstone.
   In a tall pillar red as fire
      Set the skull, our saint,
Magnus who orders the seven unruly crewmen.

In my smithy, I will beat out
   My blood-crusted axe, to shine
      Candlestick and cruet in our kirk,
My net will hang at the wall.

I desire an ark to carry this people
   To Golden Jerusalem (I am to sail there soon
      In a fleet of fifteen ships,
A frail flutter of poems).

Sir, you will be paid in good Rhenish gold.
   Be at the port of Leith in Scotland
      On the Saint's day, mid-April.
Three ships, ample-holded,

Will carry your score of masons,
   Your gear (flutes, chessboards, tankards too)
      All things apt and needful
To build this great red psalm in the islands.

St Rognvald's Journey to Jerusalem
*Rognvald's epic voyage was the inspiration for a major artistic
event in the 1993 St Magnus Festival. Fourteen sails painted
by local artists were hung in the nave of St Magnus Cathedral.
Drawing their inspiration from the poet's laconic text, each of
the sails celebrated a 'station' on the great Viking pilgrimage
to Jerusalem. This artistic enterprise has now acquired a
musical dimension in a sequence of orchestral and choral
works composed by Sir Peter Maxwell Davies for the BBC
Philharmonic Orchestra.*

    I   Fifteen keels laid in Norway for Jerusalem-farers
   II   In Kirkwall, the first red Saint Magnus stones
  III   An Orkney wintering. Stone poems in Orkahowe:
        'great treasure . . . '
  IV   Bishop William: a blessing on the pilgrim sails
   V   Westerly gale in Biscay, salt in the bread broken
  VI   The bishop's ship a small storm-tossed kirk
 VII   Rognvald and Ermengarde: roses, lyrics in Narbonne
VIII   The winter burning of a Spanish castle
  IX   Eindred's desertion, five sails dwindling eastward
   X   A dromond taken, the torrent of molten gold

Saint Magnus Day: The Relics
*The cleft skull of the martyred St Magnus was discovered in
one of the central piers of the cathedral during a major
restoration in 1919.*
  *Bishop William the Old was the first Bishop of Orkney, and
occupied the bishopric for well over 50 years.*

The standards – Andrew, Columba, Olaf –
Flutter
Like great seabirds outside the door of the kirk.

The torches cluster that were invisible flames
Out in the wind and sun,
Red now inside the cave of the kirk,
One by one, a torch in a socket
Under the branching arches,
A torch for the altar,
A torch for the great pier,
Laved in its own red light,
All but the one
Red stone of burial.

Is that music? Listen, listen.
The jargon
Is far off still between
Peerie Sea and Cornslip,
Fiddles, pipes, a drum,
The beat of ocean in it,
And louder (listen!)
And here in the kirk the harp stands,
A silent angel, waiting
For a meshing of the sea music.

Open the door wide. Open
The west door.
Lights of April – lagoon and lift – light, lap
The feet of the bishop.

But now, red light of stone, torches, tapers.
He comes, Gulielmus Episcopus,
'A clerk of Paris',
And Eynhallow with him, the abbot
And canons and deacons
And last
The little old priest of Egilsay,
He that was in his kirk
That night of cold vigil.
What does the bishop carry
Besides his crozier?
An oaken box with an intricate cleft bone.
See, they process
In gold, scarlet, ivory, jet
To the high altar.
A young monk drifts to the harp. He sits. He waits.

A tumult outside. Listen.
Who makes riot on such a day?
Last scars of snow
Silver are on the hill. Scars
Of fire are on a hill.
They acclaim the death of winter:
Per the fisherman and his crew,
Ikey from the tinker quarry,
Skaf that sweeps leaf and shell from the street,
Vik who cargoes a ship among the islands,
Skald who thongs planks
        above curving
        keel, curve on
        rising curve, and
        caulks and tars,
Bluenose the taverner, Swart the smith,
Sigg of the milk and butter
And men from under the cliff.
Why can the town not come in?
They make a clamour at the mercat cross.
The doorkeeper offers a sign.
They rush, shoulder, stumble, grumble,
Then all ingathered, doucely folded.

The white hood stoops to the harp
Like a swan to a loch.

The Harp in the Glebe

This poem was specially commissioned to celebrate the
residency in Orkney of the Scottish National Youth Orchestra
in 1989.

1

Then, after longships, torch and axe,
The skirmish in shore waves, scattering
   Of broch-stones, came a month
   Of hunger, hardship, the yoke

2

On the stubborn ox, a stumbling
On stony furrows, seed-cast, harrows,
   Charting of perilous salt for
   Lobster and ling, long

3

Moor cuttings that a hearthflame
Fail not in the fall and fell of winter.
   Then, the tilth greening,
   Links littered with lambs,

4

Hearthstone and threshold set sure,
The earl spoke. 'Now this steading
   Requires the seal of song,
   A concord of pipes and strings

5

That the rooting of this folk in Orkney
Be at one with the star streams.'
   That night in the long hall
   Young hands, young mouths, beseeched
   Earth-ore, sun-gold, the cornstalk.

Come in September. Then is harp
   Loosed from cobwebs at the wall,
   It rejoices among fires and ice.

Come in September. You will know soon
   Have you come to a hospitable house
   Or will it be thin ale in snow-time.

The poets here will curl their lips.
   They know this, the best bards
   Sail to me from Iceland in September.

Thorbjorn, I will have an ale-mug
   Struck for you. A new lamp,
   In September, beside your scrolls.

Here, in September, over stubble,
   Burnished hand clasps bone hand.
   That treaty, we know, is poetry.

Thorbjorn, you will have sea salt
   In September, on beard and harp.
   And you will be tired of fish.

Inga, that girl, will bring you brightness,
   Sweet well water. Helga,
   In September, will break you a gold crust.

Autumn Cruise

Rolf left stream for streams.
The miller grinds salt.

Sven set foot on a rock, he's
Crabs, cold shells.

Arn's eye
Would have cherished the pure flight and cry of the bird that
   quenched it.

Wolf stooped under a lintel.
There is a lower stone.

Thord? We keep silence.
Thord was soon out of the story.

Aud, silver seeker,
Ten weeks till the snow, Aud.

'Sea sluts, Gerd,
Unravel your Thord . . .'

The ship lies, furled, off More.
Of twenty, seven dry cold oars.

The First Castle: Edinburgh

Set up tents on the slope of this crag, twigs and skins.
   Leave the wounded with wolves, far back.
      'Rain in the south? Or dust of hooves?'
      'There are springs of cold sweet water. Dig deep.'
      'Dig deeper till iron rings on stone.'

They make of stones a small sun prison, a smithy.
   (Barns must wait, the smithy comes first.)
   They build first, a keep on the crag, a stone eagle.
   In old words our story has been uttered, in secret, to the
      strong stones.
   They build a house for the daughters of the chief.
      'Make swords, blacksmith, strokes of winter sun.'
   Quarrymen labour at first dawn.
   The masons square stones at sunset, still.
   The women pluck wool, they spin a thin line from the fog
      of wool, they sit at wooden frames inside a tent.
   The young men live in the fortress, in the sign of the
      eagle, high.
Three or four have gone laughing into the forest. Three
      drag a blood-snortled boar. 'Girls, go with oil and
      leaves to the wounded hunter.'

A mule brought baskets of shifting silver,
   Fishermen stood at the loch under the crag.
     Protect us from the Saxons . . .
     Horsemen broke our keels at a shore in the west . . .

Forge roars, a beast in darkness. The rock reels with black
       music.
   The eagle has iron beak and claws.
   A known tribe then, driving swine and cattle north.
    'We will give you this cow of a hundred
      cheeses for hanks of that wool.'
  Why are you hurrying north?

(They urge pig and ox to the shore of the firth, going north.)
   Girls dance to a swart music. The anvil utters bits of
      strong sun. The eagle will overshadow the Saxons.
   The eagle will tear horse from horseman.
   Girls and warriors turn about the black sun, a Celtic wheel.
   Ice hung gray nails from the stone lintels.

The horsemen came at the time of the first dropped lambs.
   Sunbursts, they blinded a winter folk. A tempest of
   ordered hooves scattered fog and dances, the high
   watcher, the loom and the sweet lost cries of children.
   Bright edges strewed the stones of the keep about the
   high rock. Then was the eagle up in the west. They
   gathered lissom girls to the strong backs of horses.
   They rode with songs into the green sun.

Gallowsha (A Witch Fire)
Gallowsha was the place of public execution in Kirkwall.

THREE OLD WOMEN

  Bring in fire! three old women cried.
  Give her the yellow and red coat! But
  no torches were lit before the throat was girdled.

NEIGHBOUR

Was as bonny a bairn as ever wore daisies, she.
What worm comes in at the mouth, when innocence
sleeps? It breeds in the heart.

THE STRANGER

Oh yes, but she cried. She skirled when she saw
the post and the rope! She stopped then. She went
to the hangman laughing like to a lover.

PREACHER

Repent ye, therefore, and turn. Behold the tree of
sinners, that the rose petals thereof wither like snow,
and are thorns and ashes soon.

ALEWIFE

Ale, penny a pot. Cool the flame the poor girl stands
in. Usque, twopence the glass. Warm a cold spirit.
It passes.

A PALACE SERVANT

He tried her this way and that last winter, all smiles
and sovereigns, then threatenings. She would not
wait under the moon, burning. Then three strangers
with paper and seal stood at her father's door.

CHILD

What's that black mask? What gray thing is shaking
under the rope? Mother, why seven torches, and the
sun so bright?

They stood there, in a small flock
At the wooden jetty in Hamnavoe,
Till the gang-plank was let down.
The heart of the small steamer began to beat
And ropes were cast off.
A few stood above, leaning on the rail –
One shepherd smoked his pipe –
All looking at the granite hill
And Hamnavoe, that cluster of stone houses.
The children
Swirled here and there on the deck like happy birds.
Most of the women were below.
They didn't speak. They looked at nothing.

*

As the great ship out of Southampton
Bore them and hundreds of others (strangers)
Round the Cape, and out
Into the Indian Ocean (such warmth and glitter!)
More deeply the new-sharpened chisels
Scored the stone of their minds with last images:
Fishing boats, seals on a skerry,
Peat hills, kestrels, the great plough-horses,
Kirk and tinker-fire and the hard hewn flame
Of St Magnus at sunset –
Rackwick, the green jar tilted at the sea.
Now here, at night, a new star wheel
Rose from the east, slowly and bound them to it.

*

For days Australia filled their horizon.
Strange birds followed the ship.
The children forgot. Their minds
Were scribbled over and again with new scenes.
But the hammer-strokes of their childhood
Cut the men and women to the heart.
And they made their hearts stone
And their lips were like stone,
As the pulse and wash of the ship drove them on.

*

A sailor pointed eastward, 'New Zealand!'
And they saw a snow mountain, far off.
The children stood for a minute,
Their faces all one way: and soon
They were clowns, dancers, disturbers of the peace!
One girl from Hoy looked west and north –
Bird-high her glance, the sun
Glittered across the prisms of her eyes.
But ancient eyes of Celtic stone
Cut through the roots
Of Himalayas, Caucasus, Atlas, Grampians,
And the curving unquiet crystals of two oceans
To a round blue hill, and seals, and a barleyfield.

Haiku: for The Holy Places

Orc

Orkney – 'orcs' – the school of sleeping whales,
To those who glimpsed it first,
Hills half-sunk in the sea.

Midsummer

Midsummer, the hills wear fertile patches,
Corn and pasture and meadow,
Long green coats from the hills' throat to the shore.

The Northern Sky

Orkney turns upon poles of light and darkness.
A summer midnight, the north
Is red with the two lamps of dawn and sunset.

Kirkyard

Always, by the shore, kirk and kirkyard.
The legends of the dead, their carved names
Faced east, into first light, among sea sounds.

Wind

Wind always, the unseen summer crystal
Compelling boats, clouds, birds.
The million whispers of fulfilment in the green ears.

Scapa Flow

Scapa Flow: great warships lie ramshackle
Under the gray floor.
And soon the veins of oil will throb and flow.

Sea and Cliffs

Sea, old sculptor, carves from the western ramparts
Stack and cave and skerry,
Sweep harpist, with sagas of salt and stone.

Fishing Bird

It waits, rock-fast, wind-flung
Wing – wind – enthirling
One flash from the sea's hoard.

Island Faces

Many masks merge here, in an island face –
Pict, Norseman, Scot
Face of a crofter, gnawed with loam
Face of fishermen, seamen –
Gray of the sea, eyes level as horizons.

Old Houses, New Houses

The old crofts ride the green hill surges,
Long arks; man and beast under one roof.
The new houses,
Will they be there at the dove's return?

Stromness

Stromness, Hamnavoe – 'haven inside the bay'
Twenty stone piers, with boats,
A street uncoiling like a sailor's rope.

Fishermen and Crofters

They hold the keys to earth and ocean,
Earth-key, the plough;
Sea-opener, the net and sinker;
Seventy years nourished with corn and fish,
They open the mysterious doors,
Go, most into earth,
A few through the door of the sea.
They gain the richness of man through the elements.

The Bridegroom from the Sea

I stopped at 'The Arctic Whaler'
To give me courage,
Also to hire a horse, Bess, at the yard.

There was that ale-house in Kirbister.
Bess wouldn't pass the door
Till we'd dug our faces deep in the grain.

Aith in Sandwick, what horseman
Could ever resist your malt?
I sat at the fire with four thirsty ploughmen.

I'd deserted *Susie*, my yawl, that day
To bespeak a bride,
A Birsay lass, well dowered.

I was wearing my best black suit.
At Dounby, didn't I set the mothballed elbow
In a pool of sour ale?

The deeper that nag bore me
Among the barley fields
The sweeter the sea sang in my ears.

Good reports of that lass –
Bonny, a baker of good bread,
A golden hand in the butter-kirn.

After the shebeen in Marwick
I had to rest in a ditch.
I woke up. Bess was away in a green wind.

I never stood at that bride's door.
I footed it home to Hamnavoe.
I said to my boat next morning,

'*Susie*, sweetheart, forgive me.
Our creels never lacked a lobster.
Your thwarts thrashed with continuous silver.

'Brutish servitude, hooves and millstones.
You and I, *Susie*, will go still
Among the blue-and-silver coursers out west.'

The Bridegroom

He spurred round the hill Kringlafiold,
Reined in his horse at croft and croft,
   Chanted the summons, was offered
   The messenger's ale-cup,

Then on, the beast flinging foam on the wind
(Wind blowing foam from ale-cup and ale-cup),
   By way of the marsh and granite,
   To the terrace of scattered crofts

Above Hoy Sound and the shining west,
Garth, Feolquoy, Don, Lingmira,
   Liffea, Legar, Dale,
   Weaverhall, Witt,

Got welcome at every door, but after
The heavy malt of Don, had wisdom
   To froth his beard only,
   And at Pow, horse clomping cobbles,

'Bring your fiddle,' added to the bell cry,
Then dropped down to Glebe, between
   Oatfield and barley
   To where Mr Clouston, minister,

Was taking combs from a hive, addressing
The firestorm of bees in Latin, with
   'Sir, if you please, we want
   The wedding on Lammas Tuesday.'

And set a shilling in the web of sticky fingers.
Then put the scatter of hooves about
   And up across the ridge
   To Castle, Croval, Langhouse,

And sat for oatcakes and cheese at Hammar
(The horse's tongue dredging the trough).
   The west smouldered, stars
   Were sketching a silver rune,

While the bridegroom lingered, and lamps
Stood in Hamnavoe windows,
   Blond squares, and a homing boat
   Struggled in the tide's honey.

The Tryst

'Kirsten' . . . (A moth-burr at a window.)
Kirsten stirs in a caul of shadows.

'Kirsten, I'm outside, it's cold.'
Kirsten sleeps, on her cheek the warm moon apple.

'Kirsten, it's me, Sander.'
Kirsten is in a country that knows no names.

'Kirsten, I've ridden four miles through the gale.'
Through Kirsten's skull it falls, a silver rain.

'Kirsten, I've brought you this rose.'
Kirsten trundles a little bee in her nostril.

'Kirsten, you promised! – O Kirsten – Kirsten!'
In a crystal cave lies Kirsten, sweetly cloistered.

Elizabeth Sweyn, widow, at her writing desk in the hall

For taking a trout out of my water: the cold hill
   water that tumbles white and brown over stones
   to the loch, and loses itself there awhile, and
   then gathers its strands and issues out again,
   tranquil and blue and reed-stained, to the sea,
     I summon you to the Hall.

For making much noise in the bothies and beyond about
the French and their setting to rights of the
frame of society (wrenched from its natural
frame by priest and tyrant): and so casting
a shadow of doubt and threat and disquiet upon
this ancient island seat, and sowing mischiefs
in simple minds,
I summon you to the Hall.

For arrears of rent. I have had much patience with
that old perverse one, your mother, who has
not two farthings to tinkle together when it
comes to Martinmas and the factor stands in
the office with his open rent-book and the
crofters come in, one by one, silver-fingered,
taking off their bonnets: no, but the same
bold lady could come back from last Lammastide
in Kirkwall with a new bonnet and gloves, and
a dozen white cups and plates with blue scroll-
work on them: and after cries to Mr Brodie my
grieve, *What way at all can I pay, and that*
Stephen of mine never turning tilth, no but
squandering every sea-sillock-cent in the ale-
house, morning to night, year-long?
I summon you to the Hall.

You understand well enough, it's bred in your bone,
it is as sure rooted in every person in this island
as the order and priority of stars – one fish
in seven, and that the best, is to be left at
the door of the Hall before sunset: and you
have gone by the door of the Hall every night
this past moon with a string of cod in your
finger to some ignorant red-mouth and sweet-
whisperer in a darkling hill croft; and so
left my five cats hungry.
I summon you to the Hall.

For continual disrespect, in that when a certain
person is horse-borne on the island road all
islanders but one doff bonnets, and crook the
knee, and cast their eyes down; no, but one
certain lump of obstinate clay turns his back,
yea and falls to studying a bird's flight, or

a flower opening, or a raindrop in a pool:
for explanation of such and other practisings and slightings
   I summon you to the Hall.

For that all summonses hitherto, delivered by sundry:
   as, the factor Mr Walter, the grieve John-
   William Brodie, Hilda the lass from the
   butter-house here, Ikey the tinker who passes
   word about the crofts in consideration of a
   sup of whisky, Mr Gilfillan the new minister,
   the Hall dog Major (who so delicately carries
   letters in his teeth), since all and every
   summons from here has been a summons to a
   stone, I intend to come with this myself,
   unfaltering from Hall to hovel, six black
   words on a white sheet,
      I summon you to the Hall
For a hundred reasons I cannot think of now, man,
   I summon you to the Hall.

You have hair like spillings of sunlight and the
   distant words of your mouth laughing among
   fishermen are a disturbance to me and (I know
   it) when you walk from your mother's door of
   mornings to the boat *Cloud-racer* the island
   seems to be yours then, and not this foolish
   widowed soon-to-wither woman's; and if I do
   not speak soon, some little slut from the hill
   or the shore will have you to kirk and to bed
   and to bairn-making; and what is authority in
   a place if a yoke cannot be put on a serf, a
   mere mingling of brief dust and spume; no
   hard yoke either, but a sweet yoke of ease
   and privilege; that being undeniably so?
      I . . .

                    *

Mrs Sweyn, the young widow, left off her writing
   here, she smiled, she tore her letter into small
   pieces and let them fall and flutter from her
   hand into the coal-fire in the study.

Unlucky Boat

That boat has killed three people. Building her
Sib drove a nail through his thumb. He died in his croft
Bunged to the eyes with rust and penicillin.
One evening when the Flow was a bar of silver
Under the moon, and Mansie and Tom with wands
Were putting a spell on cuithes, she dipped a bow
And ushered Mansie, his pipe still in his teeth,
To meet the cold green angels. They hauled her up
Among the rocks, right in the path of Angus,
Whose neck, rigid with pints from the Dounby Market,
Snapped like a barley stalk . . . There she lies,
A leprous unlucky bitch, in the quarry of Moan.

Tinkers, going past, make the sign of the cross.

A New House

They shall sit at the fire,
Neighbour and tramp
And such as seek shelter from the sea.

A fiddle at the wall.
A deep bed.
In the cupboard, a loaf and a bottle.
The Word in the window.
Two cows, ladies of butter, in the long silk summer grasses.

Twelve sheep on the hill.
At the lee wall
Net and plough and peatstack.

And a lucky boat on the shore.

May the rat in the field be chaste and a lover of thistles.

The Guardians

May a strong guardian
Stand at the door
With sword and olive branch.

May the keeper of the windows
Be eager-eyed
For dawn and the first star,
    snow-light and corn-light.

May the keeper of the fire
See a loaf on the table
And faces of travellers lit with welcome
    and shadow-of-flame, in winter.

May the keeper of the beds be resolute
Against the terror that walks by night,
And herd with gentleness the flocks of sleep.

In a blue-and-silver morning
On the first winter step
Those guardians, and others who hold a finger
    to the lip, smiling
Came about her who holds now the key of the house.

The Finished House

In the finished house a flame is brought to the hearth.
Then a table, between door and window
Where a stranger will eat before the men of the house.
A bed is laid in a secret corner
For the three agonies – love, birth, death –
That are made beautiful with ceremony.
The neighbours come with gifts –
A set of cups, a calendar, some chairs.
A fiddle is hung at the wall.
A girl puts lucky salt in a dish.
The cupboard will have its loaf and bottle, come winter.
On the seventh morning
One spills water of blessing over the threshold.

Cragsmen

Cragsman
   He wears the long blue wind for a coat.

Shyness
   Wart is such a shy boy
   He turns aside
   From hag or honeymouth or even a small girl on the road.
   Wart has taken, though,
   The she-kestrel in his fist.

Pinleg
   Sam'l fell, broke his leg.
   He sat a morning
   Among broken gull-eggs, shattering waves.
   Now (lacking his leg)
   He breaks burning peats with a long wooden toe.

Hatchling
   Tammag said to the naked thing
   Blinking
   Out of a broken shell,
   'You and me, buddo,
   May have business with each other
   In a twelvemonth maybe.'

Cliff Fall
   No. Never look. Is no
   Kist or kirkyard stone for Mansie.
   Seventeen summers corn-lissom
   He plummeted
   To meet the singing seagirls.
   One bore him off, brided him
   In a cell beyond Hoy or Suleskerry.

Fight
   'This was my bird
   And my eggs. I was eyeing
   This ledge since last winter . . . '
   'No, but the bird
   Stretched her neck into my hand,
   The bird
   Kissed my neck – look – till it bled . . . '

That cliff talk
Came to flung fists, torn blood, later
In the horizontal ale-house
As if a stinking fulmar
Had been Jean of Fea, bonniest of the lasses that year.

The Test
Before a cragsman can put a ring on a girl's finger
Let him
Teeter on one leg on a high ledge,
Launch himself
Up and round in a wheel
And stand (fluttering)
Facing the bird-hung crag-face,
The mother, gaunt
Giver of life and death.

The Last Step
And Bertak said,
'I know every step in that crag.'
And he said,
'I could go up and down
Blindfold.'
And avouched, into his third mug of ale,
'I don't need a star either.'
He said,
'I think I work better without women.'
That same winter
Bertak went up with a full sack of eggs.
There was a bud of love in his heart.
On the last step
Rose and eggs and Bertak went their ways.

The Challenge
Once I had a race with Andro
Up the crag.
Andro, being first, got
Marget for wife, the lass
That was half a swan.
I kiss, forty winters on,
The wrinkled cheek and chin of the Gray Head.

Dunce

Ten mistakes in grammar! Two
Multiplications wrong!
'Helsingfors,' I stammered, 'capital of Greece . . . '
I was thrust
Forth from the House of Learning, a dunce.
I hung, all morning,
Between a wave and a cloud.

Home-sickness

Chaldru is back from New York.
Mother and father and sisters
And brother
He left behind in America
(The brother
With a desk job in a lawyer's office in Boston).
'I missed the cliffs,' said Chaldru,
Lighting a fire in the ruin of the old croft.

The Bigger Cliffs

'I have to say,' said James the fisherman
In the reeking ale-house,
'Hoy has higher crags than ours.'
And Chaldru's ship
Had passed St Kilda, going to New York.
'Cloud-rakers, star-rakers . . . '
That night
James and Chaldru bought their own booze.

A Drowning

He struggled into a gray and silver coat of sea.

For Jean of Fea: A Love Song

An egg or two for the minister.
Three eggs for the factor.
And a hatful
For Sam'l to crack on his wooden leg.
An egg for Blind Magso
And one for Skatehorn the tramp.
Where
(Among what reeds, on what lost islet)
Will I get me a swan's egg to take to a croft
On the far side of Fea?

Crag Talk
    'Seapink, bonny lass, is this thee . . . ?'
    'Mistress Fulmar, spitting stink at me,
    Tonight
    Jean will break two of your eggs in the spitting pan . . . '
    'Mister Limpet,
    What news in your tent today?'
    The crag
    Whispered and laughed and thundered
    Red answers all about Kelpie.

Relics
    'If I die,' said Kelpie,
    (For maybe death's a dream
    Everybody dreams
    Except the withering man himself)
    'Put me under the hill
    With a few raven-shells and the skull of a gannet.'

Last Cragsman
    Nobody knows
    The way down the red stair now
    But myself and Kelpie
    (I wouldn't put it past that new taxman)
    And the nose-twitcher (the rabbit)
    And the tinker's old goat.

House of Sea Stones
    Sig drove his wife and two daughters the long way round
    To the foot of the Gray Head
    And up again, salt stones in their baskets,
    To build his croft.
    (That was a hundred years ago.
    In a sea-haar, the floor-stones shine like mirrors.)

Schoolmaster
    'The prudent ones, they plough and they
    Gather into barns . . . '
    'The average ones, they
    Hammer planks together with nails, they fish . . . '
    'A few, the best,
    Sit at an office desk in Kirkwall with soap-bright fingers . . . '
    'About the gatherers of crag-fruit
    I have nothing to say.'

Sunset
 When sun meets sea
 The crag is twelve ladders of fire.

Peter Maxwell Davies: 60
8 September 1994

There: the Rackwick boats
Are round Rora now
(See the patched sails, how
 They drink the wind!)

And the women count sixty
 boxes on the
 stones: haddock,
 cod, a huge
 halibut.

Summer's end: the patched
Fields of Rackwick
 Hold sixty stooks, in
 burnished ranks.
 No one in the valley
Will lack bread and porridge
 At the time of the first snow.

Orpheus in his cottage
 Near the crag edge
Ponders
The mystery of being and time; all
 His years a net
Of dancing numbers and notes.
 But sixty: this September
 All the birds of Hoy will sing blithely.

Achievement
The Old Man of Hoy (455 feet) was first climbed in 1966.
These lines celebrate a much later American ascent of the
famous sea stack.

Through spindrift, blizzarding birds,
The salt-eaten stone,
And the great bell of the Atlantic
Beating far below,

They have broken now
Into the high wind and the sun,
Where the eagle
Might linger in the great arc of his flight, to salute
them.

The Rackwick Dove

A pigeon was hurled from its course
Into the valley of salt and corn . . .

Will it leap over the hill's shoulder again?
Ah, it hasn't the strength.

Bide awhile then, bird of peace,
About the thresholds of Rackwick.

The bird hesitates between sixteen gables.
Too many crofts are empty skulls.

Go, there's Lucy up at Glen.
Lucy will scatter you crumbs galore.

The knight of music, up at Bunertoon. Sir Peter,
All birds are his friends. Fly there.

Twenty children of summer on the beach.
One could make a salt branch of her arm.

On Mucklehoose roof it flutters, falls.
Hutch has hammered a fish-box house.

Alan threw grain on the flagstones.
It lived like a prince on gold tithes.

But it pined for the broken flight,
Longed for the lost gray company.

After breakfast, one morning, we find
It has shaken our abundant salt from its wings.

Gossip in Hamnavoe: About a Girl

'I tell you, man,
A mermaid's been taken in the nets!
Go along to the fishermen's pier.'

'She must be somebody from the fair –
The girl
They draw a star of flaming daggers round.'

'Oh no, no. I think she's
The new minister's niece, a bonny lass,
On holiday from the college.'

'A girl with honey-coloured hair?
No girl like that here.
Oh, who's the princess at the end of the close?'

'The pity is, a girl's beauty
Stacks in this heart and that
Such honey-loads of pain.'

'One old poet doesn't grumble. She
Quickened a dead tree.
His pen flowered among the gales and snow.'

'Oh, she'll be back. That dear one
Is gold of our corn,
She's Orkney rain and spindrift . . . '

A Hamnavoe Man

A child in a sea-close, the salt on his tongue

A boy on a pier, taut dripping line
and twist of silver (a sillock)

A young man under Yesnaby, saving
creels from the purpling west

A man and a woman, lamplight, the
plate with haddock and tatties
and butter, and the bairn in
the boat-shaped cradle

An old man on a fish-box
smoking his pipe,
eyes level as horizon

The stone in the kirkyard
The voices of ocean all around.

The Old Woman in Number 20

Sons? I'll tell you about my five sons.
The oldest, Bill,
He keeps a sweetie shop at the end of the street.
He visits with a half-pound of tea at the weekend
And a packet of Rich Tea biscuits.
His wife hoards every ha'penny.
She stopped visiting a year ago,
We'd had words.

Dick, he's a fisherman. Well,
I never lack for haddocks.
Martha, his wife, she comes with fish in a pot, up the pier,
And tatties laced golden with butter.
And they have eight growing bairns.

Andrew, he's the clever one.
Andrew stands at a blackboard in the school at Norday,
Smelling of chalk and ink.
His Edinburgh wife, she's too grand to visit.

One morning thirty winters ago
Sam's bed was empty. I got
One letter from Napier, New Zealand. Silence ever since.
Bert Wylie the sailor saw Sam once
On the wharfs of Dunedin, patches on his coat.

Poor Jimmag, he's no good to anybody, except
He might take me a bunch of mayflowers from a ditch.
He's never had a job.
I give him a pound from my pension
Every weekend for a pint and a packet of Woodbines.

Kirk Bell

Dove, unfurled 'twixt ark and sun,
Give Sabbath tongue!

Folk wind-burdened, folk wind-blown.
Dang-dang, ding-dong.
Birds howk long worms from the lawn.
The bronze vibrates.

A family goes, one long black line.
It romps and reels, the steeple.

Old Tabby licks the kipper bone.
'Come pray, good people!'

Six fine hats down one small lane,
The high mouth brims, berates.

The organ preludes, a solemn paean.
The bell is a folded dove again.

Fundamentalist

An ordinary day in the parish

The pub opened and shut
A hen quizzed a dandelion
One swan lit the water

Everything was in its place

But Amos crossed the hill
Certain that arks, pillars of salt, apocalyptic beasts
Would any moment
Cover the boring landscape.

Old Tins

Be reverent, dustman.
   That tin
Was Spain and oranges,
   And that
The Atlantic samurai, the lobster.
   And there
With an ignorant yell you throw,
Among ashes and *Sunday Posts*,
The holy cell where brooded

   The bruised monk Barleycorn

   Who shrived our thirsts.

Neighbours

When I've uttered the old grave words in the true order,
Maurya
Goes gravely across the field between our two doors.
I know the things mouthed
In that cottage with the wireless aerial.
The crofter is saying, 'I told you,
Keep away from that old liar, the cat wife.'
And the mother,
'Bedtime and not a schoolbook opened!'
The black Ford, like a shark,
Has taken the brother into its maw of oil and rust.
Old Grand-da tells (but nobody listens)
How a boy and a girl – neighbours – raked pools
In the golden time, for whelks and mussels . . .
Maurya sets a first daffodil
In a jam jar in her window.
Hesper hangs a lantern over the sea.

What it is to be an old one going with her rune
On the long road between flower and star.

The Mother

On Monday she stood at the wooden wash-tub,
Suds to the elbow,
A slave among the storm-gray shirts and sheets.

Tuesday, she pegged the washing high –
The garden a galleon in a gale!
Then lamplight, the iron, the crisp sun-smelling folds.

The rooms thrummed with Gaelic rhythms,
A low monotone, on a Wednesday
(And every day), ancient Celtic work-spells.

She was never free like the lipsticked shop-girls
On Thursday afternoon; all her tasks
Were like bluebells in a jar on the window-sill.

On Friday she rose above textures of oat and barley
Into the paradise of cakes.
I licked cream from the wooden spoon.

Saturday night, I followed her basket and purse.
The grocer, silver-spectacled, was king
Of the apples, cheeses, syrup, sweetie-jars, cloves.

We sat, seven, in the high pew on Sunday.
After the psalms, her paper poke
Made sweet thunders all through the sermon.

*Many church-going families depended on a poke of sweets to
survive the longueurs of the traditional Presbyterian sermon.
In his autobiography,* For the Islands I Sing, *the author
remarks that 'the rustling of the bag sounded like a small
electric storm in the pauses of the minister's discourse'.*

Trees

A certain child is out of the island,
Her with spillings-of-sunlight hair.
She has gone to the city.
The old man, thin from stokeholds,
Ventures as far as the peatstack.
Every house but one
Has had its postcard, blots and chunks of script.
Dogs bark lonely. Wind blows poorer, I swear.
You would see his black beard on the shore
In a smoulder of sunset, faced south.
(The ring of pure elements that is an island
Suffers a breach
From the subtraction of sweet bright dust.)
The road goes idle from north to east.
Occasionally
It has some unimportant person on it.

       *

Emmeline is back! She has taken the skyway home.

       *

Women from every croft but one
Troop to the door of new experience.
Their tongues ring with welcome in the threshold,
Nine separate bellmouths.
You can see, in the dark corner, the cheese-cutter cap.
(Hong Kong to Leith,
He has wandered by many forests of masts.)
He asks no questions.
He sparks fierce matches at an unbroken pipe.
The mouths of the women peal with inquisition.
'The house I lived in was high as a crag.'
'The clouds under the wing
Were just like the froth in Merran's ale-bin.'
'Three whole days
I could not know what the wife in the sweetie shop said.'
'A blind man with a quick white stick.'
'Did you like the postcards I sent?'
'There was this one gray patch of sky
Above the Castle.'
'And one day we walked through a wood.'

'Never a sheep or a cow or pig,
Just red shapes on a hook.'
'I bought that pipe for Grandad. Look.'

The women go, their ears brimming with marvels.
The old one endures his varnished pipe.
She's in her nightgown soon.
She lights a candle.
   Kisses the beard.
      Whispers.
'I hope I dream about the trees all night.'

He nods beside the glow of a bog-drowned forest.
He puffs on till the pipe is sweet.

The Sons and Daughters of Barleycorn

THE YOUNG MEN

The Griefs of the Young Men

I

I swore, after the third pint,
   To lift more creels than Thorf –
     Crammed every Yesnaby creel with the blue lobster fruit.
Thorf, six boxes despatched in ice to Billingsgate,
   Was buying whisky to all the fishermen in 'The Arctic
     Whaler'.

I drank the sixth pint, alone.

When I launched the *Whitemaa*
   After the tenth pint of Flett's strongest ale,
We ended on the reef Hellyan.
Whitemaa and I
A laughing stock in Hamnavoe all that winter.
'Twenty pounds,' said Stanger the boatbuilder,
'To fit a new strake.'

Whitemaa, smashed, still lies on the noust.

I signed on with Thorf at the end of December.

I have lost my boat and my lass.

2

'Listen,' said Mr Stove, the factor.
'Listen well.
Listen to what I have to say, man.

We had no trouble at all with your father,
That good man who's dead.
You should think shame
Whenever you pass your father's grave in the kirkyard,
Unquiet dust.

You didn't mend the hill dyke after lambing.
Swine snortled in the burn.
The white bull
Stood throat-deep in the green oats.
The first summer wind
Blew down your scarecrow.
More seriously,
You have paid no rent for the croft Leaquoy,
Neither in May nor Michaelmas.
Do you want to stand out on the road
With your goat and six hens
And your mother's sticks of furniture . . . ?'

How can I tell the old scum, all summer
    I've been pleading with Peterina of Smelt,
And if Peterina marries me
Leaquoy will be like a ship in a green sea?

3

The registrar licked his pencil
And wrote 'Andrew James' in his register.

'How many sons is it you have now, William?' says he.

'Ten sons,' said I,
'And three lasses.'

'Well,' said the registrar,
'You look in the dumps. Have
A drop from my phial?'

He blew stoor and a spider
Out of two dirty glasses.

When I topped the hill
I could see the five youngest
Brawling about in the barnyard.

I got to the stile. The dog barked.
My wife, Jemima,
Was singing above the small bagpipes
Of Andrew James, our newborn.

4

But when I got to the wreck
The hold was a wooden cave, sloshing sea.

Every pig-sty and empty well
Stuffed with apples
And kegs of Swedish spirits.

I thought to get a few baulks of wood
To make tables, a door,
A few rafters to keep the roof solid.
(No timber so seasoned
As Baltic merchantmen.)

Then the factor arrived
And four excisemen from Kirkwall.

5

I was signing on for a whaler.
The quill in my fist.
Stumbling, stammering across the page,
Scattering blots,
When a shadow fell on the book.

I followed my mother like
A young dangerous dog
Back to plough, peat-bog, crab creels.

6

Blood in the beer! I sat
   All weekend in the Hamnavoe jail
For fighting with Thorf, my friend . . .

About? Lobsters or lasses or the Liberal candidate,
I forget. I must
   Stand in the dock on Tuesday first.

7

The *Albion* on Graemsay. I turned
   A swathe of seaweed
And there a face remote as a star,
The mouth strung with hair.

I think I'll grow to be an old man,
And that star
Trembling in the rockpool always.

The Joys of the Young Men

1

Last winter I drained the bog.
   It had drowned, lately,
   A dog and a ram.
   Now it's a patch of young corn.

2

A hard thing, being
   Small and ugly, and a heart
   Like red iron, with love, in a forge.

And a strong coarse brute
   Coaxing her, ignorant urgings,
   At Harvest Home outside
   Under the cold stars.

And winter fell on the red iron.
   Rose leaves spilt on my hand,
   Standing in the kirk beside her.

And the coarse brute, the ploughman,
  Trudged to the smithy
  To get him a strong plough.

3

Three years since I rented the shop
Lic^d to sell Tobacco and Spirits –
Choicest Indian Teas – Coffee
Fresh-ground on the Premises

With the few sovereigns
My poor grannie kept in a kist under the bed.

I dropped the plough in the furrow
The day she died
And walked the six miles to Hamnavoe, to the lawyer there.

I spent a month sweeping cobwebs from a hovel,
Nagging a joiner
To make wood shavings curl and whisper
For counter and shelves,
Licking a pen
With lists for the wholesale merchant, commercial travellers.

This morning
The bank agent was smiling like a sour lemon – 'Mister
    Halcro,
You've made three hundred pounds this year.'

4

I woke up. The croft
Had winged up near the sun, into pure dazzlement.

I opened the door,
The hill was a white whale.

I dug seven ewes out of seven blinding graves
Before the old wife
Cried, *The broth's on the table.*

Her withered face, that snowfall,
Shone like an angel.

The three bairns building the snowman,
Their mouths shivered like small silver bells.

5

I am the laird's son
And I am new out of Lancing.
I ride my chestnut over the parish
And the crofters' women
Bow shawled heads on Greenay Hill,
When Sven, my horse, strikes a spark from a stone,
    Going with my gun after grouse.

Today a girl in an oatfield
    Made no curtsy,
    She looked me flush in the teeth, unsmiling.

I smiled, going on the sheep-path with my falcon.

I think I won't tell my father
He has a radical virago on his estate.
    'Worse than the black worm,' he'd say.

How shall I find out the name of the temptress?

6

'Drunk and incapable. Assault and battery.
Resisting arrest.
Together with co-accused Thorfinn Voe, fisherman.'

The sheriff had a beetroot face, only
Brandy and port wine
Could have patched his cheeks that colour.

The sheriff listened merrily to Swann the publican and Dass
    the constable
And witnesses, a few fawners and lick-boots.

The sheriff shuffled papers.

The sheriff looked at Thorf and me, Thorf
Says 'sternly', but
As sure as I sit here, in 'The Crab and Creel'
With my dram and scooner of ale,
That sheriff winked at us.

'*Not proven*,' says the sheriff.

And down he brought his gavel on the bench
Such a smack
I thought it might take two joiners
A fortnight to patch the woodwork.

7

The old women at the pier steps,
Cleaning fish

In a demented blizzard of wings
– 'That gull furling his wings,
    That's Peter Thomson . . .'
'It might be or it mightn't
    But I ken Bert Isbister
Though he's a whitemaa
And lacks a clay pipe in his beak . . .'
– 'I know Willag Simpson.
He made
That exact same outcry
Every Saturday night, being
Thrown out of 'The White Horse'.
Here, Willag, whitemaa, here's
A tail and a fin for thee . . .'
So my mother and the pier women,
Putting a name to every gull,
A fisherman dead or drowned.

And here I am
Setting my basket of cod on the pier steps,
Alive and in love,
Just before the old women come in a flock with flashing
    tongues and knives.

1

'Fish,' said the old wife, 'I swear
    I can hear choirs of them in the mouth of Hoy Sound
        Pleading for the hooks!'

But I put on my black suit
    And I took five shillings and threepence –
        ha'penny from the loose stone in the wall
And I set out for the Fair.

My mother, Jane 'Clip-cloots', raged at the end of the
        close.

2

'No,' said I to Bella-Ann,
'I'll darken the door of not one ale-house.
    You must bide and milk the cow.
    You must be here
When the bairns come home from the school.'

'Last Lammas,' says Bella-Ann,
    'You darkened seven pub doors in Hamnavoe
    And when the sun was still high
The pubs had put complete darkness on you, man.'

I all but went on my knees to Bella-Ann.

In the end we trailed into Hamnavoe, me
    And Bella-Ann and the five bairns.
    We passed the doors of pub after pub.
Even when Bella-Ann slipped away
    To have her fortune told
    (Secret words, shadow of silver on a hand)
I couldn't get near the doors
Brimming like hives
For the five laughing howling coconut-gnawing kids.

The steamer *Hoy Head* from Hoy, Flotta, Fara, Graemsay
   Full of folk,
     The men in black suits, every lass
Like a butterfly from the laird's garden,
Their mouths all rose curls and dew.

The coaches from Birsay, Harray, Sandwick, Stenness,
Likewise laden.

And I at the coal store
Shovelling a mountain of coal into hundredweight sacks,
   Black as the King of Africa,
   Black as the marketman licking the red-hot poker.

4

The most wonderful thing I ever saw
   – And I stuck a harpoon in four whales last summer
   In Davis Straits,
Besides lifting a thousand creels in the west,
   Purple with lobsters,
   Like ancient knights in dungeons,
And passing a million haddock and herring
Through slime-silvered hands –
   Most amazing,
A little fish yellow as a Chinaman
   Gowping and gaping
   Round and round in a small glass bowl.

5

All the world's in Hamnavoe this day –
A line of Indians selling silks,
Charlie Rigolo, Italian, whirling his wheel and numbers,
Six Jews with their shooting booths (china teapots for prizes),
The Prince of the Congo
In a leopard coat crying 'alabakalavia',
The Persian fortune-teller
With planets and a black cat painted on her booth,
Guilio with the ice-cream barrow,
Cockneys and gypsies and Mrs Gold from Germany.

Jock the sailor says
   You wouldn't see the like of this throng
   On any waterfront, 'Frisco to Shanghai.

6

I thought this, spurring Betsy
  Through the Scorradale gap
  To the masks and the music,
'Now the root has drunk the rain
  First green shoot
  Is soaked in sunlight,
    The tall bronze whisperer
Is a dancer in the wind,
  And all stand stooked
Against the white siege of winter.
  It was Betsy's hoof
That spanned the ripening summer
   (Betsy is my mare)
Hlafmas – Lammas – 'feast of the loaf'.

Feet that have ploughed, feet
  That have followed the scythe,
Come in in hundreds to dance on this day,

Throats sun-dry, devout,
To tap the barley oozings.

7

The nine parishes are here
  And the five islands,
A thousand faces
  Patched red with drink and laughter.
  And I go all day
Seeking one face like a star.
  There it was, red under a flare
Taking a coarse kiss
From Jock of Curquoy, that
  Red hunk of peat-bog.

The Grief of Island Girls

1

Why am I sad,
   of all the island girls?

I have brought my pail home,
   empty from the hill.
   Buttercup the cow
   was sold last week at the mart.

2

No one saw me
   lifting my apron to my eyes
   the day Thorf
   was rowed out to the tall ship.

Darkness and dew.
   Secretly, in silence, the dew falls.

3

I am not to be married
   to Rob and his hundred acres
   till the time of snow and stars.

I wanted
   to walk across the burn to the kirk
   through marigolds
   and larks singing over Ernefea.

4

This the grandmother left me,
   her spinning wheel,
   and I expecting a bag of crowns and sovereigns
to buy a sweetie shop in Hamnavoe.

5

His fiddle woke me,
    among the drunks in the village inn
    – their slurpings and howlings!
I danced alone in my attic.

6

At first dawn of May
    I climbed Kringlafiold,
    I soaked my face in the dew.

'Merran,' says the rockpool at sunset,
    'You're as plain as ever you were.'

7

Six silly girls
    sit in the new school
    learning letters and numbers.

Soon they'll be prim
    as the lady and her daughter up at the Hall.

Because I'm fifteen
    I mend creels at the sea-wall, and spit.

Island Girls at Harvest Time

1

Oats in my hair,
    dust of oats in my mouth,
        fingers torn with sharp stalks.

I'm half blinded too
    with the flaming scythe in front.

I would sit down, but Tomas
    goes on and on,
        circled with flame from knee to shoulder.

2

Why do I have to bide here
   stirring bitters in a black pot?

   All the island lasses
   are out in the sun and wind
   bending, binding sheaves.

'Merran, your turn this year
   to brew ale for the Harvest Home.'

3

Jessie goes round with the last oatcakes.
   There's a black cloud over the sun
   like the patch on a sailor's eye.

Betsy drives the cork
   into the stone ale-jar.

The men sharpen the blades on a stone.
   The blades are dull.
   Jean holds out a hand for the first raindrop.

4

Benna, foolish creature,
   has scattered a sheaf,
gone screaming
   from a rat unlocked from its green house
   by a singing scythe.

5

Betsy is princess today.
   All the valley crofters
   are cutting her father's barley.

Betsy stands in the door of Garth
   with the ale-crock
   and the basket of cheese and oatcakes.
Betsy, princess,
   will bestow gifts on the sweating serfs.

The old queue
mutters inside. She counts pennies and shillings.

6

'How many bannocks in this field?'
A thousand.
'And how many tubs of ale?'
A hundred or more.

And somewhere, hidden, the oats
that will make the oatcake
that will be broken
above the head of a winter bride.

7

There was only one shower, at noon.
The uncut oats
were hung with raindrops.

Now the field's all cut.

'Tomas, come up to the ale-house.'

Tomas lingers beside a corngold girl,
She sucks a drop of blood from her finger.

The Joy of Island Girls

1

Look, Madda! – a puff of smoke!
– the *Hoy Head*
from Hamnavoe coming
with chocolates, apples, bottles of scent,
and ribbons from the Lammas fair.

2

I unlocked the door this morning.
A great trout lay streaming on the step.

If you go by the croft of Quoy
   Tell Andrina
there'll be two places at this table.
Tell that girl
the old mother who baked the cake won't be there.

4

I unlatched my door one morning
   and covered my eyes!
My bridelace so dingy in the dazzle of new snow.

5

Dawn and a stiff westerly.
   Three fishermen, my brothers, on the rock, teetering.
   I scattered them with a word.
      I came back with twenty lobsters.

Rob and Jock and Mansie
   were in the ale-house.

And I hauled up *Fulmar*, alone.

6

I unlatched the door.
Tessa the tinker read in my hand
a town house, horses and a coach,
a golden beard,
a desk and ledgers in Hamnavoe.

Well, it only cost sixpence.
Tessa's palm wasn't rich like mine.

7

They stopping the peat-heave at noon,
   the women went here and there
with oatcakes and ale.
Sando said, *That pot with the blue stripe going round it,*
   it has the best ale.

The faces of the women
    would have soured a honeycomb.
    Three went home, unbidden.

When Sando lifted his face from the wet black bank
    I wanted to give it a sunset kiss.

Shrove Tuesday

The fiddlers, they were suddenly there,
Three fiddlers
More eager for ale than dances.
'The cloth's not off the kirn yet . . .'
'The sun's still up . . .'
They stamping feet with rage!
Then Merran brought to the barn a lantern.
The old fiddler
Stoked his thirst at the farm fire.
His two boys went out to the hill to gather in girls.
(The ox stood, a black flame, in the winter byre.)

Soon were fifty under the barn rafters,
Under the russet splash of the lantern.
Six farm women
Going with baked fish and bannocks on a board,
Merran following with the ale-bowl,
The old dragging in from the twilight like snails
The children a wheel and whirl of birds.
And all laughing,
The young fiddler lost, last seen
Black against sunset bars.
(The farmer stood alone,
Solemn between harness and harrows.)

Too much should not be said about that night.
Was there merriment?
Was one bad fight, with red wet stars on the whitewash,
An old man thought him a boy again
In a whirling, skirling giggle of girls,
A child weeping in a corner,
Reel after reel on the threshing-floor,
Two fiddles throbbing,

Merran mad – the goosegirl has dropped
An ale-crock on a flagstone,
A wild flung star of malt.
'Tinkers hungry this March night, tented poorly . . .'

[497

          *

Out with them, out and off, before midnight,
Merran-herded,
Off home under The Plough,
Drunks, fiddlers, bairns on sleep fallen,
The gray-faced eld
Hirpling to a dozen doors before the last door.
(The stars like scatterings of corn seed.)
All's swept into one corner,
Crusts, fishbones, the fiddler's bonnet,
The tooth of a fighter,
The dust of twenty farms about.
Mice cheepered in the wall.
Then board and bowls to the house brought in.
The lantern lost in circles of dawn-light.
Wind of Hesper
Swept the barn of last echoes of folly.

          *

Merran, hearth-bent,
Sees, beyond cold cinders, sun and bread.

Ash Wednesday

Remember, man, that thou art dust.

The earl kneels, the ash of the end is written on his brow.

A captain of ships kneels, to be put in mind of a death in a far
    port, or at home, or on a rock of the sea.

And the boy that holds cinders for the priest,
His forehead is smeared,
Who wears a coat of fourteen Aprils.

The lady of Paplay
Thinks, most mornings, she will live forever; kneeling now
Is touched with the grave-stoor.

The ploughman folds sun-grained hands,
He tilts his face
To the dust drained of warmth and light.

Fisherman, the spindrift
Will wash the ashes from you tomorrow.
Still you remember, between two waves,
St Peter and the fire of his denials.

And the old bishop, 'I know this,
One God-ground deed or thought
Endures, when the circle of diamond-and-gold on my finger
is dust.'

In the kirk of Magnus
Stood a multitude of islanders, death-farers, that day,
Hungry, after, for *panis angelicus.*

And unto dust thou shalt return.

Chinoiseries

SMALL SONGS FOR THE BEGINNING OF LENT

I

Snow on Orphir hills, a shawl.
I have broken old cake, old shortbread, on the balcony.
And the birds dance past my window.

The sun
Two steps up from cinders.

Soup and bread and ale, at Hopedale,
At two o'clock.

An old man has died in the House of the Old People.
They will bury him this afternoon.

He travelled far, young.
He came home to be a fisherman. At last
He was coal merchant, magistrate.

His wife died weeks ago.
    A cold burial at the end of winter.

3

The way it is with old poets: swift ebbings, swift floods.
It was a low ebb this morning,
    The spirit a beachcomber
        – Dark swathes of seaweed.

Now, after bread and honey and tea,
    Spirit urges,
        'Write a few small Lent songs.'

4

Good, the surge of the year
    Towards equinox.

Some say, winter ends with January.
    But I think it is February.
    February begins to unlatch the gate,
        Feeling with frail hands.

Still, she is the daughter of Winter,
    Cordelia of the Crocuses.

5

Two days in the valley of the shadow
    Since Ash Wednesday, two days

And still I haven't unrolled
    The chart of threnodies
        That shows a way through the place of bones
    To the garden.

Now, on the third day,
  Old bones finger the pen.

6

A hundred Lents from now
  Who will remember us?

What is a carved name, some numbers?

  Sand sifts through the skulls.

    Who shall know the skull of a singer?
Silence is best. Song
Should be rounded with silence.

Another tongue of dust will rejoice
  A hundred springs from now.

7

Now the old sky woman
  Plucks her chickens. Flakes
Drift past my window from north-west.

Between cold sunbursts
  Old Bessie sits on her doorstep
    And strews white feathers on the wind.

Three days into Lent,
  Sun and snow mesh airily
    From the hovel on Brinkie's Brae.

Bessie Millie sold favourable winds to visiting sea captains from her hovel on Brinkie's Brae in eighteenth-century Stromness.

Via Dolorosa: A Beggar

I

I know when there's a trial,
A sentence given.
There are three strokes on a black drum then.

2

There's always a cluster of bronze greaves,
A ring of hooves.
Today, at the roadside,
A column of pure silence.

3

Being blind, I know better than most
A butterfly lighting on a rose.
I know
When a man has stumbled on stones.

4

A rare thing in women, such silence.
(All women know it, the hour after a birth.)
Pray for me, mother, on the way.

5

Pray for the stranger
They have dragged out of the mob
To lend a hand (I know his country smells).

6

The girl from the linen shop, surely!
The unfolding,
A bright sweetness in the wind,
The fabric fallen on blood and sweat.

7

The road is steep now. The dancer
Measures his length again in the hot dust.

8

That pure silence still
Among lamentation the wildest keening I've ever known.
A penny, sir. Thank you. I think
It may come to thunder later indeed.

9

I know. I've heard it. This man
Went from hill to hill, lord of the dance.
His dance is broken today.

10

They've taken his dancing coat away.
For the patchwork coat of wounds.

11

Now they are nailing his dancing feet,
A threefold iron clang.

12

But the song goes on for three hours,
World's woe,
The psalm of the black sorrow of the shepherd king.

13

Lady, out of your death-bearing stillness,
Pray for us sinners,
All our deaths scattered through history.

14

I heard the man they are burying
Put light into a blind man's skull lately.
I am content not to see
The man evils done under the sun.
(Thank you, sir. It has been a rough day, indeed.)

The Poet's Year

He can make his mouth chime –
Drops from a gray nail of ice

His silences
Are like the first cold root stirrings

His verse a trumpet in March
To widen the sun circles

Children come in a dance to his images:
Daffodil, lamb, lark

He wears the lyric coat
Cut from blue bales of sea and sky

He has knowledge of furrows
Beyond ploughmen

Can thrift sing, can herring?
He tongues their pink and silver silences

Sweeter than beeplunder, oozing,
The fairground fiddle

He knows the horncall, near sunset
For Hesper and Orion

He goes by stubble fields,
Tongue rich with shadows

He graves names of the dead
Deeper than kirkyard stones

What now, midwinter bellmouth?
Christus natus est.

Four Kinds of Poet

I

'Here, now. A new time, a new place. Write something. This
is expected by publisher, readers. Try to render both actuality
and soul of the place, look, and write. Quick. Time passes. The
place is changing as I look and write. I wither. The place ingath-
ers in a mesh of words. Words, keep me, keep all, now: a poem.

2

'This place is boring, like most places. There's nothing I feel inclined to say about it. When (out of boredom) I try to find equivalent words, the place changes: a fog shifts, lifts. There are the stones, piers, windows, chimneys, children of light and water that once he saw in a good dream – long forgotten: a poem.

3

'What happened here? Congregate, ghosts, among the weathered and cracked stones. Take my mouth, speak. Dance. There was nothing but ritual on earth once. I imagine ceremonies. I will make masks: among those shadows buying and selling: a poem.

4

'Creation of a word, this place. What word? The word is streaming across time, holding this place and all planets and all grains of dust in a pattern, a strict equation. I am always trying to imitate the sound and shape and power of the unknowable word. Dry whisperings: a poem.'

A Song for Winter

'Go,' said the bird to the boy.
'Go down to the ship now.'

    Far the shore, bitter the salt,
    Beautiful the long curve of ocean, and
        the islands a broken string of emeralds.
    The bird fluttered about the mast
    Or sat, furled,
        Or sang at night to him on watch.

He was set ashore
    With a flute and a purse of silver.
That island
    Was a great mountain in the sea.
    'Give your strength to the mountain . . .'

He gave his songs
    To the striking of a road through high snows,
    To star configurations,
    To talk with eagles and goatherds,
Then saw below him
    Village roofs that shone in the green sun.
    The bird
Sang of girls and apples and flagons.

How long at the inn? He sat long
    Among the guitars,
    Among card games and tobacco pipes.

Autumn flames showed the branching blue of his veins.
    The talk of the men
Edged with danger and enchantment.
His silver sea-wealth
Melted like snow, and no bird sang.
    And his flute was broken.

A daughter of music
Took the withered hand of the voyager
    To a narrow house
With a tree and a well
    And a lamp on the table.
    'Here is the place, father.
    Here you must write the story.'

He laboured over the page, a hundred cold words.
    (His flute was lost.)
    He slept. When he woke
    The lamp and the fire were out.
It was the dazzling solstice of winter.
On the tree outside
    The lost bird sang.
'We have come to the place, friend.
    Tomorrow, bell and candle,
    A light, a silence
Further than sun-keel and star-chart.'

The Warbeth Brothers at Christmas
The remains of a monastic chapel can still be seen in the old
Stromness Kirkyard at Warbeth. It features in many of the
author's poems, and most prominently in his novel Vinland.

1

We have wandered, unfaithful
Even at ploughtime
Leaving the ox in the half-made furrow.

And in the time of green shoots
We turned away
From the black wings, from worm in the root.

We presumed
To sit and eat with harvesters at lowsing-time.

Now, in the time of blackness and hunger,
Do not forget us.
Lantern and hay are brought to the ox.

2

Wake us, midnight bell, from our dreaming.
Turn us
From the comfort of the five folded senses.

Let the first unbroken snow
Take the prints of our foot.

We would go out soon
Bearing a sheaf of unlit candles under a cold star.

3

Did we not always return to the seed sack?
We did not suffer the plough
To languish in the half-broken field
Eaten with the cold fires of rust.

We remembered the black wings
And broke their congregations.

Though late, we sharpened our sickles,
And had a cave
To store a jar of wild honey for the poor.

Therefore, this winter midnight,
We will rejoice in The Bread.

The Kirk in Orphir

*The remains of the Round Church stand in the Orphir
Kirkyard. It was reputedly built by Earl Hakon, slayer of
St Magnus, following his penitential visit to Jerusalem.*

Winter in Scapa. Five seamen
Hauled the boat high. The skipper
   Wrung salt and snow
   From his russet beard.

They stood, wrapped, on the Orphir shore.
The skipper considered the stories –
   The burning forts,
   A battle on the ice,

Churches in the Celtic west
Cleared of chalice and candlesticks,
   Chant and saga
   In red blood scrawled . . .

Stars pierced them like nails.
In the Round Kirk, candles,
   A bell, boys' mouths:
Gloria in excelsis . . .

Travellers

After the rockpools, beyond the cliff of Rowe
Nothing but moor, the wind too sharp
   To light sticks under the kettle,

Far less stew this rabbit. Sunset
With sleet covered the hasty tent.
　　Too cold for sleep that night.

Mile after mile, bog, and the donkey
Trudged, rattling with cans.
　　At Yesnaby, in a green hollow,

We put crabs in the kettle, and sang
And were sleepy, but couldn't wait,
　　The waves pealing from west

At the caverned crags, and we had
A hundred Hamnavoe doors to knock on.
　　Stars lit us over the Black Crag,

Lamps in farmhouse windows then
Till we came to the bell and candles at Warbeth.
　　There, at midnight, we knelt.

Three Sons

Five cod from the west. The boy
　　Beaches the boat, brings
The bunched fish up to the bothy.
　　The mother guts, cleans,
Lays the silver in salt, in smoke.

A lantern in the barn. A boy
　　Threshes two sheaves, oats
Spatter the floor, a golden rain.
　　Then winnowing, millstones,
The mother with crusted loaves.

Skull-food, swine-husk, till The Word
　　Drew chaos to a dance
Of shepherds, angels, kings,
　　Plough and net in a chapel
The Word, the Star-child, Mary.

One said, 'I thought I heard on the stone a midnight keel.'
(It was the Yuletide bell.)

One said, 'So cold! I heard the chain of ice in the burn.'
(The bell unleashed its tongue, *Christ is born*.)

One said, 'A bairn, surely, a cry at the sea wall.'
(Through their salt sleep the bronze echoes fell.)

One said, 'A wave broke, white on black, far out, on the
    Breckness Rock.'
(The bronze reeled and brimmed with another stroke.)

One said, 'I dreamed an angel stood in our door.'
(Brightness on brightness unfurled through the bleak air.)

One said, 'Five fish on my hungry doorstep I found.'
(There are waverings deeper than sound.)

One said, 'I baked two sun-cakes on my hearth.'
(*Gloria*, cried the bell to the village and all the earth.)

Christmas

'Toll requiem', said sun to earth,
As the grass got thin.
The star-wheel went, all nails and thorns,
Over mill and kirk and inn.

The old sun died. The widowed earth
Tolled a black bell.
'Our King will return,' said root to bone,
To the skeleton tree on the hill.

At midnight, an ox and an ass,
Between lantern and star
Cried, *Gloria . . . Lux in tenebris . . .*
In a wintered byre.

Epiphany: The Shepherd

'No,' said Jock and Howie and Jimmag in 'The Selkie',
'There'll be no snow.'
The two fishermen said nothing. There will be snow.

Last year six sheep disappeared
In the gray drifts.
We dug four out, dazzled with blue and gold.

Two months till the lambing. Sometimes
I go down to 'The Selkie'.
We play dominoes, between the lamp and the fire.

Yesterday, a bar of pale gold on the floor,
The climbing sun. No wind.
But incense of ice at sunset.

Trek of a funeral past my door, the hill croft
Estquoy shuttered.
Eight wraiths in a first flurry of flakes.

'Foolish flock,' I say to the queen ewe, Flossie.
'Huddle them under the lee hill.
I can't see every fleece in a blizzard like this.'

No snow to speak of this winter, though.
A tinker
Supped a bowl of porridge at the table.

A man came by with a map.
I didn't know the ruin he was looking for.
A sailor, I think.

There was another stranger. He thanked me
Under the first star.
Those three came just before the big snow.

The Three Kings
This Epiphany carol was set to music by the American folk
singer, Pete Seeger.

They're looking for what, the three kings,
Beyond their border?
A new Kingdom, peace and truth and love,
Justice and order.

> *One was black and one was brown*
> *And one was yellow.*
> *A star crooked its jewelled finger.*
> *The three kings follow.*

How did they fare, the three kings?
Where did they dine?
They lived on a crust or two
And sour wine.

> *One was yellow and one was black*
> *And one was brown.*
> *They passed a scorched and rutted plain*
> *And a broken town.*

Whom did they meet, the three kings,
Among the thorns?
Herod's captains hunting
With dogs and horns.

> *One was brown and one was yellow*
> *And one was black.*
> *Here's what they found, a refugee bairn*
> *Wrapped in a sack.*

What did they do, the three kings,
When they got home?
In Vietnam, Rhodesia, Kashmir, troubled they bide
Till the Kingdom come.

Snow blossomed,
Snow withered and shrank the heart.
One year an old man at the fire
Nodded upon silence.
I remember a child
And an apple
And many stars outside,
A first cradle-load.
The tree was green.
The tree was tall.
The tree was broken into lights.
There was a winter
Of no trees,
But soldiers stayed in this house and that.
Even the king,
It was said, lacked
And was moved from town to town.
I know, most winters
The rich children got silver dolls and birds
And a poor child
Clapped hands over a coloured stone.
Plenty of stars and beggars always.
In the year of the soldiers
There was no beggar,
All held out hands, mute, like bare twigs.
When I was a child
The snow was higher than me
And bell-cry and bird and candle
Brighter than snow.
Life, a cartload of days, at last, thankfully
Draws to winter,
To silence and to darkness.
For new breath, soon,
The snow, the bells, anguish, the birds and the gifts.

FOURTEEN DRUIM CHINOISERIES
(POEMS FROM THE CHINESE)

*Druim House is in Nairn. Pluscarden Abbey is in Elgin.
Macbeth met the three witches near Forres.*

1

Rain falls and falls.
A beautiful horse grazes in the meadow,
How high, the lime tree!
The house is full of friends and laughter.

2

The starlings in the chimney,
So far
They haven't dropped into my room
To waken me with matins.
There was one bluebottle.
Alas! he is lying legs-up under the mirror.

3

I hear more guests arriving.
They are all sitting
Round a log fire, laughing.
Soon
I must go out and join the wedding guests.
This is selfishness,
Writing poems alone before a mirror.

4

The monks are chanting
Their office at Pluscarden.
Between here and there
King Macbeth met the witches.
An Orkney earl
Went to meet the Scottish king fearfully.
I think of the monks
With the light of storied glass
On praising mouths.

5

If the sun comes out
I will walk through the beautiful garden.
When it rains outside
It is perhaps better
To drink wine with friends round a log fire.

6

Yesterday the trees were like ghosts.
Today the Black Isle is a blur.
In Orkney
Does the sun shine? More likely
A storm is prowling among the hills and firths.

7

Lovely the yellow lanterns of laburnum.
Lovely the great rich clusters of rhododendrons.
I didn't know
The lime tree would be so kind to us.
Last night, late,
We drank tea from French lime-blossom.

8

How pleasant, to eat Shetland salmon with friends
And talk about poetry.
I saw a beautiful cat two days ago,
Then it flowed up the stairs.
I have not seen it again.
I must tell my black cat Gypsy all about this.

9

The sun is driving gray flocks
To water the earth.
Trees and grass are glad of the rain.
Tomorrow, they know
The sun will throw a golden coat over them.
Today the wind is at home.

What more could I ask for?
A little white room
A bed, a chair, a lamp.
I sit at the window
Writing verses on small white squares of Pluscarden paper.

11

There's a wild sweet blackbird.
He sings and sings
Between a leafy branch and broken crystals of cloud.

12

In the mirror in the window
I see
A thousand gray hairs.
Don't look any more!
Quick, write a new verse
Before another black hair turns to ash.

13

Where are the two big dogs?
They wrestle
Boisterously and merrily.
Nuff the black dog
Is like a cloud to them
With an occasional rumble of thunder in his throat.
As we break biscuits
They crack open huge bones.

14

Lilac and juniper and lime
Talk to me
More convincingly than politicians
Who are husting.
Today, in the rain,
The beautiful Arab horse, El Callil,
Crossed the field to us.
Then we had to turn our faces
To the mountains and firths.

Three Songs of Success (in a Chinese style)

1

This is bitterness.
Knowledgeable men are praising you for a thing accomplished
(Except for an envious one
And another you have unknowingly hurt),
To have to turn away from the wine-glasses at last
And live with the lonely certainty of failure.

2

This is bitterness too –
To have burned much oil
And broken many pens,
To make a precious thing for a friend:
Then to have her flick a page,
And give her passing beauty back to the sun.

3

There is a third bitterness –
To put more and more of one's joy,
As the flesh shrivels,
On a white page with black markings on it,
So that the young
May learn the various categories of joy.

The Friend

Stone, tree, star, fish, animal, man,
All gathered
Within one circle of light and fire.
And think in Orkney
Of the old friendship of stone and man,
How they honoured and served each other,
The fire on the hearth, blue tremblings
Of water in well and wall-niche,
The stone bed,
The stones that children enchant on the shore
To ship or castle,

Querns that ground corn,
The Book of the Dead –
Stone pages, celebrations in the kirkyard.

The Elemental Stone

'I am blessed by stone and the water in the hollow stone. Light beats about the stone. The stone has come from the fire at the heart of earth.'

Here, offered, over and over, the stone of our beginning and end.

The bride: 'I have taken a white rose from his hand' . . . (And air and fire and snow laboured and danced also at the forging of root and petal.)

Ploughman and plough unlocked the stone. 'The stone stands tall in sun and wind and rain, stone broken into cornstalks, multitudes.'

The fisherman holds a course clear of reef and crag. 'I will come soon to the well-built stone pier – wind in the sail – with the bounty of salt and water.' (The quarry, beyond, is a broken wave of fossils.)

The gravedigger turns his key. Sun and air and water of grief have fallen briefly on the dead. And, 'This stone will be carved with a new good name,' he says.

And the monk, 'Here we will build arch upon arch, stone fountains. A candle will burn and shine in a niche. There will be water of blessing in a worn eight-sided font. The air between red pillars will move, night and morning, with the ordered cry of our mouths.'

The Solstice Stone

'All were locked in me,
   Silence and darkness.
   I was a thing of winter.
   Hollowed, I might lodge a skull.
   I was barrenness.
   I was the block rejected by mason, carver,
      shaper of querns.'

A star unlocked the stone.
   The stone was a white rose.
   It was a dove.
   It was a harp with a hundred carols.
   It was a cornstalk.
   It was the candle at sunset.
   It was a fountain, cluster of arches.

On that stone lie the loaves and the cup.

Waters

'All the rivers run into the sea' –
From high Grampian gleams,
From dawn-dew, springs in rocks,
Atlantic clouds
Plucking harps in the Gaelic west,
From stone throats in ancient rose-gardens,
From burn and loch where trout
Make insect circles at sunset,
From juices of buried creatures
Purified in the deep cells of clay,
From the eye brightness
That seeped upon a stone through the small knuckles of Inga
After her blackbird died –
All gathered earth lucency
Seeps on and out
To the seven bitternesses of ocean:

That the ships may cross
Freighted with corn and guns and voyagers.

A Dream of Christmas

In his garden, under white roses, an old man
Confused by the seasons, cried –

   'For my last Christmas, a dance of children only.
   One will be masked as a snowflake,
   One as a star,
   One as the red-beaded holly,
   One as a dove,
   One as an ox housed from sun and furrows,
   One as a surging-crested-breaking wave
   – Masks of all natural things
   I bid to the feast,
   All but the mask of ore, that has withered
   History to the root
   And wintered me, hearthstone and heart.'

Time opened. It covered the sleeper
In whitest drifts.
   At the garden gate
A black boy stood with a golden apple.

Uranium 1
*This and the following poem were written at the height of the
controversy arising from a proposal by the nuclear industry to
make test drillings in the West Mainland of Orkney. (1977)*

We passed through the Door of Stone.
We stayed a while, with tusks and ashes.
We left.
The stones fell, silently.

The Door of Bronze opened to us.
In the square
Masques were danced: battle, harvest, hunt.
Time dimmed those pillars.
The streets lay empty.
The tribe had moved far on.

Always the Door of Salt
Had stood open.
We entered, returned with fish.
Quick thrustings, takings:
Always a few did not return.

The Green Door –
A man forged a key to that,
After fire, brimmings of iron music.
The barns lie fair to the sun.
Here
We have broken bread a winter or two.
This, we are assured,
Is not the place still
Where the tribe
Will write history on skins
And seal it in a jar, cave-kept.
A horseman
Returned across the desert this morning.
On the far side
He had stood before a door that had no name.

Uranium 2

A fist beat on a winter stone.
Let the sun in!
Wind and rain and sun, let them in!

The stone opened.
Plough and ox went in at the door of stone.
Stone and seed mixed pure grainings.
That was the House of Corn.
The sun burned on the hearth.
A man, a woman, a child broke bread (the sun) at a board.
This dance of earth, air, water, fire
(Though threatened always
By soldier and rat and worm),
This has circled
For six thousand summers, a green dance.

The great sun-key,
The plough,
Lies in the barn
Till the green word is uttered, each spring.
The earth door opens.
The ceremony of bread begins again.

*

A stranger
Knocks today at the ancient door.
(He does not smell of roots or rain,
He smells of nothing.
His face is a blank mask.
$E = mc^2$ is the mark on his key.)
Under your furrows, islanders,
A treasure richer than cornstalks.
At the hearth, grandmother and child.
There was once a dragon and it came to the king's gate.
Shall we barter dove and the ear of corn
For dragon eggs?
Shall we open the door? What story, the old or the new?
We have lived so long and so well
In our green fable.
Shall we open the doors?

Bird and Island

A bird visited an island,
Lodged in a cliff,
A stone web of mathematics and music.

Bird whirled, built, brooded on
Three blue eggs.

A bird visited the island,
Sun by sun, aloof
From wild pig and dolphin and fossil
But woven into
The same green and blue.

The bird returned to the island,
Saw curves of boat and millstone,
Suffered fowler and rock-reft.

The bird, sun-summoned,
Turned slow above
The harp, the fire, the axe.

Bird and boy
Shared crust and crab.

Bird brooded
On a million breaking rock songs.

Bird visited, hesitant,
The island of wheels.

Bird entered
The heavy prisms of oil.

Flame now, bird, in your nest
Of broken numbers.

Summer and Winter

I was happy, one afternoon in summer,
When a kind lady
Asked me to write a poem for the *National Schizophrenia
  Newsletter.*

It was a day of carnival in Orkney,
All around
There was music and laughter
And children abroad in the sunshine
In coloured dresses,
Happy as flowers or the blue waves on the pier.

Life, I know, is not
All happiness like that day.
We must all
Endure dark times and onsets of winter.
No person born but has
Storms, barren branches, and darkness.

We should know that always and everywhere
The seed is under the snow,
Waiting,
And always it thrusts up, unfolding in the garden
Like this carnival throng
In the sunlight, in blown music and colour and laughter.

Each one
Has sat with curtains drawn against winter.

Each one has thought then
The bleakness and cold never-ending.

Listen to the summer music!
The sea is blue again, the grass is green.

Children in Need

May this Greenland child
Be holding an orange and a loaf in her hand soon.
May this child from wars far east
Get a fish in his thin yellow hand.
Twins in a burnt African forest
In a cold wind
Look, a van has driven their way
With coats, blue and green.
I think, some sunset
A child dumb with grief
    May be given a guitar,
Then all children in need
    Dance under the stars
Till the bread-burdened sun rises.

To the Tibetan Refugees

May the house be firmly founded.
And I hope there's a well,
Ever springing, near the door.
There should be a fire for cold nights
And a clear window, too,

To see the stars snapping silver fingers!
I imagine a cupboard
With bread and cheese and fruit in it,
So that a lost traveller may eat too.
A good bed, chairs, a table.
A jar with flowers and a book.
And may the angels of mountain and of snow
Bend perpetually over that good house.
(So wishes
One with a house beside a cold Northern sea.)

Poem for Three Peoples

On the Balkan mountains
Sat clouds like doves.

The Adriatic shore
Washed by waves, endless harps.

On the mountain passes
Folk went with their goats and baskets of eggs.
Along the shores, nets drying,
Boats and children and seabirds.

And all blessed by sun and stars.

Suddenly along the mountain passes
Come women, weeping.
Houses and churches and barns burning, below.
Guns in the cornfields.

And on the shore boats broken
For irregulars to feed flames
In the first snow.

Cities of Croatia, Bosnia, Serbia,
May children climb
Out of your ruins into the sun

And the doves
Fly down upon their thin hands, soon.

I, Ikey Faa, being of whole and sound mind, (nobody
       thinks it but me),
do hereby bequeath and leave my possessions
to the following persons, heartily praying that
those beneficiaries make full use
of the same, to their own hearty good and the
good of all the world beside.

Item: the birds of the isle, hawk and swan,
       eider and blackbird and dotterel, to the
       child JOHN SWEYNSON that gave me and the birds a
       bite to eat in last winter snow, and I in the
       high winds of March gave the said John a
       kite I had made out of sticks and paper for to fly among
          the
       said birds.

Item: the fish in the tides and rips and
       races about this isle, to JOCK SINCLAIR fisherman in
          the
       said isle: that he having to return the
       fattest fish to the laird's plate and kitchen, in
       exchange for a farthing or a halfpenny:
       since also the fingers of the laird have not baited hooks,
                                 nor his lady's fingers
       to my knowledge stunk with fish-guts,
       and there is no true truce and tryst-time
       as between hall and haul:
       which season and compact are well
       kent to the fishermen. I have had this and that cod-
          head
       from John's goodwife.

Item: the flowers of the sun, from the first
       snowdrop to the last blown rose petal,
       to GERDA FLAWS, for I have not
       seen such delight in flowers in any
       house-bound creature, no, not in butterfly and
       bee; and I pray the said Gerda to
       ensure and guarantee all traffic as between
       bee and butterfly, sun and raindrop and

the feast in the open bud. I wish for her
a long happy butter-time and
bannock-time and bairn-time, happy among flowers.

Item: I leave the land of this isle from the
lowest rooted tangle in the ebb to the
hawk over the hill to MANSIE GRAY and all others who
changed it, in a thousand years and more,
from a bog to a green-and-gold patchwork;
and yet it wears Mansie Gray
out, the land, it grinds him down and it
grays him, bows and breaks him, to keep the big
laird's house with nine empty echoing rooms and
another in the city of Edinburgh; and forbye
to stock the said dwellings
with beef and bread and wine, silk and fiddles and
    etchings and harps.
I have eaten croft-crusts with thankfulness from Mansie
    Gray's table.

Item: The bums and the winds to millers.

Item: Rain and sun and corn to the makers of ale.

Item: to the factor, a breath and a heartbeat and
a breath, calculations, one at a time: as far as the last
    breath:
such as are never noted among the ciphers and in the
    ledger in his office.

I, Ikey Faa, write this with a stick on snow and
mud in the quarry, three days before Yule,
having a hoast on me that does not
mend, and a fiercer burning in the
blood than I have known.

I have rejoiced greatly in the
elements that are soon to shake me out and away, all but
    earth – 'twixt
Yule and Hogmanay, as near as I can
guess – and I leave what is all mine and all men's and
    God's to them that
will enjoy and use it best.

As *Witness* – a sparrow (his splash in the ditch)
    a mouse (his scurry and snow mark)

(Will I manage to struggle to the ale-house
before closing time? If I do, will the thin-lipped
prevaricator that keeps the place give me the loan of a
last whisky?)

528]

Glossary

Alba ancient kingdom of the Picts and Celtic Scots
Alexander Graham local hero who won economic independence for
     Stromness
bason basin
Bessie Millie spaewife who sold favourable winds to visiting sea captains
     from her hovel on Brinkie's Brae
Black Pat Patrick Stewart, much feared and hated Earl of Orkney
     (1565–1615)
bog cotton attractive white moorland flower
brairds first shoots of a crop
Brodgar stone circle near Maeshowe, Stenness
caisie basket of woven straw or heather
City of the vanished race Skara Brae
claggam twist of home-made toffee
cuithe older coal-fish
curragh boat similar to a coracle
death by fire an abbot of Newbattle loved a girl of the neighbourhood.
     Her father, a knight, forbade their meetings. For a time they went
     their own ways, then began to meet secretly, by night, in a house not
     far from the Abbey. One night the girl's father, having discovered
     their meeting place, set it on fire, and the lovers both perished.
demptions downpours
dromond swift medieval man-of-war
drouths drunkards
enthirling binding, enslaving
Euclidian geometrical
glebe land attached to a parish church
gowping gaping
grimling twilight, gloaming
haaf deep-sea fishing ground
haar cold sea mist
Henry Moore, etc. the poet's contribution to a Tate Gallery Anthology
     (1986)
Hesper evening star
holm small island

holy cards attendance cards distributed by Presbyterian Church elders to
    members of their congregation prior to Communion

howe prehistoric burial mound

John Gow notorious Stromness pirate, hanged at Wapping in 1726

kamiks knee-length sealskin boots worn by Vikings

Lammas old feast-day celebrating the first fruits of the harvest

lappered loppered, curdled

laverock skylark

Leif Ericson eleventh-century Viking explorer who discovered Vinland

lowe flame

lowsing time end of the working day

makar poet

mercat market

muirburn annual burning of moorland heather to promote new growth

noust sheltered inlet for small boats

Orkahowe Viking name for Maeshowe

orraman farm worker, kept to do any odd job that might occur

peerie small, peedie

pertelotes hens

reiving robbing, plundering

roost powerful current caused by conflicting tides

scrieving writing, gliding swiftly along

scrithe proliferate

scunner disgust

share ploughshare

shebeen illicit liquor shop

sillocks young coal-fish

silver orb nuclear reactor at Dounreay, Caithness

skerry reef of rock, small rocky island

stour dust

tang seaweed

The Drowning Brothers Rackwick's depopulation accelerated in 1952 fol-
    lowing the tragic death of two young brothers, the last children of the
    valley, in a drowning accident in the Rackwick Burn. Thirty years were
    to pass before a new child, Lucy Rendall, was born into the valley in
    1981.

thole put up with, suffer

three-mile line fishing limit for larger boats

tilth soil

Tir-Nan-Og land of the young, the Irish Elysium

trauchled bedraggled

tuskars peat-cutting spades

uncan strange, unknown
usque whisky
vennels lanes
whitemaas gulls
withershin rotating against the sun (regarded as unlucky)
wore the red coat was burnt as a witch
yole Orkney variant of yawl, a fishing boat

Index of First Lines

Index of Titles